Research and Practice in Applied Linguistics

General Editors: **Christopher N. Candlin** and I
Macquarie University, Australia

CW01455370

All books in this series are written by leading researchers and teachers in Applied Linguistics, with broad international experience. They are designed for the MA or PhD student in Applied Linguistics, TESOL or similar subject areas and for the language professional keen to extend their research experience.

Titles include:

Dick Allwright and Judith Hanks
THE DEVELOPING LANGUAGE LEARNER
An Introduction to Exploratory Practice

Francesca Bargiela-Chiappini, Catherine Nickerson and Brigitte Planken
BUSINESS DISCOURSE

Francesca Bargiela-Chiappini, Catherine Nickerson and Brigitte Planken
BUSINESS DISCOURSE, SECOND EDITION

Christopher N. Candlin and Stephen H. Moore
EXPLORING DISCOURSE IN CONTEXT AND ACTION

David Cassels Johnson
LANGUAGE POLICY

Helen de Silva Joyce and Susan Feez
THEORY, RESEARCH AND PRACTICE OF LITERACIES

Alison Ferguson and Elizabeth Armstrong
RESEARCHING COMMUNICATION DISORDERS

Lynne Flowerdew
CORPORA AND LANGUAGE EDUCATION

Sandra Gollin-Kies, David R. Hall and Stephen H. Moore
LANGUAGE FOR SPECIFIC PURPOSES

Sandra Beatriz Hale
COMMUNITY INTERPRETING

Geoff Hall
LITERATURE IN LANGUAGE EDUCATION

Richard Kiely and Pauline Rea-Dickins
PROGRAM EVALUATION IN LANGUAGE EDUCATION

Marie-Noëlle Lamy and Regine Hampel
ONLINE COMMUNICATION IN LANGUAGE LEARNING AND TEACHING

Jemina Napier and Lorraine Leeson
SIGN LANGUAGE IN ACTION

Annamaria Pinter
CHILDREN LEARNING SECOND LANGUAGES

Virginia Samuda and Martin Bygate
TASKS IN SECOND LANGUAGE LEARNING

Norbert Schmitt
RESEARCHING VOCABULARY
A Vocabulary Research Manual

Helen Spencer-Oatey and Peter Franklin
INTERCULTURAL INTERACTION
A Multidisciplinary Approach to Intercultural Communication

Cyril J. Weir
LANGUAGE TESTING AND VALIDATION

Tony Wright
CLASSROOM MANAGEMENT IN LANGUAGE EDUCATION

Research and Practice in Applied Linguistics
Series Standing Order ISBN   978–1–4039–1184–1 (hardback)
978–1–4039–1185–8 (paperback)
(*outside North America only*)

You can receive future titles in this series as they are published by placing a standing order. Please contact your bookseller or, in case of difficulty, write to us at the address below with your name and address, the title of the series and one of the ISBNs quoted above.

Also by Jemina Napier

INTERPRETER EDUCATION IN THE DIGITAL AGE
Innovation, Access & Change (*co-edited*)

INTERPRETING RESEARCH METHODS
A Practical Resource (*co-authored*)

SIGN LANGUAGE INTERPRETING
Linguistic Coping Strategies

INTERNATIONAL PERSPECTIVES ON SIGN LANGUAGE INTERPRETER EDUCATION
(*edited*)

THE SIGN LANGUAGE INTERPRETING STUDIES READER (*co-edited*)

INTERNATIONAL SIGN (*co-edited*)

Also by Lorraine Leeson

LOOKING FORWARD
EUD in the 3rd Millennium – The Deaf Citizen in the 21st Century (*edited*)

IRISH SIGN LANGUAGE
A Cognitive Linguistic Approach (*co-authored*)

EXPERIENCING DEAFHOOD
Snapshots from Five Nations (*co-authored*)

WORKING WITH THE DEAF COMMUNITY
Education, Mental Health and Interpreting (*co-edited*)

SIGNED LANGUAGE INTERPRETING
Preparation, Practice and Performance (*co-edited*)

SIMULTANEITY IN SIGNED LANGUAGES (*co-edited*)

Sign Language in Action

Jemina Napier
Heriot-Watt University, UK

and

Lorraine Leeson
Trinity College Dublin, Ireland

palgrave
macmillan

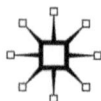

© Jemina Napier and Lorraine Leeson 2016

All rights reserved. No reproduction, copy or transmission of this publication may be made without written permission.

No portion of this publication may be reproduced, copied or transmitted save with written permission or in accordance with the provisions of the Copyright, Designs and Patents Act 1988, or under the terms of any licence permitting limited copying issued by the Copyright Licensing Agency, Saffron House, 6–10 Kirby Street, London EC1N 8TS.

Any person who does any unauthorized act in relation to this publication may be liable to criminal prosecution and civil claims for damages.

The authors have asserted their rights to be identified as the authors of this work in accordance with the Copyright, Designs and Patents Act 1988.

First published 2016 by
PALGRAVE MACMILLAN

Palgrave Macmillan in the UK is an imprint of Macmillan Publishers Limited, registered in England, company number 785998, of Houndmills, Basingstoke, Hampshire RG21 6XS.

Palgrave Macmillan in the US is a division of St Martin's Press LLC, 175 Fifth Avenue, New York, NY 10010.

Palgrave Macmillan is the global academic imprint of the above companies and has companies and representatives throughout the world.

Palgrave® and Macmillan® are registered trademarks in the United States, the United Kingdom, Europe and other countries.

ISBN: 978–1–137–30975–4 hardback
ISBN: 978–1–137–30976–1 paperback

This book is printed on paper suitable for recycling and made from fully managed and sustained forest sources. Logging, pulping and manufacturing processes are expected to conform to the environmental regulations of the country of origin.

A catalogue record for this book is available from the British Library.

Library of Congress Cataloging-in-Publication Data

Napier, Jemina, author.
    Sign language in action / Jemina Napier, Lorraine Leeson.
        pages cm.—(Research and practice in applied linguistics)
    ISBN 978–1–137–30975–4 (hardback : alk. paper) –
    ISBN 978–1–137–30976–1 (pbk. : alk. paper)
    1. Sign language. 2. Deaf – Means of communication. 3. Applied linguistics.
    I. Leeson, Lorraine, author. II. Title.

HV2474.N367
2016 419—dc23   2015025769

For Andy, Tilda & Haaris

Contents

List of Figures and Tables

Figures

Tables

General Editors' Preface

Research and Practice in Applied Linguistics provides the essential crossover between research in applied linguistics and its practical applications in the professions. Written by leading scholars and practitioners, the series provides rapid and authoritative access to current scholarship and research on key topics in language education and professional communication more broadly. Books in the series are designed for students and researchers in Applied Linguistics, TESOL, Language Education, Communication Studies and related fields and for professionals concerned with language and communication.

Every book in this innovative series is designed to be user-friendly, with clear illustrations and accessible style. The quotations and definitions of key concepts that punctuate the main text are intended to ensure that many, often competing, voices are heard. Each book presents a concise historical and conceptual overview of its chosen field, identifying many lines of enquiry and findings but also gaps and disagreements. Throughout the books, readers are encouraged to take up issues of enquiry and research that relate to their own contexts of practice, guided by reflective and exploratory questions and examples that invite practical connections to their work.

The focus throughout is on exploring the relationship between research and practice. How far can research provide answers to the questions and issues that arise in practice? How should we warrant the relevance of research to practice? Can research questions that arise and are examined in very specific circumstances be informed by, and inform, the global body of research and practice? What different kinds of information can be obtained from different research methodologies? How should we make a selection among the options available, and how far are different methods compatible with each other? How can the results of research be turned into practical action?

The books in this series identify key researchable areas in the field and provide workable examples of research projects, backed up by details of appropriate research tools and resources. Case studies and exemplars of research and practice are drawn on throughout the books. References to key institutions, individual research lists, journals and professional organisations provide starting points for gathering information and embarking on research. The books also include annotated lists of key works in the field for further study.

The overall objective of the series is to illustrate the message that in Applied Linguistics, there can be no good professional practice that isn't based on good research, and there can be no good research that isn't informed by practice.

Christopher N. Candlin and David R. Hall
Macquarie University, Sydney

Acknowledgements

No book is ever written in a vacuum, and this one is no exception. Apart from the obvious cooperation we have had with one another in writing this book, we have so many people to thank for their support – for helping us to generate, critique and develop our ideas.

Firstly we would like to thank the late Christopher Candlin and the late David Hall for their invitation to write this book and contribute to the Palgrave Applied Linguistics and Professional Practice series. We are thankful for Christopher's feedback on earlier chapter drafts and are sad that neither of them were able to see the book come to fruition. Thanks also to Libby Forrest and Rebecca Brennan from Palgrave Macmillan for their patience while we took a lot longer than expected to complete the manuscript due to various work and life commitments.

We'd like to send heartfelt thanks to Andy and Tilda Carmichael for their support to Jemina all the way through the project, but particularly in the last stages of frenetic writing and proofreading, and to Haaris, Asim and Neelofar and Ashfaque for the support and sustenance of Lorraine during this period. Lorraine would like to thank colleagues and students at Swarthmore College, Pennsylvania, USA, where a portion of this book was prepared while she served as the Julian and Virginia Cornell Distinguished Visiting Professor, 2013–2014. Thanks also go to Trinity College Dublin, who supported her Leave of Absence during this period. Jemina would like to acknowledge the support of Macquarie University in Australia, where she was employed while she conducted much of the research reported in this book.

Thanks to Heather Mole, a PhD student at Heriot-Watt University, for her last-minute help in formatting the final reference list, and to many friends and colleagues for the discussions concerning the topics raised in this book, including (in no particular order) Robert Adam, Noel O'Connell, Rosie Oram, Alys Young, Robyn Dean, Cynthia Roy, Betsy Winston, Della Goswell, Karen Bontempo, Suzanne Ehrlich, Adam Schembri, Trevor Johnston, Breda Carty, George Major, Jihong Wang, Stacey Webb, Yvonne Waddell, Heather Mole, Clare Canton, Mark MacQueen, Steve Emery, Graham H. Turner, Gary Quinn, Rita McDade, Svenja Wurm, Robert Skinner, Oliver Pouliot, Brigitte Francois, Jeff McWhinney, Kal Newby, Danny Stubbs, Liz Scott Gibson, Myriam Vermeerbergen, Tobias Haug, Christian Rathmann, Jens Heßman, Beppie van den Bogaerde, Sherman Wilcox, Phyllis Wilcox, Barbara Shaffer, Terry Janzen, John Bosco Conama, Teresa Lynch, Carmel Grehan, Patrick A. Matthews, Sarah Sheridan, David Little, Jim Kyle, Bencie Woll, Kearsy

Cormier, Lucia Venturi, Asim Sheikh, Haaris Sheikh, Mary Phelan, Ilana Rozanes, Markku Jokinen, Colin Allen, Andrew Wiltshire, Alastair McEwin, Alex Jones, Leonie Jackson, Audrey Cameron, Joseph Sheridan, Melinda Napier, Philippa Merricks, Andy Carmichael, Rachel McKee, David McKee, Donna Jo Napoli, Neil McDevitt, Mark Wheatley, Christopher Stone, Jeremy Brunson, Debra Russell, Stacey Storme, Christopher Tester, Brenda Nicodemus, Lindsay Ferrara, Torill Ringsø and Anna Lena Nilsson. We would also like to acknowledge the influence of sadly missed colleagues, the late Christopher Candlin, David Hall, Mary Brennan, Elena Pizzuto and Laura Sadlier, on segments of the text.

For graciously supplying us with personal quotes to feature throughout the text, we would like to thank Robert Adam, Colin Allen, Caroline Conlon, Tobias Haug, Peter Hauser, Leah Kalaitzi, Jeff McWhinney, David McKee, Philippa Merricks, Rebekah Rose Mundy and Melinda Napier.

We acknowledge the support of various funding bodies that funded several of the projects referred to throughout this book, including the European Commission's Lifelong Learning Programme, the Australian Research Council and internal grants from Macquarie University and Heriot-Watt University.

Finally we would like to pay tribute generally to members of the worldwide signing community, deaf people, sign language interpreters and researchers, for their support and encouragement of us both in our work. We dedicate this book to them, and also to Christopher Candlin and David Hall, for their pioneering work in applied linguistics and their never-ending recognition and support for sign language research.

1
Introduction

1.1 Aim and readership of the book

The idea for this book came out of our long association with the international deaf community as sign language professionals, educators and researchers. We have learned, used and experienced sign languages in different ways and have therefore developed an overview of the range of issues faced by sign language users, learners and teachers internationally. We have both felt the benefit of being bilingual in (at least one) spoken and signed language, enriched and privileged by our participation in the deaf world. We have both been involved in leading the development of research in *applied sign linguistics* (which we define in Chapter 2) but have noted something of a 'silo effect', whereby publications in the related fields of Deaf Studies, sign language linguistics, sign language teaching and sign language interpreting and translation tend to be concentrated in certain vehicles for publication, and researchers tend to cluster in these fields. We feel very strongly that there is a high level of interconnectedness between these areas, but there has been very little discussion of these issues under the broader umbrella of applied linguistics. Thus our goal in writing this book is to draw together these fields and give consideration to the potential 'strands' of applied sign linguistics. Our aim is that anyone who may have an interest in languages can pick up this book and get some insight into the research and language practices of one particular minority language community – that is, the (signing) deaf community – and the wide range of people who come into contact with that community in everyday contexts. Although the book is targeted primarily at students of sign languages and sign language interpreting students, teachers of sign languages, researchers, sign language interpreter practitioners and educators, Deaf Studies teachers and students, educators working with deaf children and policymakers, we believe it will also be of interest to other people working with minority language communities and to scholars and practitioners in applied linguistics research more generally. As with

1

Spencer-Oatey and Franklin (2009, p. 2) with their book in this series on *Intercultural Interaction*, we perceive that 'this book will provide a very helpful "mapping of the field", accessible analyses of [applied sign linguistics], and pointers for the journey towards greater intercultural competence [between deaf and non-deaf people]'.

1.1.1   A note on conventions

The prevailing convention in the literature with respect to discussions of deaf people and 'sign languages' is to refer to non-deaf people as 'hearing' people; a convention we also adopt throughout this book. Some readers may also be aware that in Deaf Studies, sign linguistics and interpreting literature there is another established convention to distinguish between deaf people who use a signed language and identify with other sign language users (Deaf) and those who have a hearing loss but do not use a signed language or identify themselves with a community of sign language users (deaf; see e.g. Lane, Hoffmeister & Bahan, 1996; Senghas & Monaghan, 2002; Sutton-Spence & Woll, 1998). However, given the complexities of sign language transmission, the evolving nature of the deaf community due to medical interventions and changes in educational policy, greater numbers of deaf people come to the community as late learners of sign language (which will be discussed later in this chapter and throughout the book). Thus, definitions of deaf community membership are changing. In order to avoid any judgements about the linguistic and cultural identity of deaf people and to put a spotlight on the use of sign languages by both deaf and hearing people, in this book we refrain from using the D/deaf convention. No judgement is made about the hearing and linguistic identity or status of people who use a sign language, and the only time we retain the D/deaf convention is when directly quoting other authors (see Chapter 2, Section 2.2, for more discussion).

1.2   Title of the book

Applied linguistics is a field that has significantly affected deaf communities, shaping language policy and practice, influencing the development of sign language curricula and assessment and describing aspects of the sociolinguistic variation that exists in sign language using communities. The applied linguistics field has also influenced studies on sign language acquisition and contributed to the field of interpreting studies. Despite this contribution, there is a significant absence of applied sign linguistics publications framed wholly within an applied sign linguistics framework. Indeed, the first applied sign linguistics conference was held as recently as 2009 at Bristol University in the UK, where the focus was firmly settled on issues of sign language curricula.

In parallel, we can say that sign linguistics is an active field of research. Since Bernard Tervoort and William C. Stokoe independently began working on the formational parameters of signs in the 1950s, there has been a move towards greater understanding of the form and function of sign languages. Yet it is only in the past decade, with the development of digital software such as ELAN (see Chapter 7, Section 7.1.5), that it has become possible to annotate and analyse large bodies of data, and this has led to large-scale corpus linguistics projects in several countries, increasing the potential for more sophisticated cross-linguistic comparison to occur. New technologies affect deaf communities beyond the scope of these research-based approaches: Digital corpora have been created in several countries to archive aspects of deaf community experience and knowledge; this allows for data that is functional for some research purposes, for teaching and learning purposes, and which serves the deaf community in terms of documenting their community and language over time. This process creates a positive feedback cycle between researchers and communities in a way that was not possible previously, particularly when online archiving of data and results of research are taken into account.

With this emergence of sign linguistics research, there has been growing interest in how sign languages are used in everyday life in different contexts; that is, how and where sign languages are used in contexts where deaf people are present. These include situations where deaf children and adults are accessing services (e.g. educational settings, healthcare or legal settings) or in the workplace. It includes settings where deaf people are the recipients or the providers of services, and as such we can consider diverse settings such as non-native signing deaf children in mainstream educational settings who are working with sign language interpreters, native deaf signers working as academics and delivering their courses via a sign language, deaf politicians, deaf people in medical contexts (as patients or health professionals) and deaf people in legal settings (as legal professionals or jurors, as criminals, as witnesses). Some of the research that will be reported on in this book (including that carried out by the authors) includes explorations of how service providers perceive their services and how sign language users experience those same services. In some cases, research findings from this kind of triangulated study (e.g. interpreters, service providers, sign language users) allow for the creation of criterion-referenced curricula for service providers and interpreters, and we will discuss some of these as case studies. We will also consider how the emerging discipline of applied sign linguistics draws upon established fields of applied linguistic inquiry.

Thus, we felt that a title such as *Sign Language in Action* encapsulates our overarching goal to describe sign language in use, sign language in context, and sign language discourses.

1.3   Authors' subjectivity, position and goals

Against this backdrop, and in line with ethnographic approaches to research, we feel it necessary to position ourselves vis-à-vis the focus of this book, as neither of us are deaf. So, here we discuss our role as hearing people doing sign language research and our goals in writing this book. First, let us introduce ourselves.

Profile: Jemina Napier

I was born in the UK deaf community into a family with multigenerational deafness. My home language was British Sign Language (BSL), and I grew up using BSL on a daily basis. I would be considered a 'native signer'. People in my situation are often referred to as Children of Deaf Adults – Codas, or as I prefer, People from Deaf Families (PDFs; see Chapter 6, Section 6.1). I am now fluent in several sign languages, acquired as the result of having lived in different countries, and I am a qualified interpreter in both the UK and Australia. I am also on the approved list of International Sign interpreters of the World Federation of the Deaf and World Association of Sign Language Interpreters. I am a practising interpreter, interpreter educator, applied linguist and sign language interpreting and interpreter pedagogy researcher, and I am currently Chair of Intercultural Communication and Head of the Department of Languages and Intercultural Studies at Heriot-Watt University in Edinburgh, where there is a large team of deaf and hearing academics involved in delivering undergraduate and postgraduate sign language interpreter education programmes and conducting research on topics related to applied sign linguistics.

My research interests and expertise focuses around three strands of intercultural communication: (1) language and communication in the context of interpreter-mediated communication – primarily with (but not limited to) sign language interpreters and the Deaf community, adopting sociolinguistic, discourse-analytic and sociological explorations of interpreting in context (particularly education, legal and medical contexts) to inform the wider field of interpreting studies and applied linguistics; (2) how deaf adults actually use sign language to communicate in their lives and the challenges this poses for sign language interpreters and (3) interpreting pedagogy, using action research to explore aspects of distance education, blended learning, curriculum innovation and discourse-based teaching practices.

Profile: Lorraine Leeson

I grew up in a non-deaf family in a locale steeped in Irish deaf history and, as a result, had an early introduction to the Irish Deaf community. I worked in a deaf school, acquired Irish Sign Language (ISL), and went on to work for local, national and European deaf NGOs (Cork Deaf Enterprises, Irish Deaf Society, European Union of the Deaf). As a result of living in several countries, I have some degree of fluency in several sign languages. I am also a practising interpreter, interpreter educator, sign linguist and interpreting researcher. I am currently serving as Ireland's inaugural Professor of Deaf Studies and was the founding Director of the Centre for Deaf Studies at Trinity College Dublin, a space where ISL is the working language. In this role, I have worked with colleagues – deaf and non-deaf – in establishing undergraduate programmes in interpreting, Deaf Studies and ISL teaching, and I have opened up opportunities for postgraduate work on a broad range of topics pertaining to the linguistic description and functionality of sign languages in society. I am also the current (and inaugural) Chair of the European Forum of Sign Language Interpreters Committee of Experts, and in 2015, I was honoured to be invited to serve as Patron to the Irish Deaf Women's Group.

My research interests and expertise focuses around three strands of work: (1) linguistics and applied linguistics of sign languages, (2) interpreting studies and (3) transdisciplinary work that affects Deaf Studies topics. My focus on the linguistics and sociolinguistics of sign languages includes work on the morpho-syntax and semantics of ISL (including issues of word order), language planning issues vis-à-vis deaf education and the use of ISL and gendered issues in the Irish deaf community, particularly in terms of language use. Cognitive linguistics interests include the role of metaphor and metonymy in ISL, the impact of iconicity on the language, simultaneity in signed languages and point-of-view predication. My applied linguistics work includes coordinating the mapping of teaching, learning and assessment of sign languages for professional purposes to the Common European Framework of Reference for Languages (PRO-Sign, European Centre for Modern Languages), and work on a corpus of L2 hearing sign language learners (with colleagues at Trinity and at Stockholm University). My interpreting studies research tends to be transdisciplinary in nature and includes a focus on the provision of interpreters in a range of domains (e.g. education, healthcare settings, legal settings), quality of outputs and assessment issues.

The involvement of non-deaf people in the deaf community has been an ongoing and vexatious issue. There has been long recognition of the value that hearing people bring to the deaf community if they embrace the values of the community and can sign fluently enough to engage with deaf people directly (see Chapters 2 and 3 for more discussion). There have been attempts to separate the identity of hearing people who are involved in the deaf community from those 'other' non-deaf people who do not use sign language and who are considered 'outsiders' (see Napier, 2002; Ladd, 2003), with suggestions that hearing people such as Codas and sign language interpreters occupy a 'third culture' (Bienvenu, 1987; Sherwood, 1987).

Some authors have suggested different naming conventions, such as subverting the D/deaf convention (as discussed in Section 1.1.1 above) to refer to 'hearing' people who are members of the deaf community and 'Hearing' people as outsiders (Napier, 2002; Ladd, 2003); or by referring to community members as 'Deaf (hearing)' and outsiders as 'hearing' (Stone, 2007, 2009). Others have suggested that there should be no reference to audiological status, and instead we should refer to a community of 'sign language users' (Bahan, 1997), 'sign language persons' (Jokinen, 2001) or 'sign language peoples' (Batterbury, 2012; Batterbury, Ladd & Gulliver, 2007). Whichever convention you prefer, we identify ourselves as 'Deaf (hearing)'; that is, as hearing people we align ourselves with deaf people and their values based on our long involvement in the community, and we bring that subjectivity to our writing.

In the field of applied linguistics, Cameron, Frazer, Harvey, Rampton and Richardson (1992) began early discussions of the unequal power relationships that can be evident in social science research. They state that researchers should develop the research process so that it benefits the 'subjects' as well as the researcher and distinguish between 'ethical', 'advocate' and 'empowering' approaches to the relationship between researchers and the researched. Essentially, Cameron and colleagues urge researchers to work *with* all stakeholders.

There is also much debate in the deaf community and among researchers about the potential oppression that deaf people face in having non-deaf people conduct research *on* their community, with emphasis on the need for research to be done *with* deaf sign language users (Sutherland & Young, 2014; Turner & Harrington, 2000) and to adopt a 'community participatory approach' (Emery, 2011; Napier & Kidd, 2013; Napier, Sabolcec et al., 2014; Young & Temple, 2014). Consequently there is an emerging body of work that explores the need for ethical approaches to conducting sign language research in order to ensure that there is involvement from deaf sign language users in conducting the research, that deaf people's views are integral to any research project and that the research is 'deaf-led' (Harris, Holmes & Mertens, 2009; Hochgesang, Villanueva, Mathur & Lillo-Martin, 2010; Mertens, 2010; Singleton, Jones & Hanumantha, 2012; see Chapter 7, Section 7.1.4, for more discussion).

We would like to frame our position as hearing applied sign linguistics researchers by drawing on some recent published debates in the field. In 2011, two hearing sign language researchers published a somewhat controversial article on their status as hearing people in the field of Deaf Studies (see Chapter 2 for definition and overview of Deaf Studies as a discipline) and their perceptions of their 'hearingness' (Sutton-Spence & West, 2011). In their article they suggest that the 'problem of Hearingness remains the elephant in the room (p. 425)' and discussed how deaf academics may in fact be in a position of power over hearing researchers in the field of sign language research, as they intrinsically belong to the deaf community and have rights and privileges not afforded to hearing people. Sutton-Spence and West's article was heavily criticised by two deaf researchers, O'Brien and Emery (2013), for not placing Deaf Studies in a much broader socialpolitical context (see Quote 1.1), and they rejected Sutton-Spence and West's suggestion regarding power dynamics, arguing that deaf people are still in the minority as academics.

> **Quote 1.1**
>
> Sutton-Spence and West's thesis, while discussing the position of hearing academics within the field of Deaf studies, failed to address the issue of the relationship of the Deaf academic to academia in general. This failure obfuscates the power relations between Deaf and hearing academics that we argue are present in the field. We further suggest that by theorising about the place of hearing academics within Deaf studies in English in a peer-reviewed journal, Sutton-Spence and West are moving the debate into an arena in which only a few privileged Deaf people can participate. They are re-affirming divisions within academia on d/Deaf-hearing lines and arguably push a 'hearing' agenda within Deaf studies. (O'Brien & Emery, 2013, p. 27)

Furthermore, another book that was written by two hearing researchers (Young & Temple, 2014) uses Deaf Studies as a case study for illustrating how to conduct social research and features much discussion where the authors problematise their position as 'hearing' researchers, their associations with the deaf community and their reasons for writing the book: Alys Young is a fluent (L2) BSL user who has worked with the deaf community for many years, and Bogusia Temple has worked with ethnic minority communities and conducted cross-cultural research but is not a sign language user. Young and Temple (2014) assert that epistemological choices affect the methodologies and methods that researchers use but are not necessarily predictive of which methodology is chosen. They go on to question the relationship between 'models of deafness' (see Chapter 2, Section 2.2) and epistemology, which can influence the nature of objectivity and the position of the researcher. They also acknowledge that identifying the position of researchers as deaf or hearing is an important issue in the Deaf Studies field and that power is central to not only what researchers reveal about themselves but also how their presence may influence the outcomes of data collection. However, Young and Temple (2014) also suggest that identifying researchers only on the basis of whether they are deaf or hearing oversimplifies the complexity of the different life experiences that researchers bring to academia, and on the very last page of the book, they state that they hope their book will open up discussion and debate in the field.

There have been two reviews of Young and Temple's (2014) book that specifically address the issue of deaf-hearing research dynamics, and these discuss the same points but from a slightly different point-of-view: one from Jemina Napier (co-author of this book) and another from Mike Gulliver (a hearing, fluent sign language user and researcher who works in the field of Deaf Studies). Napier (2014a) notes that Young and Temple do not pay close enough attention to the politics concerning the status of researchers in Deaf Studies, but they present their position honestly. Gulliver (2015) also notes their lack of recognition of the inherent deaf-hearing politics in Deaf Studies and goes further by criticising them for not bringing in a deaf co-author on the book – see Quotes 1.2 and 1.3 for pertinent extracts from each review.

Quote 1.2

It is interesting that although they [Young and Temple] do establish their position, they do not acknowledge the political debates that are particularly current in the Deaf Studies sector concerning the status of researchers (see e.g. O'Brien & Emery, 2013; Sutton-Spence & West, 2011). Although they do cover this issue later in the book, I think it should have been mentioned earlier in the book to expose 'the elephant in the room'. Young and Temple might find themselves criticised by some (deaf or hearing) researchers in the field for not having a deaf co-author, but they transcend the issue by honestly discussing their position and the complexities of conducting social research in Deaf Studies. (Napier, 2014a, p. 1)

Quote 1.3

Although Deaf-centred epistemologies are present, there is insufficient exploration of the wider participatory and representational politics of Deaf Studies or how its methodologies have been shaped by a legacy of hearing hegemony within (and surrounding) the discipline. The last few years have seen a surge in Deaf-led moves to 'reclaim' Deaf Studies for Deaf people and although, given the delay between manuscript and publication, it is hard to see how they might have fully captured this movement, it is disappointing to see them reference a paper that clearly alludes to it (Sutton-Spence & West, 2011) without digging into such an important area more thoroughly.

Secondly, I am disappointed that Young and Temple did not bring in a Deaf (co-) author and then felt they could deflect obvious criticism about this by means of apology. To me, this causes two problems. Firstly, it suggests that it is acceptable for hearing people to appear as representatives of Deaf Studies in toto, as long as they clearly display their discomfort at doing so. Secondly, by representing their hearingness as something they need to be uncomfortable about, they do Deaf Studies and themselves an injustice.

Recent exchanges within Deaf Studies suggest that neither hearing representations of the Deaf community nor hearing self-effacement are acceptable. Deaf people have had enough of hearing people working out their own insecurities within a field where they should be guests…Deaf Studies is now calling for an honest and transparent exploration of a Deaf-led future, its relationship with the academe and the Deaf community, and its need – within that future – to argue (confidently), define (boldly), question (transparently and honestly) the roles, responsibilities, privileges and places of both Deaf and hearing researchers and how each will separately, and cooperatively, contribute to the field. (Gulliver, 2015, p. 315)

We therefore feel it is important to acknowledge this issue up front at the beginning of the book, put forward our position and address several points in relation to those raised by O'Brien and Emery (2013), Napier (2014a) and Gulliver (2015) with respect to the status of hearing researchers in sign language research.

Firstly, neither of us see ourselves as positioned only in Deaf Studies. As linguists and interpreting studies researchers, we see our work within a broader context of applied linguistics and intercultural communication, and the languages that we happen to work with happen to include signed languages. In challenging 'hearing hegemonies' in Deaf Studies, it is possible to draw parallels with Black Studies, where the field emerged in response to the struggle of black people and the need to promote a black intellectual framework and the role of white researchers is questioned (Bailey, 2007). In the 21st century, Black Studies still exists (and is often reframed as African-American Studies, African Studies, Afrocentric Studies, etc.), and black intellectuals have a central role (Christian, 2006). Sutton-Spence and West (2011) and O'Brien and Emery (2013) both refer to White Studies and Black Studies in their publications in examining the position and advantage of white people as compared to hearing people. The key difference, however, is that white people cannot become black, but hearing people can learn to sign. Thus our focus is on *sign language use*, not *deafness*.

Although deaf identity and sign language use are intrinsically linked (as discussed in Chapter 3, Section 3.1), when promoting the use of sign languages as minority languages, it is not just deaf people who use those languages, and therefore it is not just deaf people who do research on those languages and the kinds of questions that arise when a number of languages, spoken and/or signed, come in contact in a range of contexts.

We recognise that the emergence of Deaf Studies was a pushback against the oppression experienced by deaf people at the behest of hearing people (see Chapter 2, Section 2.1), and we wholeheartedly believe that deaf people should be centrally involved in sign language research but that, at present, Deaf Studies 'remains in its infancy, still not fully accepted by the academy' (O'Brien & Emery, 2013, p. 29).

On the other hand, applied linguistics is very much established as a discipline with a strong community of practice in the academy, with 'a plethora of publications ... scientific credibility ... [and] sociable liveliness' (Candlin & Sarangi, 2004a, p. 1). So, this book provides an opportunity to showcase sign language in action in the context of applied linguistics, not just Deaf Studies. Drawing on frameworks of discussion in applied linguistics generally, we focus in this book on asking questions about sign language in practice, aptly captured in Quote 1.4 about applied linguistics.

Quote 1.4

What we want to ask of applied [sign] linguistics is less what it is and more what it does, or rather what its practitioners do... What may be more novel is to take *doing* a step further and address the question of with whom one does the doing, for what purposes, and with what anticipated outcomes and impacts. So, while acknowledging the goal of cumulative coherence, the need to establish principle and not just catalogue practices, and the need to address the issue of whether applied linguistics is more like a research space than it is a tightly defined discipline, we return to relevance, and ask what it is that we do, how, and why. How this relevance may be characterised, how it can be appraised, how it can be disseminated. (Candlin & Sarangi, 2004a, p. 1)

Secondly, we acknowledge that although we are allies of the deaf community, we are not deaf and therefore do not have a shared life experience with deaf people. We are guests in the deaf community (as suggested by O'Brien & Emery, 2013), but we do have a strong philosophy of collaboration with the deaf community collectively and individually in all our research and practice. We believe that it is important for deaf and hearing researchers to work together for the best interests of the worldwide deaf community, but we recognise the power we have as hearing people in the community and the historical backdrop of hearing researchers dominating the field. O'Brien and Emery (2013) provide a useful framework for considering the role of deaf and hearing researchers by drawing on Bourdieu's (1977, 1997) categories of 'habitus', 'field' and 'capital' (see Quote 1.5).

Quote 1.5

The combination [of Bourdieu's categories] of habitus, field, and capital could be used to explore why many deaf people who work in academia chose to work in the field of Deaf Studies. In this field, it may be that they have the linguistic capital that comes with mastery of BSL to succeed, either as teachers or as researchers who can appreciate the nuances of the language that can arise from research interviews or in linguistic analysis of the language. The 'd/Deaf habitus' could also confer benefits, possibly making d/Deaf researchers more empathic to their d/Deaf informants in research interviews, or better able to interpret research findings due to their social proximity to research participants. Hearing researchers, in contrast, can use the strength of their institutionalised cultural capital (i.e. academic degrees and qualifications) and linguistic capital in the official language of the institution to justify their involvement or claim on the field of Deaf studies, advantages which, for reasons discussed earlier, Deaf people may not have. (O'Brien & Emery, 2013, p. 34)

We agree that we have institutional cultural and linguistic capital, and therefore we have 'hearing privilege' (see Concept 1.1), but privilege does not always have to occupy a negative position. We would assert that we accept the responsibility of having hearing privilege (Storme, 2014), and we use our hearing privilege positively to broker engagement and educate inside and outside the community.[1]

Concept 1.1   Hearing privilege

Hearing privilege can be best explained quickly by saying it's similar to the concept of white privilege (McIntosh, 1989). In a nutshell, white privilege is 'a way of conceptualizing racial inequalities that focuses as much on the advantages that white people accrue from society as on the disadvantages that people of color experience.' It's different than racism and prejudice; racism and prejudice are essentially when a dominant group actively seeks to oppress or suppress other racial groups for its own advantage. It is a privileged position; the possession of an advantage white persons enjoy over non-white persons. White privilege is everywhere...

Similarly, hearing privilege is when hearing people view their social, cultural, and economic experiences as a norm that all deaf people should experience. It is a privileged position; hearing people possess an undeniable advantage over deaf persons. The quick reader will rightly point out that whites have an unearned advantage (skin color) while hearing people have a physical advantage (being able to hear), but the privilege itself remains. (http://www.deafecho.com/2010/12/ hearing-privilege/)

Because of our hearing privilege, we get invited to do things like write a book, but we believe that we act in a way that is congruent with deaf cultural norms and values, and one of those values is reciprocity. So, all the royalties from this book will be donated to the World Federation of the Deaf to support their ongoing work with deaf sign language users throughout the world. We are using our hearing privilege to give back to the deaf community.

We have also taken a community participatory approach in writing the book by engaging with deaf people to contribute different aspects to the book. Throughout the book, we feature case studies and quotes from deaf experts who have influenced applied sign linguistics research or practice. Some people may argue this is tokenism, and we know that we may be criticised for not having a deaf co-author. But we also wanted to avoid any potential tokenism when the primary goal of the book is to share our thoughts in defining what we mean by applied sign linguistics (developed over many conversations) and to illustrate those thoughts by showcasing our own research.

In this book, we explore in depth in Chapter 3 the complexities involved in relation to sign language and identity in order to frame the rest of the discussion, and we give examples from our own experiences. This is not a Deaf Studies book; it is an applied linguistics book, drawing on the life, professional and academic experiences of the authors. Our focus is on *sign language in action*; where and how it is used, who uses it, and how we can research sign language in action in order to better understand the relationship between sign language use, culture and identity. For us, we have deliberately focused our discussion on how deaf *and* hearing people use sign language and the implications for learning and teaching and professional practice.

Our respective expertise in various research projects that describe *sign language in action* means we are well placed to collaborate on a project such as this book.

1.4   Overview of the book

This book is the first of its kind, discussing a range of sign language data in applied linguistics contexts. Drawing on data from projects and publications that have explored sign language in action in various domains, the book fills a gap by offering professionals working with signed languages, sign language teachers and students and research students and their supervisors authoritative access to current ideas and practice, emphasising the integration and interdependence of research and practice in a usable way. Throughout the book, we discuss issues of sign language in action throughout the life cycle of deaf and hearing sign language users, considering how sign languages are used by children and adults, deaf and non-deaf, in everyday life and in different contexts.

The book offers a 'map' of the field and developments in applied sign linguistics, providing:

- research evidence for the main ideas and concepts;
- an overview of competing issues and unaddressed and unsolved questions;
- discussion of the range of practical classroom and curriculum applications available in a variety of linguistic and cultural contexts that draw on such concepts and ideas and may challenge them;
- an overview of important models or concepts for practice-based research;
- a synopsis of the applied sign linguistics research conducted to date, and the variety of research methodologies and different research sites;
- a reference list of resources available to support applied sign linguistics research, including listings of vehicles for dissemination, emerging

research networks in this developing field and professional and community partners.

Part I of the book provides an overview of key concepts and research issues in Chapters 2 and 3; Part II discusses practical applications in Chapters 4, 5 and 6; Part III focuses on research into applied sign linguistics in Chapter 7; and Part IV finishes up with information about further resources in applied sign linguistics in Chapter 8.

Part I: Key Concepts and Research Issues

Chapter 2: Understanding Applied Sign Linguistics

Chapter 2 frames the rest of the book by providing an explanation of the sociolinguistic and sociocultural identity of deaf sign language users, who are contrasted with people with hearing loss who are non-sign language users in order to foreground the reason that this book focuses on sign language research. The chapter also defines and frames applied sign linguistics by placing it within the context of the wider applied linguistics field. We contrast *applied* sign linguistics, in terms of the description of sign languages in use and in professional practice, with sign linguistics, in terms of language description, in order to distinguish the need for this book along with its focus on *sign language in action* and research in this domain. The history of sign linguistics research that led to the emergence and development of applied sign linguistics research is described, and we consider the 'inter-relationality' (Candlin & Sarangi, 2004b). The chapter is closed by bringing readers full circle back to the wider field of applied linguistics, highlighting how applied sign linguistics research aligns with current themes in applied linguistics and can inform and augment what we know about language use generally.

Chapter 3: Sign Language in Action

Chapter 3 discusses the notion of sign language in action in depth. Initially we explore the notion of deaf identity, and the importance of sign language use to that identity, to highlight the relationship between deaf people as a linguistic and cultural minority group and the wider majority of non-deaf people. We use this chapter to tease out the complex layers of sign language, identity and belonging in relation to the deaf community, and we suggest that a more appropriate term might be to refer to 'signing communities' in order to embrace the fact that sign language is used by deaf and hearing people within the community. Describing attitudes towards sign language, we then provide a context for considering the policies that influence the uptake of sign language usage

Part II: Practical Applications

Chapter 4: Learning and Teaching Sign Languages

Following on from Chapter 3, in this chapter we concentrate on the issues around first and second sign language acquisition for deaf and hearing people; who can be defined as a 'native signer'; what we know about teaching sign languages; what makes a successful learner of sign languages; and how the teaching, learning and assessment of sign languages, including the use of sign languages for professional purposes, have been mapped onto recommendations for teaching any (spoken) language as a 'foreign' language.

Chapter 5: Sign Language in Everyday Life

Chapter 5 provides an overview of research that reveals how sign languages are used in everyday life and in professional contexts. Initially we explore how professionals working in various contexts (such as interpreters, schoolteachers, community workers, academics, counsellors) can benefit from the understanding of knowing how a sign language is used 'in action' and in context. We also contrast where sign language is known to be used with where deaf sign language users would like to see it used. We continue with the description of sign language in action through the life cycle by outlining how deaf children can begin to use sign language in everyday life at home and progress to using sign language at school and in the workplace as adults. The chapter includes case studies about deaf children and families and everyday interaction at home and at school as well as deaf people who function in different professional roles, such as deaf pilots, politicians, doctors, academics, poets, teachers and lawyers.

Chapter 6: Sign Language in (Professional) Practice

Chapter 6 explores sign language in non-professional and professional practice by discussing the work of deaf and hearing applied language professionals, with a focus on language brokering and sign language interpreting and translation, the relationship between sign language interpreters and deaf sign language users and sign language interpreter identity. In the chapter, we focus on sign language in professional practice from an applied linguistic perspective, so we take some issues for granted regarding the status of the sign language interpreting profession and the nature of service provision.

Part III: Research into Applied Sign Linguistics

Chapter 7: Conducting Research in Applied Sign Linguistics

In Chapter 7 we outline approaches to conducting research in applied sign linguistics and emphasise the importance of the research and practice research cycle, with each feeding into and learning from the other. With reference to Candlin and Crichton's (2011) five-perspective model of inter-discursivity, we suggest multiple possible entry points for research and analysis: we consider the text perspective, the participant perspective, the social and institutional perspective, the social action perspective and the analyst's perspective. We give an overview of applied sign linguistics research that has been conducted in relation to each stage of the life cycle, and we conclude with some suggestions for applied sign linguistics research topics.

Part IV: Further Resources in Applied Sign Linguistics

Chapter 8: Key Resources

In Chapter 8 we provide a comprehensive list of key resources that may be of interest to readers who wish to follow up on the topics and concepts that we have covered in this book on applied sign linguistics. We provide an overview of recommended readings and other relevant resources, including: journals, book series, research centres, associations or organisations, conferences and websites.

Part I
Key Concepts and Research Issues

2
Understanding Applied Sign Linguistics

'The uses and practices of sign languages are strongly related to scientific research on sign languages and vice versa. Conversely, sign linguistics cannot be separated from Deaf community practices, including practices in education and interpretation.' (Meurant, Sinte, van Herreweghe, & Vermeerbergen, 2013, abstract)

2.1 Defining Deaf Studies

The term Deaf Studies was coined in 1984 at the University of Bristol after the establishment of the Centre for Deaf Studies in 1978, and the first International Deaf Researchers Workshop was hosted at the same university in 1985 (Marschark & Humphries, 2010). Researchers interested in exploring the language, culture and lives of deaf sign language users from the perspective of a social rather than medical model began to identify as Deaf Studies scholars, and the field focused on the following areas: sign language and sign linguistics; sign language acquisition; the deaf community and deaf culture; cognition, mental health and education; and communication-related technologies (Marschark & Humphries, 2010). Scholars such as Carol Padden and Tom Humphries (1988, 2005) and Harlan Lane (Lane, 1993; Lane, Hoffemister & Bahan, 1996) have trailblazed explorations of deaf culture and the fact that deaf sign language users form a linguistic and cultural minority group based on shared experiences. Since that time, scholars have branched out and specialised in different aspects of research with deaf people, so that now the term 'Deaf Studies' is more synonymous with 'sociological, anthropological and ethnographic explorations of deaf lives' (Marschark & Humphries, 2010, p. 2). It is beyond the scope of this book to discuss the range of literature in Deaf Studies, so we refer readers to other excellent sources, including Ladd's (2003) theoretical discussion of 'Deafhood', Bauman's (2008) edited volume featuring various Deaf Studies scholars' discussions of different aspects of language, culture and community; and Young and

Temple's (2014) exploration of social research methodologies within the field of Deaf Studies.

Nevertheless, it is important to refer to, and define, Deaf Studies in order to contextualise the advent of applied sign linguistics. One area of specialisation borne out of Deaf Studies has been in sign linguistics, where researchers concern themselves only with describing the various sign languages of the world. Over time, researchers further specialised by focusing more specifically on applied aspects of sign linguistics. Before we provide an overview of how we define applied sign linguistics, give an historical breakdown of the development of sign linguistics and discuss the relationship between the two research strands, we discuss the socio-cultural position of signed languages and deaf people in order to frame the discussion throughout the rest of this book and align with applied linguistics in providing a platform that 'strives to be larger than language, embracing wider concerns of culture and communication' (Candlin & Sarangi, 2004b, p. 225).

Concept 2.1   Social model of deafness

The social model of deafness suggests that individuals who are deaf suffer disability as a result of their environment, not of their physical limitations. Social models of deafness often stress the importance of deaf education for individuals diagnosed with the condition, which should ideally start at a very young age. In fact, research suggests that children who receive deaf education starting at the age of four years will have an easier time communicating with both hearing and non-hearing members of the community than those who do not receive similar types of education. Deaf education often focuses on interaction with others who have similar conditions and learning how to navigate in a society that is not designed for the deaf and hard of hearing. (http://www.deafwebsites.com/deaf-culture/models-deafness.html)

2.2   The sociocultural position of sign language and deaf people

This section provides an overview of the key theories and historical developments that serve to frame our understanding of what it means to be a deaf sign language user in the 21st century. Over time, perceptions of 'deaf identity' have changed significantly, based on linguistic, sociological, anthropological, educational and medical research, and the recognition (and increasingly, legal protection) of deaf people as sign language users.

At this point, we want to ensure that readers understand that when we talk about deaf people, we are not referring broadly to the estimated 360 million people worldwide with a 'disabling' hearing loss, who may manage their capacity to hear through the use of technology such as hearing aids and cochlear implants (World Health Organisation).[1] Instead, we are referring to those who do not identify with the wider (dominant) society based on their hearing status (see Chapter 1, Section 1.1.1). People with a hearing loss tend to speak the spoken language of the majority in their country and rely on their assistive devices and lip-reading to communicate, depending on the level of their loss (described in terms of decibel loss). This group of people are typically referred to as being 'hard of hearing' and some will have an acquired hearing loss, having lost their hearing either in their childhood or early teens or, more commonly, as they age (presbycusis; International Federation of Hard of Hearing People).[2]

Instead, we are referring specifically to people who are deaf and whose first or preferred language is a sign language. They may be profoundly deaf; they may choose to wear hearing aids or have a cochlear implant; they may also be able to speak and make use of some residual hearing; but ultimately they prefer to communicate via a sign language and identify with wider society based on the fact that they are a deaf person (World Federation of the Deaf).[3]

2.2.1   Who are deaf people?

Historically, a biomedical model of health and illness and medical model of disability has influenced and medicalised general thinking on deafness. Such perspectives tend to define deafness in pathological terms, viewing deafness as deficiency, with the result that the medical focus must be on cure or rehabilitation. This kind of thinking considers society and the environment to be unproblematic for deaf people. Practical applications in this vein, which aim to deal with deafness, include the provision of hearing aids, speech therapy, cochlear implants, special education and so on.

These perspectives also view deafness as a characteristic of the individual rather than a community, and as a result, the existence of deaf communities or peer relationships is not relevant to proponents of this model. The ultimate goal of the medical model is to support the deaf person in achieving integrated socialisation into the hearing world insofar as possible. Ladd (2008) suggests that this kind of thinking remains dominant in today's world and has not shown any signs of fading over the last 120 years. It is important to point out that for people who are deafened or hard of hearing, their orientation may indeed be towards the majority hearing society rather than the deaf world, and these people are more likely to base their identity and status in the hearing world. For them, being deprived of hearing may be a threat to their identity as hearing people and their status in that world because talking and listening are prerequisites for participation in the hearing world. For example, in March 2014, the International Federation of Hard of Hearing People welcomed the WHO call on countries to invest in prevention and care for hearing loss.

Quote 2.1   On deafness as a preventable or treatable disability

According to the World Health Organization (WHO), the highest prevalence of disabling hearing loss is found in the Asia Pacific, South Asia and sub-Saharan Africa. About half of all cases of hearing loss worldwide are easily prevented or treated.

However, a report published by the agency on the occasion of International Ear Care Day, observed on 3 March, says that just 32 of the 76 countries who responded to a WHO survey have developed plans and programmes to prevent and control ear diseases and hearing loss.

Many countries lack trained health personnel, educational facilities, data and national plans to address the needs of those living with ear and hearing problems. The gap between need and services is greatest in sub-Saharan Africa. (www.ifhoh.org/actualities/)

Thus, the scope of practice for hearing-related professions such as speech pathology and audiology (Lubinksi & Hudson, 2013) is well suited to those people who do not identify with sign language or the deaf community, as the focus is on speech and hearing and often hearing loss prevention; but it is not necessarily suited to deaf sign language users, as any attempts to frame their experience by 'what is normal' relates only to hearing and speech and not to sign language use.

Lane (2005) suggests that the 'technologies of normalisation' are created within the frame of eugenically driven viewpoints, where the technologies of normalisation refer to attempts to 'cure' or eradicate deafness through technological and medical interventions, including cochlear implantation, stem cell research and genetic engineering. The common theme is the goal of eliminating deafness – and by extension, deaf people and sign language use. These approaches also have the impact of stigmatising deafness, and by extension, sign language users and deaf communities. For some people, these attempts to eradicate deafness remain controversial because they are viewed as deliberate, experimental attempts at eradicating deafness and, consequently, limiting the biodiversity of humanity. On the other hand, some view these practices as genuine acts to meet the wishes of individuals who do not want to have a hearing loss (i.e. these are typically people who have acquired a hearing loss).

A case in point is the European Brain Council's proposed research strand of brain science, entitled 'From Deafness to Brain Mechanisms of Hearing' (Olesen et al., 2006).

Quote 2.2   Assessing the 'economic burden' of deafness

Deafness is 'rarer than other nervous system pathologies, sensory disturbances represent a substantial economic burden that is probably underestimated and

> often not taken into consideration in statistical assessments of health costs. For example, severe to profound hearing loss affects 1 in 1000 newborns, another 1 in 2000 children before they reach adulthood, and 60% of adults over 70.' (Olesen et al., 2006, p. 140)

This argument clearly mirrors a social Darwinist discussion of economic burden, but as we have seen, for those with acquired hearing loss, Olesen and colleagues' call for investment in stem cell implants may be welcomed. At the same time, deaf communities may see such activity as eugenic, with the potential 'genocide' of deaf culture and sign languages (Skutnabb-Kangas, 2000) – a theme we will return to later.

In his discussion of the technologies of normalisation, Lane (2005) claims that professionals use technology to enhance their expertise and control over disabled people to continue their employment. This aligns with McDonnell's (2001) discussion of *technocratic expertism*. McDonnell describes the situations where experts' views are often favoured over the experientially driven views of individuals. He suggests that experts use and apply their technological knowledge to reinforce their beliefs. For example, medical professionals often see deafness as a disability, and this viewpoint has been enshrined in legislation that forbids the selection of deaf embryos over non-deaf alternatives in certain contexts in the UK (Emery, Middleton & Turner, 2010). In parallel, cochlear implantation (CI) levels have risen significantly over the past 20 years, although today it is rare to find medical professionals who will claim that CIs 'cure' deafness. However, there is still a tendency to promote the false belief that if children use a sign language, they will damage their capacity to develop speech (Marschark & Spencer, 2009).

2.2.2 Who are deaf sign language users?

Deaf communities began to emerge in the late 18th and early 19th centuries as a result of the Industrial Revolution and the establishment of deaf schools throughout Europe in the mid-18th century, but historical archives that document the existence of deaf sign language users dates back over 2,000 years (McBurney, 2012). Sign languages are natural languages that have evolved through contact between deaf people. They are not invented sign systems. Different sign languages are used by deaf people in every country throughout the world, with new sign languages still being discovered (Woll, Sutton-Spence & Elton, 2001) and created. An example of this is the case of Nicaraguan Sign Language, which is emerging as a new sign language after deaf children from all over the country came together for a new school programme (Senghas, 2003; Senghas & Kegl, 1994).

Since the first research on sign languages in America (William Stokoe) and the Netherlands (Bernard Tervoort) in the 1950s and 1960s, researchers have provided extensive evidence demonstrating that sign languages are syntactically complex languages with morphological, phonological and sociolinguistic features, which are distinct from spoken languages. In fact, sign linguists argue that we now know more about language in general as a consequence of research into sign languages (Wilbur, 2006). As a result of such work, myths about sign languages and deaf people (e.g. that sign languages were just manual representations of words on the hands) have been dispelled. It is now widely accepted by linguists, anthropologists and sociologists alike that deaf people belong to a linguistic and cultural minority group and identify with one another on the basis of using the natural sign language(s) of their country. For example, Brennan (1992), as a linguist; Ladd *et al.*(2003), as a sociologist; and Senghas and Monaghan (2002), as anthropologists, have all argued that any discussion of the life, communication or experience of deaf sign language users must be framed within the notion of deaf culture and community and the use of sign language as a linguistic right.

Deaf people are regarded as belonging to a community with its own culturally accepted norms of behaviour based on shared experience (Padden & Humphries, 2005; Lane, Hoffmeister & Bahan, 1996). It is accepted that (almost) every country has its own national sign language (indeed, many countries have more than one sign language) and therefore its own deaf community and culture with its own local influences. It is also widely recognised that deaf people belong to a 'transnational' deaf community (Murray, 2007), as their deaf identity transcends the fact that they come from different countries and the visual-gestural nature of sign languages means that deaf interlocutors can find common ground for transnational communication (Adam, 2012a). Adam goes on to tell us that cross-national sign communication was first reported in the early 19th century. Quote 2.3 comes from Laffon de Ladebat, who describes the meeting of the Frenchman Laurent Clerc with British deaf children at the Braidwood school in London in the early 19th century.

Quote 2.3   Transnational engagement

As soon as Clerc beheld this sight [the children at dinner] his face became animated; he was as agitated as a traveller of sensibility would be on meeting all of a sudden in distant regions, a colony of his own countrymen. [...] Clerc approached them. He made signs and they answered him by signs. This unexpected communication caused a most delicious sensation in them and for us was a scene of expression and sensibility that gave us the most heartfelt satisfaction. (Laffon de Ladebat, 1815, p. 33)

Adam (2012a) reports that such cross-linguistic communication can be regarded as a pidgin, in which deaf people from different communities communicate by exploiting their awareness of iconicity and their access to visual-spatial expression via what is usually called International Sign (IS). However, complex meanings are not easily conveyed via IS. Thus, 'Use of the term International Sign, rather than International Sign Language, emphasises that IS is not recognised as having full linguistic status' (Adam, 2012a, p. 853).

Concept 2.2   Defining deaf culture

One of the first definitions of deaf culture: 'Members of the Deaf culture behave as Deaf people do, use the language of Deaf people, and share the beliefs of Deaf people toward themselves and other people who are not Deaf' (Padden, 1980).

Turner (1994) critiques Padden's (1980) definition as being self-referential and over-simplistic criteria that serves as a 'Bingo Card model'.

Padden updates her definition: Deaf culture describes the social beliefs, behaviors, art, literary traditions, history, values, and shared institutions of communities that are affected by deafness and which use sign languages as the main means of communication. (Padden & Humphries, 2005)

2.2.3   The role of education in the development of deaf sign language users

Although tensions and debate remain in the area of deaf education, the legitimisation of sign languages as 'real' languages has also had an impact in the educational sphere. Over time, there has been a shift by some educational providers in recognising that deaf children can be educated in a sign language (rather than requiring them to attempt to hear, speak and lipread the majority spoken language with the assistance of technical aids; Takkinen, 2012). Along with research evidence that children who grow up bilingual with 2 or more spoken languages may have a cognitive advantage (Chin & Wigglesworth, 2007), some educators have acknowledged that deaf children will not be disadvantaged by learning a sign language, and in fact may benefit from developing bilingual skills in a sign language and the written (and perhaps spoken) form of the majority language. Additionally, a social rather than medical model of deafness has led to acknowledgement that deaf children should be encouraged to identify as deaf and not as 'broken' (and therefore inferior) hearing people (Ahrbeck, 1995; United Nations 2006). Thus, the bilingual deaf educational philosophy was born, mirroring bilingual educational approaches of spoken languages (especially of minority groups; e.g. Helmberger, 2006; Rolstad, Mahoney & Glass, 2005). This philosophy essentially means that whether educated in a segregated deaf school or integrated into a local school with hearing children, more deaf children have the option to access their education in a sign language (directly via teachers or indirectly via interpreters), rather than through auditory-oral methods (see Chapter 3).

We can also suggest that mainstream education potentially places deaf children under pressure in terms of social, emotional and identity development (Kyle, 2012; Rogers & Young, 2012; Vermeerbergen, van Herreweghe & De Weerdt, 2012). We also need to be aware that the consequences of mainstreaming do not only affect deaf students and their families. There are far-reaching consequences for deaf communities, too. These include pressure being placed on the stability of sign languages due to inhibited transmission paths, and with this a marked destabilisation of sign languages, which some linguists consider one of the factors that pushes some sign languages into the category of endangered languages (e.g. Johnston, 2006, for Auslan). In part, this arises as a result of a number of factors:

- Deaf children are typically born to hearing parents in 90–95% of cases, so their acquisition of a sign language does not take place naturally, as is the case for deaf children of deaf, sign language–using adults.
- Deaf children growing up in hearing families may use gesture as the basis of communication with hearing family members. This typically is conventionalised within the family sphere, creating a 'home sign system'.
- Deaf children who come in contact with other deaf children typically generate – often predicated on their collective home sign systems – conventionalised sign languages (the generation of Nicaraguan Sign Language is a case in point; see Senghas, Senghas & Pyers, 2004, and www.youtube. com/watch?v=pjtioIFuNf8).
- Where deaf children have access to deaf sign language using role models, they have input from native signers, who can correct and influence language use.
- Where deaf children typically attended the large schools for the deaf in each country, sign language variants were associated with attendance at specific schools. However, within the areas where these sign variants were used, the languages were robust, despite the threat to sign language use during the heyday of oral education.
- Today, given limited access to other deaf children and deaf adults, the potential for accessing fluency in a national sign language is reduced, and with this, the potentiality for school-specific generated signs increases.

Unless there is action to facilitate the engagement of deaf children from mainstream schools with the adult deaf community and children from other mainstream schools, there is real potential for fragmentation of national sign languages (Leeson & Saeed, 2012a). This has consequences for community engagement across generations and, in real terms, the potential for diminishing the social engagement of deaf people due to a decline in community membership. At worst, then, from a deaf community perspective, mainstreaming potentially facilitates a path towards 'language death' (Crystal, 2002), or as others put it, can be taken to demonstrate 'linguistic genocide' at work (Skutnabb-Kangas, 2000), which may be interpreted as an overly politicised argument but represents the feelings of many deaf people nevertheless.

2.2.4 Contemporary position of sign languages

In essence, what we have witnessed is a 'linguistic turn' in Deaf Studies (Thoutenhoofd, 2000). Several countries have legally recognised the indigenous sign language of their country while others have given *de facto* recognition to their national or regional sign language in the form of statements in policies or relevant legislation (Krausneker, 2000; Wheatley & Pabsch, 2010, 2012), such as disability discrimination acts or language policies. A survey of 93 countries, conducted by the World Federation of the Deaf (Haualand & Allen, 2009), sought to identify which countries have given recognition to their national sign language, and in what form, as part of a wider study of the human rights of deaf people across the world. Table 2.1 below (taken from Haualand & Allen, 2009) gives a snapshot of the nature of sign language recognition according to region.

According to Haualand and Allen (2009), 'sign language' is mentioned in the constitution of 10 countries, and in 19 countries, it is mentioned in one or more laws. In another 19 countries, 'sign language' is mentioned in some form of policy, and 7 countries mention 'sign language' in guidelines. Among those who have given detailed information on where and how a sign language is formally recognised, most refer to educational laws/policies or laws/policies regulating social and/or welfare services. The survey revealed that the term 'sign language' is mentioned in legislation in only one-third of responding countries. Although the numbers are small, they are growing, and consequently, attitudes towards sign language have become more positive (Burns, Matthews & Nolan-Conroy, 2001).

Table 2.1 Snapshot of sign language recognition by region

Region	Constitution	Legislation	Policy	Guideline	Other
Eastern Europe and Middle Asia		5			
Asia and the Pacific	1	3	5		
South America	3	2	1		
Mexico, Central America and the Caribbean		2	4		
Southern and Eastern Africa	3	3	9	2	
Western and Central Africa		1			
Arab Region	3	3		5	1
Total	10	19	19	7	1

We can also add a snapshot overview of the European context. In 1988, the Irish European parliamentarian Eileen Lemass chaired the committee that prepared the European Parliament's Resolution on Sign Languages. The European Union (EU) then comprised 11 member states with an estimated deaf, sign language–using population of 500,000 (today, there are 28 member states and an estimated 750,000 deaf sign language users[4]). Originally, the scope of the committee was to develop a document to promote the standardisation of sign languages across the EU member states. Following from a prolonged period of consultation with organisations of deaf people and service providers across Europe, it became clear that standardisation was not what deaf people wanted. They wanted recognition of their languages, and they wanted access to civil society and to education via sign languages.

Quote 2.4   European Parliamentary Aspirations Resolution on Sign Languages, 1988

In practice, official recognition of sign languages could lead to the following: schools, colleges and universities providing deaf students with the support services that ensure them equal educational opportunities; employers accepting deaf job applicants on their merits and providing the necessary support services; health, welfare, legal, police and other statutory services providing sign language interpreters as required; television broadcasting services including sign language interpretation in their programmes; political parties, trade unions and professional bodies providing sign language interpretation at their conference and meetings. (Eileen Lemass MEP, Plenary Address to the European Parliament, 17 June 1988)

Quote 2.4 is aspirational, alluding to the key themes addressed in the European Parliament's resolution. In 1998, the European Parliament reiterated their 1988 resolution, explicitly calling for 'the Commission to make a proposal to the Council concerning official recognition of the sign language used by deaf people in each Member State; ... the Member States to abolish any remaining obstacles to the use of sign language'.

Other key issues raised, alluded to in Quote 2.4 above, include the need to provide training for sign language interpreters and to ensure that there is provision of sign language interpreting across the EU; the need to ensure that sign languages are represented on TV; the need to ensure that hearing people have the opportunity to learn sign languages; and the need to ensure that sign language dictionaries are created and that sign language exchanges are facilitated. Finally, the resolutions called for European commitment to fund such enterprises. And, indeed, the institutions have funded some significant projects relating to deaf communities, sign languages and interpreting. However, there are still institutional barriers to participation on several fronts, including, crucially, the funding of interpreters.

Despite the significant 'win' that the European Parliamentary resolutions represent, there are shortcomings, too. The most significant shortcoming is the fact that the resolutions are non-binding. Because of the principle of subsidiarity, which determines the level of intervention that is most relevant in the areas of competences shared between the EU and the member states, the EU may only intervene if it is able to act more effectively than member states. Therefore, the EU has no legal basis to enforce the recognition of any language in any member state. Therefore, while they can encourage member states to recognise their sign languages locally, the EU cannot enforce this (as they can with issues covered in European Directives, for example). As a result of this, there is no pan-European port of call for deaf communities whose member states do not recognise their languages as a result of these resolutions. Instead, deaf communities must take legal action (if required) on the basis of discrimination due to disability, using EU disability legislation (e.g. Article 19 of the Treaty on the Functioning of the European Union) or via national equality legislation (e.g. the Americans with Disabilities Act) or, for those countries who have ratified it, via the United Nations Charter on the Rights of Persons with Disabilities (UNCRPD; United Nations, 2006; we say more on this below).

Other pan-European avenues that have been explored in the pathway to recognition of sign languages include the Council of Europe Parliamentary Assembly. The Council of Europe is a separate political entity from the EU. It has 47 member states, including the EU member states, the Baltic states, Turkey and Russia. In 2003, the Council of Europe's Parliamentary Assembly passed a resolution on sign languages. This was spearheaded by the Scottish parliamentarian Malcolm Bruce (UK; see Leeson, 2004; Timmermans, 2005, for further discussion). However, as with the European Parliamentary resolutions, the Council of Europe's Parliamentary Assembly's resolution is non-binding for member states. However, the Council of Europe has a quite powerful, legally binding treaty which relates to regional or minority languages: the European Charter for Regional or Minority Languages (CRML) (Council of Europe, 1992). Unfortunately, despite efforts on the part of several countries, the Council of Europe argues that the CRML extends only to the indigenous *spoken* regional and minority languages of Europe. Thus, for over a decade, the European Union of the Deaf (EUD) has called on the Council of Europe to extend the scope of the CRML to include sign languages. It may be that a Charter for Sign Languages will emerge – this would have binding status, as it would have legal standing as a treaty. Timmermans (2005) was commissioned by the Council of Europe to write a report on the status of sign languages in the Council of Europe territories. She notes that the report:

> ... could serve as the starting point of a wider study of the needs of sign language users in Council of Europe member states. Reference to such

a needs analysis is made both in Recommendation 1598 (2003) of the Parliamentary Assembly of the Council of Europe 'Protection of sign languages in the member states of the Council of Europe' and the reply of the Committee of Ministers thereto (c.f. Appendices 3 and 4). Such a study could, in turn, form the basis for any debate on a possible future Council of Europe legal instrument to protect the sign languages and the rights of their users (p. 11).

The most recent review of the European situation on recognition of sign languages comes from the EUD (Wheatley & Pabsch, 2012), outlining the constitutional, legal and *de facto* recognitions of sign languages across the continent. An updated overview of the situation is summarised in Figure 2.1.

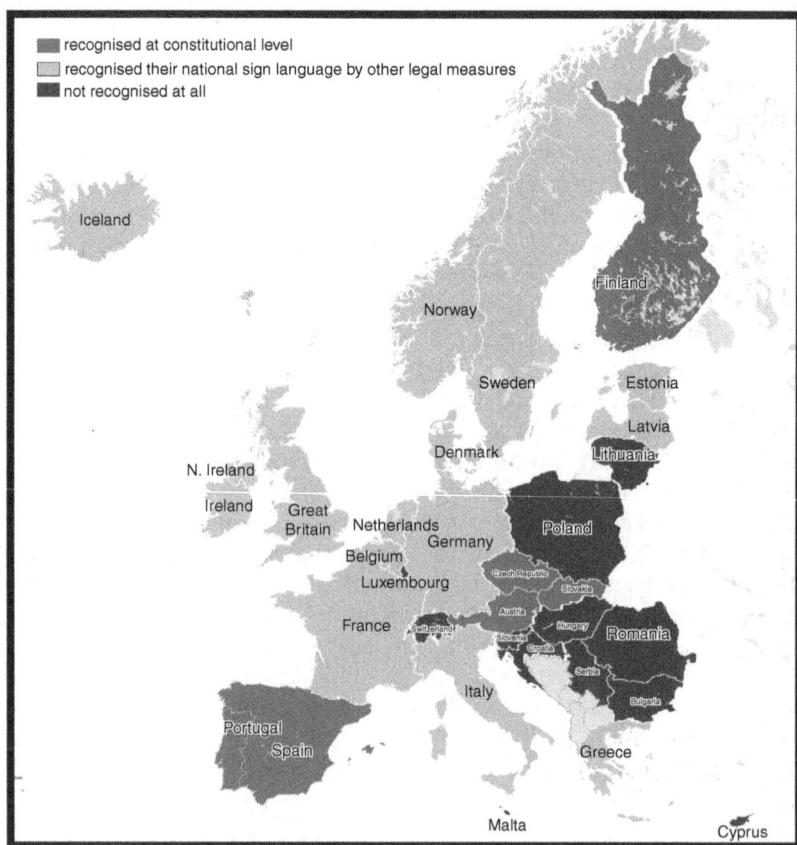

Figure 2.1 Legal recognition of sign languages in Europe[5]

At the global level, a key document pertaining to global recognition of the importance of sign languages for deaf communities is the United Nations Conventions on the Rights of Persons with Disabilities (United Nations, 2006). On 19 December 2001, the United Nations General Assembly established an *ad hoc* committee to consider proposals for an international treaty on the Rights of Persons with Disabilities. In considering why deaf people needed to be represented by this particular UN Convention, we can say that many deaf people across the world are still not guaranteed their human rights at present (Haualand & Allen, 2009). Further, there is a clear need for a paradigm shift from the medical model to the human rights model of disability (which we see as including a 'linguistic rights' model of deafness). Therefore, a Convention was needed to secure a commitment to non-discrimination against and protection of the human rights of people with disabilities and to securing the linguistic rights of deaf people.

Between 2002 and 2006, the committee, which was made up of representatives of member states, UN special agencies like UNESCO and the WHO and many NGOs, including wide representation from the international disability movement (the International Disability Caucus [IDC]) met to discuss the content of the Convention (Leeson & Sheikh, 2010). The interests of deaf sign language users were represented by the World Federation of the Deaf (WFD), who participated at all levels in the process of drafting the Convention. In its final form, the Convention aims to guarantee equal rights for persons with disabilities to enjoy physical, social, economic and cultural rights covering issues related to the environment, health, education, information and communication. WFD's objective was to ensure that deaf people would be able to enjoy all human rights and fundamental freedoms that are experienced by all other citizens. Their key goal, however, was to ensure that deaf people's linguistic rights would be recognised within the Convention.

Ultimately, WFD's objectives on sign languages were approved within the framework of the Convention. Many rights are mentioned in a general way, and these can be interpreted together with those articles where sign languages are explicitly referenced. For example, non-discrimination on the basis of language and linguistic rights is mentioned in many segments of the Convention, including in the preamble, and sign languages are mentioned 8 times in 5 different articles:

- Article 2 – Definition
- Article 9 – Accessibility
- Article 21 – Freedom of expression and opinion, and access to information
- Article 21(e) – Recognising and promoting the use of signed languages
- Article 24.3(b) – Education

- Article 24.3(c) – Education
- Article 24.3(e) – Education
- Article 30: Participation in cultural life, recreation leisure and sport.

Because of the importance attached to the UNCRPD by deaf NGOs, we run through each article in turn.

In relation to Article 2, which deals with definitions, WFD informants report that it proved difficult to convince all members of the *ad hoc* committee that sign languages were (are) 'real' languages (Kauppinen, 2013; Leeson & Sheikh, 2010). Many State delegates wondered why several sign languages exist alongside a single system for Braille. Some proposed that in our time of globalisation, we should only have one international sign language. Even members of the EU discussed the use of the term *sign languages* (plural form) versus *sign language* (singular form) for 2 hours in their own group meeting (Leeson & Sheikh, 2010).

Article 9, which focuses on accessibility, notes that persons with disabilities shall have the right to 'participation in all the levels of society'. Many items listed in this article also emphasise the right to freely access communication and have access to communication and information through intermediaries.

Quote 2.5   Provide sign language interpreters

State parties shall: 'Provide forms of live assistance and intermediaries, including guides, readers and professional sign language interpreters, to facilitate accessibility to buildings and other facilities open to the public.' (United Nations, 2006, Article 9)

The reference to 'professional sign language interpreters' means that States who ratify the Convention have responsibilities to promote and develop sign language interpreter training, degree programmes and registration processes, to facilitate interpreter services and to promote access to sign language interpreters (see Chapter 6, Section 6.2).

Article 21 aims to secure freedom of expression and access to information through all forms of communication, including public services in sign languages, in media and via the Internet. Sign languages are mentioned in paragraphs 21(b) and 21(e) of this Article, as outlined in Quote 2.6.

Quote 2.6   Freedom of expression and opinion, and access to information

21 (b) Accepting and facilitating the use of sign languages, Braille, augmentative and alternative communication, and all other accessible means, modes and

formats of communication of their choice by persons with disabilities in official interactions.
21(e) Recognizing and promoting the use of sign languages. (United Nations, 2006, Article 21)

WFD felt it important to emphasise not only that sign languages are languages used by deaf people in their interaction but that they should also be approved for official interactions: People must have the right to submit a document in a sign language and to receive a response in a sign language; to act and to receive information in court and in interaction with the police; to carry out transactions and to get consumer instruction in sign languages as well as to receive access to treatment and other services in sign languages. Quote 2.7 illustrates how this language policy maps to the reality faced by deaf sign language users in 2013, as reported by the EUD.

Quote 2.7   UNCRPD implementation in Europe – A deaf perspective

The Netherlands, as one of the last countries of the EU to not have ratified the UNCRPD, is one of the countries with the biggest problem of Deaf awareness. Over 50% of respondents claimed that the biggest issue in the workplace was no Deaf awareness. By contrast, this number is as low as 12.5% in the Czech Republic.

The UK (11.11%) and Denmark (5.4%) both have reportedly very little problems with governments or employers not paying reasonable accommodation. For other countries such as Greece or Luxembourg, the number rises to 100% of respondents. Luxembourg, although having ratified the UN Convention, does not have any legislative protection of their national sign language (German Sign Language).

Furthermore, access to reasonable accommodation for example in the form of sign language interpreters is often inflexible and only covers a portion of a full workweek. Often the application procedure to receive services is too complex to be readily understood by all Deaf workers. By contrast, Deaf people who worked in Deaf environments reported little to no problems. (European Union of the Deaf, 2013 UNCRPD Report, p. 12)

The UNCRPD's Paragraph 21(e) states that sign languages should be recognised either in legislation or in public policies and programmes. It also means that deaf people of all ages have the right to use a sign language: Children should not be forced to change their language while growing up. Promotion also covers support for publications in sign languages, education, research and general usage – that is, securing the use of sign languages to the extent that deaf people's human rights are realised. The reality remains far from ideal, as we can see from Quote 2.8.

> **Quote 2.8   'I had no support'**
>
> When I went to third level...I failed first year because there was no interpreter provision. I felt it very difficult on my own amongst all these hearing people. It was a very confusing time for me: I had no support, no tuition, then I left [college]. My mother tried to find an interpreter. Thankfully we found a tutor for some subjects. Then I was able to pass the [repeat] year. ... Then in second year I passed. ... I feel that there is a severe lack of interpreters. (Deaf woman, Ireland; Leeson, 2007)

Article 24 of the Convention focuses on education. Paragraph 24.3(b) states that State parties shall engage in facilitating the learning of sign language and the promotion of the linguistic identity of the deaf community. They specify that use of a sign language should not be prohibited in learning, which sadly remains a reality in the majority of countries of the world. Indeed, WFD estimates that currently only 17% of the world's 72 million deaf people have access to education, and of these, just 3% access sign bilingual education (Allen, 2013).

> **Quote 2.9   Make use of 'most appropriate languages'**
>
> State parties shall engage in 'Ensuring that the education of persons, and in particular children, who are blind, deaf or deafblind, is delivered in the most appropriate languages and modes and means of communication for the individual, and in environments which maximize academic and social development.' (United Nations 2006, Article 24.3(c))

Article 24.3(c), outlined in Quote 2.9, means that education, for example for deaf children and across the life span, should be in those languages and in such environments which guarantee maximum cognitive and social development. For deaf people, WFD argued the case that this means a sign language/bilingual learning environment. Quote 2.10 illustrates what this can mean in practice.

> **Quote 2.10   Linguistic access breeds success**
>
> I had a deaf lecturer and when there were hearing lecturers, we had an interpreter provided, and this gave me great access to everything that was happening in the classroom. I really enjoyed the course so I decided that I would move on to the Diploma course [from a Certificate course]...I remember how I had been before I started the course, saying that I didn't want to study again. This was due to my experience of school when I was younger. However this [more recent] course has

really opened my eyes to education. I'm not saying it was easy, but I did have access to supports like note-taking. Now I'm studying for my master's degree and I will be finished in another two years. (Interview with Carmel Grehan, deaf academic; Sheikh, 2009)

Sign languages are also referenced in Article 24.4, which deals with who should teach children. Quote 2.11 provides the UNCRPD vision.

Quote 2.11   Appropriate teachers

In order to help ensure the realization of this right, State Parties shall take appropriate measures to employ teachers, including teachers with disabilities, who are qualified in sign language and/or Braille, and to train professionals and staff who work at all levels of education. Such training shall incorporate disability awareness and the use of appropriate augmentative and alternative modes, means and formats of communication, educational techniques and materials to support persons with disabilities. (United Nations, 2006, Article 24.4)

Implementation of this paragraph will potentially prove challenging for teacher training in many countries and for national and regional policy setting with regard to the competencies required by teachers with respect to appropriate levels of fluency in a sign language skill. The need to ensure that deaf people have access to teacher training is also key; in many countries, there remain barriers to participation in third-level education generally and teacher training specifically. When this can happen, deaf children get to 'sit up and take notice', as Irish deaf teacher Sean Herlighy points out in Quote 2.12.

Quote 2.12   Sitting up and taking notice

Some teachers did provide information in ISL when I was at school, and when they did, we really sat up and took notice, for it was in those moments that we really learnt. It is in this environment, I knew that as an adult, a Deaf adult, I could make a difference in the Deaf child's learning process. (Sean Herlighy, deaf teacher; AHEAD conference, 2012)

Finally, Article 30 of the Convention is concerned with participation in cultural life, recreation, leisure and sport. Paragraph 30.1 is concerned with ensuring that the right to take part in cultural life on an equal basis with others is facilitated. This means that cultural materials such as TV programmes, movies, theatre and other cultural activities and cultural venues and places (such as museums) and information should accessible by deaf people. Leeson and Sheikh's (2010) informants report that when the *ad hoc* committee came to discuss this article, it raised a lot of discussion among indigenous peoples who also wanted to include their own rights under this Article. Paragraph 30.4 makes specific reference to the right to cultural participation by deaf people, and specifically to the right to recognition and support for sign languages and the identity of deaf people as members of a culture.

Quote 2.13   On cultural participation

Persons with disabilities shall be entitled, on an equal basis with others, to recognition and support of their specific cultural and linguistic identity, including sign languages and deaf culture. (United Nations, 2006, Article 30, Para. 30.4)

These articles, together with other human rights treaties (where discrimination based on language is denied), strengthen the position of sign languages and deaf people's human rights, critical goals of global, pan-continental and national NGOs representing deaf sign language users. It is for this reason that deaf leaders believe that the UNCRPD has the potential to revolutionise deaf people's lives in a majority of countries once it has been ratified and implemented in national legislation.

As of October 2015, the Convention has had the following response[6]:

- 160 signatories to the Convention
- 93 signatories to the Optional Protocol
- 159 ratifications of the Convention
- 88 ratifications of the Optional Protocol

This situation would not have come about without the tireless work of WFD representatives, most notably Honorary WFD Presidents Emeritus Liisa Kauppinen (who in 2013 was a recipient of the United Nations Human Rights Award Prize) and Markku Jokinen. The baton for continued work relating to the monitoring of the implementation of the UNCRPD now lies with WFD President Colin Allen, whose work on human rights we cited earlier in this chapter. And there is a great deal of work to be done. For example, while Australia, Canada, El Salvador, New Zealand, Russia, and the United Kingdom have ratified the Convention, the United States and Ireland have not yet done so. And where the Convention is ratified, the work of ensuring that appropriate responses to sign language users are instantiated and supported over time will require ongoing monitoring.

Thus, we can suggest that deaf citizens in the 21st century are living in a world that is in many ways more politically aware of and responsive to the linguistic and cultural position of sign language users than at any previous time in history. Ironically, as we have seen, due to technological, scientific and medical advances, the traditional deaf community is also under threat as either fewer people are being born deaf or more people receive cochlear implants as babies, so fewer deaf children are being exposed to sign language from birth or a very young age (Johnston, 2006).

Concept 2.3   Linguistic Human Rights (LHRs)

Skutnabb-Kangas (2000) talks about the concept of linguistic human rights (LHRs) as a combination of language rights and human rights that are necessary to satisfy people's basic needs. Wheatley and Pabsch (2012) suggest that this includes the right to one's mother tongue, including the right to positively identify with and be educated in that language. They argue that for deaf people, 'the learning of a national sign language and the national (spoken) language, albeit in its written form, should be facilitated' (2012, p. 25).

Concept 2.4   Legal recognition of sign languages

The legal systems in the various EU member States are as diverse as the legal status of its sign languages. Sign languages are recognised and mentioned across a large range of different pieces of legislation: from constitutional recognition, to separate sign language acts, or no reference at all ... All countries have in common that recognition was only achieved through the continuous efforts of Deaf organisations (National Associations of the Deaf, NADs) and Deaf individuals. (Wheatley & Pabsch, 2012, p. 37)

2.2.5   Contemporary position of deaf people

Conferences have been organised to celebrate academic and artistic analyses and expressions of deaf culture, with subsequent publications; for example, the Deaf Nation (UK) and Deaf Way (USA) conferences (Erting, Johnson, Smith & Snider, 1994; Goodstein & Brown, 2004). Books have also been written discussing deaf identities (e.g. Breivik, 2005), deaf history (e.g. Van Cleve, 2007) and deaf sport (e.g. Atherton, Turner & Russell, 2000) and their cultural significance for deaf people. There is a burgeoning recognition of the uniqueness of sign language poetry as an art form (Sutton-Spence, 2005; Pollitt, 2014), and we are witnessing an increase in funded research that explores aspects of deaf identity, sign language use in context, sign language bilingualism and multilingualism (see Chapter 3 for more discussion).

This book focuses on how sign languages are used in context and how the use of sign languages in everyday life is shaped by the identities of the deaf and hearing people who use those languages and with whom they interact.

Although we have framed the rest of the book by establishing the socio-cultural position of deaf people, it is important to note that there are likely larger numbers of hearing people who use sign languages in everyday life: parents and family members of deaf children and adults, work colleagues of deaf adults, teachers of deaf children and adults and sign language transla-tors and interpreters. In this respect, we give consideration to all of these people as sign language users, regardless of their hearing status.

2.3   What is applied sign linguistics?

This section is concerned with introducing the idea of applied sign linguis-tics. To do this, we first need to consider the development of the field of sign linguistics in the 20th and early 21st centuries, as applied sign linguistics has evolved in parallel with considerations about how deaf children acquire signed and spoken languages, discussion surrounding bilingual deaf educa-tion, the training of sign language interpreters and the teaching of sign language to hearing adults.

It is not our intention to draw a sharp line between sign linguistics and applied sign linguistics, as this would not capture the close mutual involve-ment and influence of the two strands on one another, as is also evident in linguistics and applied linguistics generally. Instead we consider the 'inter-relationality' (Candlin & Sarangi, 2004b) between sign linguistics and applied sign linguistics before we discuss the praxis (i.e. the process) by which theories presented from the two strands of research are embodied, enacted and realised in sign language use in everyday life and professional practice.

Concept 2.5   Sign linguistics

Before the beginning of sign language linguistics, sign languages were regarded as exemplifying a primitive universal way of communicating through gestures. Early sign linguistic research from the 1960s onward emphasized the equiva-lences between sign languages and spoken languages and the recognition of sign languages as full, complex, independent human languages. Contemporary sign linguistics now explores the similarities and differences between different sign languages, and between sign languages and spoken languages. (Pfau, Steinbach, & Woll, 2012, p. 1)

Concept 2.6   Applied sign linguistics

Over the past decade, sign language research has been presented at a wide range of academic conferences, and special sign language sessions or workshops have been held in conjunction with many professional conferences in related disciplines (including child language acquisition, bilingual acquisition, gesture studies, minority languages, endangered languages, sociolinguistics, language typology, laboratory phonology, corpus linguistics, computational linguistics, anthropology, psychology, and neuroscience)... Without question, research into sign languages has enriched our understanding of the human mind and its capacity for language. (McBurney, 2012, p. 938)

2.4 The difference between sign linguistics and applied sign linguistics

While sign linguistics has focused on the development of robust descriptions of sign languages, often framed within linguistic, psycholinguistic or neurolinguistic theoretical perspectives, applied sign linguistics focuses on the applications of findings in these realms to understanding the relationships that hold between sign languages and society (sociolinguistics), how children and adults acquire languages and the (typically positive) outcomes associated with acquiring a language in the visual modality as a first, second or subsequent language. Applied sign linguists are concerned with the development of curricula for the teaching and learning of sign languages, with assessment issues, with the creation of dictionaries and with interventions for those with learning disorders. Therapists engage in applied linguistics work when they encounter sign language users who have suffered strokes or brain injuries. Sign language interpreters and translators are also applied linguists in that they utilise their languages in practice, making complex decisions about the relationship between their source and target languages in the process, influenced by many situational and contextual demands (see Chapters 5 and 6). All of these practitioners could be considered researchers, what Daniel Gile (1994) has termed 'practisearchers' in relation to interpreting practitioner-researchers. There are also crossovers both ways, from sign linguistics to applied sign linguistics and vice versa, and applied sign linguistics does not just apply new knowledge but formulates original contributions to our basic knowledge.

2.5 The history of sign linguistics

Until the 17th century, deaf people communicated mostly using home sign or gesture unless they happened to live in a village or community where a larger population of deaf people resided, leading to the development of a village sign language (McBurney, 2012). It was not until the establishment of public schools in the 19th century that more formal signed languages seem to have developed. McBurney notes that during the Enlightenment, deaf people became a source of 'cultural fascination' (p. 914), and for the first time, consideration of sign languages and deaf people was a matter of concern.

In the 20th century, Ben Tervoort's (1953) doctoral dissertation regarding the signing of deaf children in the Netherlands and William Stokoe's (1960) description of the linguistic structure of American Sign Language (ASL) marked the beginning of modern sign linguistics. By the 1970s, several American and European linguists had begun to independently study their local or national signed languages.

Bencie Woll (2003) has described research on sign languages as falling into three broad categories: (i) the modern period, (ii) the postmodern period, and (iii) typological research.[7]

Following Leeson and Saeed (2012b), we must bear in mind that while the categories suggested by Woll are not absolute, they offer a useful framework for considering how the field of sign linguistics has evolved, and they provide us with a timeline against which we can plot the development of applied sign linguistics.

We can say that early research in the 'modern period' tended to focus on the description of individual sign languages, with a concentration on what made sign languages similar to spoken languages rather than on what differentiated them from each other. For example, early research focused on the linearity of expression in sign languages without reference to issues like manual simultaneity or iconicity (e.g. Fischer, 1975; Liddell, 1977) – issues that today we recognise as modality-related features of sign languages and so on. This development had an impact on work on word order in sign languages (see Quote 2.14).

Quote 2.14   Word order in ASL

Fischer (1975), for instance, describes ASL as having an underlying SVO pattern at the clause level, but also notes that alternative orders exist (such as the use of topic constructions in certain instances, yielding OSV order). In contrast, Friedman (1976) claims that word order in ASL is relatively free with a general tendency for verbs to appear sentence-finally, also arguing that the subject is not present in the majority of her examples. However, Liddell (1977) and Wilbur (1987) questioned Friedman's analysis, criticising that she did not recognise the ways in which ASL verbs inflect to mark agreement, a point of differentiation between spoken and sign languages, which we can align with Woll's [later] post-modern period of research. (Leeson & Saeed, 2012b, p. 250)

This 'postmodern period' had its beginnings in the 1980s, when researchers began to look at how signed and spoken languages differed from each other, leading to work focusing on the impact of language modality. Focusing on the issue of word order, Leeson and Saeed (2012b) point out that the beginnings of work on British Sign Language (BSL), for example, fall into this timeframe. During this period, Margaret Deuchar (1983) raised the question of whether BSL, like English, had an SVO patterning. (In the end, she argued for a more functional topic-comment analysis.) Deuchar's work also compared BSL with ASL, representing an early move in the direction of typological work on sign languages, again illustrating that Woll's categories are not watertight silos but rather that they leak into each other. Similar patterns hold true for early work on Australian Sign Language (Auslan) in the late 1970s and early 1980s (for example, Johnston, 1989). By the late 1980s and into the 1990s, work on ASL also began to make greater reference to issues of differentiation such as simultaneity (e.g. Miller, 1994). Miller's work also focused on Quebec Sign Language (LSQ), marking a move towards cross-linguistic, typological studies (Leeson & Saeed, 2012b).

Of course, some parts of the world were ahead of others, not least as a result of rising deaf community consciousness around their language and culture, leading to (in the USA) an era that pushed forward the linguistic rights of deaf Americans in the 1980s, inspired by the civil rights movement in the 1960s. While ASL research may have entered into the postmodern stage in the early 1980s, the fact that the point of reference for comparative purposes has frequently been ASL or BSL implies that for many other under-described sign languages, some degree of cross-linguistic work has always been embedded in their approach to description (Leeson & Saeed, 2012a). However, it is only in the 21st century that we see a conscious move towards typological research.

Work carried out by sign linguists in the late 20th century and early 21st century tended to be cross-linguistic in nature, often focusing on how modality effects can be considered a point of differentiation between spoken and signed languages. Moreover, Leeson and Saeed (ibid.) tell us that studies sought to identify points that differentiated between individual sign languages while also acknowledging the impact that articulation in the visual-spatial modality seems to have for sign languages, which leads to a certain level of similarity in certain areas. This typological research period has thus led to a significant leap forward in terms of our understanding of the relationship between sign languages and the ways in which sign languages are structured (Leeson and Saeed, 2012b).

At the same time, we need to be mindful that the research results from the early days of sign linguistics were heavily influenced by a spoken language linguistics lens, which may, in part, have led to a belief that sign languages seem remarkably similar across the world. Quote 2.15 provides some insights that help us to understand why sign languages may be similar.

Quote 2.15   Why sign language structure may be similar across language boundaries

If sign languages are really as similar as has been claimed, we need to enquire why that may be so. Five mutually compatible and probably overlapping reasons suggest themselves:

- the relative youth of signed languages (including creolisation)
- iconicity
- a link between sign languages and gesture
- linear syntax intrinsically creates greater differences than spatial syntax
- differences are there but researchers haven't noticed them.

(Woll, 2003, p. 25)

Vermeerbergen and Leeson (2011) build on this, noting that in the past, 'cross-linguistic work' often entailed a comparison of spoken and signed languages but that since the beginning of the 21st century, there has been an increase in cross-sign language comparison ('typological research'), which has led to the point where we see a small number of sign languages compared, leading to the emergence of preliminary typological projects that involve a larger number of sign languages (e.g. Zeshan, 2006; Zeshan & Perniss, 2008). However, there are many challenges that remain, including the fact that many sign languages are undocumented or under-described for the purposes of typological description.

Quote 2.16   Multiplicity of terminologies

Another challenge is the fact that for many phenomena no consensus on labeling has emerged, leading to a multiplicity of terminologies. This lack of agreement regarding terminology, coupled with the lack of a written form for signed languages or a universally adopted, conventionalised system for notation, complicates the process of interpreting the outcomes of seemingly similar studies. Are, for example, the purported differences between signed languages real, or are they the artefact of different interpretations of the raw data? (Vermeerbergen & Leeson, 2011, p. 283)

Other key questions that sign linguists are considering today include:

- Analysis of sign languages as heterogeneous systems in which meanings are conveyed by using a combination of elements, rather than as homogeneous systems where all major elements of signing behaviour are considered to be equal parts of a morphosyntactic system (e.g. Schembri, 2001);

- The analysis of sign language structure as incorporating both linguistic and 'gestural' elements (e.g. Armstrong, Stokoe & Wilcox, 1995; Emmorey & Reilly, 2002; Janzen & Shaffer, 2002; Liddell, 2003; Schembri, Jones & Burnham, 2005; Vermeerbergen & Demey, 2007; Wilcox, 2004a,b);
- Usage-based approaches to sign linguistics, made possible because of technological developments that facilitate work with digital corpora, marking a significant shift in the processes that sign linguists adapt (Quote 2.17, and evidenced in publications like Johnston & Crasborn, 2006; Schembri et al., 2010);
- Typological work that classifies languages on the basis of their structural and functional features, with the goal of describing the structural diversity of the world's sign languages (e.g. Zeshan, 2006; Zeshan & Perniss, 2008).

These fields of focus are very much a hallmark of early 21st century research. Thus, today we see researchers drawing on the results of work emanating from the modern and postmodern periods, consolidating knowledge and rethinking theoretical assumptions with reference to cross-linguistic studies on aspects of syntax, semantics and pragmatics (e.g. Perniss, Pfau & Steinbach, 2007; Vermeerbergen, Leeson & Crasborn, 2007).

Quote 2.17   On how things have changed for sign linguists

[When we started out we had] pencil and paper! I did a study once looking at body sways and I had to put a transparency over the monitor from the VHS video, and put lines on it. And I physically marked how far away something is in this way...and I'm sure you wouldn't do it like that today...I wish I were 30 years younger now. Because I think it's a wonderful time in terms of technology. Um, we're working closely with people from Hamburg on corpus technology, and I think it will have a huge influence, especially if you have people involved in your teams who really know about that kind of technology, and it's become a little bit cheaper, some of this stuff, so I would love to be a young researcher now. (Penny Boyes-Braem, Back to the Beginning Project interview, July 2013)

Yes, I already [had] this notebook, handwritten notebook going back and forth between Bill Stokoe and myself. But also, we had this big video machine – very complicated, that even now it's difficult to save. We just started to try to save all the incredible amount of film – old films that we have at our lab. And it's, it's...a bit expensive, but I want to – this is my new challenge – try to save the incredible big corpus that we have. But it was also very difficult to film people because you need[ed] lights, you need[ed] special rooms, you need[ed] expensive machines...(Virginia Volterra, Back to the Beginning Project interview, July 2013).

The early 21st century has also seen an increase in the number of deaf researchers completing doctoral-level work on sign languages, bringing native signers from the very heart of the deaf community to positions of leadership vis-à-vis academic analysis of their languages. The issue of 'deaf-led' work on sign languages is highly topical, not least due to the fact that in some countries, approaches to research on sign languages still persist without the involvement of deaf people. Further, while many sign linguists are sign language users, there have been generations of linguists working on sign languages with very limited sign language proficiency, and many barriers still remain in many countries regarding access to university education for deaf people who may wish to pursue linguistics or applied linguistics as a career, leading to too few deaf native signers being positioned in leadership roles in academia.

In early 2014, this led the WFD to state:

Quote 2.18   On the fundamental need for engagement with deaf communities

The WFD considers exclusion of [any] Deaf Community and their national organisations from sign language work (such as production of [a] sign language dictionary, sign language interpreter training or sign language research) is a violation of the linguistic human rights of deaf people. Decisions regarding sign languages should always remain within the linguistic community, in this case deaf people. Sign language work should under all circumstances be contrived and realised in cooperation with national associations of the deaf. (World Federation of the Deaf, 2014)

Thus, while we have come a long way, there is still clearly a great deal of work to be done in ensuring that that deaf researchers are welcomed and supported, that their academic progress is encouraged and supported and that the contribution of deaf sign language users is respected and acknowledged – even within the field of sign linguistics research.

Today, we see an ever-increasing awareness of the scope of simultaneity in word order, and we see sign linguists taking on board findings from the field of gesture research. We find usage-based approaches to the description of sign languages, made possible by technologies that allow for digital corpus development, refining and sometimes rebuking previously held beliefs about the nature of sign language grammars. These fields of focus are very much a hallmark of early 21st century research. Thus, today we see researchers drawing on the results of work emanating from the modern and postmodern periods, consolidating knowledge and rethinking theoretical assumptions with reference to cross-linguistic studies on aspects of syntax, semantics, and pragmatics (e.g. Perniss, Pfau & Steinbach, 2007; Vermeerbergen, Leeson & Crasborn, 2007). Indeed, in Part II of this volume, we explore some of the ways in which these changes affect what we now know about sign languages in a range of contexts and what these developments have meant for sign language users in practice.

Leeson and Saeed (2012a) report that work carried out in the late 20th century and early 21st century tended to be cross-linguistic in nature, often focusing on how modality effects can be considered a point of differentiation between spoken and sign languages. Moreover, they tell us that studies sought to identify points that differentiated between individual sign languages while also acknowledging the impact that articulation in the visual-spatial modality seems to have for sign languages, which leads to a certain level of similarity in certain areas. This typological research period has thus led to a significant leap forward in terms of our understanding of the relationship between sign languages and the ways in which sign languages are structured (Leeson & Saeed, 2012a).

2.6 The development of applied sign linguistics research and sign language practice professions

While we date contemporary sign linguistics research from the 1950s, the history of applied sign language work in the shape of the practice professions has a more visible, long-term trajectory. We can trace the history of deaf education back to the late 1600s and 1700s (Lane, 1984). At this point in time, we know that sign languages played a central role in many countries and deaf teachers were at the forefront of deaf education, often leading the establishment of schools for the deaf far from the shores of their homes (Leeson & Saeed, 2012b). During this period, several deaf individuals of note emerge from the pages of history. While we cannot introduce our readers to each of these figures here, we refer you to Lane (1984) and Lane, Hoffmeister and Bahan (1996) for excellent overviews of the history of the American deaf community. Lane (1984) presents a window back in time to the flourishing of French Sign Language courtesy of the man who is frequently regarded as the 'father' of (sign) deaf education, Abbé de l'Epée.

Here, we offer a more schematic timeline of key figures and milestones relating to sign languages and their use in the world.

1760 – Abbé de l'Epée establishes school in France.

1760 – Braidwood establishes a school in the UK.

1771 – First record of someone functioning as a sign language interpreter in court (Stone & Woll, 2008).

1816 – School established in Ireland.

1817 – School established in America.

1880 – Congress of Milan takes place.

1889 – First International Congress for the Deaf and Dumb takes place.

1880–1970s – Strict oralism introduced and maintained across much of the world, leading to the suppression of signed languages and 'colonisation' of Deaf bodies (Ladd, 2003), leading to the de-intellectualisation of Deaf communities.

1924 – Royal National Institute for the Deaf and Dumb established in the UK.

1928 – Deaf Welfare Examination Boards established in the UK, which included a sign language interpreting assessment.

1940s – First sign language interpreter education in the USA (Ball, 2013).

1950s – Tervoort is thinking about how deaf children acquire language and notes that signs have decomposable parts.

Late 1950s – Stokoe is working at Gallaudet College and suggests that signs can be broken into smaller component parts.

1960s – Response to Stokoe's 1960 publication asserting that sign language is a language in its own right is not positive, even at Gallaudet.

1960 – Sweden establishes SLI programme (initially 2 weeks).

1964 – Registry of Interpreters for the Deaf established in the USA.

1970s – SALK institute begins working on sign languages (SLs); Edward Klima and Ursula Bellugi publish detailed overview of ASL, including early findings on neurolinguistics and SLs in 1979, followed by more in-depth psycholinguistics findings in the early 1980s. They bring Harlan Lane into the field.

1970s – Switch towards 'Total Communication' in schools.

1973 – Brita Bergman publishes (in Swedish) on the linguistic status of signed languages.[8]

Mid-1970s onwards – Work on interpreting curricula in the U.S. underway.

1975 – Mary Brennan suggests that the sign language used by deaf people in the UK should be known as British Sign Language.

Late 1970s – Scott Liddell publishes on the role of non-manual features in ASL.

1978 – Margaret Deuchar completes the first PhD research on language planning and BSL.

1978 – First Centre for Deaf Studies established at University of Bristol.

1979 – Klima and Bellugi publish *The Signs of Language.*

1979 – In Ireland, the 'Blue Book' (a glossary, presented as a dictionary) attempts to standardise ISL to make it easier for hearing people to learn the language.

1979 – Conrad's study on deaf children's literacy is published in the UK. Jim Kyle is a research assistant on this project, and the process raises many questions for him about BSL. He – with Bencie Woll – established the Centre for Deaf Studies at Bristol University.

1980 – Baker-Shenk and Cokely publish *American Sign Language: A Teacher's Resource Text on Grammar and Culture.*

1980s – A move towards bilingual education happens in Northern Europe.

1980 – Mary Brennan and research team establish the first funded BSL research project at Moray House at the University of Edinburgh.

1980 – Sharon Neumann Solow's book on sign language interpreting based on observations and practice is published.

1981 – Coleville, Brennan and Lawson publish on BSL phonology.

1982 – Dr Glenn B. Anderson becomes first African American deaf person to complete a PhD (in rehabilitation counselling from New York University).

1984 – Deuchar publishes on BSL syntax.

1985 – Kyle and Woll present their overview of the British Deaf Community and BSL.

1988 – The Deaf President Now protest at Gallaudet gains international coverage.

1988 – Dorothy Miles publishes a volume on BSL with the BBC.

1988 – Publication of the Vista Signing Naturally Curriculum (Smith, Lentz & Mikos, 1988).

1988 – European Parliament passes resolution on sign languages.

1989 – Trevor Johnston completes a PhD on Auslan.

1990 – Mary Brennan completes a PhD on word formation in BSL at Stockholm University.

1990 – Nancy Frishberg's volume on sign language interpreting is published.

1992 – BSL dictionary is published (David Brien).

1992 – Student interpreters and student sign language teachers from Greece, Ireland, Israel, the Netherlands, Portugal and the UK undertake training at Bristol University's Centre for Deaf Studies. European-funded programmes like this influence slow-growing but significant change across the continent.

1994 – Lars Wallin presents his doctoral dissertation on polysynthethic verbs in Swedish Sign Language. He is the first deaf person in Sweden to complete a PhD.

1995 – South African Sign Language formally recognised.

1995 – Finnish Sign Language formally recognised in the Finnish constitution.

1998 – European Parliament reiterates resolution on sign languages.

2001 – Centre for Deaf Studies established at Trinity College, Dublin.

2003 – Council of Europe's Parliamentary Assembly passes resolution on sign languages.

2004 – Trevor Johnston secures funding to create a corpus of Auslan as a mechanism for documenting the language, which he argues is endangered.

2006 – United Nations Convention on the Rights of Persons with Disabilities is adopted. There are 4 paragraphs that make explicit reference to signed languages and their community of users.

2006 – Deafness Cognition and Language Research Centre established at University College London with funding from the Economic Social Research Council (ESRC).

2008 – UK ESRC funds the BSL Corpus project (www.bslcorpusproject.org).

2009 – First deaf member of the European Parliament elected (Dr Adam Kosa, Hungary).

2010 – International Congress of Educators of the Deaf offer apology for the consequences of oralism on generations of deaf people.

2010 – National Science Foundation in the USA funds the Visual Language and Visual Learning Science for Learning Center, which is hosted at Gallaudet University.

2010 – European Union of the Deaf sign the Brussels Declaration.

2010 – Carol Padden receives MacArthur Prize ('Genius Grant').

2013 – Bristol University closes its Centre for Deaf Studies.

2013 – Liisa kauppinen awarded UN Human Rights Prize.

2.7 Understanding applied sign linguistics: concluding comments

In this chapter we have given an overview of the discipline of Deaf Studies to contextualise the field of sign language research, and we have discussed the emergence of sign language linguistics research. We have also defined what we mean by applied sign linguistics and chronologically mapped out various activities that have affected the way that sign languages are used in the world.

Starting with this chapter, and for the rest of this book, we can see how applied sign linguistics research aligns with current themes in applied linguistics and can inform and augment what we know about language use generally. In particular, themes covered in the Palgrave *Research and Practice in Applied Linguistics* series of books will also be explored in this book within a framework of applied sign linguistics, including language for specific purposes, children learning a second language, language teaching, corpora and language education, communication disorders, classroom management, language testing, developing the language learner, language policy, online communication, intercultural interaction and community interpreting.

Given that applied linguistics focuses on 'the theoretical and empirical investigation of real-world problems in which language is a central issue' (Brumfit, 1995, p. 27), we draw on Turner (2005) to ask the following questions:

- How has language, in the community and in institutions, been pivotal in shaping deaf lives?
- What is the role of applied sign linguists in responding to communities' circumstances?
- How have sign languages been studied in applied linguistic ways?
- What impact can the recognition of applied sign linguistics have on linguistic scholarship and on signing communities?

These are questions that we turn to in coming chapters, with the first considered in Chapter 3, where we explore some aspects of sign language in action.

3
Sign Language in Action

'Harry Potter does not know who he is. He arrives at Hogwarts to find that he is a hero in the wizard world, after living as a "nobody" in the muggle world. This parallels the different status given to people depending on the "center" (hearing, deaf, wizard, and muggle) ... Another parallel is the tendency that wizards (and perhaps all humans) have to establish binary relationships as in "us and them." The urge to create taxonomies that define the world as either wizard or muggle reflects a common outlook that many minorities use to define their own world. This compartmentalization of every-thing as either Deaf or hearing, Black or White, gay or straight, and so forth demonstrates the power of identity especially as it applies to the worldview of minorities.' (Czubek & Greenwald, 2005)

Sign language in action is a term that we have coined to encompass how sign languages are used in everyday life. In Chapter 2, we framed the notion of *sign language in action* against the backdrop of the fields of Deaf Studies and applied linguistics and by introducing the concept of applied sign linguistics. In this chapter, we will discuss the concept of *sign language in action* in depth, exploring sign language identity, attitudes and policy. Initially, we will explore the notion of sign language and identity to highlight the relationship between deaf people as a linguistic and cultural minority group and the wider majority of non-deaf people. By describing attitudes towards sign languages, we can then provide a context for considering how sign language policy and planning is shaped by attitudes towards deaf people from within and outside the deaf community.

3.1 Sign language and identity

In Chapter 2, we introduced the concept of deaf culture and the fact that due to the recognition of the linguistic status of sign languages, deaf sign language users are considered to be members of a linguistic and cultural minority group rather than a disability group. There are problems, though, with such a binary distinction, as there are still tensions in how deaf people identify themselves that affect social inclusion and exclusion (Skelton & Valentine, 2003). The key to the notion of 'deaf identity' is the relationship between the use of sign language and the wider 'hearing world', whose construct of deafness is typically very different from that of deaf sign language users. As discussed in Chapter 2, the field of Deaf Studies emerged in the 1980s in order to give status to deaf people and their language and identity rather than reduce them to the level of their hearing loss. Although it has been suggested that the emergence of the field of Deaf Studies has been centric to the U.S. (Myers & Fernandes, 2010), it has still provided a wealthy forum for discussion and exploration of sign language, culture, community and sign language in action.

Over this period (1980–present), the body of academic knowledge about sign languages, deaf people, their identity (identities), their culture(s) and their relationships has given rise to a notion of 'Deaf epistemologies' (Hauser, O'Hearn, McKee, Steider & Thew, 2010; Paul & Moores, 2012). Although Supalla (2013) believes that Paul and Moores' (2012) focus on 'deafness as specialised knowledge' is too narrow, it is a useful umbrella concept to explore the knowledge that we share about sign language and identity and how that knowledge has been framed differently over time.

In the next section, we describe the language that has been used by Deaf Studies and applied sign linguistics scholars to assert changing deaf epistemologies and, given our applied linguistic focus, the integral part that sign language plays in these epistemologies. What follows, then, is discussion of signed languages as embodied languages, the notion of deaf citizenship and the nature of deaf and hearing identities in relation to sign language and the deaf community.

3.1.1 Language to talk about sign language and identity

The language used to talk about deaf people and research involving deaf people is important, especially given the 'fuzziness' of deaf identities (Young & Temple, 2014). The work of Deaf Studies scholars in the 20th century used language in a certain way to defend the position of deaf sign language users and their linguistic and cultural identity and to reclaim a forgotten history (Bauman & Murray, 2009, 2010). Recognition of the full linguistic status of sign languages was transformative in enabling researchers to shift perceptions of deaf people as 'outsiders in a hearing world' (Higgins, 1980) to people with a sense of belonging, who identify with one another based on shared experience and the use of a sign language, regardless of how well they actually know each other; a situation described by Schein (1989) as being 'at home among strangers'.

Quote 3.1   Exploration

Deaf culture needed Deaf Studies to explore itself. (Bauman & Murray, 2010, p. 211)

An increasing amount of literature pushed back against the perceived historical oppression from hearing non-signers by putting language and culture front and centre in talking about deaf sign language users. The 'frame' of Deaf Studies during that time was clearly to distance deaf sign language users from the label of disability. A scan of seminal book titles of that era reveal various metaphors used to highlight either the visual nature of sign languages or the fact that deaf sign language users can be considered collectively as a group.

Concept 3.1   Variations on a theme

Terms used	Reference
Seeing Voices	Sacks (1989)
When the Mind Hears	Lane (1984)
A Place of Their Own	Van Cleve & Crouch (1989)
Deaf in America: Voices from a Culture	Padden & Humphries (1998)
Mask of Benevolence: Disabling the Deaf Community	Lane (1992)
A Journey into the Deaf World	Lane, Hoffmeister & Bahan (1996)
Forbidden Signs: American Culture and the Campaign Against Sign Language	Baynton (1998)

The emergence of Deaf Studies, and the recognition of the importance of language and culture, led to a distinction between describing deaf people who use a sign language and those who identify solely on the basis of their hearing loss. This distinction manifested in a written convention of using the letter 'D' in upper or lowercase to reflect identity, initially suggested by the sign linguist James Woodward (1972): 'Deaf' people who use sign language and who identify themselves as members of the Deaf community and regard themselves as culturally 'Deaf', whereas 'deaf' people are those who do not sign and who regard themselves as having a hearing impairment or 'loss' and associate themselves more closely with the wider hearing majority. This definition has been widely utilised in the literature by deaf and hearing writers alike.

Quote 3.2 **Early definition of Deaf culture**

The culture of Deaf people...is more closed than the Deaf community. Members of the Deaf culture behave as Deaf people do, use the language of Deaf people, and share the beliefs of Deaf people towards themselves and other people who are not Deaf. (Padden, 1980, p. 93)

Other writers have also proposed conventions for identifying non-deaf people who are involved in the deaf community, who (although they are not deaf themselves) are very fluent signers and who embrace the cultural values of the deaf community. The proposal by Napier (2002) and Ladd (2003) involves inverting the D/deaf convention to refer to H/hearing people. So, 'Hearing' people are those that are part of the wider majority, identify most closely with the values of the wider majority and may not be familiar with Deaf culture; whereas 'hearing' people are those who are family, friends and work colleagues of Deaf people, are 'culturally Deaf but audiologically hearing' (Stone, 2009), and who are accepted into the community and seen as being different from 'Hearing' people, who are associated with the historical oppression of Deaf people and their signed languages (see Chapter 2). Stone (2009) offers a different convention: 'Deaf (hearing) people' (see Chapter 1, Section 1.1.1).

Quote 3.3 **A familiar scenario**

Many will be familiar with the following scenario: A hearing person (child of Deaf parents, sign language interpreter, etc.) is engaged in conversation with Deaf people who are criticizing the hearing majority for their ignorance of the Deaf community and its culture, and the hearing person receives the comment, 'We don't mean you, you're different – not like those hearing people.' (Napier, 2002, pp. 144–145)

Interestingly, however, these days many writers use the double convention of 'D/deaf' to convey the fluidity and complexity of identity (Skelton & Valentine, 2010), with recognition that although sign language and identity are intertwined, not all deaf people choose to be labelled as such. Or else they opt to use 'deaf' to refer to people, and 'Deaf' to refer to the community and culture, to avoid any ambiguity or assumptions in labelling the identity of deaf people. See for example, Napier's (2009b) editorial and introduction to the inaugural issue of the *International Journal of Interpreter Education* and our discussion in Chapter 1 of this book. This convention is one that is endorsed by the WFD President Colin Allen.

Quote 3.4   Diversity in the international Deaf community

I believe that we should recognise the diversity in the international Deaf Community and not label people as 'Deaf' as we cannot assume that a person is culturally Deaf. I think that by using 'deaf' this is more accepting of all deaf people, regardless of their sign language skills, whether they come from a deaf family, when they learned to sign, whether they choose to speak as well as sign, or whether they have a cochlear implant. There are so many people that come to the Deaf Community later in life that we should not exclude them. Using the term 'Deaf' could potentially exclude people. Using the term 'deaf' includes all individuals, but we can use the term 'Deaf' when referring to community and culture. We, a diverse group of deaf people, are all part of the Deaf Community and should enjoy the richness and variety of life. (Allen, personal communication, 29 August 2014)

This shift is noteworthy in relation to sign linguist Trevor Johnston's (2004a, 2006) observations that the core of the deaf community in Australia – that is, native sign language users who have acquired Auslan from before the age of 5 years old – may be 'withering'. He argues that due to advances in technology and better medical preventions, there are fewer people who are born deaf, and those who are do not necessarily learn to sign at a young age. Other international linguists, anthropologists and educationalists have countered Johnston's arguments with their own: that the same phenomena is not evident in their own countries, that deaf culture and sign language use is rich and abundant; that the nature of the deaf community is changing and boundaries should be broadened to include those who learn sign language later in life, have a cochlear implant and position themselves bilingually and biculturally at the nexus of the deaf and hearing worlds (Burke, 2006; Carty, 2006; Hyde, Power & Lloyd, 2006; Mitchell, 2006; Moores, 2006). However, one author has acknowledged that a similar pattern to that described by Johnston could be seen in Norway (Vonen, 2006).

An increasing number of non-deaf people learn to sign as a second 'foreign' language, with ASL listed as the fourth most commonly studied language at college in the United States in 2009 (Quinto-Pozos, 2011). As a result of this phenomena, estimates of sign language–using populations often now include deaf and non-deaf people. For example, the British Deaf Association (2014) estimates that more than 250,000 people use BSL daily in the UK, 70,000 of whom are deaf and use BSL as their first or preferred language. Thus, the notion of 'the Deaf community' is becoming more fuzzy and perhaps can include non-deaf people if the focus is on sign language use rather than audiological status.

In her earlier seminal work, the anthropologist Carol Padden focussed her discussion more on 'boundaries' between deaf and hearing people and among deaf people themselves (Padden, 1990, 1992, 1994). However, her later work (Padden & Humphries, 1998, 2005) has noted the changes in the deaf community and that more 'co-existence' with hearing people has created more 'bicultural' deaf people. Her later discussions of the deaf community re-emphasised the concept of boundaries but suggests that where in the past, there were physical boundaries between deaf and hearing people, there are now intangible boundaries created by language and culture. Therefore, the distinction between deaf and hearing people is less clear.

In considering, then, the relationship between sign language and identity, it is not surprising that other emerging literature uses a different language and is moving away from describing people as 'deaf' at all. Some activists, leaders and academics have argued that we should focus on the fact that sign language use is salient, as any reference to the word 'deaf' still evokes a relationship to audiological status. Instead, it has been suggested that people should be referred to as 'sign language users' (Bahan, 1997), 'sign language persons' (Jokinen, 2001), 'sign language peoples' (Batterbury, 2012; Batterbury, Ladd & Gulliver, 2007), 'people of the eye' (Lane, Pillard & Hedberg, 2011; McKee, 2001), and a 'visual variety of the human race' (Bahan, 2008).

3.1.2 Focus on cultural identity

Interestingly, however, the explorations of sign language and identity have led to the resurgence in Deaf Studies, drawing on other disciplines, theories and frameworks to bring an interdisciplinary perspective to our field, and to focus discussions on identity – what could be considered as 'Deaf Studies Mark 2.0' – with the word 'Deaf' squarely situated within the title of the theoretical framework. Ladd (2003) has criticised the emphasis on sign linguistics for diverting attention and enquiry from the exploration of deaf cultures in their own right and reducing our understanding of deaf culture to characteristic language use and its consequences, which could explain the continuing 'ownership' and use of the term 'Deaf'. As we stated in Chapter 2, this is not a Deaf Studies book, so we will not focus discussion on the theories that have been developed in any great depth. Instead, here we provide a snapshot of the current theoretical frameworks that are informing debates on identity in order to frame the broader field of applied sign linguistics and discussions of sign language use.

We have seen leading scholars in the field discuss the 'new wave' of Deaf Studies in an edited volume entitled *Deaf Studies Talking* (Bauman, 2008): a collection of chapters from linguists, anthropologists, sociologists, psychologists, political theorists, educationalists and historians who explore the relationship between deaf culture and identity.

Paddy Ladd's (2003) theory of 'Deafhood' is one of the seminal works that has been widely adopted, and it has led to the establishment of the Deafhood Foundation,[1] to teach, share and promote the values of deaf culture(s). Ladd's work essentially provides an anthropological and socio-political overview of what is meant by deaf culture and focuses on the journey on which deaf people need to embark in order to feel a linguistic and cultural sense of belonging in the Deaf community.

Concept 3.2   The process of Deafhood

'Deafhood' is 'a process – the struggle by each deaf child, deaf family and deaf adult to explain to themselves and each other their own existence in the world'. (Ladd, 2003, p. 3)

A central theme of Ladd's theory is the power struggle between deaf and hearing people and that deaf people have historically been controlled and oppressed by hearing people for their own self-interest until the 'Deaf Resurgence', where deaf people began to stand up for their rights. This tension described in Ladd's work builds on the theory of *audism*, first coined by Tom Humphries in his 1977 doctoral dissertation and later expanded on by Harlan Lane in his book *The Mask of Benevolence* (1992). Audism is the attitude perpetuated by a person who believes that he or she is superior based on his or her ability to hear, and it can be applied to deaf or hearing people who behave in the (oppressive) manner of the hearing majority (i.e. they are 'audist'). Ladd's notion of Deafhood as a transformative sense of belonging has also been explored through a 'Deaf lens' on the literature (Czubek & Greenwald, 2005), drawing parallels between the Deaf world and life at Hogwarts (from the famous *Harry Potter* book series), where deaf people born into a hearing family can identify with the struggles of wizards who come from 'muggle' families.

Additional interdisciplinary explorations of deaf culture have also been framed in terms of:

- 'Deaf citizenship' and the extent to which deaf people participate politically in society (Emery, 2006, 2009);
- 'Deaf ethnicity' (or Deaf ethnos/Deafnicity), constituted of bodily features, genetic inheritance and social identity (Eckert, 2010; Ladd & Lane, 2013; Lane, 2005; Lane, Pillard & Hedberg, 2011);
- 'Deaf geographies' that enable visual people not only to occupy geographical, physical space but also to explore metaphorical spaces through the

identification of deaf-oriented spaces (Gulliver, 2005, 2006; Harold, 2012; Mathews, 2011);
* Deaf culture as arts, performance, literature, folklore and heritage (Brueggemann, 2009; Sutton-Spence, 2011).

Essentially, all these theories of deaf identity draw on wider social constructs (Humphries & Humphries, 2010), with a focus on the cultural aspects of identity.

Quote 3.5 Discourses of Deaf identity

...the processes of [Deaf] identity construction and the recent discourse of Deaf identity are not unique phenomena at all but echo the experiences of other embedded cultural groups around the world, particularly those that are stressed by the assertion of hegemony over them by others.

...living embedded in a hearing society dominated by others that insist on defining deaf people differently from the way that Deaf people define themselves creates pressure and tension that puts the identity of the group and individuals within it into question...

We recognize the experience of Deaf people in struggling to understand and, equally important, to express identity as an experience like that of other groups that have been 'owned' by others, for example, African Americans who were a captured people, displaced and literally owned, bought and sold, as commodities...

Initially, the questioning evolved around who is 'DEAF' (here, all caps denote a sign from American Sign Language, which poorly translates into English as 'deaf'). DEAF (the sign) is the name in ASL for Deaf people and is what they call themselves. It is not the same as the English word 'deaf,' which refers to a physical condition of being without hearing. DEAF is the way Deaf people identify themselves to one another. It is the meaning of DEAF that has been the subject of public discourse since the 1970s. The ASL question, 'Who is DEAF?' or its ASL counterparts, 'Is he/she DEAF?' and 'Am I DEAF?' have simmered and erupted periodically over the decades since then. (Humphries & Humphries, 2010, pp. 153–154)

So what does this mean for applied sign linguistics? Although there is a body of work that focuses on identity in terms of cultural constructs, there are also conversations that relate to the way people relate to one another and the rest of the world visually; that is, the focus is on sign language as the identifying feature, or what could be termed *sign language as identity*.

3.1.3 Sign language *as* identity

The latest theory of 'Deaf Gain' emphasises the ontological aspects of being deaf as a visual variety of the human race (Bauman & Murray, 2009, 2010). Deaf Gain essentially positions deaf people and their language positively on the spectrum of human biodiversity. Bauman and Murray argue that the visual orientation of deaf people offers opportunities for 'exploration into the human character' and that 'deaf people and their sign languages are vast resources with significant contributions to the cognitive, creative, and cultural dimensions of human diversity'. What is particularly ground-breaking about their work is that Bauman and Murray assert the value and contribution of a visual orientation to various fields of human activity; that is, the world is a better place because it has deaf sign language users in it.

Quote 3.6   Reframing deafness as Deaf Gain

Frame Theory can be applied to the concept of 'deaf'. Deafness has long been viewed as a hearing loss – an absence, a void, a lack. It is virtually impossible to think of deafness without thinking of loss. And yet Deaf people do not often consider their lives to be defined by loss. Rather, there is something present in the lives of Deaf people, something full and complete. They view their lives through a frame that is diametrically opposed to the frame of hearing loss. We call this opposing frame Deaf Gain ... Deaf Gain is defined as a reframing of 'deaf' as a form of sensory and cognitive diversity that has the potential to contribute to the greater good of humanity. There are three different signs that we use to mean Deaf Gain. The first can be glossed as DEAF INCREASE, and it expresses the opposite notion of hearing 'loss'. It emphasizes that Deaf people have something of importance. The second sign can be glossed as DEAF BENEFIT, and it emphasizes that deafness is not just a loss but a benefit as well. The third sign can be glossed as DEAF CONTRIBUTE. This sign emphasizes the importance of considering all the ways that Deaf people contribute to humankind. (Bauman & Murray, 2009, p. 3)

In arguing how deaf people contribute to cultural diversity, Bauman and Murray note that there is a shared experience across international deaf communities through the mutual use and understanding of sign languages. Re-emphasising the focus on sign language users, scholars recognise the nature of inclusivity in communities of sign language users: that is, people identify with one another because they can sign rather than because they are deaf *per se*.

Deaf people have been described as 'global citizens' and the deaf community as a 'transnational community' (now a key concept in applied linguistics) with a sense of identity that crosses national (ethno)linguistic and cultural boundaries (Breivik, 2005, 2006; Murray, 2007; Bauman & Murray, 2009, 2010). This 'transnationality' is made possible because of the visual nature of sign languages. Although sign languages are different in every country, deaf people can 'communicate across mutually unintelligible language boundaries' (Supalla & Webb, 1995, p. 334) using 'cross-national signed communication' (Adam, 2012a, p. 852): a pidgin sometimes referred to as International Sign (IS). Essentially, IS is a form of 'foreigner talk' (Quinto-Pozos, 2007) where different sign languages come into contact. (See further discussions of IS under Section 4.3.1, Learning to sign cross-culturally, and Section 5.4.5, Sign language in politics).

Quote 3.7 Exploiting iconicity

In a sign pidgin, Deaf people from different communities communicate by exploiting their awareness of iconicity and their access to visual-spatial expression. (Adam, 2012a, p. 853)

The key is that people identify with one another based on the fact that they can communicate visually through sign language. This is not surprising given that hearing people visiting a new country where they do not speak the local language will often resort to visual gestures to communicate. Gesture is a natural communicative instinct, one that is increasingly attracting attention from spoken and sign language linguists (e.g. Armstrong et al., 1995; McNeill, 1992; Vermeerbergen & Demey, 2007; Wilcox, 2004a) – perhaps another element of Deaf Gain.

Example 3.1 A serendipitous meeting

Whilst back-packing across Europe in the mid-1990s, Jemina boarded a train in the middle of the night while travelling to Prague with her (hearing) brother and (hearing) partner, who also grew up with deaf parents and works as a sign language interpreter. As they made themselves comfortable, a man and a woman opened the carriage door and pointed to the other empty seats, querying if they were available. Given they were in the middle of Eastern Europe, Jemina and her two companions assumed that the people did not speak English, so responded by gesturing to the seats and nodding. As the people sat down, nodding and smiling, Jemina came to the conclusion that they were deaf because of the way they oriented to their surroundings (see Quote 3.8 below) and because they used no verbal communication at all. She turned to one of them and used the internationally recognised sign for 'DEAF?' The man and woman nodded enthusiastically and repeated the question back to Jemina and her companions: 'YOU DEAF TOO?' Jemina shook her head to indicate no, then explained using a combination of BSL signs, gesture, and International Signs that they were all hearing, had deaf parents, and that she and her partner were also sign language interpreters. The other two travellers indicated that he was American and she was originally from South Africa but was living in the UK. They had just been attending the World Deaf Games (now known as the Deaflympics) in Bulgaria. As Jemina and her partner both knew some ASL, the conversation then continued using a mix of BSL, ASL, IS and gesture. It was not long before they discovered mutual friends and connections in the international deaf community: Jemina had grown up with a deaf man who was a close friend of the American man, and Jemina's partner had once worked as an interpreter at a college where the South African woman had studied.

Example 3.1 neatly encapsulates the notion of sign language *as* identity, but it is more than just the use of sign language that orients sign language users to one another, as demonstrated in Quote 3.8.

Quote 3.8 I see deaf people

In New York City, a father and daughter sat in a café people-watching out the window and drinking coffee. 'Look across the street', signed the father. His daughter quickly scoped the busy street packed with people bustling to and fro before quizzically looking back at her dad. 'One of them is deaf...which one is it?' he asked. She looked back and scanned the crowd. She noticed one man's eyes glancing from side to side. 'The one with the brown overcoat', she guessed. 'I agree. Let's watch and see', he suggested. The man in the brown overcoat was about to cross the street, but sensed the sudden shift in the crowd of people around him as they simultaneously looked in the same direction. He decided he too should check in that direction and saw sirens and flashing lights accompanying a speeding ambulance. After the commotion subsided, he crossed the street and continued walking past the café. The father waved his hands in the man's periphery. In the middle of a bustling city, the man in the brown overcoat noticed a flutter of hands through the window and quickly turned to see the father and his daughter. 'You deaf?' signed the father. The man was astounded and asked, 'How did you know?'

The characters in this short story are unique in that they inhabit a highly visual world. They use a visual language to communicate and have developed a visual system of adaptation to orient them in the world that defines their way of being. (Bahan, 2008, p. 83)

In his story, Ben Bahan recounts how deaf people recognise one another through their visual orientation. Interestingly, Example 3.1 demonstrates that it is not just deaf people who recognise each other in this way. The evaluation of visual orientation can occur between sign language users regardless of their audiological status. This sharing of identity based on sign language use (sign language in action) is the foundation of the transnational deaf community, and it could explain why there is evidence of 'inclusive communities' where members identify with one another based on their sign language use and not necessarily their hearing status. These communities have been variously referred to as 'assimilating communities', 'assimilative societies', and 'integrated communities', but the current preferred term is 'shared signing community' (Kisch, 2008; Kusters, 2010; Nyst, 2012), which aligns with notions of transnationalism, multilingualism, and identity in applied linguistics (Duff, 2015).

3.1.4 Identity in shared signing communities

There are examples of places where deaf and hearing people use sign language as a regular occurrence, and it is embedded within community language practices. Communication is adapted, and hearing and deaf people alike use signs, gestures and written and spoken communication. This phenomenon occurs in communities with an unusually high incidence of deafness, and these communities are regarded as using 'village sign languages' rather than 'macro-community sign languages' (Nyst, 2012). Kisch (2008) argues that these communities should not be classified as types of deaf communities but rather as types of 'signing communities', in recognition of the mixed identities of their deaf and hearing sign language users.

The earliest record of such a shared signing community is the island of Martha's Vineyard, off Massachusetts, on the East Coast of the United States of America. For over 250 years, deafness was commonplace on the island. A recessive gene for deafness and frequent intermarriage among islanders meant that in some parts of the island by the middle of the 19th century, 1 in 4 residents were deaf (Groce, 1985). As Sacks (1989) notes, the result was a natural fusion of deaf and hearing cultures to the point where Groce's research found it difficult to define who was deaf and who was hearing as everyone used sign language to communicate. There were apparently no social or language barriers. and deafness was considered ordinary, not a sickness or a deficit. However, Groce's work was conducted 'post-factum' (i.e. after the situation ceased to exist) so there is no way of knowing exactly how the community members interacted (Kusters, 2010).

Kusters (2010) and Nyst (2012) have mapped various research that has identified similar behaviours worldwide in islands such as Providence Island near Colombia, Grand Cayman Island in the Caribbean and the Amami Islands near Japan; in villages including Bengkala (Desa Kolok) in Bali, Adamorobe in Ghana, Nohya (Yucatec Maya) in Mexico, Ban Khor in Thailand, Kosindo in Suriname and St Elizabeth in Jamaica; and in social groups such as the Al-Sayyid Bedouins in Israel, the Urubu of Brazil and the Enga of Papua New Guinea.

Kusters (2010) cites Bahan and Nash (1995) and notes that these contexts are referred to as 'signing communities' and are often perceived as a 'utopian place' for sign language users. She also points out, however, that the majority of research on these communities seems to have been conducted by hearing people who construct what they want to see. When exploring issues in these villages in more depth, Kusters (2010) suggests that they may not automatically provide a utopian experience. Hearing people can still choose not to sign, which is a key issue that many other researchers may have overlooked. Furthermore, in her observations of the Al-Sayyid Bedouins, Kisch (2008) states that 'a sign language shared by many hearing people does not erase the asymmetry... Despite hearing people's familiarity with sign language, it still remains the case that deaf people need mediation of what is being spoken' (p. 308).

Nonetheless, deaf *and* hearing people are present in deaf communities, so given this inclusivity, for the rest of this book we will adopt the term suggested by Bahan and Nash (1995), *signing communities*, to refer to communities of sign language users, regardless of whether they are deaf or hearing.

The campus of Gallaudet University in Washington, D.C., could be considered a shared signing community. Gallaudet is the only 'deaf' university in the world and has been funded at federal level by the U.S. government since 1864. Gallaudet's mission statement is that it is 'a bilingual, diverse, multicultural institution of higher education that ensures the intellectual and professional advancement of deaf and hard of hearing individuals through American Sign Language and English'.[2] The bilingual learning environment of the university is a hub for deaf and hearing sign language users from all over the world. Students take a range of courses, and ASL is the language of instruction in virtually all classes. New hearing members of staff are expected to achieve minimum levels of ASL proficiency within a certain time frame as part of their probationary requirements, and hearing students are only permitted to study certain targeted courses (e.g. teaching, linguistics and interpreting). Example 3.2 demonstrates a response from a hearing undergraduate student at Gallaudet University to a question posted on the Yahoo Answers page: 'What is the experience for Hearing students at Gallaudet University?'

Example 3.2   A hearing undergrad at Gallaudet

As a Hearing Undergrad (HUG) soon to graduate from Gallaudet University, in my years here for my degree, I have seen plenty of hearing students with different attitudes. Attitude in the Deaf community is huge. Some previous comments imply that Gallaudet is a scary place for any hearing person to go. That would depend on your attitude and language skill.

From my experience, Gallaudet is a small-town of it's own. When you ask if the Deaf students are accepting, think to yourself: Half the campus is involved in each other's lives and have been together since Deaf school, or their years at Gally (estimated statistic). It takes time to get to know anyone, and they have already had years of friendship. Like any college experience if you get yourself involved on campus, in the dorms and take time to genuinely spend time with people, you will meet a TON of great friends.

Also think of this: I was once told while applying to Gally that it isn't a place where hearing people enroll to learn ASL (unless for ASL class). They go there to

USE ASL. This was interesting to me because I often see new hearing signers have negative experiences on campus. A stronger knowledge of Deaf culture and the ability to fluently communicate is important and should be seriously considered. (lakebaby, https://answers.yahoo.com/question/index?qid=20100821215115AAy A45c)

More recently, Gallaudet has begun to accommodate the needs of non-signing deaf and hard of hearing students, but this has been the subject of debate between administrators and the signing community who value a campus steeped in deaf culture and dominated by signing (see Quote 3.9).

Quote 3.9   The 'Hearing-ization' of Gallaudet?

The influx of 'non-signers,' who can hear and speak or who read lips or text, may be necessary for Gallaudet's survival. Yet it has sparked passionate debate on whether the university is becoming 'hearing-ized' and whether deaf culture is slipping away. 'We want a signing environment, because how often do deaf students get that environment?' said Dylan Hinks, 20, student body president. 'This is the place where I want to have comfort and ease in my communication.' (www.washingtonpost.com/local/education/gallaudet-university-adjusts-to-a-culture-that-includes-more-hearing-students/2011/09/23/gIQAC3W9tK_story. html)

Although the notion of identity is heavily influenced by visual orientation and sign language use, when we consider sign language in action, there are still observable differences between deaf and hearing sign language users and their status and identity in signing communities. First, we address how hearing signers may be considered as intercultural interlopers in signing communities, followed by discussion of how some deaf people themselves may also be regarded in the same way.

3.1.5   Hearing signers as intercultural interlopers

Here we come back to a point addressed in Chapter 1 (Section 1.3) about the position of hearing people in signing communities and the level of acceptance of hearing people in the deaf world. There are two distinct types of hearing 'identity' in signing communities: those who grow up as signing community members through dint of birth (i.e. they have deaf parents) and those who come to the community later in life after having learned a sign language as a second language.

People who have grown up with deaf parents are often referred to as Children of Deaf Adults (Codas) and often grow up using a sign language as their first language in the home (see Section 3.4). Codas could be considered as automatic members of signing communities because of their native sign language use, but the situation for Codas is not as simple as that. Their 'hearingness' does in fact influence perceptions of their identity and status of signing community membership.

Concept 3.3   Codas

Codas are 'Children of Deaf Adults' and have the potential to grow up bilingual and bicultural, sharing both the language and culture of their deaf parents and that of the majority hearing society around them. (after Singleton & Tittle, 2000)

Codas often feel a tension because, although they have grown up in a signing community and using a sign language, they are not actually deaf (Bishop & Hicks, 2008a). There are several autobiographical descriptions that detail what it was like to grow up as a Coda (e.g. Corfmat, 1990; Sidransky, 2006), that typically describe the conflict that was felt in terms of identity: 'Am I deaf? Am I hearing? Where do I belong?' Some Codas have described this conflict as having a 'passport without a country' (Davie, 1993).

Two studies of Codas' experiences of growing up with deaf parents in the U.S. (Preston, 1994, 1996) and the UK (Adams, 2008) have explored these tensions in terms of sign language and identity. The best-known study is that of Paul Preston (1994), a Coda himself. Preston found that his 150 U.S.-based informants had both positive and negative experiences and a shared cultural perspective of signing communities. Adams (2008) – a non-Coda – collected narratives from 26 Codas to examine their experiences at key life stages. Adams sought to moderate past definitions of Codas in terms of their cultural affiliation and community membership and instead focus on patterns of experience. She classified 4 unique patterns of experience particular to their situation as Codas – 'go-between', 'misfit', 'foreigner' and 'glass ceiling' – and states that these should be considered the life experiences which define Codas. Both Preston (1994) and Adams (2008) also report that many Codas grew up with feelings of conflict.

However, Codas also report growing up in a signing community as a positive experience (Mudgett-DeCaro, 1996) due to being raised bilingually and biculturally, much like children who grow up speaking another language at home (Napier, in press). Another positive aspect is that Codas can be afforded status that may not be easily given to other hearing people. Being able to explain a connection in the community can provide the necessary credentials for acceptance (see Quote 3.10).

Quote 3.10   Opening doors to the Deaf community

When we moved to Australia, my husband and I knew nobody. An Australian deaf person, whom we had met at a conference in the United Kingdom, met us at the airport and proceeded to introduce us to members of the deaf and interpreting communities. In some ways, the transition was difficult, as nobody knew who we were. People would ask if I had deaf parents; when I confirmed that I did, they would automatically ask, 'Which school did they go to?' Then I would explain that I was British, so my parents went to school in England. Nobody knew my family, so I could not make connections with people based on mutual and historical friendships. I did not have any shared experiences with the Australian deaf community. I did not understand the nuanced communication which was embedded in Australian deaf history and culture. Yet growing up in the British deaf community actually made it easier, because of the perceptions of community ties. Even though people did not know me or my family, as soon as I mentioned that I had deaf family members, I was accepted. There was an implicit understanding that I was a member of the community. (Napier, 2008, pp. 226–227)

From an intercultural perspective, Mindess (1999) would suggest that the example recounted in Quote 3.10 occurs due to the understanding that some hearing people have empathy with the deaf experience, ally themselves to the signing community and engage in reciprocal relationships with deaf people (e.g. interpreting in exchange for being taught the language).

Many Codas grow up acting in a language and cultural brokering role for their deaf parents, and often go on to become professional sign language interpreters (Napier, in press). Bienvenu (1987) suggests that hearing sign language interpreters occupy a 'third culture' in that they come from a different culture but they have a foot in both the deaf and hearing worlds; therefore, the 'third culture' allows for deaf and hearing cultures to 'meet in the middle' and, as a consequence, establish mutual understanding.

Having a 'good attitude' is a phrase often used to describe hearing people who are accepted into signing communities, in relation to Codas and interpreters in general (see Quote 3.9). Napier and Rohan (2007) and Napier (2011a) asked deaf Australians about their perceptions of (hearing) interpreters and found that having an appropriate 'attitude' was an important factor in trusting those interpreters and allowing them 'in' to the signing community.

If someone is not a Coda, he or she is typically considered an 'outsider', a second language learner, and notions of reciprocity from the signing community in exchange for sharing language and culture have to be learned and demonstrably valued (Mindess, 1999). This situation presents the reverse of Higgins' (1980) definition of deaf people as 'outsiders in a hearing world', with a view that hearing people can be outsiders in the deaf world. For example, Harris (1995) talks about her journey into deaf culture, having to overcome traditionally 'hearing' behaviours and accept that boundaries of space are different.

Earlier, we mentioned the importance of 'attitude' and also the theory of 'audism' which relates to people's demonstrated behaviours that are patronising, oppressive or discriminatory towards deaf people on the basis that they cannot hear. This term has typically been used to refer to hearing people who serve in roles where they try to 'fix' or 'save' deaf people; for example, teachers of the deaf who promoted linguistic imperialism in the form of banning sign language and promoting only speech. Hearing 'interlopers' into signing communities are judged on whether they have the correct attitude, if they align with the values of the signing community and if they give something *to* the community as well as *take* (i.e. access to the language and culture given to them by members of the community). Audists are not welcome in signing communities, but if someone is judged to have the right attitude and wants to join the community for the right reasons, then deaf sign language users display unfailing levels of patience with hearing people as they acquire sign language skills and deaf cultural knowledge (Harris, 1995; Gesser, 2007).

Interestingly, it seems that hearing people newly entering signing communities may experience a reverse form of audism and encounter more problems with other hearing people than with deaf people. Gesser's (2007) account of his ethnographic observations at Gallaudet University revealed a culture of linguistic imperialism – from hearing people against other hearing people. He noted that deaf people displayed patience with his developing ASL skills, but he experienced and observed oppression of hearing non-signers (or rudimentary signers) by hearing signers who would mock people for lack of signing proficiency, or demand that they sign at all times even if no deaf people were around. Example 3.3 reveals a response to the same question on Yahoo Answers about hearing students' experiences at Gallaudet University.

Example 3.3   Attitude goes a long way

Typically, the problem tends to stem from hearing students who think they're fluent in the language when they aren't, or who think they're Deaf when they aren't. Attitude goes a long way. There's good and bad in every group. (https://answers.yahoo.com/question/index?qid=20100821215115AAyA45c)

Some would argue that this behaviour is not linguistic imperialism but respectful in prioritising the use of sign language. For example, a

British (hearing) clinical psychologist who is also a BSL/English interpreter recently wrote a 'manifesto' stating that hearing professionals who work with deaf people should always sign for themselves in meetings, even if they cannot sign fluently and sign language interpreters are present (Cromwell, 2014).[3] The Conference of Interpreter Trainers (CIT) in the U.S., which is attended by deaf and hearing interpreter educators (but is dominated by hearing participants), also promotes a policy of sign language use, with preferential treatment given to conference presentations in ASL (see Example 3.4).

Example 3.4   An ASL-inclusive environment

CIT continues to move towards the goal of creating a more ASL-inclusive biennial conference. ASL remains the official language of the CIT conference and over the past several conferences more and more speakers have chosen to use ASL as their presentation language. To foster this trend even further, priority consideration will be given to speakers who will present in ASL. Presentations in spoken English will also be accepted; the number selected depending on space availability in the schedule. (www.cit-asl.org/new/conference/call-for-presentations/)

Regardless of whether hearing people are considered 'interlopers' or not, they do make up a proportion of the signing community, and it is significant to note that many hearing sign language users take action to ensure that sign language use is not oppressed.

Another factor for assessing the credibility of a hearing person in the signing community is their sign language fluency (see Examples 3.5 and 3.6 and Quote 3.11) – not only how they use sign language, but where and how they learned it (see Chapter 4 for a more detailed discussion).

Example 3.5   Find real deaf people

...learn the language and culture from the REAL deaf people – the grass roots deaf community. Find them and explore ways that you can immerse yourself into their lives to learn their language, culture and history. They will respond with sincere interest if you express a sincere desire and persist. (https://answers.yahoo.com/question/index?qid=20100821215115AAyA45c)

Example 3.6   Am I hearing or deaf?

I sign well enough that Deaf people usually don't know from my signing whether I'm hearing or deaf. (http://deafness.about.com/od/learningsignlangu age/a/deafattitudes_2.htm)

Quote 3.11   Water or wood?

When people sign, especially sign language learners, I think of them as 'water' or 'wood'. People who sign like wood are more rigid and stiff and I often think they will find it harder to become fluent in sign language. People who sign like water have a smooth flow to the way they sign, it's comfortable to watch, and 'easy on the eye'. These people will often develop sign language skills that look almost near native, like the way a deaf person signs. (Caroline Conlon, Australian deaf performer, director, sign language teacher, translator)

This same criteria may be used to assess the identity and membership status of deaf people themselves. As mentioned briefly earlier in this section, there is another group of potential intercultural interlopers who are deaf: people who could also be considered as 'outsiders' or on the periphery of the signing community – deaf non-signers or late sign language learners.

3.1.6   Deaf intercultural interlopers

In addition to hearing (signing and non-signing) people who have been considered outsiders in signing communities, deaf people themselves have often used this term to describe how they felt when they first discovered a signing community. Initially, these people tended to be 'oral' deaf people who had grown up relying on hearing aids and communicating through speech and lip-reading, and who had therefore spent most of their life in the hearing world, especially if they were 'late-deafened' as an adult (Graham & Sharp-Pucci, 1994). Typically, these deaf people would be referred to as 'hard of hearing' or 'hearing impaired'. For example, Hurwitz, Weisel, Parasnis, DeCaro and Savir (1997/1998) noted that one aspect of a 'Deaf' label is an expectation of using sign language to communicate, whereas the label 'hard of hearing' may have an expectation of successful communication using spoken language. Earlier assumptions in the literature perpetuated the idea that there were only two possible identities and that all deaf persons fit into one category or the other, that is, 'Deaf' or 'deaf' (McIlroy & Storbeck, 2011); representative of a typical Western, postmodern approach to identity classification without recognising the complexity of identity (Ladd, 2003). Therefore, if you were 'deaf', you were an outsider.

Even if these 'deaf' people chose to learn a sign language later in life (see Chapter 4 for more discussion), their sign language skills would be judged as inadequate because they were not fluent enough; they did not have the range of vocabulary; they used a form of sign language where the grammatical structure is seen to be 'contaminated' by the grammar of the spoken language, for example, in Australia referred to as 'Signed English' or in the UK and Ireland as 'Sign Supported English'; or they signed and spoke at the same time (simultaneous communication).

These 'oral' deaf people were often assessed by members of the deaf community as being not really 'Deaf enough' and therefore considered as interlopers in a signing community. Gesser's (2007) ethnographic account of his experience at Gallaudet University relates the perception of hard of hearing people in a deaf signing space (see Quote 3.12).

Quote 3.12   Privelege of choice

[A Hard of Hearing student] told me that he feels angry with some Deaf people because he thinks that they are behaving in the same way hearing people did in the past when they insist he use ASL on campus. 'Why?' he says 'If I am in Japan do I have to use Japanese? What about my right of privacy? I can speak both ASL and English, what's the problem if I privilege one over another?' (Gesser, 2007, p. 274)

Many of these people have shared their journey of being accepted in to signing communities through blogs[4]; what has been described as a 'process of becoming' ('Deafhood'), and was the crux of Paddy Ladd's work, which we outlined earlier in this chapter. Ladd himself has documented his own process of becoming, as he too grew up using oral communication methods.[5]

Quote 3.13

As we struggle to agree on appropriate names, we must ever be aware that labels exclude and that rather than defining ourselves we may actually be reducing ourselves only in a different way. As a cultural description, 'Deaf' captures the experience of an identifiable group, but when it is used to question, invalidate or trivialise the authenticity of someone else's cultural experience, it can in itself be an oppressor's term. (Jordan, 1993, p. 69)

Over time, increasing numbers of deaf adults and children are receiving cochlear implants as assistive hearing devices (Leigh & Christiansen, 2006). So, not only are they 'oral', but they have an additional aspect to their identity – they are even more identifiable by the large magnetic receiver placed externally on their heads. 'Oral' deaf hearing aid or cochlear implant users were initially perceived as 'outsiders', as second language sign language learners, because they were not really 'Deaf' linguistically and culturally. The upsurge of cochlear implantation was initially particularly controversial because it was promoted as an 'either/or' option – members of signing communities worldwide lobbied against this intervention, as typically children receiving implants were 'banned' from using sign language. Opponents perceived cochlear implantation as a form of genocide against deaf people and against the use of sign language as a human right (Christiansen & Leigh, 2002).

Quote 3.14   Trapped between two cultures

The danger with existing cochlear implants is that they risk depriving such children of full membership of any culture. Implantees may end up trapped 'between cultures,' unable to function effectively in a hearing context but also lacking the facility with sign language available to those who grow up with it as their first language. (Sparrow, 2005, pp. 143–144)

Most, Wiesel and Blitzer (2007) have debunked earlier claims with results from their study of 115 deaf and hard of hearing adolescents who completed a demographic questionnaire, the Deaf Identity Developmental Scale and a questionnaire on their attitude towards cochlear implants. The results revealed that participants' bicultural identity was strongest and marginal identity was weakest, and that those with bicultural identities also had a high acceptance of their cochlear implants. Spencer, Tomblin and Gantz (2012) found similar results in their study of 41 children with cochlear implants, where they used the Satisfaction with Life Scale and the Deaf Identity Development Scale to measure the children's experience of growing up with an implant in relation to their identity. They found that the group obtained high educational achievement and reported a very high level of satisfaction with life. They also found that most participants reported feeling comfortable with signing deaf people as well as with hearing people; that is, they had a 'dual identity'.

Given these results, we can say that the attitude towards 'other' deaf people is changing. The international signing community is beginning to embrace members who are oral or have cochlear implants but who choose to use a sign language. This is clearly demonstrated by WFD President Colin Allen's comment in Quote 3.4.

Therefore, deaf late sign language users or non-sign language users are no longer necessarily considered 'interlopers'. More sophisticated discussions of deaf identity now encompass representations of the complexity and diversity that we see in the international signing community (Leigh, 2009) and less polarity with identity as an 'either/or' option; that is, 'Deaf' or 'deaf'. For example, Bat-Chava's (2000) research suggests fairly static clusters of 4 deaf identities: deaf, Deaf, negative/ambiguous identity, and bicultural identity; Breivik (2005) frames identity in terms of 'hybridity' based on diversity and heterogeneity; Brueggemann (2009) proposes the idea of 'in-betweenity', or deaf people living 'between spaces'. As noted by Skelton and Valentine (2003), 'the binary categories of D/deaf/hearing, Deaf/deaf are not really very useful in capturing the complexities and 'in-betweenity' of young D/ deaf people's identities. Their identities are deeper than these binaries allow space for' (p. 464).

Language policies (see Section 3.4) around sign language and cochlear implants are changing, and sign language is now increasingly recognised as having a crucial role for deaf children with cochlear implants, preferably through bilingual education (see Chapter 5 for more discussion), in order to develop linguistic and cultural competence (Swanwick & Tsverik, 2007). The notion of a signing community is broadening to encompass the variation seen throughout the world (Myers & Fernandes, 2010).

Maxwell-McCaw and Zea (2011) suggest that various factors can influence whether deaf people develop a deaf, hearing, marginalised or bicultural identity and that the nature of their identity can be measured using a 'Deaf acculturation scale'. Drawing on racial identity theory, they further developed Glickman's (1993) Deaf Identity Development Scale and normed the scale on a sample of more than 3,000 deaf people in the United States. Maxwell-McCaw and Zea's sample revealed that deaf individuals with deaf parents tended to show greater deaf cultural identification, deaf cultural involvement, deaf cultural knowledge, language competence in ASL and deaf preferences than those who grew up in hearing homes. Similarly, those who grew up in hearing homes showed stronger identification with, and preferences for, hearing culture as well as better language competence in English than those who grew up in deaf homes. There was no significant difference between the two groups with regard to their knowledge of hearing culture. It has also been suggested by McIlroy and Storbeck (2011) that the development of deaf identity is influenced by educational experience.

Quote 3.15 Identity politics

The increasing awareness and understanding of what it means to be deaf, which extends beyond the outdated 'first-wave of identity politics' (Davis, 2002), is far more nuanced than the medical/social model. The newer approach allows for an appreciation of the complexity and range of deaf ontology. (McIlroy & Storbeck, 2011, pp. 496–497)

Quote 3.16 DeaF identity

[We] propose a bicultural 'DeaF identity', which represents the cultural space from which they transition within and between both the Deaf community and the hearing community. Hence, the capital F in DeaF highlights the deaf person's fluid postmodern interactions and engagement and dialogue across the conventional dividing line between Deaf and culturally hearing identities and communities as an authentic bicultural DeaF person. (McIlroy & Storbeck, 2011, p. 497)

As can be seen, the notion of identity in signing communities is complex and multifaceted. The discussion of identity goes beyond the division of deafness and hearingness. It can clearly be seen, however, that the use of sign language is at the core of identity, used as the vehicle to *perform* identity (Willie, 2003; Leeson et al., in press). Signed languages – like spoken languages – can also be said to be *embodied*, an idea that we turn to next.

3.2   Sign languages as embodied languages

Sherman Wilcox (2004b) reports that while linguists have concluded that signed and spoken languages manifest the same characteristics, including a belief that 'human language ability depends on abstract, modality-independent and purely linguistic abilities' (p. 119), this ignores the ubiquity of iconicity, and his suggestion is that 'signed and spoken languages are united by their common basis in embodied cognition' (p. 120). Wilcox is referring here to a significant idea that has emerged from the field of cognitive linguistics, an idea that suggests all languages – spoken and signed – are embodied (Evans & Green, 2006; Johnson, 1987).

Concept 3.4   Embodiment

Embodiment is the idea is that language users' physical experience of being and acting in the world, of perceiving the environment, moving bodies, exerting and experiencing force, etc., allows them to form basic conceptual structures which then are used to organise thought across a range of more abstract domains. (Lakoff, 1987)

Thus, the principle of embodiment suggests that our organic nature – as humans who have bodies – influences our experience of the world (Leeson & Saeed, 2012a). For example, we talk of the positions of things in the world with respect to how they relate to us: *in front of, behind, facing towards, facing away from*, and so on. Our bodies and our gaze have natural orientations, and we project this onto other entities like houses and natural features in the landscape which can, via metaphoric extension, be said to 'face' a certain way. In this way, embodiment underpins language because of a second important cognitivist assumption: that semantic structure incorporates and transmits conceptual structure.

Quote 3.17   Iconicity

There seems to be a strong tendency to see iconicity in sign languages as typically involving some kind of pictorial representation of meaning. This is why the terms *pictorial* and *iconic* are often used almost synonymously. (Brennan, 2005, p. 362)

Quote 3.18 Creative resource

...iconicity is a central creative resource in sign language formation, maintenance and productivity... (Thoutenhoofd, 2000, p. 261)

Quote 3.19 Construals

Iconicity is not a relation between the objective properties of a situation and the objective properties of articulators. Rather, the iconic relation is between construals of real-world scenes and construals of form. (Wilcox. 2004b, p. 123)

Quote 3.20 Visual motivation

...I suggest that the myths espoused by many hearing and indeed Deaf people derive from an intuition about the nature of human gesture and the visual world. Sign languages are visually motivated, and Deaf people exploit and respond to this visual motivation on a daily basis. In recent years considerable work has been done in the field of gesture, including work on coverbal gesture. Such research has provided insights into the ways in which natural gesture can work along with speech to express meaning. In particular, it has been argued that this phenomenon is often metaphorical in nature and that gestural metaphor provides a key component of meaning. I propose that sign languages exploit similar mechanisms. In particular, sign languages make use of metaphorically motivated gestures that are actually integrated into the linguistic system. As with coverbal gesture, these metaphors often provide visual images that incorporate cultural information. (Brennan, 2005, p. 362)

One of the key elements of the work of Lakoff (1987) and Lakoff and Johnson (2003) has been an analysis of metaphor as a system for conceptual mapping. Moving away from traditional ideas of metaphor as poetic and novel, they present an experientially based view that sees metaphor as a systematic conceptual thought process or, as Lakoff and Johnson put it, 'metaphor means metaphorical concept' (2003, p. 6), with this work preparing the way for a significant body of work that demonstrates how metaphor is 'shaped to a significant extent by the common nature of our bodies and the shared ways that we all function in the everyday world' (p. 245).

This approach has been applied to studies of a range of sign languages, with one of the most notable researchers working on conceptual metaphor in sign languages being the deaf linguist Phyllis Perrin-Wilcox. Quote 3.21 picks up her thinking on the relationship between iconicity and conceptual metaphors that relate to how we conceive of thought via the metaphors MIND IS A CONTAINER and IDEAS ARE OBJECTS.

Quote 3.21   Conceptual metaphor and iconicity

In ASL, handshapes lend themselves to metaphoric constructs through their phonological forms and productive morphemes. The handshape icons not only reveal iconicity that is prevalent in spoken languages (Armstrong, 1983; Bybee, 1985; Fauconnier, 1985; Givón, 1991; Haiman, 1985; Langacker, 1981) but also use the corresponding movements to add visual images to the linguistic spectrum. ASL phonemes and morphemes are isomorphic, with corresponding handshapes having the same appearance of form. (Perrin-Wilcox, 2000, p. 268)

Perrin-Wilcox (2000) argues that we have to differentiate between iconic and metaphoric conceptual relationships, suggesting that an iconic relationship would hold where for example, a signer cups their hands to indicate the relative size of someone's brain/skull, while a metaphoric relationship between sign and concept holds in a case where a signer 'told a friend that if he continued to think lascivious thoughts, he should remove his skull cap and give the entire inside of his brain a thorough scrub. After the cleansing, the friend should then plop the lid back onto his brain (shaped by the non-dominant cupped hand) and revert to a more pious mode of thinking' (p. 269).

While iconic depiction is evident in both descriptions of skulls, in the figurative (skull-cap) example, the source is an actual brain while the target domain is a container, as conceptualised by the deaf signer; one which holds an immaterial substance – in this case, lewd thoughts! As Perrin-Wilcox points out, ideas are abstract and do not have physical structure, and, as a result, one cannot literally pick them up and handle them. In this way, the MIND IS A CONTAINER conceptual metaphor assists in distinguishing between iconic and metaphoric usage in ASL – and in other sign languages (see e.g. Russo, 2004 for Italian Sign Language; Brennan, 1990, for British Sign Language; Perrin-Wilcox 2000, Taub 2001 for American Sign Language).

Discussing embodiment in Irish Sign Language, Leeson (2010) describes how signers present what is before them as the most focussed elements in a discourse, thus exploiting a relationship between narrative perspective and the position of the signer's body. Less salient information is presented more distantly from the signer's body (Leeson, 2010; Leeson & Saeed, 2012a). Similar behaviour in ASL has been described as a metaphor – SPATIAL DISTANCE IS CONCEPTUAL DISTANCE (Janzen, 2010). Janzen (2010) suggests that ASL signers present items that they consider to be conceptually distant from each other as being physically distant in signing space, while items considered conceptually similar or identical are presented at adjacent or the identical point in space. Leeson and Saeed (2012a) talk about this as the 'privileging of signer perspective' (p. 180) and suggest that this can be identified in the tendency to encode actor-led activity on the signer's body (that is, signer = actor). In this way, action is led by the signer (as him- or herself, as narrator or, as we shall see in Chapter 4, a character in a constructed action).

Very recent work on embodiment, iconicity and metaphor suggests that there is also a link to emotion: Perniss and Vigliocco (2014) believe that iconicity is central to embodiment because it is through iconic links that language may become connected to events in the world. In this way, they propose that iconicity offers a key to understanding language evolution, development and processing.

Quote 3.22   The bridge of iconicity: from a world of experience to the experience of language

In language evolution, iconicity might have played a key role in establishing *displacement* (the ability of language to refer beyond what is immediately present), which is core to what language does; in ontogenesis, iconicity might play a critical role in supporting *referentiality* (learning to map linguistic labels to objects, events, etc., in the world), which is core to vocabulary development. Finally, in language processing, iconicity could provide a mechanism to account for how language comes to be *embodied* (grounded in our sensory and motor systems), which is core to meaningful communication. (Perniss & Vigliocco, 2014, p. 1)

This knowledge about how sign languages are embodied languages, and how sign language embodies identity, has come about as a consequence of research. Research influences language attitudes, and shifting language attitudes, in turn, have an impact on identity (Hill, 2013a).

3.3   Attitudes towards sign languages

As documented in Chapter 2, sign languages were not previously viewed as 'real language', but instead as wholly gesturally based and as a last option for those considered 'not intelligent enough' to speak (see e.g. the Irish government's 1972 policy document on education for deaf and hard of hearing children (Department of Education (1972)). These attitudes were often internalised by signing communities who came to view natural sign languages as some kind of pidgin signed variety of 'real', high-status spoken languages. Thus, many signing communities did not even name their languages until the 1980s. This attitude also affected community relations – those who used signed forms of spoken languages were considered to be more intelligent than those who did not.

The rise in 'Deaf consciousness' in the 1970s in the U.S. and in the 1980s in Europe led to a raft of changes, including the establishment of the European Union of the Deaf and a host of national associations of deaf people. These have a primary goal of securing recognition for natural sign languages (see e.g. Wheatley & Pabsch, 2010, 2012). With rights-based legislation and disability-related legislation, formal recognition of sign languages (in many countries) and access to education with interpreting and other provisions provided, the situation regarding the status of sign languages has shifted.

Attitudes towards signing communities and sign language identities have changed significantly as a direct consequence of sign linguistics and Deaf Studies research. Although applied sign linguistics research has been used as evidence to support the recognition of sign languages as legitimate languages (Burns, Matthews & Nolan-Conroy, 2001) in many countries, there are still some countries where linguists need convincing (Bartha, 2003). But, generally, it could be said that sign languages are no longer taboo. As we have seen in Chapter 2 (Section 2.2.4), the 2006 UNCRPD has 5 articles that specifically relate to sign languages out of a total of 30 articles, and sign languages are also mentioned in another 8 articles.

Several countries, including New Zealand, South Africa, Thailand, Uganda, Uruguay and many in the European Union, have legally recognised the natural sign languages of their countries (Haualand, 2009; Timmermans, 2005); most recently, Finland (March 2015) and Scotland (September 2015). Other countries indirectly recognise their national sign languages in the form of statements in policies or relevant legislation, such as the UK, Denmark and Finland (Haualand, 2009; Krausneker, 2000; Wheatley & Pabsch 2010, 2012).

Nevertheless, even if a country has made provisions for the recognition of sign language, this does not always translate into policies and provisions within states of the country, something that Hill (2013a) identifies as the difference between attitude and structural reality. This is particularly the case in the education of deaf children, where the use of sign language is not always encouraged and sometimes is still actively suppressed (Hill, 2013a; Leeson, 2006; Small & Cripps, n.d.; see Chapter 5, Section 5.2, for more detailed discussion of sign language at school). Furthermore, signing communities can be regarded as being in a constant state of emergency 'caused by a backlash in institutional attitudes' as a result of cochlear implants and the pervasion of oralist attitudes (Tapio & Takkinen, 2012, p. 288).

3.3.1   Language attitudes *within* signing communities

In parallel to the broader positive attitudes towards sign languages, one other aspect of language attitudes that is particularly interesting from an applied linguistics perspective is the attitudes towards sign language use *within* signing communities. This issue was mentioned briefly in Sections 3.1.5 and 3.1.6, where we discussed how members of signing communities make judgements about the way that others actually use sign language.

Quote 3.23   Attitude object

Attitude is defined as 'a psychological tendency that is expressed by evaluating a particular entity with some degree of favor or disfavor' ... The particular entity being evaluated is called the *attitude object* ... the attitude object [can be] a deaf or hard of hearing person's signing. Because the attitude object is a language [there are] affective, cognitive, and behavioral types of evaluative responses toward particular language varieties (that is, languages, dialects, pidgins, and creoles) based on stereotypical perceptions of social groups who use those varieties ... Responses toward language varieties, which are attitude objects, are based on two perceptions: a sensory perception of linguistic items in a language variety and a stereotypical perception of a social group that uses these items. (Hill, 2013b, p. 21)

Quote 3.24   Attitudes and social identities

The attitudes toward signing varieties are tied with the perceptions of social identities related to deafness and signing abilities. (Hill, 2013b, p. 25)

These attitudes come about primarily because of historical language planning and policies (see Section 3.4) and the use of various forms of sign language: either what is considered to be 'pure' sign language (Woodward, 1972), as examined by sign linguists and used by native signers, or 'mixed' signing, described by linguists as a form of language contact primarily between spoken and signed languages, where signers blend grammatical features from each language to produce 'contact signing' (Lucas & Valli, 1992; Quinto-Pozos, 2007); for example, borrowing English into BSL through mouthing, fingerspelling or signing in English word order, or manual artificial codes such as Signed English, which effectively represent lexical items in exact spoken language word order (Bornstein, Saulnier & Hamilton, 1980). Attitudes within the community may also be influenced by social factors and the sociolinguistic variation witnessed in sign languages, based on gender or generational difference (Grehan, 2008; Leeson, 2005b; Schembri et al., 2010), regional variation (Schembri et al., 2010) or race (McCaskill, Lucas, Bayley & Hill, 2011).

Joseph Hill (2013b) conducted an exploratory analysis of a range of ASL users' attitudes towards other deaf and hard of hearing signers in an attempt to find patterns in linguistic and social factors in the perceptions of and attitudes towards signing variation in the American signing community based on the users' race, age and age of acquisition of ASL. His study built in 4 different components to explore ASL attitudes and to assess the linguistic and social factors: (1) subjects' perceptions of people signing and whether they used 'Strong ASL', 'Mostly ASL', 'Mixed', or 'Non-ASL'; (2) effects of social information on whether the subjects' perceptions of signing changed; (3) use of evaluation scales for subjects to rate different signers with respect to language and social characteristics and (4) participants' description of the signing that they watched. Hill found that participants produced varied judgements of signers' ASL use and that social characteristics had a bearing on language attitudes. He also found that if participants perceived signers to have come from a deaf family or to have been to a deaf school (and therefore had been exposed to sign language from an early age), their signing skills were rated and described more positively.

Therefore, it can be seen that attitudes towards sign language users are very much related to perceptions of identity. Attitudes also influence sign language policy and planning.

3.4   Sign language policy and planning

As with applied linguists generally (e.g. Lo Bianco, 2004), applied sign linguists are concerned with language policy and planning in a deliberate effort to influence the function, structure or acquisition of languages or language variety within a community. Any discussion of sign language policy and planning needs to be placed within a historical context. As documented in Chapter 2 and earlier in this chapter, sign language use worldwide has been greatly influenced by attitudes towards whether sign languages are legitimate languages and medical or cultural perspectives on deafness. Massive shifts in language politics have influenced policies typically created by non-deaf people about how, when and where sign language can be used.

Concept 3.5   Language politics, policies & planning

From certain language politics, a certain language policy will follow, which will be implemented through some type of language planning. In other words: language politics refers to the why, language policy to the what, and language planning to the how. (Schermer, 2012, p. 890)

These language politics have not only been influenced by medical and cultural perspectives on deafness but also from general politics and values surrounding multilingualism and the status of minority languages (Tapio & Takkinen, 2012). Nonetheless, Turner (2009) suggests that there are some issues particular to sign language planning as a consequence of the socio-political landscape of signing communities, many of which have been eloquently described in Timothy Reagan's (2010) book *Language Policy and Planning for Sign Languages.*

Quote 3.25   On sign language planning

Around the world, sign languages have long been treated as requiring planning. In short, either the language or its users, or both, have commonly been seen as inadequate for effective social intercourse and authorities have felt the need to take action in various ways. (Turner, 2009, p. 245)

Reagan (2010) states that '[sign] language planning as an applied sociolinguistic activity has the potential to function either as a tool for empowerment and liberation or as a means of oppression and domination' (p. 157). Previous frequent and pervasive language planning methods of creating and implementing the use of artificial manual codes in deaf education are considered to have been oppressive to signing communities and their natural signed languages (see Herreweghe & Vermeerbergen, 2009; Reagan, 2010). Perhaps because of this practice, along with other pushes to standardise signed languages (see Case study 3.2 later in this chapter with respect to Pan-Arab Sign Language), sign language planning is often perceived to be a problematic concept driven by hearing people that has the potential to control deaf people and their language use. As noted earlier, sign languages incorporate variation as a norm of discourse, but historically it has been reported that hearing teachers of deaf children, second language learners and interpreters have difficulties with such variation (Eichmann, 2009; Leeson, 2005a; McKee, Major & McKee, 2011; Schermer, 2012).

In this section, we touch on three aspects of language planning that have affected signing communities and present relevant case studies: (1) status planning, (2) corpus planning and (3) acquisition or educational planning (Schermer, 2012).

3.4.1   Status sign language planning

Status planning focuses on the development of policy, legislation and the recognition of language, typically with attempts to change language use and function. Signing communities have been lobbying, with various success, for governmental recognition of their natural sign languages. Recognition does not always lead to equality and access, but it is considered an important symbolic step towards these goals (Behares, Brovetto & Crespi, 2012; Geraci, 2012; Hult & Compton, 2012; Parisot & Rinfret, 2012; Quer, 2012; Reffell & McKee, 2009; Schermer, 2012a, 2012b). Status planning for sign languages in countries such as Belgium, New Zealand, and Germany was the focus of a special edition of the journal *Current Issues in Language Planning* in 2009 (Turner, 2009) and has seen two volumes published by the EUD (Wheatley & Pabsch, 2010, 2012).

At the time of writing, more than 40 countries (out of approximately 200 worldwide) have formally and legally moved forward to award their national sign language(s) official status (Krausneker, 2009). The WFD has conducted a major project to investigate the status of sign languages worldwide, and many national deaf associations have the goal to lobby for the recognition of the legal status of their national sign language. As Schermer (2012) points out, however, status and/or legal recognition does not necessarily resolve the barriers encountered by sign language users.

3.4.2   Corpus sign language planning

Corpus planning concentrates on 'the prescriptive intervention in the forms of a language. Corpus planning is concerned with the internal structure of a language, that is, with matters such as writing systems, standardisation, and lexical modernization' (Schermer, 2012, p. 36). Large amounts of language data (typically using a range of elicitation tasks) are collected for categorisation and codification, either to describe aspects of the grammar and lexicon (e.g. the BSL, Sign Language of the Netherlands (NGT), ISL, German Sign Language (DGT), Belgian-Flemish Sign Language (VGT), French Sign Language (LSF), Auslan, NZSL corpus projects – see Chapter 8 for resource information) or for the purposes of promoting standardisation.

For example, standardisation is used for projects that seek to develop various sets of specialised vocabulary in response to increased use of a sign language in a new domain, a process known as 'vernacularisation' or 'lexical modernisation' (Reagan, 2010). Many countries have had projects to develop new standardised terminology in sign language, such as science, maths or astronomy signs.[6]

Case study 3.1   Medical signbank

The Medical Signbank project, an innovative project in Australia, set out to bridge the gap in the Auslan lexicon for health-related terminology and to help improve health outcomes of deaf Australians as a result of improved interpreting in medical and mental health settings.

Taking a bottom-up approach, a website was established which allowed for the proposing of new vocabulary items and discussion of same (Johnston & Napier, 2010; Napier, Major & Ferrara, 2011) by members of the Australian signing community (deaf people, interpreters and anyone else who signs). The rationale for this approach was underpinned by anecdotal information suggesting that the health lexicon of Auslan is strikingly under-developed (Major, Napier, Ferrara, & Johnston, 2012).

In addition to establishing the online Medical Signbank, which serves as a resource for Auslan users and interpreters, additional research examined health terminology from the perspective of deaf people and outlines some of the strategies that deaf Australians report using when communicating about health concepts that do not have established signs in Auslan (Major, Napier, Ferrara et al., 2012). These include the use of fingerspelling, depiction and explanations, which deaf Australians report utilising to circumnavigate lexical gaps when talking about health matters.

In a review of the outcomes of the project, Napier, Major, Ferrara and Johnston (2014) report that they found it hard to get the Australian signing community to engage with the Medical Signbank. They surmised that this was primarily due to a lack of confidence in suggesting signs to be uploaded and concerns from interpreters about perceptions of them 'imposing' signs on deaf people (and thus perpetuating historical, oppressive language planning endeavours).

More about the Medical Signbank Project: http://new.auslan.org.au/about/medicalsignbank/

A more controversial form of corpus sign language planning can be seen in Quote 3.26 and in Case study 3.2, which focus on the attempted unification of a Pan-Arab Sign Language.

Quote 3.26   No one has the right to force us to accept unified signs

Why do interpreters and hearing people insist on forcing us to accept the unified dictionary despite us not understanding these weird signs? Sign language is our language and no one has the right to force us to learn the signs of Al Jazeera interpreters. Instead of forcing us to learn the signs of the unified dictionary, interpreters should learn Emirati Sign Language that we cherish and of which we are proud. Deaf Arab people stand united on one front and demand that immediate cessation of the unified dictionary and the prohibition of interpreters from interfering in sign languages. (Emirati deaf informant cited in Al-Fityani, 2010, p. 136).

Case study 3.2   Designing a 'Pan-Arab' sign language

Reference to a pan-Arabic Sign Language (ArSL) can be traced back to 1980, when it was mooted as a mechanism that would allow deaf Arab people to understand each other across national boundaries and for them to access television media to increase their awareness of current events (Al-Fityani, 2010). The recommendation to establish ArSL was documented in the minutes of a meeting of the Arab Federation of the Organs of the Deaf (AFOOD), an organisation whose objective is to coordinate the efforts of medical, educational and social work organisations that attend to deaf people across the Arab region. But by 1993, AFOOD, while continuing to hold the long-term goal of a unified sign language, had recommended that each Arab country document the sign language(s) used within their borders and release a dictionary, which would in turn serve as the foundation for a single unified language, ArSL.

By the turn of the 21st century, the unification project had moved forward with pan-Arab governmental bodies and support from Al Jazeera, the satellite news network (Al-Fityani, 2010). In 2002, Al Jazeera began offering on-screen sign language interpretation in ArSL in a bid to provide access to Arab deaf people across the region. This decision followed soon after the release of the unified ArSL dictionary in 2001. Al-Fityani reports that the project was framed as a human rights effort to advance the welfare of deaf Arab people, with governmental bodies playing a role in pushing for adoption of the unified sign language at schools for deaf children. At the same time, Al Jazeera played a complementary role in harnessing the power of television to promote the unified language as the official language of deaf Arab people.

Quote 3.26 above is indicative of the fact that many deaf Arab people were unhappy with these moves toward unification. By 2009, awareness of the project had raised concern at the highest levels, leading the World Federation of the Deaf to issue a statement outlining their concerns.[7] WFD saw the attempt as a violation of the linguistic human rights of Deaf people in the region and an unwanted interference with linguistic diversity. They argue that language planning decisions should always remain with the linguistic community and advised that planning activities in the region should be contrived and realised in cooperation with National Associations of the Deaf. Drawing on the WFD statement on the unification of sign languages, '[The] WFD Board wants to state firmly that any forcible purification or unification of Sign Languages, conducted by governments, professionals working with Deaf people, and organizations for or of the Deaf, is a violation of the UN and UNESCO treaties, declarations and other policies, including the recent UN Convention on the Rights of Persons with Disabilities. Deaf people in every country have the sole right to make changes, if necessary, in their own local, provincial and national Sign Languages in response to cultural changes. The control of the development of any Sign Language must be left to any social group where the particular Sign Language is used.'

The WFD called for the unification project to cease, suggesting instead a greater level of consultation with deaf people in the region alongside cooperation with WFD's Ordinary Members from 130 countries around the world. WFD also encouraged all parties to achieve mutual understanding for better recognition of national sign languages in the Arab region.

However, the project continues, and while it is unlikely that individual signing communities will cease using their national or regional sign language in favour of ArSL, some communities (e.g. in Iraq, Egypt and Jordan) have already borrowed elements from ArSL; at the same time, Arab signing communities continue to seek to document and receive official recognition of their indigenous sign languages. (Al-Fityani, 2010)

3.4.3   Educational sign language planning

Acquisition or educational planning is primarily concerned with learning and teaching of languages and 'is required to change the status of a language and to ensure the survival of a language' (Schermer, 2012a, p. 904). We discuss the learning and teaching of sign languages, and the role of sign language in education, in more depth in Chapter 4. Here, we only talk briefly about one way that educational sign language planning manifests in signing communities: through the development of bilingual education policies and provision.

Sign bilingualism is an inherent part of deaf citizenship and social justice (Emery, 2007), and ever since Johnston, Liddell and Erting (1989) promoted a sign bilingual approach to deaf education in their widely cited manuscript *Unlocking the Curriculum*, educational sign language planning has focussed on introducing deaf children to sign language as early as possible and promoting sign bilingualism, either with a signed and written language or a signed and written/spoken language, depending on the capabilities of the child.

Much research has delved into how to ensure that deaf children can be educated bilingually (see e.g. Mayer & Akamatsu, 1999; Mahshie, 1995) and the role for manual communication systems such as simultaneous communication and cued speech to introduce students to phonological, lexical and grammatical rules of spoken/written languages (e.g. Marschark & Spencer 2009; Marschark 2007).

One of the important issues to consider in instigating sign bilingual policies in education is that it does take a lot of planning: Incumbent teachers need to learn to sign, staff recruitment policies need to be changed to ensure minimum sign language fluency and resources need to be developed to support teachers and students.

Case study 3.3   Developing sign bilingual resources

At the end of the 1990s, Thomas Pattison School Bilingual Program for deaf children in Sydney, Australia, commenced a pilot of the Auslan Resources project. The remit of the project was to produce translations of various books targeted at children of K–2 reading level (5–7 years old) for parents and teachers to use as a resource in reading books with children of this age group, as it had been identified that development of bilingual resources was essential to the success of the program (Johnston, 2004b) and the bilingual proficiency of the deaf students (Johnston, 2004c).

The translation of resources involved stages of forward and backward translations in consultation with various stakeholders at the school to create deaf-culturally appropriate translations, with consideration given to the goal of each translation. Each translation progressed from the initial draft, through consultation with children, teachers, interpreters and linguists, to achieve the final product. (Conlon & Napier, 2004)

3.5   Sign language in action: concluding comments

In this chapter, we have discussed various aspects of sign language in action by examining the relationship between sign language and identity, shared identity in signing communities and the complex layers of deaf and hearing identities in signing communities. We explored sign languages as embodied languages and attitudes towards sign languages and within signing communities as well as the various elements of sign language policy.

In establishing key concepts, this chapter lays the foundation for the next part of the book, where we focus on the practical applications of sign language in action: where and how sign language is learned and taught, how sign language is used in everyday life and how sign language is used in non-professional and professional practice.

Further reading

Bauman, H-D. L. (Ed.). (2008). *Open your eyes: Deaf Studies talking.* Minneapolis, MN: University of Minnesota Press.

Ladd, P. (2003). *Understanding Deaf culture: In search of Deafhood.* Clevedon, UK: Multilingual Matters.

Ladd, P., & Lane, H. (2013). Deaf ethnicity, Deafhood, and their relationship. *Sign Language Studies, 13*(4), 565–579.

Lane, H., Hoffmeister, R., & Bahan, B. (1996). *A journey into the Deaf World.* San Diego, CA: Dawn Sign Press.

Mahshie, S. N. (1995). *Educating Deaf children bilingually.* Washington, DC: Gallaudet University Press.

Part II
Practical Applications

4
Learning and Teaching Sign Languages

'There is no evidence to back up the claim that sign languages are easier to learn than spoken languages or that if a child learns a sign language, that child will lose motivation to work at gaining speech skills' (Humphries et al., 2012, n.p.).

4.1 Acquiring a sign language as a first or preferred language

---

Quote 4.1   Scaffolding sign language learning

...for a child to learn sign language effectively, there needs to be available language models who are able to provide exposure to and interaction in that language. (Napier, Leigh & Nann, 2007, p. 85)

There are many issues to consider regarding the acquisition of signed languages, including the critical issue of transmission of language. As we saw in Chapter 3, an estimated 90–95% of deaf children are born into hearing, non-signing families, and as a result, these children may have a haphazard route to sign language acquisition. In addition, an estimated 80% of deaf children born in the developed world receive cochlear implants, and for a variety of reasons, many of these children will receive limited or no access to a sign language during what is considered to be the critical period for language acquisition (Blume, 2010; Humphries et al., 2012).

Further, approaches to the teaching and learning of sign languages are often under-informed by empirical evidence in the field of applied linguistics generally, and specifically, they do not harness recent findings from sign linguistics. This is evidenced by the lack of formal educational pathways to sign language teacher education in most countries, heightening the gap between theory and practice; in this case, sign language teaching practice. Some work is being done to try to address this difficulty, for example, the European Commission–funded project Sign Teach (www.signteach.eu) and the European Centre for Modern Languages project PRO-Sign (www.ecml.at/F5/tabid/867/language/en-GB/Default.aspx).

Compounding this matter, there are very few formal routes to training for sign language teachers in many countries and few minimal requirements in place to restrict who can call themselves a sign language teacher. In part, this may reflect the status of sign languages and point towards a body of work yet to be done in order to ensure that sign languages have equal standing with spoken languages in teaching and learning settings.

Despite historical and, in many countries, ongoing contemporaneous debate around the assumed superiority of spoken languages over sign languages, the empirical evidence does not support this (see Quote 4.2).

Quote 4.2   Oral-manual debate in deaf education

Issues associated with language have been contentious in deaf education for centuries. ... however, the 'oral-manual debate' is not at issue as *there is no evidence that one language modality or another is universally superior for deaf children nor, contrary to popular claims, that language acquisition in one modality interferes with language acquisition in the other.* (Marschark & Spencer 2009, p. 206; emphasis added)

Further, acquisition of a sign language has not been shown to impede potential acquisition of a spoken language (or vice versa), a claim which has been made many times throughout the history of deaf education and which is still used in some quarters to 'encourage' parents to select a sign-free environment for their children (Humphries et al., 2012; Mathews, 2012). In contrast, a feature of signing communities is the presence of 'bimodal bilingualism'.

Concept 4.1   Bimodal bilingualism

Separate perceptual and motoric systems provide speech–sign or 'bimodal' bilinguals with the unique opportunity to produce and perceive their two languages at the same time. In contrast, speech–speech or 'unimodal' bilinguals cannot simultaneously produce two spoken words or phrases because they have only a single output channel available (the vocal tract). In addition, for unimodal bilinguals both languages are perceived by the same sensory system (audition), whereas for bimodal bilinguals one language is perceived auditorily and the other is perceived visually. (Emmorey et al., 2008, p. 43)

Indeed, Marschark and Spencer (2009) tell us that early sign language, with or without accompanying spoken language, is generally associated with better early outcomes for deaf children. While this is something that signing communities have known experientially and argued for in terms of policy for a long time, the evidence has never been compiled in so clear-cut a manner before. This is vitally important because so very few deaf children are born into families where a sign language is their 'mother tongue': statistics suggest that only 5% of deaf children (in the U.S.) have early exposure to a sign language (Mitchell & Karchmer, 2004) because their parents are themselves deaf sign language users.

For these children, the acquisition of a sign language generally follows the same milestones as those attained by hearing children acquiring their mother tongue in a typical manner from their parents or caregivers. As Chen Pichler (2012) notes, a major theme of early sign acquisition research was to draw parallels between L1 acquisition of natural sign languages by native-signing deaf children and more traditional L1 acquisition of spoken languages by hearing children. This work emphasised the underlying similarities in acquisition, regardless of modality. It also contributed to the argument that sign languages are fully complex natural languages, autonomous from and equal in linguistic status to the spoken languages that surround them (Marschark, Schick & Spencer, 2006). Chen Pichler (2012) reports that despite striking parallels in the L1 development of speech and sign, modality effects nevertheless exist. The most obvious modality effect is that sign and speech each require the use of different sets of articulators, and each set might develop at different rates and be subject to different motoric limitations.

Quote 4.3   Lifelong sign language users

...it is only children with an early and profound hearing loss, and many with an early severe hearing loss, who are likely to be lifelong users of sign language. (Johnston, 2006, p. 138)

For the other 95% of deaf children, then, key questions include how early – and if – they are exposed to sign language, who they use it with and for what purposes. Goldin-Meadow (2003) suggests that deaf children bootstrap their acquisition of sign language onto 'home sign', a highly idiosyncratic and systematised use of gesture developed in individual hearing families to bridge the language gap for day-to-day communication. She argues that for fully grammatical signed language use to develop, a deaf child must come in contact with other deaf children and adults.

Case study 4.1　The birth and development of Nicaraguan sign language[1]

While some contemporary sign languages can be traced back to the 18th century (Meier, 2012), others are relatively recent. Nicaraguan Sign Language is a well-documented example of an evolving sign language whose roots can be traced to the 1970s (Meier, 2012; Senghas & Coppola, 2001). Before the 1970s, deaf Nicaraguans had little contact with each other. This was a result of several factors, including the lack of a unified national education system and societal attitudes that isolated deaf people. Further, marital patterns that tended to preclude hereditary deafness also prevented contact across the generations and the formation of a deaf community (Senghas & Coppola, 2001). Senghas and Coppola (2001) report that in 1977, a school was founded in Managua. Initially, it had 25 students, but numbers grew to more than 400 by 1983 (Polich, 1998; Senghas & Coppola, 2001). While all of the children had hearing parents and none knew any deaf adults who were sign language users, the children communicated with each other (outside the classroom, where lip-reading was used) and their interaction began to converge, allowing for the evolution of an early, rudimentary sign language (Senghas, 1995; Senghas, 1997). Since 1980, every year has brought an additional cohort to the school, which in turn has prompted the rapid development of Nicaraguan Sign Language. What makes this situation so unique is that each cohort acquires and develops Nicaraguan Sign Language among their peers from a language model that was not a fully formed language (Senghas & Coppola, 2001).

The Nicaraguan Sign Language example in Case study 4.1 gives us a rare window onto the evolution of a new sign language, but it is perhaps surprising to know that systematic comparisons between early and late L1 signers in childhood remain rare. This is also the case for studies of bilingual acquisition by both deaf and hearing children (Chen Pichler, 2012). While early studies on L1 sign acquisition focused on hearing sign-speech bilinguals (e.g. Siedlecki & Bonvillian, 1993), researchers are now beginning to consider how grammar in two modalities develops, Chen Pichler (2012) notes that even fewer researchers have examined sign–sign bilingualism, a developing phenomenon resulting from greater mobility (Pruss-Ramagosa, 2001). Indeed, WFD President Colin Allen suggested in 2013 that a mere 3% of the world's 172 million deaf sign language users access a bilingual education, but most deaf people are expected (though this is not always recognised) to function bilingually. However, there are no figures available suggesting the range of bilingual or plurilingual capacity that exists amongst the global deaf population, and little is known about bilingualism in the visual modality (Mayberry, 2006). What research can tell us is that there is a significant positive relationship between sign language proficiency (ASL proficiency, in the study we cite here) and reading skills in a second language (in this study, English; Freel et al., 2011). This suggests that the idea of establishing a sign language as a mother tongue is related to the development of competency in a second language. A second significant indicator emerging is maternal educational achievement: Freel et al. (2011) report that 'maternal education level significantly predicted deaf children's bilingual abilities, with higher education levels corresponding to more proficient abilities in ASL and written English' (p. 21). This would suggest that native signers, especially those with better-educated mothers, are best placed to develop strong bilingual capacity across language modalities. This begs the question: How do we define the category of 'native signers'?

4.1.1 Who is a native signer?

Cynthia Roy (1986) problematised the question of who might be considered a native signer, given the language transmission challenges that prevail, leaving only a small percentage of the signing community in a situation whereby they acquire a sign language from birth from deaf parents. In a more recent study (Freel et al., 2011), a native signer was classified as someone who has deaf parents and who reports that their acquisition of (in this case) ASL began prior to age 3. The age of 3 is specified as it maps onto what is taken to be the critical period for acquisition of native-like competency in a language, and thus, this cut-off point is frequently referenced in linguistic studies of sign languages that draw on native signer competence (e.g. Mathur & Rathmann, 2006). For other studies, especially neurolinguistic analyses, research groups often seek out informants who are at least second-generation deaf-of-deaf signers (Costello, Fernández & Landa, 2008; MacSweeney et al., 2002; Neville et al., 1997; Petitto et al., 2001).

What we can say is that growing up in a deaf family offers a context that facilitates normative transmission of language for native signers, be they hearing or deaf, from parent/caregiver to child. Mayberry (2006) reports that the vocabulary sizes of babies learning a signed and spoken language simultaneously is similar to those of babies learning only one spoken language. This, she says, is especially true when one considers the lexical items of the two languages, as is the case for babies learning two spoken languages. Thus, when we talk about normative sign language acquisition, we are referring to the situation of deaf or hearing children with deaf signing parents (sign language as a home language). In such instances, children acquire a sign language as their mother tongue in an age-appropriate manner. And, as Freel et al. (2011) point out, 'the criterion of having deaf signing parents creates the sociocultural experience of full access to a visual language by adults who understand how to guide visual attention' (p. 19). Deaf parents who are sign language users have also been shown to effectively support ('scaffold') language learning during the critical period of language acquisition (Corina & Singleton, 2009; Mayberry, 2007).

However, as Trevor Johnston notes in Quote 4.4, we should also remember that there are many hearing native signers too, an issue that we discussed in Chapter 3.

> **Quote 4.4   Hearing native signers**
>
> It is important to remember that there are significant numbers of hearing people who are users of various community sign languages. Indeed, there are probably as many 'native sign language users' who are hearing (having grown up using sign language with their deaf parents) as there are deaf native sign language users. (Johnston, 2006, p. 138)

The presence of Codas in signing communities presents the opportunity to examine sign language in action from a different perspective. Like deaf children who grow up with families who are also deaf, children of deaf adults often acquire a sign language as their first language.

There is a growing body of linguistic research that explores the way young Codas acquire spoken and signed languages (Baker & van den Bogaerde, 2014; van den Bogaerde & Andrews, 2008), their communicative strategies (Singleton & Tittle, 2000) and the fact that Codas function not only bilingually but also bimodally (Bishop & Hicks, 2005, 2008b; Emmorey et al., 2008; Pyers & Emmorey, 2008).

The key point of interest of all these studies is that Codas who are native signers will often utilise language contact and code-blend between a spoken and sign language, especially when they are talking to other Codas.

> **Concept 4.2   Code-switching**
>
> In many of the world's bilingual communities, fluent bilinguals sometimes engage in code-switching by producing discourses which, in the same conversational turn or in consecutive turns, include morphemes from two or more of the varieties in their linguistic repertoire. (Myers-Scotton, 2008, p. 149)

For sign language–spoken language contact situations, Adam (2012a) reports that code-mixing and code-switching are seen as context- and content-dependent (Ann, 2001; Kuntze, 2000; Lucas & Valli, 1992) with code-switching occurring inter-sententially; that is, switching between languages at a sentence boundary. In contrast, code-mixing occurs intra-sententially; that is, within the sentence (Adam, 2012a). In adapting terminology between spoken and signed languages, we must be mindful that sometimes there is no easy one-to-one mapping of label, form and function. Indeed, Ann (2001) notes that code-switching and code-mixing in sign language–spoken language contact would require a person to stop signing and start speaking or vice versa, but this rarely occurs in interaction between bilinguals who know both a spoken and a sign language (Emmorey et al., 2008).

Concept 4.3   Code-blending

Code-blending in sign language–spoken language contact has unique properties because of the different language modalities involved. Because the articulators for spoken languages and sign languages are different, it is possible to use both types of articulators at the same time. This is not only found in contact between spoken language-dominant and sign language-dominant signers, but also between native signers who are also fluent in a spoken language. (Adam, 2012b, p. 845)

Quote 4.5   Deaf parent: Coda interaction *is* intercultural communication

As one considers the cross-cultural conflict that can occur between Deaf and hearing individuals, we tend to think only of interactions involving a Deaf adult and a hearing provider/educator. However, we must also be aware of the cross-cultural communication issues that can occur within the nuclear family between parent and child when those parents are Deaf and the child is hearing. (Singleton & Tittle, 2000, p. 224)

Deaf parents are effectively raising 'foreign' children. (Singleton & Tittle, p. 227)

In some instances, Codas do not access sign language at home. Reasons reported for not signing to a hearing child include assumptions that one simply should not sign to a hearing child, or because deaf parents may have internalised negative views of signing (Hoffmeister, 1985), or because parents don't want to create a situation where they are overly reliant on their hearing child to interpret for them (Jones, Strom & Daniels, 1989). As Singleton and Tittle (2000) report, in many cases this leads parents to speak to their children with probable reduced speech and grammatical clarity, leading to a situation whereby parents and children do not have a shared language for daily discourse. In short, 'parent-child discourse becomes restricted and asymmetrical' when what is desirable is that 'Deaf parents ought to use their best mode of communication, the one they are most comfortable using, with their children, to ensure clear family communication, effective parenting, and to promote natural language acquisition for the child (regardless of whether it is a signed or spoken language)' (Singleton & Tittle, 2000, p. 226).

Within deaf families, there are tendencies for the eldest hearing child, most typically a daughter, to take on the role of interpreter for their parents, taking on responsibility for negotiating communication for younger siblings, family members and others in their community (Preston, 1996). However, an unintended outcome of this can be that younger siblings do not develop fluency in their parents' sign language (Preston, 1996; Singleton & Tittle, 2000). What should be emphasised is that if the primary language of the home is a sign language, a hearing child can and will learn the spoken language of the territory from other sources.

4.1.2   Non-native deaf signers

As we mentioned in Chapter 3, for an increasing number of deaf children and adults, a sign language is acquired as a non-native language. While there are some deaf adults who elect to learn a sign language as an L2, having mastered the ambient spoken language in childhood, for many deaf children, acquisition of a first language is delayed, with consequences for cognitive activities like mathematics and the organisation of memory as well as for purely language-related activity (Humphries et al., 2012; Mayberry, 2006).

Quote 4.6   Delayed L1 acquisition is not L2 learning

The important point to remember is that sign language learning for many deaf children and adolescents is not L2 learning but is in reality L1 learning begun at an abnormally late age, i.e. after early childhood. (Mayberry, 2006, pp. 744–745)

Such delayed learning can occur in late childhood, in adolescence or in adulthood. This happens for a number of reasons, but increasingly, it happens because deaf children are 'mainstreamed' in inclusive educational programmes with no access to sign language input, and some 80% receive pre-lingual cochlear implants (Humphries et al., 2012). Mayberry (2006) reports that this group are acquiring bilingual capacity in a sequential fashion (i.e. having already acquired a first language). She reports that, if parents do not sign to them, the majority of babies born deaf are isolated not only from the languages around them but also from sign languages. As the age of L1 acquisition increases, the ability to understand and remember sign language sentences and stories decreases; late learners often make phonological errors such as producing signs in a way that violates the semantic and syntactic framework of the sentences they wish to produce. They also have a reduced capacity to understand sign language and operate at near-chance levels on grammatical tasks (Mayberry, 2006).

With this in mind, we might ask what it means for the community of sign language users to have an increasing number of non-native deaf signers engaging with the community and what it means for late learners to engage with the signing community. While we are not aware of any empirically driven discussion of the impact of a linguistic shift, we do know that several linguists, most notably the Australian Trevor Johnston, have raised concerns about changes to the demographics of signing communities. Australia has one of the world's highest rates of mainstreaming of deaf children in the world (Power & Hyde, 2002). Johnston (2006) notes that while many children have failed to attain the linguistic and educational goals anticipated by mainstreaming, this educational approach has meant that significant numbers of Australian deaf and hard of hearing children have not grown up with Auslan, do not identify with the Australian signing community and do not mix within that community. As a result, Johnston has argued that the Australian signing community's linguistic survival is compromised.

Quote 4.7 Compromising signing communities

In addition to simply reducing the number of potential signers, mainstreaming has also had the important effect of seriously disrupting the generational and peer-transmission of Auslan. Thus, from the linguistic point of view, mainstreaming has also negatively affected the integrity and perhaps the long-term viability of the already numerically reduced signing community. (Johnston, 2006, p. 151)

This situation of compromisation has consequences for community engagement across generations, and in real terms, the potential for diminishing the social engagement of deaf people due to a decline in community membership. At worst, then, from a deaf community perspective, mainstreaming potentially facilitates a path towards 'language death' (Crystal, 2002) or, as others put it, can be taken to demonstrate 'linguistic genocide' at work (Skutnabb-Kangas, 2000). Johnston (2006) notes that as a Coda from a vibrant, predominantly deaf family, he experiences deep sorrow at the impending loss of language that may arise in Australia, but he also suggests that 'sorrow at the potential cultural loss need not be compounded by inability or refusal to act appropriately' (p. 170). He goes on to suggest that the act of creating a corpus of Auslan is a moral imperative required in response to the threat of language loss, arguing that a refusal to take this task seriously 'would display a profound indifference towards our cultural heritage, and a lack of appreciation of the most basic principles of scientific research' (p. 170). Of course, there are other perspectives on the contemporary position of sign languages, as discussed in Chapter 3.

For those mainstreamed deaf people who do take the step of engaging with the signing community, language use is just one of the indexical markers which map to identity, and feeling like an 'insider' or an 'outsider' can shift, depending on one's own perspectives – and on how the host deaf community views you (see e.g. Corker, 1996, 1998; Drolsbaugh, 2008).

Quote 4.8   Julianne Gillen – SIGNALL II project

Some days I feel like I'm a member of the Deaf community, but on other days, I still feel like an outsider. It varies. (SIGNALL II Project interview, European Commission Lifelong Learning Project)

4.1.3   Cultural interlopers revisited: non-native hearing signers: learning a sign language as an L2

Quote 4.9   'Everything depends on you'

Everything depends on you. You, the language learner, are the most important factor in the language learning process. Success or failure will, in the end, be determined by what you yourself contribute. (Rubin & Thompson, 1994, p. 3)

Hearing people learn to sign for all sorts of reasons: they have deaf neighbours, colleagues, classmates or a deaf love interest; it seems like a fun thing to do; they are influenced by signers they have seen on television programmes; they may want to 'help' deaf communities in some way; more recently, they may see learning a sign language as an avenue to a career or, in some countries, as a means to fulfilling language requirements at college level. For example, in the U.S., ASL is accepted as a 'foreign language' by more than 170 universities, including several Ivy League schools such as Yale and Stanford, which in turn primes interest in learning the language.[2] Indeed, ASL is now reportedly one of the most used languages in the U.S., with the Modern Language Association reporting that there had been a 30% increase enrolment in ASL classes between 2002 and 2006 (Peterson, 2009). Lane, Hoffmeister and Bahan (1996) report that estimates of ASL users range from 500,000 to 2 million in the U.S., with many more in Canada. They suggest that ASL is the leading minority language in the U.S. after the 'big four': Spanish, Italian, German and French. In other parts of the world, interest in learning sign languages has also grown over the past decades, but there are few reliable figures available to help track this in any meaningful way. We talk more about the teaching and learning of sign languages in Section 4.2.

Case study 4.2   Learning ISL as a young adult (LL)

Lorraine grew up in Cabra, the area most associated with deaf people in Ireland. The country's two main Catholic deaf schools and (since 2013) Deaf Village Ireland (www.deafvillageireland.ie) are based there. It is also just up the road from where the Irish Deaf Society was formed (Smithfield) and where Claremont School, the Protestant school for the deaf, was located (Glasnevin). Lorraine's maternal grandmother had a deaf neighbour and knew the British two-handed alphabet, which had been used by Protestant Irish deaf people. Her paternal grandfather had set up the local football team, which played against St. Vincent's (deaf) football club. Her local shoe mender was deaf, and there were several well-respected deaf people who lived on streets adjacent to hers. So, for Lorraine, deaf people were just part of the local environment. She didn't think about them or their community in any detailed way until she was 17 and signed up for a sign language class while on a college placement. Her teacher, Tony McElhatton, was a third-generation deaf person and well-known presenter of News for the Deaf on RTÉ, the national broadcasting company. As was then the norm, he wrote English sentences on the blackboard and proceeded to teach the students how to sign each word, each morpheme. Lorraine didn't realise it at the time, but she was learning Signed Exact English. At that time, the prevailing attitude was that this was the only appropriate form to teach hearing people and, as the thinking went, this was the form that educated deaf people used.

Later, Lorraine went to work as a housemother at St. Joseph's School for Deaf Boys. She was 18. The 16 boys she worked with on a daily basis were aged 15–20 and were *not* impressed to greet another hearing person who couldn't sign fluently. Fortunately, they took it upon themselves to teach Lorraine. They also endeavoured to make her sign less like an 'old deaf man' (as they put it)! She owes them a great deal. They opened her eyes to how members of the signing community used ISL (though very few people talked about ISL at that point, just 'sign' or 'the deaf way') and were always the first to commend her improvements and point out where more work was needed.

Another key person in Lorraine's language learning process was Joe Stringer, the shoe mender she had first met as a child of 3. He and Lorraine started working in St. Joseph's School on the same day and became fast friends. They would meet for tea and he, with the boys in the school, greatly influenced her sense of injustice with regard to how sign language users were portrayed ('less intelligent', 'less capable'). Lorraine experienced caring, intelligent people who were excluded and not given the chance to shine. Through learning ISL, her eyes were opened to the remarkable capacity that went untapped right in the space where it should have been celebrated and encouraged.

In 1992, Lorraine was fortunate enough to be selected to participate in Ireland's first interpreter training programme, run between Trinity College, Dublin, and the University of Bristol's Centre for Deaf Studies, in partnership with the Irish Deaf Society. This was a life-changing opportunity. They were suddenly learning about the grammar of British Sign Language – and extrapolating about how the grammar of Irish Sign Language worked. They were learning in a multilingual setting (with signers of BSL, ISL, Portuguese SL and Greek SL amongst their peers), living and studying alongside Patrick A. Matthews and Senan Dunne, two pioneering Irish deaf men who became the first trained teachers of ISL. They were immersed in a visual world and taught to think differently about sign languages. For Lorraine, this constituted a paradigm shift in thinking about deaf people and sign languages that has fuelled her work ever since.

4.2   Teaching and learning sign languages

Quote 4.10   Developing competence

Learners of a (foreign) language need to achieve the following competence to be able to communicate actively and efficiently:

- general competence like declarative knowledge (*savoir*), skills and know-how (*savoir-faire*), awareness (*savoir-être*), and abilities to learn (*savoir apprendre*);
- communicative language competence like linguistic competence (lexical, grammatical, semantic, phonological, orthographic, orthoepic), sociolinguistic competence (varieties of languages, register differences, etc.), pragmatic competence (discourse competence, functional competence, etc.);
- the capacity to implement these two dimensions of competence; and
- the capacity to use strategies to apply and adapt these competences in all possible contexts. (Piccardo, Berchoud, Cignatta, Mentz & Pamula, 2011, p. 15)

While Piccardo et al. (2011) are not focusing on learners of sign languages in their commentary, the competences they list are not language- or modality-specific, and indeed, these principles underpin the broad range of work now underway relating to the Common European Framework of Reference for Languages (CEFR; Council of Europe, 2001), including work specific to sign language teaching, learning and assessment (more on this in Section 4.2.1).

In recent years, the ideas that successful learners are autonomous learners (Little & Ushioda, 1998), that learning happens best when it is relevant and that successful communication in the target language scaffolds and motivates towards further language use have been leveraged in many approaches. Learner autonomy is based on the principle that autonomy is the goal of all developmental learning. As such, the assumption is that language learning should focus on knowledge *of* language, not *about* language, and that language learning occurs through language use, not least as the result of engagement in meaningful language use (e.g. group work). The focus is on meaning *and* form; autonomous learning draws on individual learners' capacity for independent, spontaneous language use where students take (and are encouraged to take) active responsibility for and involvement in learning (after Little & Ushioda, 1998).

4.3   What makes a successful sign language learner?

While we are all self-conscious when beginning a new activity, the development of metacognitive awareness and being an autonomous reflexive learner are key (Council of Europe, 2001; Piccardo et al., 2011). These come into play when we look at the strategies and practices that make for successful language learning. Peterson (2009, pp. 151–154) outlines several key strategies and practices that will support success, which he lists as suggestions for learners. He says:

- Be proactive as a learner.
- Form a study group with other students from your class.
- Read your syllabus and class texts carefully.
- Set time aside every day to practice receptive and productive tasks.
- Set goals for yourself and evaluate what you can do.
- Take advantage of the resources available to you outside the classroom – online and in your local signing community.
- Discover your personal learning style and adopt your classroom experience to this.
- Make sure your teacher knows who you are.
- Realise that your classmates are dealing with the same issues that you are.
- Keep a journal of your language learning process.
- Reinforce successful behaviour: Let your teacher know what exercises you got a lot from.

Practical issues that have been suggested as improving skill development include engaging with the signing community socially (using the language you are learning in authentic contexts) and engaging with materials such as the myriad of sign language corpora and other e-tools now available (Cresdee & Johnston, 2014; Fischer & Muller, 2014; Kaul, Griebel & Kaufmann, 2014; Leeson, 2008). Ensuring progress and successfully evaluating how one is progressing in language learning requires capacity as an autonomous language learner and awareness around what marks progress as a language learner, which we discussed in Section 4.2.1. Readers may also be interested in reading more about the European Language Portfolio as an internationally recognised tool for documenting and tracking plurilingual language development over time (www.coe.int/t/dg4/education/elp/). This is a framework that is equally applicable to the documentation of sign and spoken language skill development, though application to sign language teaching is still, in practice, at a very early stage.

4.3.1 Learning to sign cross-culturally

In Chapter 3, we introduced the concept of 'embodiment' and noted that this relates to language users' physical experience of being and acting in the world, of perceiving the environment, moving bodies, exerting and experiencing force, and so on. This allows them to form basic conceptual structures which then are used to organise thought across a range of more abstract domains, typically by metaphoric extension.

This has consequences for language learners too: As we have said earlier, we learn languages by using them, and we can learn most about the target culture, cultural heritage, tradition and ways of being within a target community by engaging with a community of practice. In this way, we suggest that when non-native signers are learning to sign, one must learn about how signers 'see' the world as 'people of the eye' (Lane, Pillard & Hedberg, 2011) and build this world-view into how sign language is used. Sign language learners must also learn to have 'Deaf heart' (Colonomos, 2014) and appreciate and inculcate the values of the 'Deaf World' (Mindess, 1999) into their own world-view if they are to be received as culturally sensitive users of the host language. Finally, and crucially, sign language learners must learn how to embody the world from a kinaesthetic and visual perspective: How do things feel when they move? How do they look? What components need to be given focus? How do we partition our body to represent different aspects of an event that we wish to recount? How do we control our eye gaze, our facial expressions, ensuring that we use them effectively in producing signed texts and in our interactive engagement with members of a signing community? Very little has been written on these subjects, and the potential for research in the domain of sign language teaching, learning and assessment is vast.

As we have also seen, in a globalised world, signers from one community may learn a second (or third ...) signed language and/or may engage with signing communities in other places. This opens up discussion about cross-cultural communication and the role of dominant signed languages (e.g. ASL) in intercultural exchanges. We have also considered International Sign and its place in the 'Deaf World' in Chapters 3 and 5.

4.3.2   Learning a sign language as a second language

Language learning is an internal process that we cannot observe directly; researchers make inferences about the nature of language learning in part based on the learner's language use (Larsen-Freeman & Long, 1991). Larsen-Freeman and Long suggest that we can improve the quality of our inferences about the language learning process by examining the nature of second language input as well as by considering factors like learner variables, differential achievement and the differences that arise between instructed second language acquisition and that occurring in naturalistic settings. While there is a great deal of literature available regarding second language acquisition and spoken languages, despite the widespread availability of sign language classes across the western world, remarkably little research has been carried out to date.

The majority of empirical work in existence focuses on phonological aspects of L2 signing (e.g. Mirus, Rathmann & Meier, 2001; Ortega & Morgan,

2010; Rosen, 2004). Of particular interest is the question of whether there are different effects associated with learning a first sign language as an L2 (M2/L2 – second modality, second language) when compared with those learning a second sign language (M1/L2 – first modality, second language). As Chen Pichler (2012) points out, such data would be critically important in considering approaches to teaching and learning for M2/L2 learners, whose number often include parents of deaf children who wish to support sign language acquisition for their child and deaf people who have been mainstreamed, as considered in Chapter 3.

Case study 4.3   Second language acquisition corpus project

At present, an exciting project is underway between a number of universities: Trinity College, Dublin (Ireland; Lorraine Leeson, Patrick A. Matthews and Sarah Sheridan), Stockholm University (Sweden; Johanna Mesch and Krister Schönström) and the University of Illinois at Urbana-Champaign (United States; Matthew W.G. Dye). The project has seen data collected from a small group of hearing students of sign languages over an extended period (2013–2015). The researchers are currently beginning to annotate their corpora and examine the ways in which learners grapple with aspects of learning sign languages over time. Their goal is to test hypotheses around the achievement of CEFR-mapped milestones in L2 learners of sign languages.

The project team is also replicating Peterson's (2009) survey of ASL learners across Europe, which will, they hope, provide some insight into the motivations of European hearing learners of sign languages for the first time.

The Irish team conducted focus group meetings with some of the students who participated in the corpus data collection, and this has led to insights into the things that students value when learning a sign language. A key concern raised by the Irish student cohort, who have completed two years of study, was the very limited opportunity they have to use ISL in authentic engagements with deaf people, despite their very best efforts to engage with the deaf community. In terms of grammar, the cohort reported finding aspects that differ most significantly from aural-oral languages the most challenging: for example, use of placement, classifier constructions and appropriate use of non-manual features (Schönström, Dye, Leeson & Mesch, 2015).

Quote 4.11   On learning a language by using the language – even with other L2 users

I think something that I found really, really helpful … was meeting up with third years [students] to have just general chit-chat conversation – two rows of chair one-to-one for three minutes and then you move on, and just interacting and their sign might not be perfect and our sign might not be perfect. But just being able to just have the chat and get the flow with someone you don't know. … Once this community spirit is better, everything is easier; the learning experience is much more pleasant. (Irish focus group respondent, Sign Language Acquisition Corpus Project, 2015)

4.4   Contexts of sign language teaching and learning

We have seen so far that the learning of sign languages – just like that of spoken languages – occurs in many guises. Depending on issues to do with attitudes to sign languages, the status of sign languages in a given place and access to educational pathways that prevail for sign language teachers and students of sign languages, where one learns a sign language and from whom can vary significantly.

While, historically, sign languages have been taught by deaf people, today it is the case that there are growing numbers of hearing people who are teaching sign languages – and this has the potential to cause conflict in signing communities. A crucial consideration, as outlined in Quote 4.12, is that of authentic representation of signing communities in language teaching.

Quote 4.12   On authenticity in teaching practice

Hearing versus Deaf sign language teachers is a hotly debated issue within the profession of sign language teachers as well as non-native versus native sign language teachers. What is the most important consideration is teaching skills and knowledge and ability to represent the language and culture authentically. Of course, if given a chance between two equally qualified teachers, a Deaf teacher should be given the opportunity first. Qualified hearing teachers can and are very capable of teaching sign language to hearing students, and often have personal insight into the challenge of learning a second language. Ideally, hearing teachers would be part of a team that includes Deaf colleagues. Feedback from sign language learners consistently shows that they highly value interaction with Deaf people as language and cultural models. (Dr David McKee, deaf sign language teacher and linguist, University of Wellington, Victoria, New Zealand)

Despite the little empirical work on the teaching and learning of sign languages, a recent volume offers insights into the current state of the art. McKee, Rosen and McKee (2014) present an international collection of research from the field of sign language teaching. They note that while sign language teaching has rapidly established an accepted place in the academic domain of second language teaching, sign language pedagogy has widely been shaped by a number of factors. These include conventional practices, available teaching curricula, and findings from descriptive linguistic research. The researchers also note that developments in curricula, teaching approaches and assessment have been relatively unmediated by applied, empirical research on learning and teaching.

4.4.1   Curricula and teaching approaches

Earlier, we noted that Larsen-Freeman and Long (1991) stated that researchers can make inferences about second language learning by examining, amongst other things, the kinds of input that learners receive, including syllabi and curricula. Richards (2001) notes that the history of curriculum development in language teaching begins with the notion of syllabus design. He writes that 'a syllabus is a specification of content of a course of instruction and lists what will be taught and tested' while curriculum development 'includes the processes that are used to determine the needs of a group of learners, to develop aims or objectives for a program to address those needs, to determine an appropriate syllabus, course structure, teaching methods, and materials, and to carry out an evaluation of the language program that results from these processes' (p. 2)

Earlier, we noted that in recent years, the teaching of ASL as a foreign language has taken off in the U.S.; indeed, Rosen (2010) reports that the take-up of ASL as a 'foreign' language increased 4,000% between 1987 and 2005. He also reports that approximately 75% of teachers who responded to his study use more than one curriculum. More than half of his respondents reported that they make their own materials, and a little less than half of respondents use commercially prepared ASL curricula like *Bravo ASL!* and the 'Green Books'. He also raises concerns about teaching strategies and awareness of underpinning philosophies embedded in various curricula, arguing that teachers must understand the ideas that guide the development of any course of study.

Quote 4.13   Lack of empirical study on ASL as L2 pedagogy

There is no empirical study of the impact that pedagogies in ASL as a second language have on learning: the empirical studies...pertain to spoken second languages. (Rosen, 2010, p. 352)

Rosen (2010) goes on to offer an overview and analysis of the range of curricula used widely by ASL teachers in the U.S. published since the 1980s. He reports that the curricula typically used can be considered with regard to their position vis-à-vis thinking from the fields of Psychology of Learning (behaviourism, linguisticism, communication) and/or Linguistic Theory (traditional grammar, generative grammar, universal grammar, sociolinguistics).

Behaviourism believed in the use of reinforcement – or conditioning – as an incentive for learning (Skinner, 1953). Rosen (2010) notes that American schools have been influenced by the behaviourist approach since the early 20th century, and this (as with other theories that have had an impact on spoken language teaching and learning) has also affected the teaching and learning of ASL (and, we suggest, other sign languages). He explains that 'linguisticism' has its basis in Noam Chomsky's (1957, 1965) thesis that humans have an innate capacity for language acquisition, which he called the Language Acquisition Device (LAD). The LAD represents the competence that surfaces in performance of a language, arising as the result of transformational rules. Communication, as a second language teaching and learning approach, was prompted by the evolution of the field of socio-linguistics and was influenced by Chomsky's Universal Grammar. An additional consideration is that of pragmatic competence, which relates to language use in context (Hymes, 1971).

Rosen also (2010, pp. 365–366) reflects on the influence of Halliday's (1978) assertion that people are motivated to acquire language because it serves a range of specific functions, namely:

(1) instrumental: an individual uses language to express needs;
(2) representational: use of language to convey facts and information;
(3) regulatory: language is used to tell others what to do;
(4) heuristic: language is used to gain knowledge about the environment;
(5) interactional: language is used to connect with others and form relationships;
(6) personal: the use of language to express feelings, opinions and individual identity;
(7) imaginative: language is used to tell stories and jokes and create an imaginary environment.

Rosen (2010) notes that ASL curricula cluster around these themes with, for example, the ASL Phrase Book comprising drills including vocabulary and sentences that students memorise and recite. This is predicated on imitative actions linked to linguistic rules, based on a traditional grammar approach and underpinned by behaviourist theories of learning.

The very popular 'Green Books', along with *Learning ASL* and *Master ASL*, are based on teaching and learning strategies associated with linguistic rules (analysis) whereby teachers provide vocabulary and sentences and explain them in terms of those linguistic rules (Rosen, 2010). Students then analyse the content, generating sentences using ASL syntactic rules. The linguistic theory underpinning this approach is generative/universal grammar, and Rosen suggests that linguisticism is the basis of the psychological theory of learning applied.

Rosen's analysis suggests that both the *Bravo ASL!* and the 'Vista' curricula are driven by sociolinguistics, a communicative approach to teaching and learning. In both these curricula, teachers present vocabulary to students and show them how it is used in conversation. Students then generate conversations about social situations via monologues and dialogues.

Given all this and, we suggest, mirroring the principles that underpin work on CEFR in Europe, Canada and elsewhere, Rosen (2010, p. 375) argues that ASL should be seen as a modern language (Quote 4.14) and that teachers of ASL need to be aware of the empirical and theoretical foundations of the range of curricula that they draw on and the precepts that frame them. Further, he argues that ASL teachers must stay abreast of current linguistic studies and pedagogical theory.

Quote 4.14   ASL as a modern living language

ASL should be approached as a modern living language for effective communication with ASL users. It serves different purposes in a variety of settings. Learners should acquire receptive and expressive skills in interactive contexts such as getting attention; negotiating a signing environment; exchanging, confirming, and correcting information; expressing degrees of uncertainty; and asking for clarification and repetition using the appropriate phonological, lexical, syntactic, semantic, and pragmatic aspects of ASL. They also need to acquire knowledge about deaf people, Deaf community, and Deaf culture. This information should be integrated into the curriculum rather than presented in a potpourri format that is unrelated to lesson topics. The curriculum should provide opportunities for learners to immerse themselves in the rich cultural activities of the Deaf community. (Rosen, 2010, p. 375)

Across the continent of Europe, a framework for teaching, learning and assessing languages has been supported by the Council of Europe: CEFR is a system for mapping curricula and assessment to learning outcomes along 6 stages of skill development from A1 (beginner) to C2 (highly educated speaker), as outlined in Table 4.1.

CEFR sets out to ensure that there is harmony amongst a range of elements, including the identification of needs; the determination of objects; the definition of content; the selection or creation of material; the establishment

Table 4.1   CEFR stages of skills development

A Basic user	B Independent user	C Proficient user
A1–A2	B1–B2	C1–C2
70% Receptive 30% Productive	50% Receptive 50% Productive	30% Receptive 70% Productive

of teaching and learning programmes; the teaching and learning methods employed and evaluation, testing and assessment (Council of Europe, 2001, p. 7). It presents a language-independent 'framework of reference' which functions as a useful tool for curriculum designers. It is also helpful in creating learning outcomes, and it is theoretical in nature. Taking a communicative perspective, CEFR presents a taxonomic approach to providing descriptors of what learners can do at various stages of learning a language. It presents global descriptors for language competence from basic to proficient user levels, as well as more detailed 'can do' statements in self-assessment grids, divided into 5 skill areas for spoken languages: (1) language production, (2) language reception, (3) reading, (4) writing, (5) interaction. CEFR has been widely adopted in Europe and in Canada for spoken languages.

Work on mapping sign language teaching and learning to CEFR began circa 2004, with France and Ireland amongst the first to explore how the CEFR descriptors could be localised for their respective sign languages (Leeson & Byrne-Dunne, 2009; see also Sadlier, van den Bogaerde & Oyserman, 2012). While the European Commission has funded a number of projects that explored elements of teaching and learning sign languages, the first Council of Europe–funded project with a focus on sign languages began in 2011, when the European Centre for Modern Languages funded the PRO-Sign Project, which looks at the teaching, learning and assessment of sign languages for professional purposes, described in Case study 4.4 and in Table 4.2.

Case study 4.4 PRO-Sign: sign languages for professional purposes

In 2011, the European Centre for Modern Languages funded a 4-year project to examine the teaching, learning and assessment of sign languages for professional purposes in tertiary education vis-à-vis the Common European Framework of Reference for Languages (www.ecml.at/pro-sign). At the outset, the goal was to focus on C-level descriptors, on the understanding that some work had already been completed for A- and B-level descriptors in a range of European Union countries. A first step was to bring together sign language teachers, mostly deaf, from across the 46 countries that comprise the Council of Europe territories to benchmark usage and blocks to further development at a conference in Graz, Austria, in 2013. A 2012 PRO-Sign Project survey of CEFR in sign language teaching and learning in tertiary education found that only 16 respondents felt that they knew a lot about CEFR ($n = 53$ from across Europe), while 12 knew either very little or nothing about CEFR. A commentary on this survey is available in both International Sign and ASL at the online Deaf Studies Digital Journal (http://dsdj. gallaudet.edu).

It became apparent that there was more limited engagement with CEFR than was desirable because of the dearth of information about CEFR *in* sign languages. As a result, a first step was the creation of podcasts describing the theoretical underpinnings of CEFR and the CEFR global descriptors in International Sign (2013).

By 2014, a second conference at the University of Hamburg saw more than 130 participants convene to discuss developments in the intervening period. Things had changed: for example, for the first time, we had data from the Netherlands that evaluated student language development and mapped that against CEFR and their own institutional expectations, as well as evidence-based results of how students performed in assessments vis-à-vis CEFR descriptors (Boers-Bisker, van den Broek & van den Bogaerde, 2014; van den Broek-Laven, 2014). Further, the European Forum of Sign Language Interpreters (Leeson, Bown & Calles, 2013) have made reference to minimum language competencies expected from graduates of a 3-year interpreting degree programme mapped to CEFR level B2 (Leeson & Calles, 2013).

In March 2015, the CEFR descriptors for sign languages were discussed and confirmed by a PRO-Signs Network Meeting at the European Centre for Modern Languages and, since June 2015, are available in International Sign and English.

A CEFR-aligned toolkit for teaching, learning and assessing sign languages, developed by the PRO-Sign team in close consultation and partnership with sign language teachers from across Europe, is available online at www.ecml.at/pro-sign in both International Sign and English. The team's goal is that the materials will be localised for rollout by regional and national communities.

Table 4.2 Common reference levels – global scale for sign languages

Proficient User	C2	Can understand with ease virtually all [signed] texts. Can summarise information from different sources and reconstruct arguments and accounts in a coherent presentation. Can express him/herself spontaneously, very fluently and precisely, differentiating nuances of meaning even in more complex situations.
	C1	Can understand a wide range of demanding, longer texts and recognise implicit meaning. Can express him/herself fluently and spontaneously without much obvious searching for expressions. Can use language flexibly and effectively for social, academic and professional purposes. Can produce clear, well-structured, detailed text on complex subjects, showing controlled use of organisational patterns, connectors and cohesive devices.
Independent User	B2	Can understand the main ideas of complex text on both concrete and abstract topics, including technical discussions in his/her field of specialisation. Can interact with a degree of fluency and spontaneity that makes regular interaction with native/proficient signers quite possible without strain for either party. Can produce clear, detailed text on a wide range of subjects and explain a viewpoint on a topical issue, giving the advantages and disadvantages of various options.

Continued

Table 4.2   Continued

	B1	Can understand the main points when clear, standard language [which, for sign language users, may be a locally used variation] is used and the topics are familiar matters regularly encountered in work, school, leisure, etc. Can deal with most situations likely to arise where the sign language is used. Can produce simple connected text on topics which are familiar or of personal interest. Can describe experiences and events, dreams, hopes and ambitions and briefly give reasons and explanations for opinions and plans.
Basic User	A2	Can understand sentences and frequently-used expressions related to areas of most immediate relevance (e.g. basic personal and family information, shopping, local geography, employment). Can communicate in simple and routine tasks requiring a simple and direct exchange of information on familiar and routine matters. Can describe in simple terms aspects of his/her background, immediate environment and matters in areas of immediate need.
	A1	Can understand and use familiar everyday expressions and very basic phrases aimed at the satisfaction of needs of a concrete type. Can introduce him/herself and others and can ask and answer questions about personal details, such as where he/she lives, people he/she knows and things he/she has. Can interact in a simple way provided the other person communicates slowly and clearly and is prepared to help.

We should add that in the field of applied linguistics, a distinction has traditionally been made between two sets of language skills; the first are required for social, conversational communication, which Cummins and Swain (1986) call basic interpersonal communicative skills (BICS). In academic settings, a different set of communication skills are required, and this is cognitive academic language proficiency (CALP). These two types of skills involve quite different language styles, or registers, and also utilise different cognitive processes. While BICS relates to the aspects of communication that are likely to be used in face-to-face communication, rather than dealing with abstract concepts, CALP is the language that is developed in a more academic environment that relates to abstract and academic concepts. CALP is a vital aspect of the ability to engage in critical thinking and using problem-solving skills that are often encountered in schools and universities. This can also be further related to the acquisition of new knowledge and new information. CALP is described as requiring both explicit learning and natural language acquisition (Cummins & Swain, 1986).

Further, the use of language is considered a very important aspect of self-representation and identity (Guiora, 1982). Indeed, the Council of Europe issued a recommendation to its 47 member states in 2014, following from a decision by the Committee of Ministers, which comprises the Ministers for Foreign Affairs from each member state.[3] This recommendation relates to the importance of competences in the language(s) of schooling for equity and quality in education and for educational success, and it notes that knowledge of the commonest types of communication, knowledge of a language or knowledge of relevant works of literature is not necessarily sufficient to ensure that a student has access to the linguistic devices necessary for building knowledge in an educational setting. The Council of Europe argues that student success or failure partly depends on such knowledge, and they point out that very often, the 'genuine importance of these linguistic dimensions in every field of knowledge is frequently ignored or left implicit' (Council of Europe, 2014, p. 17). They later add that 'the specific relations between subject areas and linguistic skills, the place of language in identity building and intellectual and aesthetic development, as well as educational traditions, all play a particularly important role as regards the language of schooling' (Council of Europe, 2014, pp. 22–23).

Fundamentally, we are saying that fluency in a language has several component parts and that the capacity to interact socially in a language is not a sufficient condition for fluency to the level required for dealing with academic and higher-order cognitive functioning via a language – and these differences are built into CEFR 'can do' statements across several topic-specific domains and across the 6 stages of skill development (A1–C2).

Despite modality differences that exist between sign and spoken languages, a language-independent model, focusing on communicative competence, captures the generalities about what learners can do. Given this, perhaps we should abandon the idea of a Common European Framework of Reference 'for Sign Languages' (vis-à-vis a CEFR for spoken languages) and propose instead that the Council of Europe amend the language of the original CEFR to better account for language use across modalities. This is certainly an issue ripe for discussion.

4.4.2 Assessment and evaluation

It is only since the 1960s that (spoken) language testing began to be seen as something that might happen separate from the testing of literary or cultural knowledge, a departure that Weir (2003) reports as the start of a 'critical change of the English language examination to one which focuses on language as against an assortment of language, literature and culture' (p. 18). As we saw earlier, trends in the teaching, learning and assessment of spoken languages tend to influence approaches to the teaching, learning and assessment of sign languages (Rosen, 2010); thus, we can expect that the assessment of sign languages draws on established work in the field of language testing.

Assessment is not simply the final step in a process of language learning; it is an integral part of the process (Noijons, Beresova, Breton & Szabo, 2011).

Language assessment refers to the implementation of language competence, and as a result, focuses on learner performance (Council of Europe, 2001). Piccardo et al. (2011) go further, separating out 'assessment' from 'evaluation' and arguing that assessment refers only to the analysis of a learner's proficiency relative to a given performance, while evaluation can refer to a broader range of issues that may affect performance, such as the quality of a course, the effectiveness of teaching and the appropriateness of pedagogical materials. They remind us that all language tests are a form of assessment, but they note that assessment also implies informal checking or verification, which can take place in a variety of ways. Weir (2005) sees language testing as concerned with the extent to which a test can be shown to produce scores that are an accurate reflection of a candidate's ability in a particular area, while Piccardo et al. (2011) remind us that all assessments include the collection of data for the purposes of making effective decisions, and these

Table 4.3   Synoptic description of assessment

Assessment purposes	Course or programme scope and expectations	Perspective on students' abilities	Assessment methods
Diagnosis and planning	• Curriculum • Resources • Learning • Communication • opportunities	• Needs analysis (initial and cyclical) • Self-assessments • Goals for learning	• Communication tasks • Surveys • Personal aims • Diagnosis of special needs
Achievement and feedback	• Taught ⬇ • Studied or practiced ⬇	**Short-term performace** • Activities • Tasks • Records • Observations • Tests **Long-term performance**	**Pedagogical activities** • Tasks • Assignments • Exercises • Observations • Responses (oral and written) • Tests
Formal certification	• Achieved • External, normative standards • Official recognition	• Accumulative, summative records • Tests • institutional requirements	**Reflective tools** • Logs • Records • Portfolios • Self-assessment **Programme completion** • Grades • Exams or tests • Passport

Continued

Table 4.3 Continued

Assessment should provide evidence of desired:
- competences
- performances
- achievements
- consequences

While acknowledging:
- cultural differences
- individual differences
- available capacities, resources and opportunities

In ways that are:
- valid (content and purpose is specified, and proved to be fulfilled without irrelevant factors or unintended negative consequences)
- reliable (consistent, comparable, equitable, and fair)
- feasible (manageable, comprehensible, and relevant)

Source: Piccardo et al. (2011, p. 43); © Council of Europe (2011), used with permission.

can include tests, checklists in continuous assessment and informal observations by a teacher (see also Weir, 2005).

Haug (2011a) reports that criterion-referenced tests (also referred to as achievement tests) and norm-referenced tests are two concepts very important to language testing.

Concept 4.4   Criterion-referenced tests/'achievement' tests

In criterion-referenced tests, the candidate's score is not compared to the performance of a normative group, but rather, to a predefined criterion that needs to be achieved. This could be, for example, the final exam of a course, where the criteria of the course (knowledge, set of skills) are a set of clearly defined objectives which should be achieved by the end of the course and are therefore independent of the performance of others (Brown, 2004; Brown & Hudson, 2002; Davies et al., 1999). (Haug, 2011a, p. 34)

Achievement measures tend to be associated with course tests, portfolio-based assessments and the assessment of course work (McNamara, 2000). In such instances, assessment is focused on student development vis-à-vis course learning outcomes, something typically seen in universities, for example. Following McNamara (2000), we can say that achievement testing has several features: (1) it should support the teaching it relates to; (2) it may be self-enclosed, that is, focusing on aspects of language grammar or use that have been covered in the curriculum rather than on language use in the wider world; (3) it can be highly innovative and (4) it is often associated with 'alternative assessment', which stresses that assessment is integrated with the goals of the curriculum, and pushes for a constructive relationship between teaching and learning.

Concept 4.5   Norm-referenced tests

Norm-referenced tests are tests where a candidate's scores are interpreted with reference to that of other candidates who formed the normative group. (Haug, 2011a, p. 34)

An example might be one where a child's results on a standardised, norm-referenced test for language development can be interpreted against those of their peer group (Haug, 2011a).

All tests have as their goal the task of measuring a trait (or set of traits) or behaviour(s); this is known as the 'construct' (Davies et al., 1999).

Concept 4.6   Test construct

A construct can be defined as an ability or set of abilities that will be reflected in test performance, and about which inferences can be made on the basis of test scores. A construct is generally defined in terms of a theory; in case of language, a theory of language. A test, then, represents an operationalization of the theory. Construct validation involves an investigation of what a test actually measures and attempts to explain the construct. (Davies et al., 1999, p. 31)

What is important to remember is that in tests, we are often not looking simply at what a candidate is doing in the moment but inferring what they may do in future settings, a point that McNamara (2000) makes in Quote 4.15.

Quote 4.15   Inferring future performance from current test performance

In judging test performances...we are not interested in the observed instances of actual use for their own sake; if we were, and that is all we were interested in, the sample performance would not be a test. Rather, we want to know what the particular performance reveals about the potential for subsequent performances in the criterion situation. We look, so to speak, underneath or through the test performance to those qualities that are indicative of what is held to underlie it. (McNamara, 2000, p. 10)

While valid test instruments are clearly needed to monitor the acquisition of sign languages by deaf children (Allen & Enns, 2013; Haug, 2011a, 2011b; Maller, Singleton, Supalla & Wix, 1999), very few commercially available tests offer robust evidence to support their psychometric properties (Haug, 2011a). But why test language development in deaf children? Following Johnston (2007), Haug lists 3 reasons:

(1) to see if a child's language development is following the expected course by comparing his or her progress against those of same-age peers;
(2) to describe the child's current language abilities to allow for individualised language therapy and school programming;
(3) to monitor and measure progress for an individual child or an educational or therapeutic programme.

When it comes to sign language testing, the waters are muddied by the relative lack of L2 sign language acquisition data underpinning approaches to teaching, learning and assessment for L2 use, though we note that there have been some tests developed to examine aspects of sign language proficiency in deaf children for a small number of better-documented sign languages, including ASL (Enns & Herman, 2011; Strong & Prinz, 1997, 2000), BSL (Herman, 1998b; Herman & Roy, 2006; Vinson, Cormier, Denmark, Schembri & Vigliocco, 2008; Woll, 2013; Woolfe, Herman, Roy & Woll, 2010) and German Sign Language (DGS; Haug, 2011a, 2011b). Tests are also available for Sign Language of the Netherlands, French Sign Language, Italian Sign Language and Auslan (http://signlang-assessment. info). However, for the majority of the world's sign languages, no standardised tests of sign language skill are currently available.

Haug (2011a) notes that while most instruments test only very specific structures (e.g. morphological and syntactic structures in the BSL Receptive Skills Test; Herman, Holmes & Woll, 1999), some tests focus on a variety of structures (e.g. phonology, morphology and syntax), such as the Assessment Instrument for Sign Language of the Netherlands (Hermans, Knoors & Verhoeven, 2009). Some focus only on language production (Herman et al., 2004), while others are concerned only with comprehension (Herman, Holmes & Woll, 1999); yet others examine both production and comprehension (Fehrmann et al., 1995a, 1995b; Hermans et al., 2009).

The BSL Receptive Skills Test and the BSL Productive Skills Test, both developed by City University, London, are arguably the best known of the standardised L1 sign language tests. The BSL Receptive Skills Test measures the comprehension of BSL grammar in children aged 3–13 years. The test includes a vocabulary check and a video-based Receptive Skills Test. The goal of the vocabulary check is to ensure that children understand the vocabulary used in the Receptive Skills Test. The receptive test itself consists of 40 items, organised in order of difficulty, which assess children's knowledge of a range of BSL structures, including negation, number/distribution, verb morphology and noun/verb distinction. Test items were selected on the basis of research on sign language development and drew on aspects of sign languages which are known to present problems to later learners (Herman, 1998a). Given that regional variation is widespread in BSL, the tester establishes what variety the child uses and, after the vocabulary check, can determine which version of the test (northern or southern UK dialect) to select for testing purposes (www.signlang-assessment.info/index. php/british-sign-language-receptive-skills-test.html).

The BSL Productive Language Test, a norm-referenced test, was developed to complement the BSL Receptive Skills Test by looking at the language produced by deaf children with a particular focus on a child's ability to produce a signed narrative, accurately incorporating the grammatical features of BSL. The child's score is determined by comparison to the mean score obtained by children in the standardised sample, allowing for an indication of how a given child's BSL production skills are developing (www.signlang-assessment.info/index.php/assessing-bsl-development-production-test-narrative-skills.html). The BSL Receptive Skills Test has been adapted for ASL (Allen & Enns, 2013; Enns & Herman, 2011), Auslan (Hodge, Schembri & Rogers, 2014; Johnston, 2003) and German Sign Language (Haug, 2011a). When applied, studies suggest that the Receptive Skills Test is an effective measure of young children's understanding of the grammar of the target language (e.g. Allen & Enns, 2013, for ASL) and can shed light on a child's overall level of comprehension relative to normative data, facilitating the identification of areas of concern (e.g. the need for further assessment and/ or intervention; Allen & Enns, 2013; Woll, 2013).

Quote 4.16   CALT and sign language testing

More research on the possible usage of CALT [computer-aided language testing] for sign language tests is needed; for example, performing usability studies, working on different task types and response formats and scoring instruments. In the future, we should collaborate more with researchers of spoken language testing and we can begin to talk about the field of 'research in sign language testing'. (Dr Tobias Haug, sign linguist and sign language interpreter educator, University of Applied Sciences of Special Needs Education in Zurich)

Tests also exist to evaluate proficiency of learners of a sign language as an L2/foreign language. A widely used example is the Sign Language Proficiency Interview (SLPI) for American Sign Language (SLPI:ASL), designed by Bill Newell and Frank Caccamise from the National Technical Institute for the Deaf (NTID), Rochester Institute of Technology (RIT), in the United States

(Newell, Caccamise, Boardman & Holcomb, 1983). The SLPI is adapted from the Language/Oral Proficiency Interview, an assessment approach used in the evaluation of spoken language competence (www.rit.edu/ntid/slpi/). The goal of the SLPI is to assess how well people are able to use sign language for communication and, as appropriate, to use this information to assist people in development of their sign language communication skills (Newell et al., 1983). It is a criterion-referenced test that uses a standard scale for rating sign language skills based on competences exhibited by highly skilled native-like signers. It sets out to evaluate communicative proficiency (a functional assessment) as well as competence in terms of vocabulary use, grammar and fluency (all components of productive competence with a focus on form) as well as receptive skill (Newell et al., 1983). The rating scale maps performance from a level where a candidate presents with 'no functional skills' (i.e. the candidate may be able to provide short single signs and primarily provides fingerspelled responses to some basic questions that are signed at a slow rate with extensive repetition and rephrasing) to 'superior plus' (i.e. the candidate's signing is native-like; they are able to have a fully shared natural conversation with in-depth elaboration on topics relating to both social situation and work; Sign Language Proficiency Interview (SLPI) Rating Scale, (National Technical Institute for the Deaf, 1999). The SLPI is also used in assessing Kenyan Sign Language (SLPI:KSL).

We should also mention that some criterion-referenced tests are mapped to national frameworks of qualifications; for example, the UK-based body Signature[4] offers BSL and ISL assessment mapped to Level 6 ('complex' language use) on the scale of National Vocational Qualifications (NVQ), with assessment criteria drawn from the UK Occupational Standards (CILT, 2010), which, it is suggested, is a level equivalent to those for modern foreign languages at honours degree level, mapping to CEFR level C1 (Council of Europe, 2001).

Tests are also used in some jurisdictions to establish whether those wishing to interpret are fit to practice. Some of these are run by associations of sign language interpreters; some by statutory bodies. In some jurisdictions, it is required to hold a statutory licence in order to practice as an interpreter, while in others no credentials are legally required in order to call oneself an interpreter. For example, the Canadian Evaluation System (CES) is only open to members of the Association of Visual Interpreters of Canada (AVLIC), who are awarded the Certificate of Interpretation (COI) on successful completion of the CES. It is not required to hold the COI in order to interpret in Canada (www.avlic.ca/ces). Across the border in the United States, another national interpreting association, the Registry of Interpreters for the Deaf's (RID) National Interpreter Certification (NIC) *is* required in some (but not all) states in order to provide interpreting services (www.rid.org/rid-certification-overview). Additionally, a licence is required in some states (e.g. Wisconsin,[5] New Mexico,[6] Kentucky[7]).

In Europe, the situation is extremely varied, a situation that led the European Forum of Sign Language Interpreters to set out learning outcomes that graduates of a 3-year university-based sign language interpreter training programme (becoming the norm in the European Union) would be expected to attain, with these threshold competencies considered as the minimal level required for entry to the profession (Leeson & Calles, 2013). However, no pan-European register of sign language interpreters (or public service interpreters more generally, for that matter) currently exists, though the establishment of the European Network for Public Service Interpreting and Translation (ENPSIT)[8] in 2013 included a call for legislation relating to public service interpreting. Further, the publication of a set of international standards on public service (community) interpreting (ISO International Standards, 2014) offers the basis for criterion against which performances could be measured.

Currently, one of the best known European sign language interpreter and translator registration processes is the UK's: Signature, mentioned earlier, also runs interpreter training to NVQ Level 6 (with criterion-referenced testing to ensure fitness to practice). The organisation also set up the National Registers of Communication Professionals working with Deaf and Deafblind People (NRCPD)[9] in both BSL/English and ISL/English. To become a member of the register, one must hold an accredited qualification as a result of completing an approved course of training and demonstrate knowledge of interpreting and professional conduct as defined in the UK National Occupational Standards in Interpreting (CILT, 2006).

In other countries, such as Australia, the assessment of sign language interpreters is not separated out from that of spoken language interpreters: the same body – in this case, the National Accreditation Authority for Translators and Interpreters Ltd (NAATI) – is the only agency that issues accreditation for practitioners who wish to work as interpreters or translators in Australia. Indeed, NAATI's stated purpose is to strengthen inclusion and participation in Australian society by assisting in meeting the nation's diverse and changing communication needs and expectations. It does this by setting, maintaining and promoting high national standards in translating and interpreting and via the implementation of a national quality-assurance system for credentialing practitioners who meet those standards. NAATI argues that their credential provides quality assurance to the clients of translators and interpreters and gives credibility to agencies that employ practitioners who are appropriately credentialed (NAATI, 2014).

These 'high stakes' tests (McNamara, 2000) – tests that have important consequences for the test taker – are thus relatively commonplace in the field of sign language interpreting. Yet the literature on testing sign language interpreting (SLI) skill is remarkably under-developed in this regard (Leeson, 2011).

Leeson (2011) notes that the assessment of interpreters is a significant issue for academic progress and also serves an important social function, namely (as we have seen) the gatekeeping of access to, and progress within, the profession. Yet the available literature focuses mainly on descriptions of assessment protocols for registration or accreditation with national bodies (Leeson, 2011; Leeson, Saeed, Shaffer & Janzen, 2013). Leeson (2011) suggests that 'the act of interpreting (i.e. "doing" interpreting) has been more highly valued than giving thought to, or theorizing about, interpreting (i.e. "knowing about" interpreting)' (p. 154), as evidenced by the relative dearth of interpreter research until the 1990s, reflecting prescriptive rather than empirically based descriptions of the act of interpreting – something particularly true of the lack of empirical data on the assessment of interpreters of spoken and signed languages. In this, we can draw parallels with our earlier discussion relating to the situation of many teachers of sign languages (Rosen, 2010).

Quote 4.17   On the lack of formal training in language testing amongst interpreter educators

Assessment of signed language interpreters is fraught with concern about fitness to practice, the competencies required to interpret effectively in a broad range of settings, idealized notions of desired competence versus minimal skill levels required to undertake the task at hand, as well as issues relating to language teaching, language status, and societal attitudes toward deaf communities and signed languages. Yet, many trainers of interpreters and many of those engaged in the assessment of interpreter quality have never had any formal training in applied linguistics generally, or specifically, in the area of language testing. (Leeson, 2011, p. 153)

4.5   Learning and teaching sign languages: concluding comments

In this chapter we considered some aspects relating to the teaching, learning and assessment of sign languages for L1 and L2/foreign language purposes. We discussed the characteristics of successful language learners, explored who teaches sign languages and issues relating to the development and deployment of curricula and considered some of the complexities associated with assessing sign languages, be they L1 or L2/foreign languages. We considered sign language interpreting as an instance where 'high stakes' testing arises and looked at a range of examples to illustrate our discussion. Across this chapter, a common theme has been the need for further research and the need to ensure that a corridor is opened up between research and practice; in this case, sign language teaching and sign language educator practice.

Further Reading

Council of Europe. (2001). *Common European framework of reference for languages: Learning, teaching, assessment.* Cambridge, UK: Cambridge University Press.

Haug, T. (2011). *Adaptation and evaluation of a German Sign Language test: A computer-based receptive skills test for deaf children ages 4–8 years.* Hamburg, Germany: Hamburg University Press.

International Standards. (2014). ISO 13611: Interpreting — Guidelines for Community Interpreting. Geneva, Switzerland: ISO.

McKee, D., Rosen, S. R., & McKee, R. (Eds). (2014). *Teaching and learning of signed language: International perspectives.* London, UK: Palgrave Macmillan.

Weir, C. J. (2005). *Language testing and validation: An evidence-based approach.* Research and Practice in Applied Linguistics. Basingstoke, UK: Palgrave Macmillan.

5
Sign Language in Everyday Life

'Without sign language/s Deaf people cannot function and participate fully in society. Because it is through sign language/s that Deaf
people communicate with the outside world. Take sign language
away from a Deaf person and s/he is "disabled" because s/he does
not have a language to communicate. Without sign language/s
Deaf people cannot "survive" in society, cannot get an education,
cannot communicate, etc.' (Stevens, 2005, p. 4)

Deaf people across many parts of the world recount stories of 'surviving' their
education because of the lack of access to the curriculum via a sign language
on the one hand, and on the other, because of the intense suppression of
sign languages that existed for many decades in many countries. Indeed, in
many places, this remains the status quo today. In the quote that opens this
chapter, we have access to the views of Helga Stevens, who in 2014 became
the first deaf woman to be elected to the European Parliament. She is also
a lawyer who has served as Executive Director and, later, President of the
European Union of the Deaf (EUD), and as a parliamentarian and a senator
in Flanders, Belgium. As a sign language user, it is clear that she is pushing
the boundaries for ever-increasing recognition and use of sign languages
across the gamut of human interaction. Indeed, she was the central public
figure behind the move to have Flemish Sign Language legally recognised
in Flanders in 2006 (Wheatley & Pabsch, 2010). In this chapter, our focus
is on where and how deaf people use sign languages in everyday life and
for what purposes, with concentration in the latter part of the chapter on
various institutional contexts where people communicate directly in sign
language or indirectly through mediated interpretation.

5.1 Where and how are sign languages used?

Signing communities use sign languages in their communities and, in
contemporary societies, in a wide range of domains from hospitals to

classrooms, from job interviews to courtrooms, from regional and state-level parliamentary meetings to the United Nations General Assembly. In this way, we can say that over the past 50 years, the functionality of sign languages has shifted significantly in many countries – from a time of intentional suppression to one of legal recognition in many places. Of course, as we have seen in Chapter 3, the status of indigenous sign languages varies from place to place. As a result, the opportunities for learning how sign languages are used in these disparate contexts, with disparate sociolinguistic norms, are not readily available to most L1 or, indeed, L2 learners of a sign language.

One reason for this is that, arising from the suppression of signing communities over time, in most countries around the world, there has been limited access to tertiary education (college, university, professional educational routes) in many spheres. For example, how many deaf doctors or nurses have you met?

While this is now changing, there is a need to have a critical mass of professionals in a sphere shaping the language of their domain. In the interim, the vocabulary of certain domains may remain in flux, with preference given over to fingerspelling concepts from the host language (Stratiy, 2005; though this depends on attitudes that prevail towards fingerspelling with individual deaf communities), borrowing established terms into the signed language from another signed language such as ASL or the use of nonce signs for context-specific purposes (Davis, 1989; Leeson, 2005b).

A broad scope of variation exists in sign languages, just as in spoken language communities. In the same way that English has vocabulary that ranges from the formal to the crude, with native speakers acquiring intuitions as to the appropriateness of usage across different settings, so too do sign languages offer a range of registers and styles for which native signers intuit usage – but which L2 learners, even fluent signers who work as interpreters, may not quite master (Padden, 2014).

Example 5.1   'You sign like an old man!'

Lorraine began to learn ISL at 17. She was taught by a deaf man who was then in his 50s. In Ireland, gender and generation combine to create highly visible variants (e.g. LeMaster, 1990). When Lorraine started work as a housemother with teenaged boys at St. Joseph's School for Deaf Boys in Dublin, they would laugh at her signing because, from their perspective, she signed like 'an old deaf man'. And they were right: Older men in the Irish signing community typically use a smaller signing space, fingerspell more than women or younger deaf men, use very little English-influenced mouthing (Fitzgerald, 2014; Leeson & Saeed, 2012a; Mohr-Militzer, 2011), and use vocabulary that is marked as gendered and generational (LeMaster, 1990, 1999, 2002; LeMaster & O'Dwyer, 1991). Learning how to sign like a young person took conscious effort, along with deliberately sought input and feedback from younger deaf people.

Thus, knowing a language – as a native signer or speaker or, indeed, as a second language learner – requires knowing a range of variants. It also means knowing who uses what, when and why and for what purposes. It means knowing what is 'insider-speak' (e.g. the use of gendered variants) and what is for public consumption. For second language learners, deaf or hearing, this requires the development of knowledge that seems intuitive for native signers, and this is a process that cannot be fast-tracked – it takes dedicated engagement with sign language users over time to really bed down an understanding of how a language works across a broad range of social settings. It also requires, as evidenced in Quote 5.1, that learning the vocabulary and the rules of a sign language is not enough. As sociolinguistic research attests, people don't use language as prescribed by textbooks, and sign language users are no exception to this rule.

Quote 5.1   Textbook sign language

Textbook ASL is not how we use our language. (Bienvenu, 2014)

5.1.1   Sign language conversation and discourse

Roy (2000) describes discourse as 'language as it is actually uttered by people engaged in social interaction to accomplish a goal' (p. 9). When it comes to understanding sign language discourse, while much has been learned about how some sign languages are used in authentic interaction (in many instances, as the result of technological developments that have allowed for corpus-building initiatives), for others, the work of documentation and description is just beginning. Indeed, while our understanding of many aspects of the sociolinguistic patterning of several sign languages has grown exponentially over the past decade or so (Schembri & Johnston, 2012), much work remains to be done (Lucas & Bayley, 2010).

Aspects of discourse that have gained attention include studies of turn-taking and style as well as work that draws on cognitive linguistic analytic frameworks to better flesh out our understanding of how discourse works in sign languages.

Research on turn-taking in sign languages has been conducted by Coates and Sutton-Spence (2001), Dively (1998) and Martinez (1995) in looking at openings, closings and pausing in conversations. In two-party conversations, a deaf signer holds the floor by not making direct eye contact with the 'receiver' (by looking into the middle distance). One strategy used to indicate a turn is for the receiver to increase the size and quantity of head nodding.

One of the most detailed analyses of turn-taking at a meeting reports on the regulators applied where Flemish Sign Language (VGT) is the language of engagement (Van Herreweghe, 2002). Van Herreweghe compares this with meetings where deaf VGT signers are in the minority, working via interpretation. She reports that eye gaze is an incredibly potent regulator of turn-taking in meetings conducted through sign language, with the current signer in an exchange using eye gaze to cede the floor to their successor. At the same time, self-selection is also possible: a would-be contributor can wave a hand, index, lightly touch the current signer on the arm, tap the table, or ask another participant to gain the current signer's attention to indicate that someone wishes to reserve the position as next speaker. Van Herreweghe notes that self-selection alone is never sufficient, however; would-be next speakers were ceded the floor only if the current speaker – but not the chairperson – looked at him or her rather than at the other participants at the meeting. As she notes, 'self-selection in all-sign meetings was never pure self-selection because the current speaker still had the power to allocate the next turn by means of eye-gaze' (2002, p. 99).

One of the fascinating aspects of discourse is the fact that individuals do not use language in the same way in all settings. Who we are, who we engage with, for what purpose, and where we are communicating – all of this has an impact on our interaction (Holmes, 2008).

5.1.2   Sign language narratives

There can be no doubt that skilled storytellers are highly valued in 'oral' cultures, where the language of a community is not written, and there has traditionally been no way of writing down sign language content in order to capture events of cultural and historical significance.

Quote 5.2   Oral traditions play a crucial part in keeping cultures alive

The oral traditions and expressions domain encompasses an enormous variety of spoken forms including proverbs, riddles, tales, nursery rhymes, legends, myths, epic songs and poems, charms, prayers, chants, songs, dramatic performances and more. Oral traditions and expressions are used to pass on knowledge, cultural and social values and collective memory. They play a crucial part in keeping cultures alive. (UNESCO; www.unesco.org/culture/ich/?pg=53)

UNESCO notes that while some types of oral expression are common and used by entire communities, others are limited to particular social groups, for example, on the basis of gender or age. UNESCO also reports that performing oral traditions is a highly specialised occupation in many societies, and the community holds professional performers in the highest regard as guardians of collective memory.

This is just as true for sign language–using communities, particularly because signing communities can be considered as having 'oral cultures' in that their heritage stories could not previously be written down (Padden & Humphries, 2005). For example, it is well documented in Deaf Studies literature (e.g. Ladd, 2003) that during the 1800s, annual banquets were convened in Paris that attracted deaf people from all over the world to celebrate the beauty of sign language and to attract attention from the wider community. This was done through speeches and storytelling. Formal and informal storytelling events have always held significance in signing communities, and deaf leaders in particular have often been described as having storytelling prowess (Carty, 2000; Padden & Humphries, 2005).

Quote 5.3   Signing banquets

These banquets became true festivals of mimicry [signing]. Signs were performed and celebrated. There even was a religious quality to these banquets; it was a religion centred on liberation and progress. (Fischer & Lane, 1993, p. 143)

Recording contemporary cultural capital – the stories, folklore, poetry and political discourse of deaf communities – and ensuring that it is repatriated to signing communities is a significant task.

Case study 5.1   Hand talk

Hand Talk is a website that presents information about American Indian Sign Language, and specifically, Plains Indian Sign Language (PISL). The stated goal is to bring together information about PISL and data in PISL, an endangered language, in one place, often for the first time.

PISL was a lingua franca commonly used across North America from the Gulf of Mexico to Calgary (Canada) in the period before European colonization occurred. Its geographic spread incorporated over 1 million square miles. The language was used by some Native American tribes as a lingua franca as they collectively spoke over 40 languages. PISL was also used within individual tribes as an alternative to their spoken language, and as a primary language for deaf community members. While there are no reliable figures for contemporary users of PISL, Hand Talk note that there remain hearing and deaf PISL signers across North America today. (http://pislresearch.com)

Until the 20th century, the technology simply did not exist to facilitate the recording of sign content, and it was only in the late 20th century that the availability of affordable technologies made it possible to video-record signers and copy materials using VHS. Into the 21st century, the development of programmes that could cope with large bodies of video-based materials and allow for time-aligned annotation opened up the way for the development of large-scale digital annotated corpora of signed languages. For example, see van Herreweghe and Vermeerbergen (2012) for an excellent overview of how sign language data is collected and handled; see Ehrlich and Napier (2015) for a discussion of the impact of the technological revolution on interpreter education. And of course, in today's world, video and editing software is now standard for phones, tablets and computers, opening up the possibility for greater usage of sign languages in distal communication (Leeson, Sheikh & Vermeerbergen, 2015).

But what of the structure of sign language discourse? Remarkably little has been written about the discourse-level norms of specific sign languages. What has been discussed are specific features that tend to diverge from spoken language structures; for example, 'role shift' or 'reference shift'. This is a feature that is typically employed in narratives where the signer uses established loci in signing space and shifts his or her body slightly in the direction of each locus to depict or enact the affect and/or action of another character (including themselves in a past or future time) in a discourse. Linguists agree that reference shift is a mimetic discourse feature and has corollaries with direct speech and with the mimetic-like use of prosody and gesture in spoken languages (Emmorey & Reilly, 1995; Liddell & Metzger, 1998; Metzger & Bahan, 2001; Sandler & Lillo-Martin, 2006). Engberg-Pederson's (1993) analysis of Danish Sign Language reveals three distinct 'reference shifting' structures that may have different functions. She notes that these structures can co-occur, but equally, they can occur in isolation:

1. Shifted reference: Pronouns are used from a quoted sender's point of view. This term is reserved for reported speech.
2. Shifted attribution of expressive elements: The signer uses his or her body and face to express the mood or attitude of a referent other than the signer. This structure is not limited to a reported speech function; it can also be found in reports of a person's thoughts, feelings or actions.
3. Shifted locus: This structure is unique to sign languages because of their spatial parameters. This structure is used when signers want to refer to their own or another's interaction with another referent that is associated with another locus.

Example 5.2, from ISL, offers a glimpse into how signers shift perspective between referents in a narrative. Here, the signer is reporting on how he watched a deaf actor, Mark, perform a role. He shifts reference by rotating his torso in signing space, and in doing so, he constructs the action of the actor (Mark), embodying his attitude and, critically, his perspective on an event.

Example 5.2   Shifting perspective in narratives

eyes down, shoulder shift
...ALSO MARK ANOTHER MARK CIGAR WALK r/s 'flamboyant-pose'
LIFTS-CIGAR-TO-MOUTH r/s 2h + w.o.w. REPEAT REPEAT SAME SAME BUT
NEVER STOP EYES-POP-OUT-OF-HEAD

'Also, there is a part where Mark – another Mark – walks on (stage) with a cigar. He walks on in a flamboyant fashion and lifts his cigar to his mouth. Wow! I've seen this scene over and over again, but it never ceases to amaze me.' (Informant S, 'ABC of ISL II' footage; Leeson, 2001, p. 60)

In this way, the idea that a 'signer's perspective is privileged' (Leeson & Saeed, 2012a, pp. 180–181) comes to the fore, not least because of the embodied nature of language (as discussed in Chapter 3, Section 3.2). The perspective that is mapped onto the signer's body and the information they present from that perspective, whether that of the signer themselves or a reported action/dialogue of another party, is the most focused element in a discourse (Leeson, 2010), while less salient information is presented more distantly from the signer's body (Janzen, Leeson & Shaffer, 2012; Leeson, Saeed, Shaffer & Janzen, 2013; Shaffer, Janzen & Leeson, 2012).

In discussing ASL, Janzen (2010) describes similar behaviour in ASL as a form of metaphor: 'spatial distance is conceptual difference', whereby signers present items that are considered to be conceptually distant from each other as being physically distant in signing space, and those that are considered to be conceptually similar or identical are presented at adjacent points in space or the identical point in space. Janzen, O'Dea and Shaffer (2001) note that non-agentive perspectives can also be marked on the body of the signer (see Quotes 5.4 and 5.5).

Quote 5.4   Reference shifting in narratives

...reference shifting in narrative is from agent to agent, that is, each shift changes the perspective from one agent to another. (Janzen, O'Dea & Shaffer, 2001, p. 299)

Quote 5.5   Passive construction in sign language

The passive, conversely, may involve a shift from one character to another, but in the passive construction, the perspective additionally shifts to that of the patient. Alternatively, the focus may remain on one character, but a shift may take place from the perspective of the character as an agent to the perspective of the same character as a patient. (Janzen, O'Dea & Shaffer, 2001, p. 299)

Similar findings have been reported for ISL (Leeson, 2001; Leeson & Saeed, 2012a; Leeson & Saeed, in press), though the use of passive (and de-transitivised) constructions in sign languages remains an under-discussed topic.

Reference shifting also called 'role shift' in the older literature is also a feature of conversations (Johnston et al., 2007) and formal lectures (Quinto-Pozos, 2007; Roy, 1989a). These shifts have also more recently been labelled as 'constructed action' (CA) and 'constructed dialogue' (CD; see e.g. Liddell, 2003), terms that are now widely used in cognitive sign linguistic approaches. In a study of hearing sign language interpreters' use of CA and CD, Goswell (2011) found that it is not entirely clear what the triggers are for using CA and CD and that there does not appear to be any clear difference in use of CA and CD between native and non-native signers.

Other features of sign language discourse include the use of manual simultaneity (Engberg-Pederson, 1993; Miller, 1994). Vermeerbergen, Leeson and Crasborn (2007, pp. 2–3) note that simultaneity in sign languages can take a number of forms, which they group into three general categories:

1. Manual simultaneity: This occurs when each hand conveys different information. This may take the form of 'full simultaneity', which they define as the simultaneous production of two different lexical items. Alternatively, one hand may hold a sign in a stationary configuration while the other hand continues signing. For example, one hand can articulate the perseveration of a topic while the other hand continues with the realisation of the comment. Examples of manual simultaneity also include simultaneous constructions involving 'classifiers'. This can take the form of expressing the relative location of actors in a motion event (each actor being represented by a distinct 'classifier') on either hand, etc.
2. Manual-oral simultaneity: This category refers to the simultaneous use of the oral channel and the manual channel and may take different forms. One form is the simultaneous articulation of lexical items from a spoken language (so called 'mouthings'). For example, as Sutton-Spence (2007) notes, the BSL sign meaning 'roll over in bed' can be combined with the silent articulation of the English word 'bed'. However, in some instances, a mouthing combined with a sign that is morphologically and lexically unrelated, such as the French words *quoi* ('what') and *après* ('after'), by virtue of their use without any lexically related sign, appear to have been introduced into Quebec Sign Language (LSQ) as oral loan words (Chris Miller, personal communication, cited in Vermeerbergen, Leeson & Crasborn, 2007). In VGT, the mouthing *op* ('on') can be combined with verb signs such as SIT, resulting in a combined meaning, 'sit on' (Vermeerbergen, Leeson & Crasborn, 2007). Simultaneous production of mouth gestures can also co-occur with manual signs. Sutton-Spence (2007) follows Raino's (2001) definition of *mouth gestures* as idiomatic gestures produced by the mouth which cannot be traced back to spoken

language. In VGT, an example of this structure would be a signer using his or her mouth to imitate the sound of a truck while signing TRUCK (Vermeerbergen & Demey, 2007). As Vermeerbergen, Leeson and Crasborn (2007) note, these subcategories cover non-manual items that exist separately from simultaneously produced manual signs, in contrast with non-manual features that combine with manual activity to create a sign.

3. Simultaneous use of other (manual or non-manual) articulators: This category extends to non-manual articulators other than the mouth, which can combine with each other or with manual and oral action. Examples that feature in several of the papers in Vermeerbergen, Leeson and Crasborn (2007) include eye gaze channel and body leans. They note that this type of simultaneity is often discussed in relation to the simultaneous expression of different points of view, which is in itself an example of simultaneity at a semantic level (see e.g. Leeson & Saeed, 2007; Perniss, 2007; Risler, 2007; Sallandre, 2007). Another example is that of the simultaneous articulation of manual signs with certain non-manual lexical items such as the ASL and LSQ 'nose-squinch WHO' (Chris Miller, personal communication, cited in Vermeerbergen, Leeson & Crasborn, 2007).

Falling into Vermeerbergen, Leeson & Crasborn's (2007) first category is a concept now widely referred to as 'buoys' (Liddell, 2003). Semantically, buoys 'help guide the discourse by serving as conceptual landmarks as the discourse continues' (p. 223) – that is, they can function as discourse markers.

While the 'list buoy' and the 'fragment buoy' (Liddell, 2003) were previously identified and discussed for a range of sign languages, albeit using different terminology, Liddell categorised additional markers such as the 'theme buoy', a marker which signifies that 'an important discourse theme is being discussed' (Liddell 2003, p. 242). In such instances, the non-dominant hand maintains a one-hand configuration with the index finger elevated horizontally as the other hand produces an independent sign. The signer then produces one or more signs related to the description of a theme of the discourse with the dominant hand while the non-dominant hand maintains the elevated index finger. In this way, theme buoys can extend across a number of signs.

Other features that have been identified as affecting the cohesion of discourse narratives include the following:

1. Episodic markers – for example, the signer may place their hands in their lap to mark boundaries between particular segments of a signed narrative (Leeson, 2010, Nilsson, 2010)
2. Mirroring – a doubling of the hands on one-handed signs for emphatic purpose (Nilsson, 2010)
3. Body partitioning (Dudis, 2004)

4. Body leans – a feature currently under analysis, with early findings suggesting that there are differences in the ways that native and non-native signers present information that maps to comparative or if/then constructions (Nilsson, 2014)

While we have come some way in identifying the norms of signed narratives, there is still a long way to go. Some of the questions that remain relate to the frequency and functionality of these features and to the interplay between features. We suggest that the growing field of corpus sign linguistics will facilitate us in answering these and other questions.

5.1.3   Child sign language

In Chapter 4, we discussed the acquisition of sign language and the issues that affect deaf children's acquisition of sign language as a first language. Here we focus on the *way* that deaf children sign and how they communicate with their primary caregivers. Although it is an under-researched area, a few linguists have described the use of sign language by young children and noted that children use discourse features such as role shift and simultaneity appropriately (Morgan, 2002). It has also been suggested that deaf children sign in a different register, which can be particularly challenging for interpreters who may not be used to this form of sign language (Schick, 2001).

Research on signed communication and interaction between deaf mothers and babies has revealed that deaf mothers use specific strategies to engage with their babies and toddlers in conversation which, it has been suggested, can be taught to hearing parents with deaf children (Spencer, Bodran-Johnson & Gutfreund, 1992). Strategies include signalling/waving for getting attention and waiting for the child to look at them before they sign (Harris & Mohay, 1997; Littleton, 2000). These strategies are also used in reading picture books to deaf children to allow them time to look at the pictures, then back at the reader for the sign language input (Van der Lem & Timmerman, 1990). There is also evidence that deaf babies exposed to sign language from birth babble manually using signs and gestures (Petitto & Marentette, 1991).

Quote 5.6   Turn-taking patterns

Children have to learn the turn-taking patterns of their language community. In a study of children learning Sign Language of the Netherlands (NGT), Baker and van den Bogaerde (2005) found that children acquire the turn-taking patterns over a considerable number of years. In the first two years, there is quite some overlap between the turns of the deaf mother and her child. This seems to be related to the child starting to sign when the mother is still signing. Around the age of three, both children studied showed a decrease in the amount of overlap, which is interpreted as an indication of the child learning the basics of turn-taking. However, in the deaf child with more advanced signing skills, at age 6 the beginnings of collaborative floor are evident with the child using overlaps to contribute to the topic and to provide feedback. (Baker & van den Bogaerde, 2012, p. 498)

Child sign language discourse is influenced by the use of sign language in educational contexts: as deaf children move into the educational environment, the way that sign languages are used by deaf children and their teachers in primary and secondary school classrooms can lay the foundation for sign language use in other contexts. By understanding the nature of sign language discourse and interaction generally, and by observing the way that deaf mothers sign and gain attention of their children, classroom sign language interaction can be observed and strategies taught to teachers (Christie et al., 1999; Smith & Ramsey, 2004).

In Chapter 4, we also highlighted the case of Nicaraguan Sign Language, where it has been observed that children may in fact have been the key instigators in developing a systematised sign language through being brought together in the first deaf school (Senghas & Coppola, 2001). See Section 5.2 for more discussion of sign language in school.

5.1.4 Formal sign language

Schembri and Johnston (2012) report that June Zimmer's (1989) work on ASL represents one of the few studies on stylistic variation in a sign language, and they caution that until further studies are carried out, no firm conclusions can be drawn about what register variation looks like in ASL, or indeed in any sign language. Zimmer's (1989) analysis draws on data from one deaf native ASL signer in three different settings: (1) giving a lecture on linguistics, (2) presenting a talk to a small audience and (3) conducting a television interview. While all of the texts are fairly formal in so far as they are not spontaneous but planned and presented to an audience, the degree of formality in each text appears to be different. Zimmer (1989) reports that the lecture was particularly different from the talk and the interview at all levels of structural organisation. Further, she found evidence of intra-textual register variation; that is, parts of each text were different from other parts. Some of the differences were considered phonological in nature: in a lecture, signing space appeared to be much larger, with signs articulated above the head, beyond the centre of the chest and beyond shoulder width. Schembri and Johnston (2012) suggest that this might be interpreted as instances of 'loud signing', following Crasborn (2001), rather than actually representing a phonological difference. Zimmer (1989) found that signs tended to be held for a longer duration in the lecture and that role shifting – sometimes called shifting reference (Engberg-Pedersen, 1993) or using surrogate space (Liddell, 2003) – presented differently in the lecture, where the signer moved a step or two, while only head movements were used in both the talk and interview.

Zimmer (1989) found that certain ASL signs considered colloquial (like PEA-BRAIN) occurred in portions of the lecture that involved direct speech and in the talk, but not elsewhere. She also noted that in the lecture, conjunctions like AND and AS were used more frequently. Other differences noted included the fact that in the lecture, exaggerated reduplication of signs was used as a vehicle to show that an action was difficult or of lengthy duration, while in the informal talk, such information was transmitted via the use of non-manual features. Zimmer (1989) also reports on several syntactic and discourse-level features that differed across her data set: topicalisation was more frequent in the informal talk, while pseudo-cleft structures arose more in the lecture. Discourse markers appeared more in the lecture, serving to segment the talk into smaller components. Finally, Zimmer notes that the signer used their non-dominant hand to point towards a fingerspelled word on their dominant hand in the lecture only. More recently, such features have been described as 'buoys' by Liddell (2003), as discussed in Section 5.1.2. For those interested in aspects of manual simultaneity and how this influences discourse in a range of sign languages, see Vermeerbergen, Leeson and Crasborn (2007).

Case study 5.2   Language contact in formal lectures

Napier (2006a) conducted a study to compare the discourse features of 'formal register' in Auslan in the context of university lectures and conference presentations. She compared the output of two Auslan–English interpreters with two deaf Australians producing equivalent formal texts in Auslan. She found that the language contact devices of fingerspelling and mouthing were used by all 4 participants in order to borrow from English into Auslan, but the main difference was between native and non-native signers rather than deaf presenters and hearing interpreters. Napier found that the one deaf and one hearing native signer participants' use of interlingual transference was less marked than the use of the non-signers, who experienced more interference from English in the structure and delivery of their formal Auslan discourse.

In Chapter 3, we saw that attitudes to sign languages are powerful indicators of how, when and where languages are promoted or suppressed in a given society. We also saw that attitudes to particular languages or varieties of languages can change over time. Sign languages have also experienced such shifts, moving from suppression and denial of their linguistic status to, in many territories, official or legal recognition (see e.g. Wheatley & Pabsch, 2010, 2012).

This is an important point because prevailing attitudes at a given time, in a given place, greatly predict how many deaf people have come to acquire or learn their sign languages (see Chapter 4). It also influences the availability and kind of spaces available for using a sign language across the life cycle (early childhood, school, college, work, with family and friends, when engaging with public services, etc.).

5.2 Sign language at school

We have already touched upon the fact that educational policy and practice significantly influences linguistic outcomes for sign language communities (in Chapter 3, Section 3.4). We can suggest also that parental attitudes to sign language use are typically shaped by the attitudes of the professionals whom parents encounter as their child is diagnosed as deaf and influenced by the advice that prevails in a given place at a given time. This in turn affects whether a parent will choose to allow their child to use a sign language or not, whether they and their family will learn to sign, educational placement decisions and support (or not) for engaging with sign language users more generally (Kyle, 2012; Marschark & Spencer, 2009; Mathews, 2012; National Council for Special Education, 2011; Veermeerbergen, Van Herreweghe, Smessaert & De Weerdt).

Traditionally, these policies and practices have been associated with the placement of deaf children in schools for the deaf, where in the pre-oralist period, sign languages were widely used in many places, as we discussed in Chapter 2. More recently, attitudes regarding the supremacy of speech over sign dominated, with a prevalent (but false) view that sign language use would potentially damage a child's spoken language development. This has been a damaging but empirically untrue claim (Marschark & Spencer, 2009). However, the fortunate irony for signing communities is that despite the official line banning sign languages, the children in the schools were together in one place, forming community, transmitting cultural norms, and doing so – albeit furtively – via sign languages. The transmission of sign languages from cohort to cohort of sign language users, with prestige vested in native signers, has been well documented and was discussed in Chapter 3.

Today, in many countries, attitudes towards sign languages are generally positive, evidenced in the legal recognitions afforded to sign languages in many places (see Chapter 3, Sections 3.3 and 3.4). In countries like Finland, such legal recognition is followed closely by state support for sign language learning, for example, via the provision of fully funded sign language classes for parents and siblings of deaf children in the family home. Even here, however, despite the stated goals of parents who want their (cochlear implanted) deaf children to be bilingual Finnish Sign Language/Finnish users, there is a struggle to provide sufficient daily use for Finnish Sign Language development in an age-appropriate manner (Takkinen, 2012).

We must also be mindful that the level of support offered in Finland is not typical: This situation must be contrasted against that in many other countries, where the prevalent educational policy towards mainstreaming deaf children in 'inclusive classrooms' brings with it the risk of isolating deaf children, leaving them without robust spoken language skills and with minimal, if any, sign language skills. There are further problems associated with assumptions that hold around how these children will acquire a sign language while accessing education. For example, in Flanders (Belgium), a deaf child in mainstream education in 2010–2011 was entitled to approximately 13 hours of interpretation in secondary school, some 11.3 hours per week in technical education and approximately 8.2 hours per week if they attended a vocational school (Veermeerbergen, Van Herreweghe, Smessaert & De Weerdt). This amounts to approximately one-third of the child's class time. Vermeerbergen et al. note that this is problematic in terms of the cultural and linguistic development of a deaf identity (see Quote 5.7).

Quote 5.7 Socialisation into the deaf community

Socialization into the Deaf community and Deaf culture can be at risk as these students have limited (if any) contact with deaf peers at school. For young children the acquisition of Flemish Sign Language (VGT) can be problematic given that outside of deaf educational placements, there are hardly any possibilities for deaf children to acquire VGT. Finally, deaf children in mainstream education can be socially isolated so that their socio-emotional wellbeing may be under threat. (Veermeerbergen, Van Herreweghe, Smessaert & De Weerdt, 2012, p. 109)

Fundamentally, like Takkinen (2012), Vermeerbergen et al. are pointing out that fewer deaf children than ever are accessing sign languages in environments that facilitate age-appropriate acquisition and, commensurate with this, access to deaf peers and the wider signing community. Taking a broader view, this raises potential consequences for national and regional sign languages more generally: fewer people using a language increases its risk of fragmentation, marginalisation and ultimately extinction (Harrison, 2010; Johnston, 2006; Leeson & Saeed, 2012a).

Further, the lack of engagement with other deaf children or adults that is typical of many mainstreamed deaf children means that cultural growth also suffers: Where can the child in a mainstream class learn to be a normal deaf person? Put another way, as Ladd and Gonçalves (2012) suggest, the mainstreamed deaf child is colonised by a hegemonic hearing society, separated from the signing community as a result of educational policy and cochlear implantation. They argue that consideration of deaf pedagogies is the way forward. Building on research they have conducted with deaf teachers in Brazil, the UK and the U.S., they suggest that deaf pedagogies, predominantly seen in contexts where deaf teachers teach deaf students, build on the principles as outlined in Concept 5.1.

Concept 5.1   Deaf pedagogies

1. The crucial role of language
2. Deaf pedagogies as dialogic
3. The importance of dialogue in discipline
4. Directness of discourse, discipline and egalitarianism
5. Discipline.

Phenomenological Properties of Deaf Pedagogies

1. Visuality
2. Use of physical space
3. Sign language, performativity and deaf pedagogies
4. The importance of humour in deaf pedagogies.

(Ladd & Gonçalves, 2012)

In the absence of deaf pedagogies, deaf children are, they suggest, disenfranchised. In other places, for example the U.S., while educational interpreters have been provided since the 1970s (Schick, 2008), there is little information available regarding how many deaf children experience an interpreter-mediated education and, as yet, we cannot consider it to be an evidence-based practice (Schick, 2008). Indeed, Russell (2010) notes that the provision of interpreting in educational settings can be dangerous if and when it provides the 'illusion of inclusion' rather than meaningful inclusion. This comes about because many school programmes do not hire qualified interpreters, which in turn negatively affects deaf students' education, including academic performance and social integration (LaBue, 2006; Russell, 2010; Winston, 2004).

Additionally, in educational settings, interpreters regularly work with students who have varying degrees of sign language proficiency, depending on when and how they have acquired sign language (see Chapter 4). In fact, many deaf children are acquiring sign language while at school; therefore, interpreters become *de facto* sign language role models. They are often the only person in the classroom (or the school) who can communicate with the deaf student (Schick, 2001).

Further, many interpreters do not have the skills to represent teachers and students' communication, the majority of public school interpreters having no post-secondary training and often not meeting minimum state requirements for practice (where these exist; Schick, 2008).

However, there are strategies that have been found to underpin successful educational interpreting (Russell, 2010). Russell notes that successful interpreters working in educational settings have more than 5 years' experience, tend to have contextual knowledge borne from prior experience and can deal with content at the teacher's pace. These interpreters:

- ask the teacher to repeat questions and answers;
- use two-handed strategies for questions and answers (questions on one hand, answers on the other); and
- represent questions and differentiate between teacher talk and student talk.

Russell (2010) argues that there is a body of work that needs to be done to ensure that we move away from a 'transmission' model of interpreting to a realisation that interpreters are co-constructing learning with teachers and students, which in turn has consequences for how an interpreter-mediated classroom is managed. See Chapter 6 (Section 6.2) for more discussion of sign language interpreting.

Case Study 5.3   Interaction in the interpreted inclusive classroom

Goswell, Leigh, Carty and Napier (2012) piloted an adapted version of Brophy and Good's (1970) classroom interaction analysis methodology to investigate the nature of teacher-pupil interaction in situations where communication is mediated by sign language interpreters. They collected 11 hours of data from authentic classrooms in a high school in Sydney with 2 deaf sign language–using students and 3 different interpreters. Using mixed methods, the researchers conducted non-participant observation, interaction analysis of filmed classrooms and interviews with the deaf students, interpreters and their teachers about their perception of interactions in the classroom. In particular, they analysed the question-answer sequences between teachers and students and the interpretation output to determine if all questions were interpreted as such. Preliminary results reveal that deaf students do not receive the cues to participate in classroom discourse due to various factors. These include: (1) time lag of interpretation, which means that by the time interpreters have interpreted the question, it has already been answered and a follow-up question asked; (2) in order to keep up, the interpreters summarise question-answer sequences as statements; and (3) students' attention is divided between watching interpreters, looking at the board (and something the teacher is writing) and writing their own notes.

5.3   Sign language and tertiary education

In considering how sign language is used in tertiary education (colleges and universities), we focus on 3 areas: (1) the academic acceptance of sign languages, (2) deaf students' access to tertiary education and (3) deaf academics.

5.3.1 Academic acceptance of sign languages

Academic acceptance of sign languages 'affords the same educational values and the same intellectual rewards as the study of any other foreign language' (Wilcox, 1988, p. 107). Despite this, the path towards acceptance has required great effort on the part of those in universities and signing community partnerships, seeking to secure the establishment of programmes and the implementation of policies that support parity of esteem for sign languages in academic institutions. By 1980, Battisson and Carter (1981, p. viii) wrote that no college or university had yet made a sign language a permanent part of the foreign language curriculum, on par with the other languages taught. Wilcox (1988), writing some 30 years after sign linguistic research had commenced on ASL, noted that things were beginning to change in the U.S. Today, some 25 years later, we find that many of the challenges faced in the U.S. in the 1980s remain for other countries. These include:

- Time associated with developing and informing/educating/convincing a network of allies within a university or college that a sign language is a subject worthy of academic study (Lamb & Wilcox, 1988);
- Time and effort associated with preparing and implementing academic proposals that lead to policy shifts (several years, in most cases we know of; Lamb & Wilcox, 1988);
- The need to ensure that affirmative action employment policies are in place to facilitate the recruitment of deaf faculty members who will become fully fledged members of the academic community (Armstrong, 1988; Wilcox, 1988);
- The need to work with those responsible for administrating budgets for supporting the provision of interpreting and other supports for deaf academics – of course, in some countries government funding covers all related costs, but this is not the case in many places;
- The need to work with those responsible for facilitating alternative examination procedures which may facilitate students taking examinations for subjects other than a sign language via a sign language (as in Trinity College, Dublin, for example).

As in 1988, the two compelling reasons for teaching ASL – or any other language – in a university setting remain true: 'One is what the language has to offer. Languages are tools, not only for communicating ideas, but for exploring ideas. ASL is, in my opinion, a wonderful pedagogical tool for sharpening the intellect, exploring the world and testing research hypotheses' (Wilcox, 1988, p. 106).

The second reason Wilcox lists is what academia has to offer the language, its culture and sign language users. He, like Armstrong (1988), argues that we must remain mindful of the fact that ASL (and, we add, other sign languages) is a minority, suppressed language, whose signers and their culture have been oppressed and poorly understood. Given this, we suggest that there is an onus on universities to ensure that they act to support community stakeholders as well as deaf students and academics, for example, via the commitment to funding the interpretation of public lectures on request.

5.3.2   Deaf students' access to tertiary education

Unless deaf students attend universities that have a critical mass of sign language users, with deaf lecturers and students and other (hearing) sign language learners who all come together to create shared signing communities (such as Gallaudet University, the National Technical Institute for the Deaf in the U.S., or the University of Central Lancashire in the UK or Trinity College, Dublin, in Ireland), and they can attend lectures delivered in sign language, then it is likely that deaf students' access to tertiary education – and their use of sign language in that context – is reliant on sign language interpreters. See Chapter 6, Section 6.2, for more discussion of sign language interpreting.

A number of other provisions have been put in place in many institutions to support deaf students in addition to the provision of sign language interpreters, including the provision of note-takers, support with reading and writing academic texts, providing for the submission of assessed work in a sign language (which may subsequently be translated to a spoken language if the academic assessing the work is not a sign language user), or the translation of academic texts into sign language (Leeson, 2012).

Research suggests that many deaf students enter university presenting at below national norms in terms of their literacy, and unless there is another deaf student in the class, they have no peer group, or at least, no accessible peer group (Barnes, 2006); that deaf students face barriers in gaining access to information in the tertiary education classroom (Lang, 2000), and comprehend less than hearing peers from interpreted college-level lectures (Marschark, Sapere, Convertino & Seewagen, 2004, Marschark, Sapere, Convertino, Seewagen & Maltzen, 2005; Schick, 2008). Therefore, the quality of such support provisions is paramount, and we point out that, ultimately, a mediated education is never the same as learning directly.

Nevertheless, studies examining deaf students' approaches to studying and their perceptions of academic quality in universities (Richardson, MacLeod-Gallinger, McKee & Long, 2000; Richardson, Barnes & Fleming, 2004) found that the impact of deafness on approaches to studying was relatively slight, and deaf students appeared to be at least as capable as hearing students of engaging with the underlying meaning of the materials to be learned. However, deaf students found it more difficult to relate ideas on different topics, and this was more marked in those who preferred to communicate using sign; also, deaf students were more likely than hearing students to adopt a critical approach and to analyse the internal structure of the topics studied. Nonetheless, deaf sign language–using students rated their academic experiences positively, as shown in Quotes 5.8 and 5.9. In Quote 5.8, Philippa Merricks, a deaf native BSL user from a multigenerational deaf family who went to the University of Central Lancashire (UCLan)[1] in the UK (where they have a suite of undergraduate BSL and Deaf Studies programmes for deaf and hearing students and a well-established interpreting provision for deaf staff and students), explains why she chose that university. In Quote 5.9, Leah Kalaitzi, who grew up oral in Greece and then went to the University of Wolverhampton[2] in the UK (where they have a similar set-up to UCLan), reveals how her university experience enabled her to realise that she was 'Deaf', learn BSL and become a member of the signing community.

Quote 5.8 Deaf native signers' experience of sign language in tertiary education

I was really struck by university life and community: the deaf and hearing signing community, and I really wanted to be part of that. [I was attracted to the university not only because of the deaf students] but also the wider community which included hearing people who could sign...there were a lot of hearing signing students studying interpreting. We would band together and organise events for the D/BSL society, we did all sorts of activities and events with the local deaf community as well as hosting a number of large events like fancy dress nights where deaf people all over the country would come to celebrate. Preston had a good vibrant community; socially it was very good. Don't forget, because there were a lot of deaf students, this also meant the University was well prepared and well equipped with interpreting support. I knew I was guaranteed interpreting support, all I had to do was hand over my timetable to the interpreting team and they would take care of it all for me. This meant I didn't have to worry about my own support needs...going to a university that had a strong signing presence was an important factor for me. (Philippa Merricks, deaf native BSL user and former President of the European Union of Deaf Youth)

Quote 5.9 Deaf non-native signers' experience of sign language in tertiary education

It was a very interesting experience for me because until that time in my life I never knew there was a Deaf community or a sign language. I was brought up orally with the help of speech therapy; I had a 'hearing identity'. I knew I was deaf but I never had the opportunity to meet other deaf people. I think it was during the first or second week at university, you know, 'fresher's week', there was a – I think, a hearing person...This person asked me if I would be up for going to the student union where there were supposed to be other deaf people. I was up for trying something new and followed along. It blew my mind when I open the door and discovered a roomful of deaf people signing. I couldn't understand anyone's signing. It was an emotional moment for me. I never knew there were other deaf people. It really hit me as a deaf person that I couldn't sign, and I felt terrible. I immediately took up learning sign language and I enjoyed every minute.

This was a whole new world to me, the deaf world. It was my 'first step' into the deaf world. My whole life changed direction. I started looking at myself and grappled with my own identity. What am I? Am I deaf? Am I hearing? Or am I both? It was such a confusing time...I was amazed and learned so much. Of course, to begin with, it was a very difficult time for me...

I don't think I was any different to any other hearing students learning BSL for the first time, when you begin your learning your style of signing is more SSE [Sign Supported English]. It takes time before you move away and you become much more visual, expressive, more fluent in BSL. I did not feel accepted by other deaf people to begin with. I found it very difficult to be accepted...There was a lot of conflict and a real struggle for acceptance. I was persistent and I kept persevering with learning BSL. I was quite stubborn as a student. People then realised they were wrong. They recognised that I was bilingual and that my BSL skills were good enough. It was a tough fight. Things changed and I became more aware and involved with the deaf community.

[At university] I found myself in the deaf world. I have to say being around other deaf people using sign language felt easier, I felt more comfortable or relaxed at communicating with other people, with people who know how to sign. This became an important part of my life...Being deaf is my life. I never had this opportunity before to develop a deaf identity or discover what it meant to be deaf. Being part of this world where I had interpreters, note-takers etc. made my life so much easier. I suddenly had equal access just like any other student who could hear at university. (Leah Kalaitzi, deaf non-native BSL user)

5.3.3   Deaf academics

Despite the significant hurdles that deaf people face in accessing and progressing along an academic pathway (Trowler & Turner, 2002), there have also been positive developments with sign language users progressing through the academic ranks, achieving doctorates and pursuing academic careers. Some of these academics work in the field of Deaf Studies and applied sign linguistics in the broadest sense; for example, as linguists documenting and theorising the structure of sign languages, as translation and interpreting studies scholars, as experts in deaf education, as well as in the fields of social policy and anthropology, to name just a few.

Quote 5.10   Deaf academics: 'Extra preparation is a fact of life'

If Deaf students have negotiated their way through undergraduate courses and have reached the postgraduate level, the problem of finding appropriate interpreters increases exponentially. Not only must they maintain their enthusiasm for a topic, often without the support of peers and advisors in informal interaction, they are likely to spend valuable time booking and preparing interpreters. Even with preparation, ASL/Auslan–English interpreters, like all language interpreters and translators, often feel out of their depth with the technical language and jargon of the field – and may even refuse bookings for this reason. Thus, in graduate school, the Deaf academic learns that extra preparation is a fact of life. ... If Deaf students overcome the many and varied obstacles and obtain higher education qualifications, more major obstacles to employment in academia will await them. Like all graduates, they will face the job market and need to maintain positive attitudes to convince employers of their suitability and potential. But Deaf graduates will have the additional burden of convincing potential employers of their ability to do the job. For example, how will they convince the academic institution that they can function as a teacher in the higher education classroom? ...

Deaf academics are usually more aware of communication requirements and limitations, not only on our part but also on the students' parts. As a result, the Deaf academic can be quite skilled and creative in teaching various concepts to diverse audiences. Nevertheless, the (hearing) academics who sit on hiring committees may have fixed opinions about the 'correct' way of teaching, either in general or in a particular subject. If ability to teach is defined by members of the hiring committee as 'teaching in the identical way we always have done', then the Deaf candidate who would teach in a different way may not be viewed as able. ...

At present, in both Canada and Australia, government funding schemes support access costs (e.g. interpreter cost) for students who are in need of accommodation in the higher education environment. However, the Deaf academic does not have access to such schemes, and funding for costs of necessary equipment (e.g. TTY, strobe fire alarm, doorbell flasher) and for interpreters may fall to the university that employs the Deaf academic. Depending on the University's budgeting practices, accommodation costs may actually be borne by the specific faculty or department to which the Deaf academic is appointed. In other universities, costs may be paid in part or in full from a central fund, so that the budget of the faculty or department in which the Deaf academic is employed is not limited by accommodation costs. At present, selection committees are economically discouraged from appointing a suitably qualified Deaf person because there is no external funding or cost sharing across departments or universities. Potential for intangible contribution aside, a Deaf candidate for a faculty position may be viewed as diminishing valuable tangible resources. Further, the selection committee may be reluctant to ask about costs of accommodation because of the risk of discrimination charges (and selection committees have reported having this type of discussion). All of these factors favour a suitably qualified, non-deaf candidate over the deaf person. (Woodcock, Rohan & Campbell, 2007, pp. 364–367)

In 2000, an organisation called Deaf Academics[3] was established to foster interaction between deaf and hard of hearing academics, regardless of their discipline. They host conferences and offer opportunities for networking. The inaugural conference, held in Austin, Texas, in 2002, was structured around panels to generate discussion of the following key topics:

- How can one maximise his or her classroom experience, i.e. receiving information and participating in the discussion?
- How can one develop and maintain relationships with (hearing) professors and students?
- Is there such a thing as a sign language academic register? (How does one express technical terms? How does one standardise technical signs? How does one adjust registers for different settings, like the classroom, presentations at conferences and conferences for the deaf?)
- What are our identities in the deaf and academic communities? (How do we deaf researchers ensure ownership and dissemination of deaf-related research? What can I, as a deaf researcher, contribute to the deaf community and to the academic community?)
- What is it like to be deaf in academia? (How do we collaborate with other research team members? How can we ensure equal access to information in an academic setting?)
- How can we ensure equal access to deaf-related international conferences where (spoken) English is declared as one of the conference languages? Do we need a lingua franca?

These topics have provided the foundation for on-going discussions at the conferences, and in other fora, about the importance of the role of deaf people in sign language research as well as the role of sign language being used to disseminate sign language research (see Chapter 7, Section 7.1.6).

A recent welcome development to account for the needs of deaf students and academics in tertiary education is the release of a position statement on 'Making Higher Education More Deaf-Friendly' by the Language and Identities in InterAction Research Unit (LIdIA) in the Department of Languages and Linguistics at York St John University in the UK (Hall, O'Brien & the LIdIA Policy Forum, 2015). The goal of the statement (see Example 5.3) is to have a positive impact on future UK policy decisions regarding deaf students and staff in higher education.

Example 5.3   LidIA position statement

Deaf people in the UK have the right to participate fully in higher education, as both students and academic staff.

The dominant language of higher education is English, which is not fully accessible to deaf people.

The preferred language of many Deaf people in the UK is British Sign Language (BSL), a language with the same expressive potential and complexity as spoken languages.

Accordingly, from the perspectives of both disability rights and linguistic and cultural rights, Higher Education Institutions (HEIs) should take steps to make higher education more Deaf-friendly.

Specifically, HEIs should:
- ensure that higher education is as inclusive as possible for D/deaf students;
- encourage members of the Deaf community to consider careers in academia, and take steps to enable Deaf academic staff to participate fully in the life of the academic community;
- take action to help ensure that the role of the Deaf community in UK public life is fully acknowledged and promoted.

Because of increasing provisions to provide interpreting support for deaf employees (see Section 5.4.6), there is a growing body of deaf academics who are working in universities in disciplines outside of sign language–related disciplines; for example, in psychology, engineering, environmental science and law. Although they may be well qualified for their work, deaf early career academics in 'mainstream academia' may face difficulties in gaining employment, tenure (permanent posts) or promotion (Woodcock, Rohan & Campbell, 2007), and end up working in deaf or sign language–related areas instead. An example can be seen in Quote 5.11 from Dr Audrey Cameron, the first deaf person in Scotland to get her doctorate, who started her academic career as a chemist but now is involved in social research and has been involved in projects related to signs for terminology, deaf education, deaf employment and deaf children's experience of domestic violence.

Quote 5.11   Finding a place in academia

I started my PhD in 1992. At that time there was no system in place to support deaf PhD students. I had the occasional sign language interpreter support for events on 'developing confidence as a PhD student', 'how to do PhD research' or 'how to get a job after your PhD', things like that. I did try to get an interpreter for my lectures but [it] just didn't work out. I had to ask my mother to come with me to classes and take notes. I didn't have much choice. The interpreters I had could not follow the chemistry lectures; they were too technical. ... Things improved when I moved on to do my post-doctoral research because I was eligible for [UK Government] 'Access to Work' funding.

Looking back, I wasn't really encouraged to use interpreters. At the time no one was really making the most of interpreters in the workplace. It's not like now, where it is common to have an interpreter in the workplace. Back then, you really had to wrestle on through doing the best you could. If you became stuck, you turned could to your manager for help. We didn't really have those kind of 'rights' back then.

We were expected to go to London every three months to report back on our research. I couldn't present on my research; at those meetings I had to ask my supervisor to speak for me. I couldn't follow or participate in the meetings; it was impossible for me. I only found out what went on when we returned to Glasgow and my supervisor would fill me in. It was ridiculous, it made me feel small, I didn't feel appreciated or equal. I had to rely on my supervisor to speak for me.

I did my second post-doctoral fellowship in chemistry at Durham University. I was still in the same field and it was brilliant. I was able to access an interpreter for meetings, but it still wasn't enough. I was involved in high-end discussions with [the company funding the research]. We would discuss topics like quicker methods for producing drugs; the team would include three other departments. The interpreter was completely lost in these meetings. It's not their fault they don't have a PhD in chemistry; it's a very specialised field. ... I created PowerPoints with subtitles and I had a friend voice over my slides. This meant I could stand up in meetings and contribute. It was important people could see it was me who did the work and not the team. I wanted to present on my part of the research. When it came to the discussions or Q&A part, I couldn't really participate. That's where I felt stuck.

I did begin thinking, *Is it worth me pursuing a career in this field when there were so many barriers?* I tried applying for an academic post, which meant I would take on lecturing duties... I saw this as an opportunity to progress. My colleagues just laughed at the suggestion. I can't tell you how small I felt. It was impossible.

I didn't let this defeat me. I kept going and I kept trying. When I was at Durham, there were two other deaf PhD researchers. They had been in the same job for 20 years and they were still at the same grade. They never lectured a class. I looked at them and thought, *Do I want to do this? Is this really worth doing?* I love being in the lab, doing research, discovering new things, but I never felt equal with my colleagues. I was always in a position where I had to ask a colleague for help. I didn't like that; I should be getting on with my career. After a lot of reflection I decided to become a chemistry teacher because I like teaching. I had an interpreter with me. I couldn't find a chemistry teacher post in deaf school, so that's why I made the choice to teach in a mainstream school. I regained my confidence, I felt equal with my colleagues. I had a full-time interpreter. The level of chemistry I was dealing with was easier compared to my previous jobs, the level of chemistry was more general stuff that everyone knows. I did enjoy the teaching job, but I did miss being involved with research. I always enjoyed working in the university, getting involved in new projects. No day was the same. Whereas teaching in a school was going over the same topics time and again... and you are dealing with naughty kids!

Then I somehow fell back in to research. I got involved in social research. I didn't expect to find myself here in a place where there's no chemistry jargon or terminology. The meetings we have are straightforward. I have an interpreter with me every day, all day, and it makes a difference. I feel part of the team.

There are less opportunities for deaf people, so I grab whatever comes my way, chemistry related or not – I don't care, I'll take it. It does help because I'm building the experience...

The world has moved on so much. It's been 10 years since I left the lab. I do enjoy the practical side of chemistry, I do miss it and I've been able to apply my chemistry knowledge with the Science Sign project – I've not let it go completely – and at Science shows. I do enjoy social research because of the direct impact it has on the deaf community. (Dr Audrey Cameron, deaf chemist and social researcher)

As seen from Quote 5.11, the interpreting needs of deaf academics in non-sign language–related disciplines are different from deaf students in academia, as they may be presenting their lectures or in meetings to predominantly hearing students or other colleagues, either in sign language that needs to be interpreted into a spoken language, or they speak for themselves but rely on sign language interpretation to understand questions from students in lectures or to interact with students in tutorials or consultation sessions (Campbell, Rohan & Woodcock, 2008).

Deaf academics' success in academia depends on the attitude of the institution where they work and their willingness to be receptive to having deaf staff and to meet their deaf staff's sign language needs (Campbell, Rohan & Woodcock, 2008).

Over the last decade, there are an increasing number of blogs and academic discussions that have centred around the role of deaf academics, their career progression and research leadership, how they acquire the necessary information to navigate the expectations of working as an academic in a community of practice and the need for capacity-building and succession planning for new deaf researchers to advance as academics (O'Brien & Emery, 2013; Trowler & Turner, 2002).[4]

Case Study 5.4   Rochester Bridges to the Doctorate Program

While the number of deaf scientists is increasing, there is a still a shortage, as deaf scientists are underrepresented in the behavioral or biomedical sciences. The University of Rochester and Rochester Institute of Technology have partnered together and established the Rochester Bridges to the Doctorate Program (http://deafscientists.com) to address this gap. With funding from the National Institutes of Health, our program aims to train and prepare eligible students while they are in one of the approved master's degree programs at RIT. [The Bridges program] aims to increase the readiness of eligible Deaf and Hard of Hearing students who plan to apply to a doctoral level program in a behavioral or biomedical science discipline.

'I am Dr Peter Hauser. I am the Bridges Program Director. The Bridges program is a wonderful opportunity. We are thrilled that the National Institute of Health awarded us grant funding with a specific focus: to foster more Deaf and Hard of Hearing scientists. This program not only teaches people how to become scientists, but also how to *be* a deaf or hard of hearing scientist and how to overcome possible challenges. Having worked with deaf and hard of hearing students who doubted they could succeed, it's exciting to watch them grow and realise that they can.' (www.youtube.com/watch?v=uBBbn1dUzUA) (See www.youtube.com/watch?v=4Xusv3UFWwQ for discussion of the Bridges Program from the Director, Dr Peter Hauser, and two of the students going through the program.)

In many countries, there has also been an increase in the number of deaf individuals pursuing careers in the professions, with a critical mass accumulating in medicine and law, allowing for the establishment of professional associations of deaf practitioners in these fields (e.g. the Association of Medical Professionals with Hearing Losses; Deaf Lawyers UK). There are also professional organisations of deaf lawyers. In Section 5.4, we discuss in detail sign language in the wider world, including legal, medical and mental health settings and the workplace.

5.4   Sign language in the wider world

This section looks at a broader range of settings where sign language is used directly and indirectly, primarily exploring a range of contexts where deaf and hearing people interact either directly in sign language or indirectly via interpreter-mediated communication. While the complexity of interaction increases when interpretation is introduced, very few non-interpreter professionals are aware of this convolution, and as a result, the functionality of specific events can be impeded. Here, we present an overview of each setting, then consider research findings relating to these domains and what the key findings mean for applied sign linguistics and sign language professional practice.

As a consequence of deaf people receiving greater access to education and to achieving higher levels of education, the use of sign language is more evident in the wider world, not only in 'deaf spaces'. More deaf people are working in different domains and are proudly promoting their use of sign language, although there are still barriers faced in some contexts where sign language provisions are not adequate. In this section, we focus on 7 key areas: poetry and performance, legal settings, medical and mental health settings, the media (television), politics, and the workplace.

5.4.1   Sign language poetry and performance

Sign language poetry has always been a part of everyday life in signing communities: at the local deaf club, in deaf schools and in social events. However, sign language is achieving greater visibility in the wider world through regular performances aimed not only at sign language users but at wider non-deaf, non-signing audiences.

Quote 5.12   Proudly unique

Through my music, I want to break prejudice and fight for equality between cultures. I want to show to people that being different can be an asset. My message is that nothing is impossible for the deaf; we can all do the same things. It doesn't matter if you are deaf or hearing. You should be proud of who you are and what makes you unique. Don't be afraid to show it. (Signmark, a.k.a. Marko Vuoriheimo, deaf hip hop/rap artist; www.signmark.biz)

Sign language poetry and folklore are interlinked (Sutton-Spence, 2012), though what is considered acceptable as a poetic form may vary across time and place, influenced by attitudes towards language and variations of same. Records suggest that the performance of sign language poetry dates back to 19th-century deaf banquets in France and the U.S., though it is not clear what form these poems took (Sutton-Spence, 2012; Esmail, 2008). Contemporary sign language poetry has its roots in the 1970s, particularly with regard to the canon of poetry of Dorothy 'Dot' Miles (Sutton-Spence, 2012).

It is important to differentiate between 'deaf poetry' and 'sign language poetry', with the former often presented in written form, and more likely to address issues to do with sound and its loss than is the case in sign language poetry (Esmail, 2008). At the same time, technology has revolutionised the potential to capture poetic signed performances for posterity: Krentz (2006) argues that the impact of video recording on sign language literature is as significant as the invention of the printing press for written literature.

Sutton-Spence (2012, pp. 1002–1003) notes that sign language poets often address the big questions – 'What is the nature of the Deaf world? And how should Deaf people live in it?' – leading to themes that address issues of deaf identity, the place of deaf people in the world, deaf values and behaviours, sign language, the ignorance of hearing society and the visual and tactile deaf life experience. Humour is a frequently utilised device. While themes arising typically emphasise the beauty of sign languages and the visual world (Sutton-Spence, 2005), Sutton-Spence (2012) notes that some young deaf people address themes of resentment towards being deaf in their sign language poetry. It is not easy to determine which aspects of sign language poetry are fundamentally textual (i.e. inherent to the language used) and which are performance related.

Quote 5.13   On aesthetic signing

As the ultimate form of aesthetic signing, poetry uses language highly creatively, drawing on a wide range of language resources ... such as deliberate selection of sign vocabulary sharing similar parameters, creative classifier signs, role shift (or characterization), specific use of space, eye-gaze, facial expressions, and other non-manual features. In addition, repetition and the rhythm and timing of signs are frequently seen as crucial to signed poetry. (Sutton-Spence, 2012, p. 1003)

The form that a signed poem will take may depend on the intended audience. The sharing of poetry with young children is considered important by many deaf poets, and this tends to focus more on repetition and rhythm than metaphor, which is considered more appropriate for older audiences (Kuntze, 2008; Sutton-Spence, 2012). Sutton-Spence (2012) tells us that audiences with no experience of sign language poetry cannot be expected to make inferences intended by poets, pointing out that 'literacy' around sign poetry must be developed and that in the absence of such literacy, signing communities may be 'overwhelmed by, alienated from, or frankly bored by sign language poetry' (p. 1004). It may also be that sign language is not as intuitively visual and 'read-able' by audiences who do not use sign language as many deaf poets may assume (Sutton-Spence & Muller de Quadros, 2014).

In terms of form, sign language poems are frequently 'lyric poems', though haiku, renga, beat poetry, rap (as in the case of Signmark, cited in Quote 5.13) and epic form arise (Sutton-Spence, 2012). Componential analysis of sign language poetry suggests that poets include use of simile, hyperbole, personification and metaphor at the level of the theme of the poem, and with regard to aspects of the lexicon – for example, signs which move upwards tend to have positive semantic meanings, while signs that have downward movements tend to have negative meanings associated with them (Brennan, 1990).

Fundamentally, sign language poetry and folklore emerges from the 'highly creative, strongly visual, entertaining and Deaf-affirming work, using sign language in novel and noticeable ways', with poets drawing on 'Neologisms and characterization through role shift work', which 'work with repetition of a range of elements to create powerful poetic effects' (Sutton-Spence, 2012, p. 1019).

More recent research from Pollitt (2014) challenges what she terms 'logo-centric readings' of sign language poetry that rely on comparing sign language poetry with traditionally written poems. She suggests that the term 'signart' is more appropriate as it acknowledges the artistic endeavour in sign language performance. In her work, she draws on translation studies, art theories and practices to focus on the performative, haptic and kinaesthetic (rather than linguistic) aspects of sign language poetry. She interviewed BSL poets and audiences attending sign poetry performances, as well as analysing BSL poems and performances, and identified the importance of movement and imagery in the poems.

5.4.2 Sign language in legal settings

When it comes to considering the position of sign languages in legal settings, we need to consider the situation of deaf victims, deaf perpetrators of crime and deaf professionals in the legal field. We suggest that the issue of problematic access to legal (and, indeed, other public services) has a basis in attitudes towards deafness and sign languages. As we saw in Chapter 3, recognition of a language is to a great extent dependent on people's attitudes towards that language and the kind of prestige associated with use of the language. And recognition, in turn, presents an opportunity for a community to potentially – and officially – use their language for a broader range of functions than might otherwise be the case. Legal support for a language may translate into service provision in that language, with commensurate increases in accessibility to information and access to content that was hitherto inaccessible. As we shall see below, serving on juries is a case in point. Before we turn to address this, we outline some of the challenges that deaf people have experienced vis-à-vis accessing legal domains.

The Access to Justice for Deaf People in the Bilingual, Bimodal Courtroom project was funded by the Leverhulme Trust and carried out by a team of deaf and hearing researchers at the Deaf Studies Research Unit, University of Durham, UK (Brennan & Brown, 1997) over a 3-year period. The study had several key components, which included the observation of trials in England and Wales and the video recording of trials in Scotland. These cases included deaf defendants and/or witnesses, and BSL–English interpreters were employed for the trials. The project team also conducted interviews with deaf people concerning their experiences of the criminal justice process, for example as victims of crime, witnesses to crime, individuals charged with crime but found not guilty and individuals in prison at the time of the interview. The team also interviewed 57 BSL–English interpreters and completed a survey of practising and trainee interpreters (Brennan, 1999a).

Brennan and Brown (1997) were amongst the first to discuss the impact of working bilingually and, crucially, bimodally in legal settings. While court interpreters are 'far from being the unobtrusive figure whom judges and attorneys would like her to be' (Berk-Seligson, 1990, p. 6), when these interpreters are working bimodally, the interpreter's presence is even more obtrusive (Brennan, 1999a). Brennan notes that signed/spoken language interpreters almost always interpret simultaneously and that a deaf participant must have visual contact with the interpreter throughout (see Chapter 6, Section 6.2 for more discussion of sign language interpreting as professional practice), a process that can prove disconcerting to legal personnel, especially to a lawyer engaged in cross-examination. She notes that direct interaction involving eye gaze is lost. Further, Brennan (1999a) points out that as deaf participants have to focus their attention on the interpreter to access the proceedings, they themselves may miss key information from the source speaker; for example, gestural activity like a shrug of the shoulders, a look of amazement, raised eyebrows, pointing towards evidence, etc. on the part of a lawyer. Any of this information may have an impact on the rest of the court but be lost to the deaf person. Brennan (1999a) also reports that gestural backchannelling on the part of a deaf witness, such as head nodding to indicate that they are following the thread of signing from an interpreter, may be misconstrued as meaning that the deaf person is agreeing to a statement of fact.

Quote 5.14   Unaware

Legal personnel are often completely unaware of what is happening before their very eyes. They are not aware of changes in message from source to target language; they are not always aware of interpreter intrusion; and they are often unaware of interactions taking place between defendants, witnesses and members of the general public, even where – as the research team observed – these actually take place within the courtroom. (Brennan, 1999, p. 228)

Studies in other countries have subsequently found similar problematic issues arising (see e.g. Kermit, Mjøen & Olsen, 2014; Russell & Hale, 2008). The impact of working simultaneously or consecutively in courtroom settings has been examined by Debra Russell (2002). She conducted 4 mock trials based on authentic court cases, and the participants included actual judges and lawyers as well as deaf witnesses and a non-deaf expert witness. The study examined the impact of interpreting mode on different kinds of courtroom discourse, namely (1) direct evidence, (2) cross-examination and (3) expert witness testimony. While post-trial interviews with participants demonstrated that lawyers and judges preferred simultaneous mode, the interpreters were the only participants who acknowledged that when working consecutively, their work product was more accurate. Indeed, Russell found that that while simultaneous interpretations were 87% accurate, the consecutive interpretations were 95% accurate. Further, Russell reports that a significant number of errors were not reported to the court, thus unknowingly leaving interpreting errors as part of the court record. She also reports that the ways in which interpreters interact can affect deaf witnesses, potentially leading to the loss of trust in a team of interpreters (Russell, 2002, 2008).

Russell's (2002, 2008) findings also mirrored those of Brennan and Brown (1997) in that legal personnel are often unaware of what is happening amongst the sign language users in court. We suggest that this serves to facilitate the existence of a parallel, but asymmetrical (in terms of access for all parties), set of proceedings, which go unrecognised and unrecorded and which can contribute to skewed processes.

Access to sign language interpretation throughout the criminal justice system is a perpetual issue (Miller, 2001). Even when an Act is in place to codify the provision of sign language interpreters in legal proceedings, such as in New Zealand, there are still problems with how interpreters are booked and whether they are suitable trained or qualified to work in court (McKee, 2011). And as can be seen by our discussion of educational interpreting (see Section 5.2), simply providing interpreters in legal settings is not necessarily an accommodation that guarantees access to information or true access to participation in legal proceedings (Brunson, 2007).

Regardless of whether interpreters are provided, one crucial point of consideration is in relation to the sign language use and literacy of those deaf people who encounter the justice system and whether they have enough sign language competency to understand what is going on, as outlined in Concept 5.2.

Concept 5.2   Minimal language competency and the legal system

Some deaf individuals have been so socially and linguistically isolated during their lifetime that they have not fully acquired either a sign language from deaf peers or a spoken language. Currently there are a variety of terms used for people in this predicament: minimal language competence (MLC), minimal language skills (MLS), High Visual Orientation (HVO), and Special Linguistic Needs (SLN)... These individuals tend not to be socially connected to a deaf community but may be encountered by interpreters at an assignment. These deaf clients have received little or no education, and their actual intelligence, knowledge or ability to absorb new information is often masked by their language deficit. They generally lack standard (commonly understood) ways of referring to concrete things or experiences and have difficulty with understanding and expressing abstract concepts.

Occasionally, a deaf person is described as MLC when they are actually an immigrant with knowledge of a foreign sign language and perhaps some literacy in the language of their home country. In these cases, using a local interpreter who also knows the client's sign language is an ideal but rarely available solution. Alternatively, you can work with a deaf person who is skilled at 'foreigner talk' and can act as a relay interpreter.

MLC clients often have an idiosyncratic system of communication, based on gestures that they use within their limited familiar social world (family, caregivers or workplace). They may also have a smattering of local sign language vocabulary. However, their limited language development will show up through gaps in their comprehension and expression of abstract information: time concepts, identifying family relationships, grammatical pronoun reference (who's doing what to whom), cause and effect, emotional states and moral concepts. Within this group, there is a range of communication abilities and styles, and working with an interpreter is not always a realistic approach...

MLC individuals sometimes fall foul of the law, getting into situations without understanding the consequences. Their communication limitations may go unrecognised by police, or even initially by an interpreter (especially where the deaf client is adept at mimicking signs and facial expression to give the appearance of reasonable sign language skills). The 1990 case of a New Zealand deaf man with limited language who was wrongfully accused of murder and imprisoned as a result of miscommunication was dramatised in a TVNZ documentary, 'The Remand of Ivan Curry'.

Living in a small rural town amongst hearing family, but relatively isolated from a deaf community, Ivan Curry was a profoundly deaf man with limited formal sign language skills and education. Based on two police interviews – the first without an interpreter, and the second assisted by an itinerant teacher of the deaf (without training in NZSL) – Curry was said to have confessed to killing his infant nephew by punches to the chest, and was held on remand in prison for 22 months awaiting trial for murder in the High Court. He was eventually acquitted in the trial, when it came to light that the infant had actually died as a result of another family member applying adult CPR to the baby's chest after finding him lifeless in his cot. Curry himself never gave evidence in court, but during the 22 months between arrest and trial, interpreters and deaf persons experienced with communicating with MLC individuals were consulted as expert witnesses and used to facilitate further interviews with Curry. As a result of a more informed picture of his actual communication abilities (as well as the weight of new evidence from family members), the two original police statements containing Curry's 'confessions' were ruled as inadmissible evidence by the trial judge on the grounds that valid communication was unlikely to have occurred. He was acquitted after a lengthy process of three full-scale hearings, including the Court of Appeal. Some people close to him claimed that during his extended period of imprisonment on remand, he did not fully understand why he was in prison. (Napier, McKee & Goswell, 2010, pp. 149–152)

The case such as that highlighted in Concept 5.2 reveals that there are potential linguistic barriers that deaf people face in the legal system, which may mean that it is decided that they do not have the linguistic competence to stand trial (Vernon & Miller, 2001, 2005). The linguistic diversity within the signing community is a key issue to be taken into account to ensure that deaf sign language users can access their due process rights (Miller & Vernon, 2001).

Case study 5.5   Justisigns – promoting access to legal settings for deaf sign language users

The project is a collaboration with several consortium partners: Trinity College, Dublin, in Ireland (Leeson, Sheikh, Lynch, Venturi); Heriot-Watt University in Edinburgh (Napier, Turner, Skinner); University of Applied Sciences of Special Needs Education in Switzerland (Haug, Shores); KU Leuven in Belgium (Vermeerbergen, Salaets), efsli (European Forum of Sign Language Interpreters) and EULITA (European Legal Interpreters & Translators Association) The project promoter is Interesource Group (Ireland) Ltd. (Sheikh).

Jemina and Lorraine are both involved in 'Justisigns': a 30-month project funded through the European Commission's Leonardo Da Vinci Lifelong Learning Programme (December 2013 through May 2016), and the aim of the project is to promote access to justice for deaf sign language users, with a particular focus on police settings.

The first phase of the project involved conducting a survey of the nature of legal interpreting provision for deaf people across Europe (Napier & Haug, 2014). In sum, it was found that although there are some established provisions for legal sign language interpreting across Europe, it is inconsistent. Furthermore, there does not seem to be a uniform approach across Europe to the training or certification of legal interpreters, and the (lack of) availability of interpreters for legal settings is a Europe-wide issue. It is, however, difficult to identify legal sign language interpreting needs when it is not possible to identify the number of deaf sign language users in the legal system.

The consortium has decided to focus on deaf people's access to interpreters in police interviews, as this is an under-researched area. The goal of the project is to collect data through focus groups and interviews with deaf people, interpreters and police officers about their experiences. The information we gather will then be used to develop training materials and to offer workshops and courses to these key stakeholder groups.

Our preliminary research has found some level of progress in the UK over the last 18 years since the Access to Justice report (Brennan & Brown, 1997). For example:

- There is legislation in place that insists on equality before the law.
- It is recommended that only qualified interpreters are used in the legal system.
- Some interpreters have received legal training.
- Some police forces have in place policies to guide officers when it comes to interviewing deaf suspects, witnesses and victims.
- A few police forces in the UK have begun to develop online videos, recognising the specific linguistic and cultural needs of the deaf community.
- Deaf professionals are now working within the legal system.

What our research is telling us is that some forms of good practice exist. Unfortunately, we are not seeing a consistent approach to ensuring that the rights of deaf people are protected. Often, good practice is achieved because individual police officers recognise the linguistic and cultural differences of deaf people, but it is not necessarily happening on a systemic level.

The linguistic challenges interpreters experience in legal settings still persist, and many of these challenges occur because of the nature of legal discourse and the lack of equivalence between spoken and sign languages. But developing research-based training materials can have a positive impact on the understanding of interpreters and police officers on how to deal with these issues.

We should also reflect on what happens to deaf people who are convicted of crimes and sentenced to serve time in prison. Oftentimes, prison authorities do not know how many deaf people there are in the system and can only make a guesstimate. For example, Gahir, O'Rourke, Monteiro and Reed (2011) carried out a survey of 139 prisons and young offender institutions in England and Wales in an attempt to ascertain how many deaf prisoners were in the system who might need a mental health assessment. It was estimated that there were 135 deaf people in the prison system at that time, but the majority were hearing aid users who did not use sign language. Only 9.6% were thought to be BSL users. The researchers found that prison staff admitted to finding it difficult to meet the needs of deaf prisoners, which corroborates Miller's (2003) earlier discussions of the need for inmates to adapt linguistically to their environment.

Vernon (2010) reports the 'horror' for deaf prisoners, who experience isolation, an increased risk of bullying and abuse, limited or no access to fluent sign language interlocutors, limited or no access to interpreting provision and limited or no access to support services (e.g. psychiatric care, counselling), as highlighted in Example 5.4.

Example 5.4   Deaf inmate sues Oregon prison system for not providing sign language interpreters

A deaf prison inmate accuses the Oregon Department of Corrections of violating the Americans with Disabilities Act by not providing him an interpreter during 13 years of incarceration.

A federal lawsuit filed on behalf of 48-year-old David D. VanValkenburg seeks $460,000 in damages for what he describes as a systematic failure to effectively communicate with him from the beginning of his prison term in November 2000. VanValkenburg's complaint alleges that the Department of Corrections failed to competently communicate with him during intake interviews and orientations, educational classes and training, and in such confidential settings as medical appointments, religious services and counseling meetings.

'Instead,' VanValkenburg's lawsuit alleges, the Department of Corrections 'required Mr. VanValkenburg to train inmates to act as interpreters for him, who were unqualified and failed to keep Mr. VanValkenburg's information confidential.'

The lawsuit, originally filed in Multnomah County in May, was moved last week to U.S. District Court in Portland. Judge Anna J. Brown will hear the case. A spokeswoman for the Oregon Department of Justice, which will defend the prison system, declined to comment on the litigation, citing its policy of not commenting on pending litigation.

VanValkenburg was convicted of sodomy and sex abuse in Washington County and sent to prison on Nov. 15, 2000. He served time at Oregon State Penitentiary and four other prisons. He's now at Columbia River Correctional Institution, a minimum-security prison near Portland International Airport.

The lawsuit acknowledges that VanValkenburg can write notes in English, with limited skills, but American Sign Language (known as ASL) is his primary language.

He served the bulk of his prison term at Snake River Correctional Institution, an Ontario prison known as SRCI, where he alleges that staffers never provided him with a qualified ASL interpreter.

In cases where he had to communicate with prison staffers, VanValkenburg was forced to use 'non-confidential, untrained and primarily unqualified inmates as interpreters, including known gang members,' the lawsuit alleges. 'After nearly 10 years of working to train his own interpreters at SRCI for free, (the prison system) paid Mr. VanValkenburg to train his own unqualified, inmate interpreters,' according to the complaint. (http://blog.oregonlive.com/politics_impact/print.html?entry=/2014/06/deaf_inmate_sues_oregon_prison.html)

Yet, despite awareness of the kinds of issues raised by Vernon (2010) and Brennan and Brown (1997), public opinion reflects a 'hierarchy of sympathy', with deaf prisoners attracting very little sympathy for their situation. For example, in 2015, Irish deaf man Edward Connors was found guilty of manslaughter and sentenced to 7 years in prison. Despite the judge accepting that there is no facility in the Republic of Ireland that can offer accessible rehabilitation to Mr Connors, no funding was made available for him to be transferred to the UK. Leeson (2015) suggests that analysis of the situation facilitates a framing of this case where institutional intersectionality has an impact on outcomes (Crenshaw, 1991). An overriding frame here is one of 'normalcy v. difference': in Ireland, there are no dedicated mental health services for young deaf people and extremely limited services for adults. This interplayed with the construction of deafness as disability (and, in this criminal case, as a partial defence). Indeed, it was reported in the media that 'Judge McCartan commented that Connors 'cannot but be described as a victim' in this case, as he was deaf since childhood. The judge also commented that he grew up in an environment where there was no opportunity for learning of any sort, leaving him with severe communication difficulties' (The Irish Times, 23 February 2015).

Further, the psychiatrist in the case reported that Connors has a 'primitive personality' arising from his lack of access to language. This is the line that played again and again in the media.[5] When Mr Connors was found guilty of manslaughter and sentenced, this generated more media coverage with, for example, the Irish Times (23 February 2015) running a headline highlighting the fact that Mr Connors was homeless (a politically salient issue in current political discourse in Ireland) – with the subtitle 'Edward Connors (30), who is deaf and cannot speak, gets seven-year sentence.' The article notes that he is homeless and that the judge said he is a 'serious danger to society'. References to the fact that he was a heroin addict with a history of offending (with syringes) was also mentioned. All of this clearly situates him in a particular way. The lack of systemic support for deaf people in this situation led the Irish Deaf Society to publish a piece in the Irish Journal, an online media source (see Quote 5.15).

Quote 5.15 Imagine...

We would ask that you imagine yourself as a Deaf person, devoid of sound in a locked cell with no ability to hear a radio, to not be able to understand subtitles on your television, to not be able to communicate effectively with staff and fellow prisoners who are unable to sign.

The Irish Deaf Society considers this to be an astounding effect on a Deaf person's mental health and well-being and urge that policy is put into place as soon as possible to combat the isolation and fear of any Deaf person in the Irish penal system. (www.thejournal.ie/deaf-dawson-st-bus-death-1959030-Feb2015/)

The distinct disdain for this position was evident in several of the responses posted on the Journal's website, two of which can be seen in Quote 5.16. These viewpoints tend to profile Mr Connors' criminal status and his membership in the Irish indigenous Travelling Community (a minority, oft-discriminated against community in Ireland), inferencing his drug addiction as counterpoints against which his linguistic rights – not to mention consideration for his mental health, arising from lack of meaningful linguistic engagement over the term of his sentence – might be considered as not worthy of consideration (or public funding).

Quote 5.16   'More do-gooder horse crap'

Again, more concerns expressed for criminals instead of victims & their families. This criminal is described as having a primitive mindset, given his background & the relative non-engagement of the travelling community with educational services then we end up in this sorry state of affairs. His violent nature will stem from a direct inability to make himself & his needs understood so frustration will lead to violence which may shed some light on his other crimes, i.e. using syringes in muggings. To be honest I pity the prison staff who will have to handle him. (Matt Donovon, 25 February 2015)

More do-gooder horse crap. Everyone living around Sandyford knows this individual and his carry on for years. He committed two muggings at syringe point while out on bail for this horrific crime, and all I hear about it is the lack of facilities in prison for him. What facilities does he need to sit in a cell or walk around an exercise yard? (Ann O'Reilly, 25 February 2015)

Let us now consider the sign language use of deaf people participating in justice in two other different roles: either as jurors or lawyers. While the inclusion of deaf people in court proceedings as witnesses is well established (Stone & Woll, 2008), most English-speaking countries do not allow deaf people to serve on juries (Napier & Spencer, 2008). Napier and Spencer (2008) note that current policy in most countries, with the notable exception of many states in the U.S. and (following from recognition of NZSL) New Zealand, suggests that deaf people are not capable of serving as jurors on account of their 'disability', i.e. their hearing loss. They also note that in the UK and Ireland, deaf people are disqualified from serving as jurors because there are common-law principles which act as a barrier to allowing a '13th person', in the person of the interpreter, into a jury room (Enright, 1999; FLAC, 2010; Napier, 2013c).

Case study 5.6   Australian deaf jurors

Napier and Spencer (2008) ran an experimental pilot study designed to replicate aspects of the courtroom experience. They tested 12 would-be Australian jurors, 6 deaf and 6 hearing, to compare their levels of understanding of a courtroom text.

They briefed their jurors with information that would have been presented at a trial and then asked them to respond to questions relating to a judge's summation from an authentic case. The goal of Napier and Spencer's study was to assess levels of comprehension received directly or indirectly via interpretation. They found that deaf jurors in this pilot were not disadvantaged by relying on sign language interpreters to access information in court, noting that while hearing jurors in the study answered almost 78% of comprehension test questions correctly, deaf jurors scored 75%. Given this, Napier and Spencer recommended that deaf people in New South Wales be permitted to serve as jurors in criminal cases, with access to be provided via interpreters as well as ensuring that deaf jurors have access to court documents in advance and transcripts at the end of each trial day. At the same time, they cautioned that deaf jurors would need to have a reasonable comprehension of English, in line with expectations of hearing jurors. They also recommended that briefing and debriefing time be set aside each day for the deaf jurors and interpreters to check for understanding, agreement regarding lexical choices, etc. Further, Napier and Spencer recommended that only experienced legal interpreters who are accredited should be permitted to interpret for deaf jurors, and they suggest that specific training be provided for interpreters regarding how to work with deaf people presenting in differing roles in court (as witnesses, as jurors, as lawyers, etc.).

Since the original study described in Case Study 5.6, Napier and Spencer (2008) have led further studies, including a survey of legal personnel and interpreters about their perceptions as to whether deaf people can serve as jurors, and follow-up interviews with lawyers, deaf people and interpreters with experience of the jury system (Napier, 2013c; Napier & McEwin, 2015). Essentially, all the studies to date have revealed that sign language should be able to be used in the jury deliberation process, as there is general agreement in principle that the courtroom discourse is translatable and understandable and that, philosophically, deaf people should be able to serve as jurors and do not appear to be disadvantaged by relying on interpreters to access the trial evidence.

The final 'piece of the puzzle' is to collect evidence of what happens in a jury deliberation room with a deaf juror and sign language interpreters present, examine how the jury deliberation process might be affected by their presence and see whether there are any changes to the typical deliberation process as a result of being mediated through an interpreter. In 2013, Napier and Spencer began a new 3-year project, funded by the Australian Research Council, working with leading legal interpreting scholars Debra Russell and Sandra Hale, to conduct ethnographic observations in U.S. trial rooms, where deaf people are part of the jury panel and engage in the selection process. They also filmed all aspects of a mock trial, including a deaf juror and sign language interpreters, to present evidence about whether having more than 12 people in the jury room is an issue. The comments in Quote 5.17 are taken from interviews with ASL interpreters, with deaf people who have served (or challenged the system because they wanted to serve) on juries and with lawyers about their perceptions of deaf people serving as jurors (Napier, 2012c).

Quote 5.17   The interpreter in the [jury] room

It's not the same as interpreting for a party, where I would ask the court to stop anytime I needed them to.

This is different because there is no normal interaction...a non-deaf juror, if they didn't understand anything, they wouldn't be saying, 'now what did he say? I missed that.' That would never happen. (Ashley, interpreter)

I think it is a challenge that any interpretation from a language to another, there is going to be some change within the discourse, you know, and I think that if jurors, you know, a lot of their role is we ask them to make their own decisions about whether people are telling the truth, whether people, you know, are – the accuracy of their testimony, etc. And so I think it is somewhat of a challenge. I think that a good interpreter, however, can work with – within that challenge and with preparation and with a lot of, you know, thoughtfulness and professionalism, can make it almost equivalent for a deaf juror to participate.

...my experience was so good because the judge was so supportive of us. From the very beginning he continually reminded the jury that we may raise our hand during the interpretation and ask for a moment or ask for clarification; he would say that all the time. He basically just put out an attitude of respect towards our needs from the very beginning, so that by the time we got to deliberations, they were just wonderful. And the California trial consultants, they said they video-taped deliberations in their mock trials and they found that jurors were much more respectful and open to listening to everybody when there was an interpreter in the room, because they were taking turns and because they were asking people, 'Are you finished? Let's let the next person sitting next to you say their piece now'. (Alex, lawyer and former interpreter)

I think if clear directions are given to the jury about the role of the interpreter as a 'non-participant but only there as a facilitator for the full and active participation of juror X', then it should not impact negatively...If anything, the interpreter's presence will impact positively by allowing the deaf juror to follow deliberations and to actively participate, thereby contributing to the administration of justice. (Jordan, lawyer)

I was elected foreperson, so I ran the [deliberation] meeting. I set up rules that all should speak one at a time and not overlap for the sake of the interpreter. Everyone agreed, and everything went smoothly. (Cameron, deaf person)

As we mentioned in Section 5.3.3, recent decades have seen an increase in the number of deaf professionals, not least in the legal domain. In their work, deaf legal professionals consult with non-deaf people and rely on mediated communication via sign language interpreters in the 'other direction';

that is, delivering rather than receiving legal services in a sign language (Kurlander, 2008). Such professionals need to develop legal discourse in sign language and think carefully about how they can participate in their community of practice in terms of conversing with other lawyers, their clients and any other personnel (see Example 5.5).

Example 5.5   Deaf lawyer makes history

A Queensland woman has made history by becoming the first deaf lawyer in Australia to appear for a client in court.

Kathryn O'Brien, a solicitor with Porta Lawyers in Brisbane, appeared last week at the Pine Rivers Magistrates Court on behalf of two clients – one deaf and one hearing – in domestic violence matters.

The court appointed a sign language interpreter, and O'Brien's supervisor briefly attended court with her to explain to Magistrate Steven Guttridge the significance of her appearance as a 'flying solo' lawyer who communicates only in sign language.

'After the introduction, I was on my own,' O'Brien told *Lawyers Weekly*. 'It was an interesting experience, because the interpreters had to figure out how to interpret for two different deaf clients simultaneously during court.'

While her appearance went smoothly, O'Brien said there was one thing she was unprepared for: call-overs. 'I am grateful to the understanding court clerk who ensured that I knew when my matter was coming up to be heard,' she said. 'The opposing legal representative also assisted me, checking for herself when the matter would be heard and informing me.'

Overcoming such difficulties is not new to O'Brien, who became a lawyer to 'break new ground' in providing the deaf community with legal advice in sign language and to ensure that their needs were being heard and met.

One of the biggest hurdles, she said, is not being able to have a spontaneous conversation with a colleague about a matter. 'Naturally, I don't expect every lawyer to know sign language, so it does pose some difficulties when I would like to sound out some concepts I may have regarding a matter,' she said.

Now that O'Brien has made her courtroom debut, she is looking forward to appearing more in the future. 'With all the teething problems with regard to interpreting costs, availability of qualified and experienced court interpreters, and everyday communication with clients [sorted out] ... I don't see why I cannot participate in court advocacy,' she said.

'This is something I would like to see more of in the near future, and not just for deaf clients but also for my hearing clients. I like the idea of thinking on my feet and doing the best for my client in such circumstances.' (posted on www.lawyersweekly.com.au, 18 March 2011)

Finally, we note that a survey conducted by the Kyle, Sutherland and Stockley (2012) on deaf people's experiences of accessing legal services found that 85% of deaf BSL users would prefer to consult with a solicitor who can sign rather than talk to a hearing solicitor through an interpreter.

5.4.3 Sign language in medical and mental health settings

'A Message Made Loud and Clear – Deafness Could Kill'. So ran the headline to an article on the experience of Irish deaf people in health care settings in the Irish Medical Times in 2014 (Reilly, 2014), which set the scene for a discussion on the fact that adequate access to sign language for deaf patients remains far from adequate in many parts of the world (see e.g. Brück et al., 2014; De Wit, Salami & Hema, 2012; Leeson, Sheikh, Rozanes, Grehan & Matthews, 2014; Nilsson, Turner, Sheikh & Dean, 2013; Rozanes, 2014; van den Bogaerde & de Lange, 2014).

Quote 5.18 Bridging terminology

It can be expected then that deaf patients may experience trouble in understanding English medical terms, much in the same way as other hearing minority-language patients or hearing English-speaking patients who have limited education backgrounds. This means an interpreter often has not only cultural but also educational gaps to bridge in addition to the linguistic task of interpreting medical terms from English to Auslan and vice versa. Additionally, interpreters may lack experience in medical contexts, or sufficient knowledge about a particular medical condition, which may exacerbate any communicative challenges. (Napier, Major & Ferrara, 2011, pp. 119–120)

While much of this work focuses on the quality provision of interpreters in such environments, there is also an emerging body of work that documents how health care professionals who are sign language users approach their task and considers mediated communication via sign language interpreters in the 'other direction' (i.e. delivering rather than receiving medical or mental health services in a signed language), and therefore needing to develop medical discourse in sign languages (Earhart & Hauser, 2008).

Quote 5.19 Connecting with patients

These [deaf] doctors connect with [deaf/hard of hearing] patients in a way that hearing physicians can't. (Darin Latimore, assistant dean for student and resident diversity, UC Davis School of Medicine, 5 February 2013; www.ucdmc.ucdavis.edu/publish/news/newsroom/7441)

When Americans with Disabilities Act was passed in 1990 (when I was 20-year-old college junior), I felt that maybe the time was right for someone like me to become a doctor and help to make hearing people and medical professionals realize that deaf people can do anything if they are given the chance to do so ... I use sign language interpreter(s) to communicate with my colleagues who do not know sign language. Some of my colleagues know sign language, but most do not. Sometimes when I do not have access to interpreter, I communicate with people who do not know sign language through writing and emails. (Dr Scott Smith, physician and doctor of medicine; www.deafis.org/faq/doctor.php)

Even with accommodations such as interpreters, deaf medical students and doctors still need to overcome significant professional barriers (Moreland, Latimore, Sen, Arato & Zazove, 2013), particularly because they spend a lot of their time making arrangements to book interpreters and so on. As with deaf academics, Moreland et al. (2013) found that institutional support was a critical to ensuring accessibility, success and satisfaction in the medical workplace for deaf doctors.

Following on from a body of discourse analytical and applied linguistic research on doctor-patient and nurse-patient discourse (e.g. Candlin & Candlin, 2003; Eggly, 2002; Holmes & Major, 2003), recent sign language research has begun to document how deaf medical practitioners using ASL consult with their deaf patients in direct communication, for example, in relation to explaining dosage statements (Nicodemus, Swabey & Moreland, 2014; Swabey, Nicodemus & Moreland, 2014). Not surprisingly, it has been found that deaf physicians use different discourse features (such as cohesive devices, restructuring the order of information, breaking down questions, providing visual examples, and emphasising parts of the text) to 'unpack' meaning and provide concrete experiential examples when compared with ASL interpreters who translate the same statements from English into ASL. The opportunity to examine direct sign language health communication, however, is rare because there are very few countries where deaf sign language users can currently become qualified nurses or doctors (e.g. the U.S., Canada, the Netherlands and Austria).

Thus, communication between health professionals and deaf patients is embedded within a cross-cultural communication framework (Barnett, 2002), with two languages and cultures at play, as well as the culture of medicine. There are a handful of discourse analytic studies that have examined interpreter-mediated health care interactions using either authentic or simulated data.

The first was Metzger's (1999) study, which used naturally occurring data and then compared that with role play simulation data. The authentic data captured the interpreter-mediated communication in a paediatric appointment between a deaf mother, her hearing child (the patient), a doctor, a nurse and a professional ASL–English interpreter. Drawing on Goffman's (1974) participation framework, Metzger analysed the frames and footing shifts of the participants and suggested that when participants share a schema for a 'medical interview' and an 'interpreted encounter', they have a similar 'frame' for what is expected in a medical interview, but that when schemas are not aligned, communication can break down. One example of miscommunication occurred when the interpreter used the first person to relay the mother's utterance about trying to help her sick child, but the doctor was unclear whether the action had been done by the mother or the interpreter. So in this instance, their frames were different, as the doctor was expecting the interpreter to use the third person to refer to the mother. Sanheim (2003) used Metzger's (1999) paediatric interaction data to analyse the interpreter's management of turn-taking and found that the interpreter tended to ignore one of the overlapping speakers and either convey that turn when possible, indicate it had been attempted or make no attempt to interpret it.

Analyses were conducted in Australia on two authentic interactions between hearing doctors and deaf patients via sign language interpreters (Major, 2013, 2014), and 10 simulated doctor-patient sign language interpreter-mediated interactions (Major & Napier, 2012). It was found that interpreters specifically used cohesive devices, unpacked some medical concepts, expanded and reduced utterances and took their own turn in the interaction to ask for clarification and repetition; it was also found that interpreters facilitated rapport between doctor and patient by engaging in humorous exchanges, thus engaging in health care interpreting as 'relational practice' (Major, 2013).

The situation of deaf patients has received quite some coverage, typically because access remains problematic. Part of the problem seems to be that, in many countries, health care workers do not fully consider the risk associated with not providing trained interpreters, or they assume that they may understand their deaf patients more than they actually do. Previous research shows that as deaf people often belong to a low-English proficiency group, they have limited access to public health information and therefore have a smaller fund of health care knowledge (Pollard & Barnett, 2009).

For example, in a study of 25 Dutch physicians and 31 of their deaf patients (of whom 84% considered themselves members of the Dutch signing community), Smeijers and Pfau (2009) found that physicians seem to view their patients as individuals with a severe hearing loss but assume them to be linguistically the same as their hearing patients. That is, the physicians are not factoring in that 45.9% of their deaf patients reported that Sign Language of the Netherlands is their mother tongue. As Smeijers and Pfau (2009) point out, 'Treating a native signer, who may not be fluent in spoken Dutch, as if they were a native speaker of Dutch may cause serious communication problems' (p.5). They also report that:

- GPs evaluated the quality of communication during consultations more positively than their patients, with 91% of GPs believing that they are often or always able to explain the diagnosis clearly to their patients.

- None of the GPs indicated that they find it harder to understand a medical problem presented by a deaf patient than one presented by one of their hearing patients. Yet only 35% of the GPs claimed to always understand the patient's reason for visiting.
- Only one of the 31 patients reported that he always brings a professional interpreter to appointments with his GP; 74% of the 31 patients indicated that they never bring an interpreter when visiting their GP.

Furthermore, in a large-scale study of deaf BSL users, funded by the UK-based organisation SignHealth (Kyle, Sutherland, Allsop, Ridd, & Emond, 2013) found that deaf people experience problems accessing health care information. They also found that deaf people often have undiagnosed or misdiagnosed illnesses or have been receiving the wrong treatment. They put this down to a number of issues: limited English literacy on the part of some deaf patients (which may not be something that health care providers consider a potential problem), the lack of provision of sign language interpreters for consultations, the fact that deaf patients may not understand sign language interpreters well enough or the fact that deaf patients do not ask the right questions of their doctor.

Another recent UK-based study on behalf of the organisation Access on Hearing Loss (Ringham, 2013) surveyed 866 people, with the majority of respondents self-identifying as deaf (251), hard of hearing (303) and deafened (78). Ringham (2013) found that:

- 77% of BSL users found it difficult to communicate with hospital staff
- 70% of BSL users were not provided with BSL–English interpretation
- 35% of deaf and hard of hearing people experienced difficulty communicating with their GP or nurse
- 32% said it was difficult to explain their health problems to their GP
- 30% of BSL users said they avoid going to see their GP because of communication problems
- 24% of patients had missed an appointment because of poor communication, such as not being able to hear staff calling out their name; 19% reported missing more than 5 appointments
- 35% of deaf and hard of hearing people had been left unclear about their condition because of communication problems with their GP or nurse
- 33% of BSL users were either unsure about instructions for medication or had taken too much or too little of a medication because of a communication problem

The issue of informed consent is one which requires that a patient is cognisant of the facts of their illness and understands the health care options being put to them in order to make an informed decision about their treatment.

In the absence of meaningful communication, no informed consent occurs (Leeson, Sheikh, Rozanes, Grehan & Matthews, 2014), potentially opening up health care providers to lawsuits.

Case study 5.7   Medisigns

In 2013, the Medisigns Project, a European Commission–funded project led by Interesource Group (Ireland) Ltd. (Sheikh) that looked at deaf people's access to health care in Ireland, Cyprus, Poland, Sweden and the UK, was awarded the EU's 'Language Label Award' for excellence. The project aimed to create evidence-based continuous professional development materials for sign language interpreters and health care professionals and to provide information to signing community members regarding their rights. The project documented what signing communities and sign language interpreters working on the ground knew – that access to health care in many countries is highly problematic and that there is a lack of targeted training available for sign language interpreters working in health care settings (Nilsson et al., 2013; Leeson et al., 2014). The team also based their peda-gogical approach on two key principles:

(1)   Interpreting shifts interaction from dyadic to triadic exchanges (Wadensjö, 1998), and this has consequences for the interaction;
(2)   Intersubjectivity – which Shaffer (2014, p. 146) defines as 'how we as commu-nicators assess each other's comprehension and adjust our interactions accordingly' – affects how participants present themselves to each other and how they understand each other.

This led to the establishment of the principle that the actors in a health care consultation were working together to establish best outcomes for patients. It also assumed that each of the participants in an interpreter-mediated health care event were jointly responsible for co-constructing a successful interaction, bearing in mind the scope of the relevant professionals' scope of practice and assuming a patient-centred approach to health care provision, expressed via the discourse norms of meetings between doctors and patients (e.g. Tebble, 2014).

Strengths of the Medisigns Project include the fact that the partners married action research with the creation of evidence-based education, and then used the evidence base to inform key stakeholders, in turn raising awareness and influ-encing policy shifts. For example, Medisigns project content was shared with interpreters across Europe via efsli, and with health care practitioners via the Cypriot partner, the University of Nicosia, and national health care providers. Project activities led to a commitment from the Cypriot government to provide sign language interpreters in hospital settings, while in Ireland, the Health Service Executive committed to ensuring that their complaints procedures information would be made available online in ISL. Dissemination to the wider community of health care professionals occurred via an Irish Medical Times article which drew on the project's findings (Reilly, 2014). Further, an app was developed in Sweden, building on a pre-existing corpus of health care data, and the project team harnessed this idea, creating a generic app which was tested by stakeholders and will soon be available on iTunes. Other materials, such as a documentary feature on some of the issues identified, PowerPoint slides developed by the multidisciplinary project team and a report on access to health care in each of the countries involved in the project, are freely available online (www.medi-signsproject.eu).

Quote 5.20   'Can you lip-read me?'

My husband was with me [in the Emergency Ward] as I was very sick. I was lying on the bed in the ward, and we had been waiting to see a doctor. Then a nurse came and opened the curtain that surrounded the bed. She asked, in a patronising way, 'Can you lip-read me?'
I was feeling so sick and just was not in form to respond. I tried to tell her that I could not, and asked my husband, Brian, to communicate with her on my behalf. As he tried to communicate with her, he signed. The nurse responded by slapping his hand, hard. Both Brian and I were totally shocked by this. In fact, Brian was furious and wanted to report her to her manager, but I told him to stop as I was too sick to make a fuss and didn't want to see Brian fighting our corner alone. Normally, I am a strong person and I always believe in securing our right to have interpreter and to ensure access, but this time was different. It was a truly horrible experience. (Medisigns Project interview with Teresa Lynch, 2013)

Case study 5.8   Access to preventative and on-going health care information

In 2010, the National Auslan Booking Service for medical interpreting (NABS) in Australia booked interpreters for 17,782 health care appointments. However, deaf people could not request an interpreter to access preventative health care information (e.g. through drop-in clinics, advertised community sessions, ante-natal classes) or on-going information after diagnosis (e.g. diabetes nutritional workshops). Deaf Auslan users could not get access to health awareness and education workshops as there were no provisions for translation of information into Auslan or for the provision of Auslan interpreters. So, NABS commissioned a study of access to preventative and on-going health care information for deaf Australians (Napier & Kidd, 2013; Napier, Sabolcec et al., 2014).
Adopting a community participatory approach, the deaf-hearing research team used a purposeful sampling approach to qualitatively survey Auslan users about their perceived health information and access communication needs through face-to-face interviews and focus groups conducted in Auslan by deaf peers. Throughout Australia, 72 deaf people were interviewed in Auslan individually or in small groups of 2–3, and each filmed interview was thematically analysed for key issues in relation to access to health care information and whether deaf people receive information directly in Auslan (e.g. from a Deaf community support worker), via an interpreter or through translated materials.
In sum it was found that deaf people:

• Had a lack of self-confidence in their English literacy;
• Desired more information on preventative or on-going health care needs;

- Over-relied on their doctor, rather than accessing health care information elsewhere;
- Had a lack of access to health-related information;
- Experienced problems in accessing health care interpreters;
- Perceived a lack of awareness by health care providers of the needs of deaf patients;
- Had clear communication preferences to give and receive health care information in Auslan; and
- Had a lack of awareness of the services available to them through NABS.

The investigation of health care needs of different generations of deaf people in Australia directly informed the policy and provision of on-going and preventative health care information to deaf people in Auslan, as NABS used the results of the study as part of their tender to the Australian government to widen their support services.

Although deaf people working in medical practice as physicians is a relatively new phenomenon, in some countries, deaf sign language users have long been involved in health care of deaf patients as mental health professionals. For example, the British and European Societies for Mental Health and Deafness hold regular conferences on best practices for working with deaf patients with mental illness or mental health problems (see Chapter 8), and many countries have sign language–specific services for members of their signing community, with support provided by deaf and hearing mental health professionals either directly in sign language or through sign language interpreters. Recommendations have been established for 'culturally affirmative' therapy (Glickman & Harvey, 2013); for interpreters and therapists to engage in a dynamic process by working collaboratively (Napier & Cornes, 2004); and dictionaries of signs for mental health terminology developed by deaf mental professionals have been published in book and video formats (e.g. Klein, 2000).

Nevertheless, deaf people needing to access mental health services experience a double stigmatisation because of their mental health issue and their deafness (Kyle, 2012). There is the added complication of how to assess deaf sign language users with standardised instruments that have been normed on hearing, speaking populations (Cornes, Rohan, Napier & Rey, 2006; Rogers et al., 2013a), so any adaptation or translation needs to be considered very carefully to ensure that the signed questions are culturally appropriate, not leading, but still elicit the required responses for the purposes of assessment (Graybill et al., 2010; Montoya et al., 2004; Rogers, Young, Lovell & Evans, 2013b).

For obvious reasons, to date there have not yet been any discourse analytic studies of mental health sign language discourse, but there has been confirmation that deaf people with mental health issues display dysfluencies in their signing (Glickman & Crump, 2013), that conditions such as autism spectrum disorder or dementia can affect sign language acquisition or sign language use (Shield & Meier, 2014; Spanjer, Fieret & Baker, 2014), and that clinicians are still getting to grips with how pre-lingually profoundly deaf schizophrenics 'hear' voices in their heads when experiencing hallucinations (Atkinson, 2006; Du Feu & Chovaz, 2014; Du Feu & McKenna, 1999).

5.4.4 Sign language on television

Article 30 of the United Nations Convention on the Rights of Persons with Disabilities (UNCRPD; United Nations, 2006) makes reference to the need to ensure access to the cultural life. Paragraph 30.1 notes that 'State Parties recognize the right of persons with disabilities to take part on an equal basis with others in cultural life ...'

In the 21st century, access to cultural life includes access to the media. While some broadcasters address the issue of access by providing subtitling, the issue of literacy arises: Many deaf people cannot access content meaningfully when it is presented in written form (Conrad, 1979; Powers, Gregory & Thoutenhoofd, 1998). Apart from this, there is also the question of ensuring that sign language programming features (or continues to feature) in mainstream media.

Although it is no longer questionable whether deaf viewers should be given access to television (Neves, 2007), the actual level of access to the media is a bone of contention for signing communities, and programming in sign languages is still, relatively speaking, rare (EUD, 2001; Kyle & Allsop, 1997). While the 'Sign On Europe' project had as its focus the status of sign languages in Europe, some relevant questions regarding television were included. The project sample included interviews with more 300 deaf people in 17 countries, using an age and gender-balanced sampling procedure. Deaf people from the UK, Germany and Scandinavia reported that television programmes for the signing community existed in their countries, while in Spain, Greece, France and Belgium, deaf people did not believe they had provision for signed programming on television (Kyle & Allsop, 1997).

Given the study's focus on the status of sign languages, questions to explore perceptions of the 'purity' of the sign language presented on television were included. Ninety per cent of deaf respondents said that they wanted deaf presenters to sign like deaf people; that is, by using a national or regional sign language rather than a signed form of a spoken language. However, Kyle and Allsop (1997) report that this priority was not shared by the mostly hearing-led organisations who responded to the same questions.

Indeed, while there are legal requirements that 5% of British programming be available in sign language (Ofcom, 2007, 2012), subtitling is the most common response to the provision of access to the media. For example, the British Broadcasting Company (BBC), a public service provider, has been subtitling programmes since the 1980s and today aims to ensure that all programmes are subtitled.[6]

In contrast, other broadcasters are required to meet the standards set by Ofcom, the independent regulator and competition authority for the UK communications industries, who are required to set 10-year targets for subtitling, signing and audio description ('television access services') as well as 5-year targets for subtitling. They note: 'The statutory targets for broadcasters are expressed as percentages of the service, including all programmes other than advertisements and programmes that have been excluded... They rise from a low level to the ten-year targets prescribed by the Act, that is eighty per cent (80%) for subtitling, five per cent (5%) for signing and ten per cent (10%) for audio description'.[7]

In the U.S., the default is also to provide subtitled programming. However, in a recent court case, a group of Californian deaf people took a case against CNN for not providing closed captioning for news video clips on their website, which they argued was a breach of state law. CNN argued that they provide closed captions on television, as required by federal law, but its CNN.com website, which includes most of its programming, does not caption video segments. The network argued that closed captioning can cause delays and inaccuracies and should be imposed, if at all, only by federal government regulations that cover all online news outlets.[8]

In contrast to the widespread production of subtitled programming, the provision of sign language on television is much more restricted. Ofcom notes that there are two approaches to signing on television: sign-interpreted programmes and sign-presented programmes. Sign-interpreted programmes show a signer, usually in the corner of the screen, who interprets what is happening in the main picture (these interpreters can be deaf or hearing; De Meulder & Heyerick, 2013; see Chapter 6, Section 6.5.1 for more discussion), while sign-presented programmes are presented in sign language and dubbed in English, often with subtitles. Ofcom notes that there are currently very few examples of sign-presented programmes, and they cite the BBC's *See Hear* programme as the best-known British example (which has been broadcast for over 30 years).

Following on from consultation with deaf audiences, Ofcom reports a community preference for investing resources in sign-presented programming rather than sign-interpreted programming on what are considered to be low-audience channels. However, they also report that broadcasters are reluctant to take this approach, citing cost and lack of appeal to mainstream audiences amongst their concerns (Ofcom, 2007). Indeed, they note that some broadcasters who attracted low deaf audience numbers felt that they should be exempt from having to provide any sign language content at all (Ofcom, 2007). Given this, from 1 January 2009, Ofcom modified the requirements for the provision of sign language on television in the UK. They did the following:

(1) Excluded channels other than public service channels with an audience share of between 0.05% and 1% from obligations to meet signing targets specified in the Code on Television Access Services (Ofcom, 2012)

(2) Required excluded channels to transmit a minimum of 30 minutes of sign-presented programming each month between the hours of 7 a.m. and 11 p.m. (as requested by deaf viewers) unless the broadcasters in question proposed alternative arrangements that would better serve sign language–using deaf people

Interestingly, given the critical mass of the signing population in the U.S. and the prevalence of sign language teaching and research, there is currently no sign language programming at all in the States, either through sign-presented or sign-interpreted programmes (with the exceptional case of State emergency notifications); but sign-interpreted programmes are broadcast in China, South Africa, Kosovo, across the Arabic world and in the UK, Ireland and Belgium.

There have been conflicting reports about the efficacy of sign-interpreted television. Steiner (1998) conducted a study with deaf BSL users to ascertain their levels of comprehension and preferences of sign language production on television by (hearing) interpreters. He recorded 70 hours of signed data and created individual profiles for each signer on a sample tape as well as a thorough description of a respondent group. He then showed video footage to three groups (deaf SSE users, deaf BSL users, and a non-signing hearing group), and carried out a comprehension test. His findings revealed that deaf people did not always understand the signers on television and had clear preferences for which ones they preferred. This finding is also being borne out in more recent work in China, where deaf people assert that the sign language used by (hearing) interpreters on television does not reflect the language used by deaf people in the signing community and that the provision of sign-interpreted programmes satisfies the Chinese government agenda but not the needs of the community (Zhao, 2015; Xiao, Chen & Palmer, 2015; Xiao & Li, 2013; Xiao & Yu, 2009).

Taking a linguistic perspective, Stone (2009) compared deaf and hearing signers' rendering of English broadcast television news into BSL and suggested that deaf translators/interpreters producing signed texts in the media employ a 'Deaf translation norm' and use particular strategies (for example, preparing 'aloud' and making target language decisions on the basis of their imagined audience) to shape their BSL text so that the evidence of translation is more covert.

A recent study, conducted by Wehmeyer (2014), used eye tracking software to examine the viewing habits of deaf and hearing adults while they watched interpreted news broadcasts in South Africa. The study revealed that deaf viewers primarily focus on the interpreter and secondarily access picture material but make very little use of subtitles or lip-reading. In contrast, hearing viewers prioritise pictorial content but also spend significant proportions of time examining subtitles, lip-reading and even watching the interpreter. Wehmeyer (2014) found that viewing patterns seem to be dependent on pictorial information density rather than comprehension. Her study confirms that the interpreter functions as a primary source for deaf viewers, but it also questions the efficiency of subtitling as an alternative information source for deaf viewers if an interpreter is present.

The other side of service provision and the statutory provisions that surround this entails consideration of the deaf actors and presenters, newsreaders and weather reporters who are effectively the public face of the signing community. There is also a small but highly skilled number of TV production professionals who are deaf who help shape the way sign language on television is presented. For example, the British company Remark! (now Flashing Lights), which was originally founded by two deaf men, is staffed predominantly by deaf BSL users in various TV production roles and makes a range of television content created and presented in BSL, including children's programmes, documentaries, current affairs and lifestyle programmes.[9] There are also increasing numbers of internet-based sign-presented programmes that have all deaf crews and presenters, such as H3, which broadcasts a range of programmes in International Sign.[10]

Perhaps the best-known deaf signing actor is the American Marlee Matlin, who won both the Oscar and Golden Globe Awards for Best Actress in 1987 for her role in *Children of a Lesser God*. Recently, she has appeared in the award-winning television series *The West Wing* and *Switched at Birth*.

Quote 5.21　On being a successful deaf actor

Every one of us is different, but for those of us who are more different, we have to put more effort into convincing the less different that we can do the same thing that they can, just differently. (Marlee Matlin, www.marleematlinsite.com)

5.4.5　Sign language in politics

Quote 5.22　Vote for whom?

I vote but I don't have the information [about] who I am voting for. (individual respondent, UK; cited in Pabsch, 2014, p. 79)

I am strongly interested in politics because it is very important to remind those lawmakers and politicians not to ignore those deaf and hard of hearing people. (individual respondent, Iceland; cited in Pabsch, 2014, p. 79)

...rendering the public sphere penetrable through the vehicle of sign language is a *sine qua non* for meaningful active citizenship on the part of Deaf people. (Turner & Napier 2014, p. 62)

The past 50 years have seen significant shifts in the fortunes of deaf people in Europe (Pabsch, 2014b; Turner & Napier, 2014) and the rest of the world, who are increasingly engaged in political activism: campaigning and protesting the status quo that saw them through the lens of a deficit model (see e.g. Ladd, 2003; Lane, 2008). At its most basic, participation in political life can be said to be an issue of citizenship, but even here, there are barriers that must be overcome to ensure that the public sphere is equally accessible to signing communities (Buxton, 2014; Costello, 2014; Emery, 2009; Gast & Nachtrab, 2014; Kósa, 2014; Stevens, 2014; Turner & Napier, 2014).

Emery (2009) following Faulks (2002), argues that despite significant advancements with regard to participatory citizenship, especially in terms of rights, responsibilities, recognition and respect, there is still a way to go to ensure that appropriate resources are invested in ensuring deaf participation in civil society.

Quote 5.23   On receiving and producing political meaning

Above all, if Deaf people were to be afforded full access to national and supranational public spheres – so that they could both 'receive' meaning from the political messages presented to other citizens, and 'produce' meaning, i.e. inject their own socio-culturally distinct contributions into public discourse – then they would need the resources either to be granted more effective educational opportunities (so that they could acquire literacy in the majority languages of their polities); or robust and communicatively efficient interpreting services; or – most likely – some combination of the two. (Turner & Napier, 2014, p. 63)

In practical terms, participation requires the provision of high-quality sign language interpreting and access to reliable technologies to support interaction between deaf citizens, public officers and elected representatives to create an effective 'third space' for deaf-hearing engagement (Turner & Napier, 2014). Work towards this goal took place with a European Commission–funded project, INSIGN, whose goal was to work to improve communication between deaf and hard of hearing persons and the EU institutions. The project took account the use of national sign languages and captioning (real-time text communication), as these are the main communication tools for deaf and hard of hearing citizens.[11] Project partners included the EUD, Designit, IVéS, SignVideo, Heriot-Watt University and efsli.

EUD report that there are almost 1 million deaf people in Europe, and for these communities, the spoken language of their country or region remains a foreign or second language. While deaf, hard of hearing and hearing signers can communicate across language boundaries amongst themselves because they may be bilingual in a number of sign languages or because they draw on International Sign for cross-linguistic engagement, a serious challenge remains in trying to integrate into educational, social and work environments, as the vast majority of non-deaf Europeans do not have signing skills.

This communication barrier also exists when deaf sign language users or hard of hearing citizens try to communicate with the European Union institutions. As the vast majority of individuals who work in the EU institutions use oral languages, sign language interpreters need to be called on, or it is possible to provide real-time text solutions (Pabsch, 2014a).

EUD notes that the organisation of sign language interpretation for each European sign language is complex, requiring advanced planning and booking, coordination and the cost of human resources (including travel and accommodation for interpreters), as well as the in-house infrastructure required to administer such provision. Given this, the INSIGN project worked towards a Real-Time Sign Language Application and Service in a bid to redress the current lack of direct communication access for deaf or hard of hearing citizens to Members of the European Parliament and the institutions of the European Union (Skinner, Napier & Turner, in press).

The other part of this story is that of representation. Recent years have also seen a rise in the visibility of deaf politicians in the mainstream political world. For example, several countries have seen deaf parliamentarians and/or senators elected (Belgium, Iceland, Canada, South Africa and Uganda), and there are currently two deaf Members of the European Union: Dr Adam Kosa (Hungary), serving his second term, and Ms Helga Stevens (Belgium).

Case study 5.9   Adam Kosa, MEP

Dr Adam Kosa is Europe's first deaf Member of the European Parliament (MEP), elected in 2009 as a representative of Hungary. He notes: 'Before my arrival, no one ever imagined that a signing deaf [person] could be an MEP at all. No one knew how to deal with me. Some people tried to speak louder or others started to write everything down on pieces of papers.'

Dr Kosa reports that sign language interpreters are seen as personal assistants rather than as 'real' interpreters/translators in the European Parliament, which creates difficulties. He also notes that it is difficult to schedule meetings with English- or French-speaking MEPs as there is no official International Sign interpretation provided in the European Parliament. As a result, his team experiences an additional administrative burden as they have to explain the linguistic situation several times a day in response to requests for meetings with Dr Kosa, which takes away time from their professional and legislation-related work.

Dr Kosa, who is President of the parliament's Disability Intergroup, was voted MEP of the Year in 2013. He reports that despite the challenges he faces, he has not experienced any negative attitudes. He reports that on his arrival in Brussels, 'No one knew that different sign languages can be found in each and every EU member state. No one realised that there are existing obligations and needs to be met which have been enforced by the new UN Convention on the Rights of

Persons with Disability since 2006. The EU itself is a party to the Convention since 2010, which means that it is obliged to provide disabled people with reasonable accommodation: in my case, with sign language interpretation.'
In 2014, Dr Kosa was re-elected to the European Parliament for a second term of office. (http://bxlconnect.com/interview-adam-kosa-member-european-parliament/)

Despite this situation, the general consensus is that there is a gap between the concerns of signing communities and their mostly hearing elected representatives, not least with regard to the need to provide appropriately qualified interpreters for political event. This issue came to the world's attention in December 2013 when a 'fake interpreter', Mr Thamsanqa Jantjie, was hired to interpret at Nelson Mandela's memorial service in Soweto (see Chapter 6, Section 6.2.1, for more detailed discussion). Deaf South Africans highlighted the problem immediately, utilising social media to bring attention to the fact that the 'interpreter' was simply waving his hands and producing gobbledygook. The World Federation of the Deaf and the World Association of Sign Language Interpreters issued a joint statement on the matter, including the extract included in Quote 5.24 below.

Quote 5.24 **Responsible responses required**

It is the responsibility of organisers to ensure that access to information is guaranteed for a deaf audience. Article 21 of the UN Convention on the Rights of Persons with Disabilities (UNCRPD) points out that deaf people have a right to choose their form of communication and State Parties shall ensure 'accepting and facilitating the use of sign languages…and all other accessible means of communication of their choice by persons with disabilities in official interactions'. The same article advises that State Parties shall take all appropriate measures to ensure recognizing and promoting the use of sign languages. Further the Article 9 of UNCRPD requires 'State Parties to take appropriate measures to ensure to persons with disabilities access on an equal basis with others…to information and communications …' This means professional sign language interpreters, who know the national sign language and deaf culture. (http://wfdeaf.org/news/wfd-wasli-joint-statement-about-the-sign-language-interpretation-at-mandelas-memorial-service)

They further underlined the need to co-operate with local deaf organisations, and like Turner and Napier (2014), stressed the need for trained, qualified interpreters to be used. Savvalidou (2010) has highlighted how difficult it is to interpret political talking strategies into sign language, so it is essential that the most qualified interpreters work in this domain. The

WFD and WASLI also call for access that is based on direction from deaf people. In short, the WFD/WASLI response calls for implementation of the '5 Rs' to which Emery (2009) referred: rights, responsibilities, recognition, respect and resources.

These 'Rs' can also be considered with respect to the fundamental respect required for sign languages, as evidenced by Case Study 3.2 (discussed in Chapter 3) with respect to the attempted standardisation and unification of a Pan-Arab Sign Language.

5.4.6   Sign language in the workplace

The emergence of a deaf professional class in the past 20–30 years (in North America) contrasts with more recent developments in other parts of the world (Hauser, Finch & Hauser, 2008; Padden & Humphries, 2005). Given this, plus evidence that deaf people are typically under-employed (Conroy, 2006; Kyle & Allsop, 1997), are 4 times more likely to be unemployed in a recession and are more likely to live in relative poverty (Conama & Grehan, 2002), this section looks at deaf people in the workplace and considers factors relating to language practices that promote or impede deaf people's participation.

Furthermore, this section offers a comparison of deaf people's access to workplace discourse as compared to hearing counterparts, given the recognition of the importance of language in the workplace to achieve transactional and relational goals (Holmes & Stubbe, 2015.

The wider acceptance of sign languages has led to an opening up of access to university and professional education for deaf people (as discussed earlier in this chapter). In turn, this has made available new pathways to employment, which contrast from those which deaf students of the 19th and 20th Century were veered towards. In the past, the discouragement (or, indeed, complete banning) of sign language in school was often extended to the workplace, with educators of the deaf advising employers to discourage fraternisation amongst deaf employees and to promote oral interaction (McDonnell & Saunders, 1993). However, sign language users continue to experience both increased unemployment (RNID, 2006) and underemployment rates (Conroy, 2006) vis-à-vis the non-deaf population.

In many countries, where deaf people are in employment, there are statutory systems that assess the need for reasonable accommodations to support access – for example, the Access to Work (AtW) scheme in the UK provides BSL–English interpreters as well as adaptations to workplace premises and equipment, amongst other things (Dickinson, 2010). Dickinson (2010) notes that while employers seem to assume that the AtW scheme provides adequately for supporting access to communication and information for deaf employees, the evidence suggests that this is not the case (see Quote 5.25).

Quote 5.25   Access to interpreters in the workplace

...the current shortage of BSL/English interpreters...means that deaf employees are struggling to secure adequate interpreting services, despite being eligible for support under the scheme...If all deaf people were assessed under the AtW programme and allocated interpreter support, it would be impossible to match supply to demand...[with] statistics suggesting that one in five people who require an SLI at work do not have access to one. (Dickinson, 2010, p. 51)

Coupled with attitudes that see deaf people as 'other' (Ladd, 2003), who require services to resolve what are perceived as problems in communication (Kyle & Allsop, 1997), the ideal of ensuring equality of access to the workplace has yet to be matched by attitudinal shifts and appropriate levels of resourcing (Dickinson, 2010). Despite the limitations that exist in the UK, levels of state-funded provision there exceed those in many European countries.

Even where legislation exists, such as the Americans with Disabilities Act (1990), this issue of reasonable accommodation is one which some fear may prove burdensome. It is suggested that in fact the ADA inhibits the employment of deaf people (see Quote 5.26).

Quote 5.26   Americans with disabilities act: what were they thinking?

I do feel that it may have prevented them [potential employers] from hiring the likes of us for two reasons: the cost of accommodation and the fear of lawsuits. That just makes it worse than it was before the ADA.

I believe ADA does more harm than good to people with disabilities. It forces employers to be responsible to pay out of their pockets for disabled employees' technology assistance and access accommodation. Therefore it makes persons with disabilities less competitive than their counterparts without disabilities. So, wasn't it a smart decision to enact this type of law? What were they thinking, really? (posted by Sarah Terras, http://deafcantgetjobs.blogspot.ie/2013/04/does-americans-with-disabilities-act.html, 10 April 2013).

A key aspect of sign language in the workplace that has received recent research attention is the role of interpreters in employment settings, with discussion of what interpreter provision practices may help or hinder the employment progress of deaf sign language users (Bristoll, 2009; Dickinson & Turner, 2008; Dickinson, 2010, 2014).

The demand for sign language interpreter-mediation in workplace contexts has meant that deaf professionals, as consumers of interpreting

services, are beginning to redefine what they want and need from interpreters. When working with deaf professionals, interpreters are required
to work in situations where the typical interpreting dynamic is reversed.
The inherent requirements of the work of deaf professionals means that
they regularly give formal presentations at conferences or seminars and
are in positions of power where they are giving, rather than receiving,
advice. Thus, deaf professionals are moving towards working with the same
interpreter(s) regularly, working with them closely to negotiate their needs
to achieve their desired outcomes, and thus co-construct. This model of
interpreting is defined as the *deaf professional-designated interpreter model*
(Hauser & Hauser, 2008).

As well as interpreting for professional consultations, meetings and presentations, the designated interpreter may also be required to work with
deaf professionals in social networking situations. When providing *diplo-
matic* or *escort* interpreting (Napier, McKee & Goswell, 2010) in this context,
the interpreter accompanies one client at an event (such as a conference
dinner) and provides a personal interpreting service throughout their interaction with others. The interpreter's main function is to enable the client
to socialise as smoothly as possible. Sign language interpreters may also be
expected to convey informal 'water-cooler' chit-chat that can be overheard
in the corridor, so that the deaf professional can keep up with the workplace
dynamics.

Dickinson's (2014) work has made a seminal contribution to the field of
applied sign linguistics by drawing on the framework of linguistic ethnography (Rampton et al., 2004) to analyse interpreter diaries, observations of
interpreter-mediated communication and general interaction between deaf
and hearing employees and interpreters in the workplace. She identified that
interpreters in workplace settings have the additional task of negotiating
disparate perceptions of workplace norms and practices, and she suggests
that the social interaction between employees, the unwritten patterns and
rules of workplace behaviour, hierarchical structures and the changing
dynamic of the deaf employee/interpreter relationship all place constraints
upon the interpreter's role and their interpreting performance.

5.5   Sign language in everyday life: concluding comments

In this chapter, we have concentrated our discussion on where and how sign
language is used in everyday life. We gave an overview of how and where
children and adults use sign language in various contexts, with a particular
focus on sign language in school and tertiary education. We also explored
how sign language is used in the wider world in various institutional and
workplace contexts, including legal, medical and mental health settings,
media politics and the workplace. One clear thread throughout this chapter
is the fact that sign language is used everywhere. When fluent signers come

together, sign language is employed in all types of discourse. Sometimes there are challenges when sign language is used in mainstream settings, where the majority of people do not use sign language, so some form of mediated communication is required. It is this mediated communication that we explore further in Chapter 6.

Further Reading

Brennan, M. (1999). Signs of injustice. *The Translator, 5*(2), 221–246.

Dickinson, J. (2014). *Sign language interpreting in the workplace.* Coleford: Douglas McLean.

Hauser, P., Finch, K., & Hauser, A. (Eds). (2008). *Deaf professionals and designated interpreters: A new paradigm.* Washington, DC: Gallaudet University Press.

Nicodemus, B., & Metzger, M. (Eds). (2014). *Investigations in healthcare interpreting.* Washington, DC: Gallaudet University Press.

Russell, D., & Hale, S. (Eds). (2008). *Interpreting in legal settings.* Washington DC: Gallaudet University Press.

6
Sign Language in (Professional) Practice

'Social, intercultural and technological developments have had a far-reaching impact on the landscape of translation [and interpreting] practices. New activities are emerging, peripheral ones are gaining visibility and the discipline of translation [and interpreting] studies faces conceptual and methodological challenges in accommodating these developments'. (Wurm, 2014, p. 1)

Previous chapters have discussed sign language and identity, how sign language is learned and taught and how it is used in everyday life. Building on these previous chapters as a foundation, we now move to the exploration of sign language in practice in terms of communication and mediation. This chapter focuses primarily on the work of deaf and hearing applied sign language professionals – interpreters and translators – in various contexts. We begin by exploring 'natural' sign language interpreters and translators – those who have grown up in the signing community as sign language brokers – before giving an overview of sign language interpreters and translators as language professionals and discussing typical and changing practices.

6.1 Sign language brokers

In Chapter 3 (Section 3.15), we discussed hearing people who have grown up with deaf parents (Codas). Ninety percent of children born to deaf couples can hear (Buchino, 1993). The small minority of deaf people who have deaf parents may also refer to themselves as Codas, but some refer to themselves as Dodas (Deaf of Deaf Adult; Jeff McWhinney, personal communication, 31 May 2013). More recently, Napier (2014b) has suggested a new term, PDF – People from Deaf Families – in order to recognise both children and adults, hearing or deaf, who grow up using sign language at home and to acknowledge that there are people who grow up in families with older siblings or other family members who are deaf, and therefore they too may have grown up using sign language on a regular basis and would consider themselves to be bilingual (see Quote 6.1).

Quote 6.1   Coda comfort

I am a 'Coda', but I have never felt comfortable with the term, as I have written elsewhere (Napier, 2008). Firstly, I am not a child, and my parents are not just 'adults', they are my parents. I don't mind being identified as someone who grew up in the Deaf community, in fact I am proud of my language and cultural heritage, but the term 'Coda' conjures up too many pejorative connotations about kids taking on responsibilities to 'take care' of their parents from a young age through brokering...

I suggest a new, more all-encompassing, convention – to refer to 'People from Deaf Families' (PDFs), which includes deaf or hearing people that have grown up using sign language regularly with one or more deaf members of their family. This term includes *both* deaf and hearing people, and also does not distinguish between children or adults, and does not focus only on people that have deaf parents... (Jemina Napier, http://lifeinlincs.org/2014/10/28/whats-in-a-name/)

The profile of bilingual individuals is complex and diverse (Hoffman, 1991; Romaine, 1995), and we have discussed sign language bilingualism in detail in Chapter 4 in the context of learning signed languages. It is important to contextualise the discussion of sign language brokering within the wider context of bilingualism and language brokering in general, so we can see how this phenomena is situated as an applied linguistic activity.

Bilinguals' language usage varies according to how they acquired their languages; whether they acquired their languages naturalistically or formally, simultaneously from birth or consecutively; whether they have bilingual proficiency in reading, writing, listening and speaking; and their degree of biculturalism (Hamers & Blanc, 2000). It is also known that bilinguals generally use each of their languages in different domains and may not have equivalent proficiency in all domains (Baker, 2011; Myers-Scotton, 2006).

Bilinguals can be defined in 2 ways: (1) *elective bilinguals*, who choose to become bilingual, and (2) *circumstantial bilinguals*, who are forced to be bilingual due to life circumstances (Angelelli, 2010). Elective bilinguals generally learn their second language through formal education or by choosing to travel and spend time in a country with a different language. On the other hand, circumstantial bilinguals are typically forced to learn a new language because they relocate to a place in which their home language is not the same as that of the new society. They must learn the society's language to function at large while maintaining their home language to communicate with their family and its language community. The relationship to the community is different for each group of bilinguals. According to Angelelli (2010), elective bilinguals typically become bilingual as an individual and do not identify with the second-language community. On the other hand, circumstantial bilinguals are a part of a community of second-language users and identify with that community while learning their new language

When considering the status of PDFs as bilinguals in signing communities, these children do not really fit either traditional definitions of elective or circumstantial bilingualism, as they do not choose to learn a signed language, but neither are they forced to relocate to a new society. Napier (in press) has argued that people who grow up using a sign language at home should indeed be considered circumstantial bilinguals, as their language situation is dictated by the fact that members of the family cannot communicate with the wider community; therefore, their bilingualism is brought about by the circumstances of their home life, but not by relocation.

Due to the fact that professional sign language interpreters are now widely available to provide access to a range of public service settings (see Section 6.1.2), it should not be necessary for deaf parents to rely on their hearing children to facilitate communication for them. However, anecdotally, we know that even if deaf parents discourage their children from doing so, sometimes their children will step in and assist as non-professional interpreters (see Quote 6.2).

Quote 6.2   Codas responsibility

My children are CODAs. Gary and I have worked hard to try and minimise any responsibility they might feel in having deaf parents. We have heard from others how they had to interpret for their parents growing up, how they grew up too soon, how they shouldered more responsibility.

In the age of the [National Relay Text Telephone Service] and access to qualified interpreters, mobile text messaging amongst other things, there just is not any reason to subject our children to being our communicators.

Despite our best efforts sometimes, we do fall into that trap. The phone rings and it is not a text-based call. The boys have to answer it. I might be talking to someone at the shop and not understand a particular phrase. Sometimes the boys step in. It is not ideal and we try to minimise it. They should be children and not taking on any extra responsibility just because we are deaf. (Deaf Auslan user Marnie Kerridge, *CODAs: The Rebuttal*, 2011)

It is widely recognised that bilingual children are natural interpreters and translators who assist their parents in a 'child language brokering' (CLB) role where 'in first and second generation immigrant families, parents may have little or no competency in the majority language. Therefore, their children act as interpreters in a variety of contexts' (Baker, 2003, p. 104). When families migrate to a new country, children often become proficient in the host language at a faster rate than their parents (Antonini & Torresi, 2012), which explains why they take on this CLB role and may continue to see the role taken on by intergenerational family members (Del Torto, 2008, 2010). The term 'brokering' (rather than 'interpreting') is used specifically in relation to CLB as it 'focuses attention on the whole cultural meaning of such an event, in which any interpretation is simply a part' (Hall, 2004, p. 285).

In a review of the CLB literature, Hall and Guery (2010) note that children act as brokers in a wide range of settings and that research on CLB makes an important contribution to our understanding of children and families generally. Research has been conducted with children from immigrant families in the UK and U.S. that are Chinese (Hall & Sham, 2007), Vietnamese (Tse, 1996), Pakistani (Hall, 2004), Hispanic/Latino/Mexican (Dorner, Orellana & Jimenez, 2008; Orellana, 2009; Valdes et al., 2003; Weisskirch, 2005), Moroccan (García Sánchez, 2010) and from the former USSR (Jones & Trickett, 2005). Studies have also been carried out in the UK (Cline, Crafter, O'Dell & de Abreu, 2011; Cline, Crafter & Propokiou, in press), Italy (Antonini & Torresi, 2012; Cirillo, Torresi & Valentini, 2010) and Germany (Degener, 2010; Guske, 2010; Meyer et al., 2010).

CLB research tends to focus on the role of children in brokering between their parents and/or other family members as minority language users and majority language users within public institutions. Children have been found to broker in various institutional and public service contexts (McQuillan & Tse, 1995), including schools (Cline, Crafter & Propokiou, in press), with mixed feelings about their experiences, sometimes feeling empowered and at other times burdened (Orellana, Dorner & Pulido, 2003).

For example, in a study of Chinese children in the U.S., Tse (1996) found that only 8% of the children reported that they did not do any brokering, with several of them indicating an older sibling did the brokering. Of the categories provided to indicate whom they had brokered for, from highest to lowest were parents, friends, relatives, siblings, neighbours, teachers and a few others. The sites they brokered in, from highest to lowest responses, were home, school, store, post office, bank and government offices. The majority of respondents reported that they had commenced their CLB role within one year of arriving in the U.S. In a similar study in the U.S., Weisskirch and Alva (2002) examined CLB experiences among 36 Mexican American children and found that all participants undertook CLB in some form, with the most frequent being translation of notes or letters from school, utility bills and medical forms and bills. The majority of CLB occurred for parents, followed by brokering for other relatives and on the phone.

In ad hoc situations, and when professional interpreters are not available, bilingual children take on the responsibility to facilitate communication. While these bilinguals can choose not to take on this role, it means that they know the individuals will be deprived of access to information if they decline. Inevitably, because they identify so closely with these individuals, it is almost impossible for them to stand by and watch this happen (Angelelli, 2010).

6.1.1   Hearing sign language brokers

Many PDFs act in a CLB role for their deaf parents and other deaf family members, and their involvement in this applied linguistic practice can be a shaping aspect of their lives (Napier, in press, in prep; Preston, 1996; Williamson, 2012). Typically the eldest hearing female child functions as the family broker (Singleton & Tittle, 2000), although this is not always the case (Napier, in press), and some choose to become professional sign language interpreters (Napier, 2008, in press). In spite of this common situation, virtually no research has been conducted specifically on CLB experiences in signing communities.

What little discussion has occurred has taken place within the context of examining hearing Coda experiences of growing up in signing communities, how they feel about their identity (see Section 3.1.5) and how brokering ('interpreting') has formed a part of that experience (Adams, 2008; Preston, 2004, 2006), or in the context of communication practices within families and language ideologies (Pizer, Walters & Meier, 2012).

Adams (2008) considers that hearing Coda experiences are unique; however, given what we know from the available CLB literature, it appears that this is not the case. Napier's (2013a, 2014b, in press, in prep) study of PDFs as sign language brokers confirms that their experience mirrors that of other children growing up speaking a minority language at home (see Case study 6.1, in Section 6.1.2), and this practice is not restricted only to children – many adult PDFs also broker for their parents in situations where professional interpreters are not available (see Quote 6.3). Napier (2014, in prep) suggests that rather than the brokering role being 'foisted' upon them by their parents, as has been previously suggested (Adams, 2008; Preston, 1994), children often offer to broker from a natural desire to help and to co-operate (see Example 6.1), although Quote 6.3 illustrates the fact that there are still some situations where PDFs feel they have no choice.

Quote 6.3   One Coda's experience

Matt Dixon is the only hearing person in his family. His parents, along with his brother Simon and sister Rebecca, are deaf. Being the only hearing person in the family, Matt had been used to interpreting English into sign language and vice versa, but never before had he been asked to interpret on a matter of life or death. It was Halloween 2008 and Matt received a text from his sister telling him that his father had collapsed and was in hospital. Matt dropped everything to be at the hospital as quickly as possible...

'Dad had been told that he had secondary cancer of the liver. He had always been a best friend to me, my brother and my sister and he was putting a brave face on it for our benefit.'...Matt remembers how the cancer centre handled the issue of booking further interpreters for his dad. 'They asked me to do it and I said

I would but only if there were no interpreters available. For all the scans, blood tests and the chemotherapy that followed they never ever booked an interpreter for him again – even though written on the front of Dad's file, in big red felt pen, it said: PROFOUNDLY DEAF.

'At the first chemotherapy appointment my dad was all smiles. I asked the receptionist who the interpreter was and she replied "Oh, really sorry, we can't get one." I just had to go with the flow. I was used to it from my life communicating for my family and I didn't know about the Equality Act back then, all that I was bothered about was my dad.

'I asked them to book an interpreter for the next appointment but they didn't and that next appointment was for the results of a scan following the first chemotherapy treatment. It was an important meeting to see if the cancer had spread or not. I relayed to my dad, acting once again as his interpreter, that the cancer had not grown.'

There was a telling early-warning sign that the failure to provide professional interpreters, especially where medicines were concerned, could have been dangerous in itself: 'The day after diagnosis, the doctor explained all the medication that my dad would have to take and there were 10 different tablets per day all at different times; it was complex,' said Matt.

'My sister Rebecca noticed that Dad wasn't taking his medication because he was confused. Looking back, I interpreted that meeting for my dad and although I understood what he needed to do – clearly he didn't. I used "family sign" (a term to describe a looser form of sign language used among family members) but not medical terms or the way to get across a complex situation, like an interpreter could.'

It took another appointment, this time with sister Rebecca and once again without an interpreter, for those potentially dangerous problems with medication to be resolved...

'We didn't complain, we're not the type of people to complain. Dad had a hard life and always got on with it. He was used to not having interpreters for GP appointments and I was used to doing it for him ...' (http://limpingchicken. com/2013/04/23/i-told-dad-his-battle-with-cancer-was-lost-because-the-nhs-didnt-provide-an-interpreter/)

Example 6.1   'Cute KODA in kindergarten holiday concert'

In December 2013, a 5-year old hearing PDF caused a sensation on YouTube, with over 8 million views of a video of her signing along in American Sign Language to a Christmas song while her parents were watching in the audience. The video received over 30,000 'likes' and over 2,500 comments about how amazing she was for providing this access for her parents. (www.youtube.com/ watch?v=zQeygYqOn8g)

The girl's father was quick to respond in a vlog post (now taken down) to the reactions to his daughter, to assure people that he and his wife never expected her to act as a broker:

'Claire's music teacher encouraged her to sign if she wanted, for her parents. It was up to Claire, and she wanted to. Just amazing. Some people have expressed concerns about using our daughter as our interpreter. No, that's definitely not

> the case. My wife and I have always agreed that since Claire is 5 years old, she will remain 5 years old...I expressly forbid her from interpreting for us...we don't allow that to happen. Absolutely not.'

6.1.2   Deaf sign language brokers

Furthermore, it is also evident that deaf people also often function as brokers, many of whom grow up in deaf families (Napier, in press). It has been reported that deaf people provided 'peer interpreting' for their class-mates when they were children in deaf schools and the teacher's signing could not be understood; that they have brokered for each other as adults by translating letters into sign language or writing letters from signed source texts; that they broker between their deaf friends and their hearing parents between a spoken and a signed language; that they broker between deaf friends and colleagues who use different signed languages and that they broker between their deaf parents and hearing professional interpreters in situations where their parents are vulnerable, such as at the doctor (Adam, Carty & Stone, 2011; Napier, in press, in prep).

In a study of 'ghostwriters' in Australia and the UK, Adam, Carty and Stone (2011) interviewed 8 deaf people who had performed language brok-ering throughout their lives and asked them to reflect on their experiences and motivations for brokering. They found that their participants brokered in the same range of general CLB contexts and were heavily invested in the role in terms of their linguistic and cultural capital. Their role as sign language brokers in the community is regarded as a form of reciprocation to the community and also as a form of leadership (see Quote 6.4).

Quote 6.4   Obligations

It was strongly felt by many of the interviewees that they had an obligation to use their knowledge of signed language, English, the Deaf community and the main-stream to benefit other Deaf people, to be role models and to pass on the Deaf value of collectivism to younger Deaf people. Some of the interviewees had learnt a sign language as a second language, because of a hearing family background or an oral education; these people indicated that their language brokering was a way to 'give back' to the Deaf Community, in return for being welcomed into the community and being given the opportunity to acquire a sign language. (Adam, Carty & Stone, 2011, p. 379)

One of the key differences, however, in the sign language brokering func-tion discussed by deaf people in Adam, Carty and Stone's study is that the deaf ghostwriters said that they never offered; they were always asked. This is the opposite of what is reported in Napier's study (2013a, in prep), who found that the hearing PDFs frequently and consistently *offered* to broker for their deaf parents (see Case study 6.1).

Case study 6.1   Sign language brokering

At the time of writing, Napier is in the process of conducting an ongoing study of sign language brokering, replicating existing CLB research with children from spoken language minority groups to compare and contrast their experiences, involving 5 key stages.

The first stage of the study (Napier, in press) involved an international survey of deaf and hearing PDFs through an online questionnaire, which replicated and adapted previous CLB surveys conducted by Tse (1996) and Weisskirch and Alva (2002). The survey sought answers to the following questions:

1. When, where and why do PDFs act as language brokers for their parents?
2. What are their comfort levels about their CLB experience?
3. How many PDF adults become professional interpreters, and why?
4. How many young PDFs plan to become professional interpreters?

A total of 240 responses were received from 14 different countries: 216 hearing respondents and 26 deaf respondents. The results confirmed that PDFs have very similar experiences to other child language brokers: 81% of the respondents reported that they regularly do language brokering, the majority of the time for parents and predominantly for their mothers. The most common language brokering contexts were at home (on the telephone, salespeople at the door, etc.), at the doctors and at the shops. One seemingly unique aspect of the PDF CLB experience is that they broker between family members at family events, perhaps between deaf parents and hearing grandparents who cannot sign. Generally, PDFs began to broker as early as 4 or 5 years old and feel proud of their brokering role. Almost 70% respondents were working as professional interpreters, but only 35% of the 20 young respondents aged 13–18 were considering a career as a professional interpreter.

The follow-up study (Napier, in prep) replicates the work of Orellana (2009) in conducting in-depth, qualitative interviews with a range of brokers. Eleven semi-structured interviews were conducted with 3 deaf and 8 hearing PDFs, aged 13–50, who had responded to the initial survey in Stage 1 and indicated their willingness to discuss their experiences in more depth. The discussion focussed on the nature of language brokering, where and how it happened and participants' feelings about why it happened, and the data was analysed using a narrative enquiry approach for key themes. Although some participants did report that they were asked to broker for their parents or other deaf family members, results reveal a clear theme of 'desire to help' and 'to be cooperative'. Many of the older participants also reported that they still broker for their parents as adults and that their feelings about their CLB experiences have changed over the years.

The next stage of the project, which took place in 2015, employed a multi-method approach, using visual research methods and vignette methodology to elicit the perceptions of young PDFs and deaf parents about brokering. This study replicates and combines the work of Antonini and Torresi (2012) on CLB in Italy (visual methods) and Crafter, de Abreu, Cline and O'Dell (2015) in examining

CLB experiences in schools in the UK (vignettes). Workshops were offered in collaboration with the organisations CODA UK & Ireland and Deaf Parenting UK. The young PDFs participated in an art workshop, where they were asked to draw pictures that depict how they feel about their language brokering experiences. In a separate workshop, their deaf parents were shown photos of various visual images and asked to select and explain the ones that best represent how they feel about their children brokering for them. Each workshop then involved a vignette task, where the deaf parents were presented with the same vignettes about young children brokering in various contexts and asked to respond about how they feel about the situation. Finally, the 2 groups were brought together to share their experience of the day and to discuss a 'take home' message.

The fourth stage of the project will involve ethnographic observations of PDFs in real brokering contexts with their parents (replicating the work of Orellana, 2009, and Valdes & Angelelli, 2003); the fifth and final stage will involve simulated interpreted tasks where young PDFs are asked to interpret for scenarios between deaf and hearing interlocutors, which are compared with the interpretations of professional interpreters in the same scenarios (replicating the work of Valdes & Angelelli, 2003, with Latino young people in America).

The exploration of CLB experiences of deaf and hearing PDFs is essential to understanding the integral role of interpreting and translation as an applied linguistic activity in signing communities. Although these brokers do not perform their role in a professional capacity, their experience and practice may well socialise them into a future role as professional interpreters and translators, as noted by Angelelli (2010) with other bilingual youngsters.

A study of 'deaf parented interpreters' experiences of accessing sign language interpreter training (Williamson, 2015) found that training courses do not always meet the needs of PDFs who do want to turn their language brokering practice into a professional career option, as most training courses are geared towards L2 sign language learners. These issues will be explored further in the next section, in consideration of sign language in professional practice (i.e. by interpreters and translators). Understanding the different types of bilinguals and their language practice is important in educating interpreting and translation students because their backgrounds and ideologies are very different (Angelelli, 2010; Napier, in press).

6.2   Sign language interpreting and translation (SL-IT)

Quote 6.5   Language use and bilinguals

Interpreter bilinguals, unlike regular bilinguals, will have to learn to use their languages (and the underlying skills that they have in them) for similar purposes, in similar domains of life, with similar people. This is something that regular bilinguals do not often need to do. (Grosjean, 1997, p. 168)

In Quote 6.5, Grosjean is referring to professional interpreters as 'interpreter bilinguals' and assumes that 'regular bilinguals' do not undertake an interpreting role. As seen in Section 6.1, however, this may not necessarily be the case, as we know that bilingual children often take on the role of interpreter or 'language broker' in their families. Sign language interpreting and translation as a professional practice has an important role in the everyday lives of deaf sign language users. As illustrated in Quotes 6.6 and 6.7, deaf people interact with the wider world via sign language interpreters in a wide range of settings.

Quote 6.6   Deaf people and sign language interpreters

Where two people need to communicate and do not have a language in common, an interpreter is required to enable communication. This often includes Deaf and hearing people or Deaf people from different countries. The interpreter's tasks are to facilitate communication without becoming personally involved in the interaction and to give both parties equal access to culturally appropriate information.

Sign language interpreters are needed in all aspects of life. Settings include schools, universities, courts, hospitals, conferences and theatres, as well as personal and business settings. Interpreting is also needed on television and in the media (including websites, web broadcasts, etc.) so that Deaf people may have equal access to information and entertainment. (World Federation of the Deaf; http://wfdeaf.org/our-work/focus-areas/education)

Quote 6.7   Different interpreters for different purposes

I use different interpreters for different work because of the varied nature of my position at Graeae. For board finance meetings I will select an interpreter who is good communicating that type of information and operates well in a business-like setting; for a schools workshop I will book an interpreter who is comfortable around young people and understands the dynamics of that environment. From my 25 years' experience working in the arts, I can safely say that different interpreters have different skills, and it is virtually impossible to find an interpreter who is ideal in every situation. (Jenny Sealey, deaf BSL user, Artistic Director of Graeae Theatre Company; www.disabilitynow.org.uk/article/access-work-deaf-employees-fear-future)

Although sign language professionals are embedded within the structure of everyday interactions within signing communities, there are many layers of complexity in relation to the professional role and function of interpreters and translators.

It is not within the scope of this book to explore the professional aspects of sign language interpreting and translation in detail; there are many other books and book chapters that explore these issues in depth, so we encourage readers to refer to the suggested further readings at the end of this chapter to learn more about the history of sign language interpreting and translation (SL-IT), the infrastructure and regulation of the profession and aspects of SL-IT education.

Instead, in this chapter we focus on SL-IT from an applied linguistic perspective, and we therefore pay more attention to the linguistic and sociocultural challenges faced by the community and sign language professionals in various contexts and to the performative aspects of professional SL-IT practice. In this section, we consider what it means to be a professional sign language interpreter. We also explore the emerging practice of professional sign language translation and the impact that this is having on signing communities, with further consideration given to changing SL-IT practices and the relationship between professional practice and technology.

6.2.1   What is professional sign language interpreting?

To contextualise the rest of the discussion of SL-IT in this chapter, we briefly discuss what is meant by professional sign language interpreting, in order to contrast the practice with the sign language brokering (non-professional interpreting) practice already considered in Section 6.1.

Quote 6.8   Sign language interpreting is...

Signed language interpreting (SLI) prototypically means interpreting between a signed language and another spoken or signed language, and is sometimes referred to as visual language interpreting. Sign language interpreters are employed in any context where deaf signers and non-deaf, non-signing 'hearing' people need to interact. One of the unique aspects of SLI is that it is often described as a 'cradle to grave' profession: even if deaf people are bilingual in a signed and a written/spoken language, interpreters will still accompany them in all aspects of their lives due to the fact that they cannot hear the majority spoken language...
(Napier & Leeson, 2015)

In some senses, the role of sign language interpreters is clear-cut, as illustrated in Quotes 6.6, 6.7 and 6.8: interpreters are required to engage in the practice of communicative mediation between deaf and hearing interlocutors in a range of contexts. However, it is not as straightforward as that. The sign language interpreting profession has evolved over time since the days that hearing church missioners used to broker for deaf people in a range of contexts as part of their wider role (Napier, 2011a; Napier & Leeson, 2015). The recognition of sign languages as legitimate languages, the various disability discrimination legislation in effect (see Chapter 2) along with the shift in thinking about deaf culture and identity (see Chapter 3), has led to the advent of hearing language service professionals – that is, professional interpreters – with a classified role who functioned differently from other professionals who continued in a 'helper' role (i.e. social workers; see Quote 6.9). Professional associations and Codes of Ethics were established, and interpreters were expected only to facilitate communication between deaf and hearing people and nothing more (Napier, McKee & Goswell, 2010).

Quote 6.9   Then and now ...

I grew up in a Deaf family, so my parents, grandparents and other family members were all Deaf ... We never had interpreters. Growing up, I never used interpreters. In those days there were no interpreters, only missioners, and they would be at the Deaf club and people would literally queue up and ask for their help. The missioners would accompany people to interviews, to court, to the doctor or the hospital to interpret for them, and they very much functioned in a 'helper' capacity. But for my family, we didn't want help, we felt we could do things ourselves, so my mother and other members of my family would write notes to the doctor or shopkeeper, or whomever they needed to communicate with, and they would carry around a special little notepad so that they could do that. So growing up I never had interpreters. Then once I got married and had children, I followed the same practice, I wrote notes and never used interpreters. Even when the missioner role changed to social workers, their goal was still to 'help' Deaf people and I didn't want help. The interpreter role still hadn't been separated out from the social worker role, so it was the social workers who did the interpreting and I didn't want social workers involved in my life, so I just wrote notes.

Also back then, although we used sign language we didn't call it 'BSL'. In formal situations, in public, we would use SSE and then more informally we would use BSL at home (although it wasn't called that); BSL was considered as just 'bad English', so as a result all the social workers used SSE when they were interpreting.

But around the 1980s, BSL was recognized as a language in its own right, and we realized that SSE was just 'signing in English word order' and was actually separate from BSL. Around the same time, the role of the interpreter got separated professionally from the role of the social worker, so Deaf people had the right to request an interpreter without necessarily needing 'help'. Agencies were established to provide interpreting services separate from social work services, so social workers could concentrate on helping those people that needed it, and interpreters just provided communication access. Even still, I continued to do without interpreters until I applied for a job at the City Lit in London, and they provided an interpreter (who used SSE) for the interview, and once I started working there we regularly booked external interpreters for staff meetings.

Although I was working with interpreters in my professional life, in my personal life I still relied on writing notes – that is, until one day I had to go to the hospital. I presented a pre-written note to the doctor to explain what was wrong with me, but she refused to read it! She walked out of the room and brought back a nurse who asked me if I could lip-read, and then proceeded to 'interpret' between me and the doctor! Next time I had to go back, I asked for a professional interpreter, and that was a first for me. So after that experience, I always make sure to book an interpreter when I go to the hospital because it's different compared to going to my local doctor who knows me well; at the hospital the doctors are always different. So now I am happy to accept that BSL interpreters are available to support me to communicate, but not to 'help' me.

Initially, professional interpreters mostly used SSE, but over time we saw a change and interpreters started to use more BSL. This was because linguistics research had identified that BSL has its own grammar and structure, so we started teaching BSL rather than SSE to sign language students. So because students were learning BSL, once they became interpreters they actually used BSL rather than SSE. Some of the 'old guard' interpreters, perhaps who had grown up with Deaf parents, still used SSE, but we did see a gradual change with newer interpreters using BSL.

We also witnessed a change in 'attitude' among interpreters, between the 'old' and 'new' model of interpreters. The old model, especially the missioners, would work tirelessly for Deaf people. They had what we would call 'Deaf heart'. Some of them had Deaf parents, but really they did their work out of affection for the Deaf community and were available any place, any time, for Deaf people. But the 'newer breed' of interpreters are more time conscious; they regard interpreting more as a professional job. Some of them do still hold that affection for the Deaf community and are involved in the community; but others don't, interpreting is their career and they do it to earn money, so once the interpreting assignment is finished they 'clock off' and leave and don't really mix much with the Deaf community. This is in stark contrast to the missioners of the old days who would spend hours at the Deaf club. There's definitely a difference between the 'old' and 'new' interpreters in their approach.

In considering the pros and cons of the old and new models of interpreting, the pros of the old missioner model were that they supported the goals and values of the Deaf community, and because they spent so much time with Deaf people on a daily basis, they were very fluent sign language users and sometimes it was difficult to tell if they were Deaf or hearing. But newer interpreters who have learned BSL as a second language typically use a 'hearing' dialect; you can tell that they are hearing when they sign; they are not as fluent. But the cons of the old missioner model are that they were often patronizing towards Deaf people, and assumed that they needed help; whereas a pro with newer interpreters is that they are more neutral, they are paid to do their job, to work 'for me' as an interpreter and that's it. But one of the inherent cons of the current model is less involvement in the Deaf community and less fluent signing skills. I should say that not all interpreters are like that now; there are many who are involved in the community. That's one of the key things now, there's a wider variety in the attitude and signing skills of interpreters compared to the old missioners, who were all a lot more consistent and similar in their attitude and sign language fluency. (Melinda Napier, deaf BSL user and former manager of sign language communication courses, Centre for Deaf Education, City Lit, London)

Many articles have been written about this shift to professionalisation (see Further Reading), so we will not discuss it in detail here. The key to defining professional sign language interpreting is that people are expected to achieve appropriate qualifications, certifications or licensure in order to practice and can expect to be suitably remunerated for their work. There are a range of routes to qualification depending on the country, with training ranging from ad hoc intensive courses to undergraduate and postgraduate programmes (see Napier, 2009a), and various mechanisms for testing inter-preter competence (Leeson, 2011; Pereira & Fronza, 2010; Sadlier, 2009). Funding is available in many countries through government departments to cover the costs of sign language interpreting provision in a range of public service settings, and depending on the level of regulation, interpreters either work in-house for public sector service providers or private fee-for-service agencies or they work freelance. Pay rates are typically determined by level of qualification and experience and can vary according to country and the cost of living in any given area, but rates can also be set by government bodies or other regulatory authorities.

From an applied linguistic perspective, with the shift to a model of 'inter-preter as professional', the discourses around interpreters, sign language and deaf people also began to change. Early literature on sign language inter-preting was dominated by discussions of 'models' of interpreting, and the language used to discuss interpreting drew heavily on metaphors to describe the role and function of sign language interpreters (Roy, 1993); that trend continues today. The models that have been 'in vogue' have been influenced by the linguistic theories that were popular at the time (Shaffer, 2014), so the models either drew from psycholinguistics to focus on the language process (e.g. Isham, 1992), from sociolinguistics to explain the various factors that influence the interpreting process or product (e.g. Cokely, 1992; Metzger, 1995), from intercultural communication to take into account how different cultural experiences influence interactions (Mindess, 1999), and cognitive linguistics to contextualise interpreting within the communica-tive act and the alignment of interpreter to the interpreted message (Shaffer, 2014, White, 2014; Wilcox & Shaffer, 2005).

Cynthia Roy's (1989a, 2000) seminal sociolinguistic sign language inter-preting research was mirrored in the work of Cecilia Wadensjö (1992, 1998) with spoken language interpreters and provided evidence that interpreters are active participants in a dialogic communicative event who co-construct the communication with the deaf and hearing interlocutors and thus cannot be neutral conduits that do not affect the message or the process of interac-tion. Most recently, we have seen a new mixed-theory model of interpreter role that draws on both sociolinguistics and psycholinguistics to describe how interpreters occupy a 'role space', so they change their behaviour and how actively they manage the communication depending on the context, the people involved and the interpersonal dynamics at play (Llewellyn-Jones & Lee, 2013). Thus, it is notable that the discourse among deaf people and interpreters themselves has now shifted from 'using' interpreters to 'working with' interpreters.

The discourse that concerns the ethical behaviour of professional sign language interpreters is also changing, as scholars have begun to examine the complexities of ethical decision making and how we should be talking about our professional practice (e.g. Cokely, 2005 Dean, 2014; Hoza, 2003;

Tate & Turner, 2002). Sign language interpreting has been defined as a 'practice profession' (Dean & Pollard, 2004, 2005, 2013), which frames the notion of professional practice in a different way than had previously been discussed in the literature (see Quote 6.10). The key to being a practice profession is the way that the professionals talk about their work and the discourse that surrounds ethical decision making. Dean (2015) has noted the importance of educating sign language interpreters to critically engage in discourse about ethical decision making, so as to give consideration not only to problems and challenges but also to what is effective practice.

Quote 6.10   Interpreting as a 'practice profession'

A new concept ... is that interpreting is a 'practice profession', like medicine or law enforcement, academic preparation and skills development precede a career in human service. We view the practice professions, including interpreting, as fundamentally distinct from other professions that do not have human service as their primary focus nor require the same degree of professional judgment *involving people* that the practice professions do. Professions such as engineering and accounting may require the acquisition of complex skills but their occupational roles are more akin to technicians than practitioners. In contrast, 'interpreters cannot deliver effective professional service armed only with their technical knowledge of source and target languages, Deaf culture, and a code of ethics. Like all practice professionals, they must supplement their technical knowledge and skills with input, exchange, and judgment regarding the consumers they are serving in a specific environment and in a specific communicative situation'. (Dean & Pollard, 2004, p. 28)

Regardless of the shift to professionalism and notions of sign language interpreting as a practice profession, there is still a tension in that the *status* of sign language interpreting is frequently misunderstood by the wider community. This may follow on from the fact that many people still misunderstand that sign languages are rich, complex languages of equal status to spoken languages (see Section 6.4). So, if sign language interpreters are 'just flapping their hands about', isn't it easy? Many readers may be familiar with the question, 'How long does it take to learn sign language, and how long does it take to become a sign language interpreter?' and the surprised response that people often give when you tell them, 'As long as it takes to learn a spoken language: if you want to be fluent enough to work as an interpreter, you're probably looking at a minimum of 5 to 6 years'. The signing community is full of anecdotes about people turning up to 'help' with communication after they have completed a level 1 beginners sign language course or less (for example, Lorraine once found herself interpreting a weekend course with a 'co-interpreter', a teacher of the deaf who had, at most, several weeks of sign language learning under his belt). If that is not acceptable for Spanish, French or German, why is it acceptable for sign language?

Essentially, sign language interpreting is not a highly regarded profession because it is unregulated. Interpreters are often regarded as being over-paid, likely due to deep-seated perceptions that interpreters are helpers and do not deserve remuneration equal to that of professional (conference) interpreters, even if they have completed undergraduate and/or postgraduate qualifications; or that deaf people can understand well enough without the need for interpreters (see Example 6.2). The fact that the field of sign language interpreting is also highly gendered may contribute to the construction of (particularly female) interpreters as 'helpers' (Leeson 2014, 2015).

Example 6.2 'Lack of British Sign Language interpreters putting deaf people at risk'

The Guardian, 7 May 2013
It is traumatic enough being rushed to hospital in an emergency, but what if you couldn't understand the doctors talking to you about what was wrong – and you woke up after an operation still not knowing the full story? That is what happened to profoundly deaf patient Elaine Duncan when she was admitted to Dundee's Ninewells hospital. Although British Sign Language is her first language, Duncan wasn't given access to a sign language interpreter at any point during her 12-day stay, which included surgery to remove her appendix. 'I repeatedly pointed to an interpreter services poster on the wall, and I handed staff a BSL interpreter's card on two separate occasions, but I was left abandoned and ignored,' she explains. 'It was a terrifying experience, leaving me feeling scared and alone, like I was in prison.'

Duncan's experience is one of many examples of deaf people being put at risk because they are not given the interpreters they need to communicate with doctors, police and other public sector professionals, says charity Signature, which campaigns to improve standards of communication for deaf and deafblind people. It says the problem is partly caused by a national shortage of BSL interpreters. Latest figures suggest there are 800 registered interpreters for 25,000 sign language users in the UK. But Signature chief executive Jim Edwards says there is also an attitude problem among public service professionals, who expect deaf people to be able to lip-read or to use the written word. 'For a deaf person, that won't be their first language, and they won't always follow it,' he says. 'Sometimes they might have a member of their family there, but their sign language may be limited – and is it appropriate that they should be interpreting when they may be distressed themselves? You need someone independent and professionally trained.'

Equality legislation requires 'reasonable steps' to be taken to ensure deaf people are not at a 'substantial disadvantage'. But Signature is urging the government to make the provision of regulated BSL interpreters a legal requirement across the public sector. Edwards says the Francis report into the Mid Staffordshire hospital scandal – which recommended regulation for all those who directly care for patients – provides added impetus. 'In the future, if you're a sign language user, the doctor treating you will have to be regulated, but the person affecting your communication – where it really can all go wrong – won't have to be,' he points out.

Duncan's case was taken to the Scottish Public Services Ombudsman, which upheld her complaint. NHS Tayside says it has since improved its procedures. But Alana Trusty, manager of the Deaf Links advocacy service, which supported Duncan with her case, says: 'This is happening all the time, across all types of service provision. If you were in hospital in France, would you be able to read a consent form or understand someone speaking French at your bedside? That's what it's like for deaf people.' (www.theguardian.com/society/2013/may/07/lack-interpreters-deaf-people-risk)

The fact that the profession is unregulated was highlighted by the case of the 'fake' sign language interpreter, Thamsanqa Jantjie, at Nelson Mandela's memorial in December 2013. Not only was Jantjie *not* a professional sign language interpreter, he could not even sign. The incident drew worldwide attention, with accusations from signing communities that he was a fraud who used 'childish hand gestures' and did not make any sense. The controversial event led to many commentaries in the news media (see Example 6.3), and social media exploded with postings about how this person who could not sign had made it on to the stage next to the U.S. President.

Example 6.3   Reports of the fake Mandela interpreter

1. Nelson Mandela memorial interpreter 'was a fake' (The Telegraph, 11 December 2013): www.telegraph.co.uk/news/worldnews/africaandindianocean/southafrica/10510455/Nelson-Mandela-memorial-interpreter-was-a-fake.html
2. Sign language expert: five ways to spot Mandela memorial interpreter was a fake (The Telegraph, 11 December 2013): www.telegraph.co.uk/worldnews/nelson-mandela/10511659/Sign-language-expert-five-ways-to-spot-Mandela-memorial-interpreter-was-a-fake.html
3. 'Zulu sign language? There's no such thing': expert reacts to 'fake' Nelson Mandela memorial interpreter (The Telegraph, 11 December 2013): www.telegraph.co.uk/news/worldnews/nelson-mandela/10511040/Zulu-sign-language-Theres-no-such-thing-expert-reacts-to-fake-Nelson-Mandela-memorial-interpreter.html
4. Sign language interpreter says he suffered schizophrenic episode at Mandela memorial (The Telegraph, 12 December 2013): www.telegraph.co.uk/news/worldnews/nelson-mandela/10514801/Sign-language-interpreter-says-he-suffered-schizophrenic-episode-at-Mandela-memorial.html
5. South Africa investigates Nelson Mandela interpreter 'murder charge' (The Telegraph, 13 December 2013): www.telegraph.co.uk/news/worldnews/africaandindianocean/southafrica/10515904/South-Africa-investigates-Nelson-Mandela-interpreter-murder-charge.html
6. Translated: what the Mandela signer was really saying (The Telegraph, 11 December 2013): www.telegraph.co.uk/news/worldnews/nelson-mandela/10511569/Translated-what-the-Mandela-signer-was-really-saying.html

From a linguistic perspective, it was obvious to anyone who is fluent in a signed language that Jantjie was not using a real sign language (as noted in many of the reports in Example 6.3). Sign language academics commented on the lack of rhythmic flow that would be expected in sign language and that none of his gestures conformed to the grammatical conventions of sign languages. Jantjie claimed that he was having a schizophrenic episode to explain why his signing looked strange, but a deaf neuropsychologist, Dr Jo Atkinson, who has analysed the sign language use of deaf schizophrenics, refuted his claim (see media release in Example 6.4).

Example 6.4   Media release

University College London

Publication date: Dec 12, 2013 01:58 PM

'Fake' Mandela interpreter claims schizophrenic episode

The Mandela memorial interpreter accused of being a 'fake' has claimed that he suffered a schizophrenic episode while on stage, and that he suddenly lost concentration and started hearing voices and hallucinating.

Dr Jo Atkinson, a clinical psychologist and researcher at the Deafness, Cognition and Language Research Centre, UCL, said:

The disruption of sign language in people with schizophrenia takes many forms but this does not look like anything I have seen in signers with psychosis.

It is not possible to make a judgment about whether or not someone has schizophrenia if they do not share your own language or based on film-clips, so this is not a comment on Mr Jantjie's mental state. There are features of signed languages, such as rhythm in the movement of the hands, the use of facial action and eyegaze, which are remarkably similar across the world's signed languages.

Therefore, it is possible for a deaf person to deduce that signing is odd, even when they don't use that particular sign language.

There were many features of Mr Jantjie's signing that do not chime with the typical presentation of disordered signing caused by a psychotic episode.

Bizarre fluidity of thought or jumbled signs are comparatively rare even among signers with schizophrenia. This typically presents as larger, more expansive, use of facial expression and signing space, and signing in a very fast and pressured way. The content of such signing is bizarre but retains aspects of sign language structure such as facially expressed grammatical markers.

By contrast, Mr Jantjie signed without facial expression and in a regimented and contained way.

Bizarre jumbling of words or signs is known as word salad and this does not come on suddenly, or switch on and off in a signer having a psychotic episode.

It would also affect his spoken language and would occur alongside significant cognitive dysfunction. Others around him would have immediately noticed that he was not making sense in any language.

It did not look like disordered signing, it looked more like someone who is not a fluent signer making it up as they went along.

Whether or not he was faking or is simply delusional about his interpreting ability, the ANC should have picked up on his poor quality signing earlier.

> *This highlights the importance of monitoring of the sign language profession around the world.*
> Dr Joanna Atkinson is a researcher at the Deafness Cognition and Language (DCAL) Research Centre and is a certified Clinical Psychologist with additional qualifications in Clinical Neuropsychology. Her work cuts across several fields including cognitive neuroscience, neuropsychology and psycholinguistics, and she has written extensively in these fields. Her published work on this subject area include:
> Atkinson, J. R., Gleeson, K., Cromwell, J., & O'Rourke, S. (2007). Exploring the perceptual characteristics of voice-hallucinations in deaf people. *Cognitive Neuropsychology, 12*(4), 339–361.
> Atkinson, J. R. (2006). The perceptual characteristics of voice-hallucinations in deaf people: insights into the nature of subvocal thought and sensory feedback loops. *Schizophrenia Bulletin, 32*(4), 701–708. (www.ucl.ac.uk/dcal/dcal-news/Mandela_Interpreter)

Not only did Dr Atkinson challenge Jantjie's statement, she also asserted the importance of monitoring the worldwide sign language interpreting profession. Other signing community representatives also took up this position and used this case as an opportunity to focus attention on the need to train sign language interpreters to a high standard and to ensure that only qualified and professionally registered interpreters should be employed at all times. WFD and WASLI issued a joint statement about the importance of using high-quality, professional interpreters by referring to the UNCRPD and the specific mention of the rights of sign language users (see Example 6.5). As a result of this incident (and also the poor level of competence of an Afrikaans–English interpreter working in the Oscar Pistorius murder charge case), the South African Government passed the South African Language Practitioners Act to regulate language practitioners and ensure quality professional standards across the translation and interpreting industry.

Example 6.5   WFD-WASLI joint statement

The memorial service for late South African President Nelson Mandela took place on Tuesday, 10 December 2013 in Johannesburg, South Africa. The World Federation of the Deaf (WFD) and the World Association of Sign Language Interpreters (WASLI) are concerned about the quality of sign language interpretation during that event.

The memorial service was followed on television by several deaf South Africans, who were disappointed on the level of interpretation of this high-level gathering. A board member of the WFD Youth Section, Braam Jordaan, described that the interpreter did not know South African Sign Language (SASL): 'The structure of his hand, facial expressions and the body movement did not follow what the speaker was saying.' He raised concerns also how this interpreter was chosen to interpret without any professional qualifications, evaluations and screening. Also, the current WFD Vice-President, Wilma Newhoudt-Druchen, followed the event on television and confirmed the poor level of sign language interpretation. She commented: 'What is he signing? He knows that the deaf cannot vocally boo him off. Shame on him.' During the television broadcasting, a proper sign language interpreter was provided on the left corner of the screen, which made it obvious that the interpreter, who was present in the event, did not know SASL or any sign language at all.

WFD and WASLI would like to announce a public statement about the importance of quality interpreter services in any public event. It is the responsibility of organisers to ensure that access to information is guaranteed for deaf audiences. **Article 21 of the UN Convention on the Rights of Persons with Disabilities (UNCRPD)** points out that deaf people have **a right to choose their form of communication** and State Parties shall ensure 'accepting and facilitating the use of sign languages ... and all other accessible means of communication of their choice by persons with disabilities in official interactions'. The same article continues that State Parties shall take all appropriate measures to ensure recognizing and promoting the use of sign languages. Further, the **Article 9 of UNCRPD** requires 'State Parties to take appropriate measures to ensure to persons with disabilities **access on an equal basis with others ... to information and communications ...'** This means professional sign language interpreters, who know the national sign language and deaf culture.

WFD and WASLI want to underline the need to co-operate with local Deaf organisations, in this case in South Africa; stress the need for trained, qualified interpreters to be used, and the emphasis on the need for access that is based on direction from deaf people. (http://wfdeaf.org/news/wfd-wasli-joint-statement-about-the-sign-language-interpretation-at-mandelas-memorial-service)

In spite of the seriousness of the issue, the case was still ridiculed in the media, with suggestions for translations of what the fake interpreter was 'really' saying (see media report in Example 6.3, Point 6), and British comedian Paul Whitehouse gave his acceptance speech at the British Comedy Awards by mimicking the incident and having a 'fake signer' stand next to him at the podium.[1] A British professional sign language interpreter who blogs under the name of 'Terpatron' wrote a post discussing the reaction to the fake interpreter incident and other media attention of sign language interpreters (see Section 6.4), and the fact that unfortunately in the UK, where the sign language interpreting profession is well established and there are several routes to training, 'in our own backyard' *unqualified* interpreters are still used in various settings, especially education.[2] Terpatron laments the fact that there is more outrage and focus on the 'spectacle of sign language interpreting' in public events than on the fact that deaf people are still not receiving the quality of access to professional interpreting services in their everyday lives. Case study 6.2 illustrates problems that have occurred in the UK, which led to the establishment of the National Union of British Sign

Language Interpreters (NUBSLI) in order to lobby for minimum pay rates and working conditions.

Case study 6.2   Access to work cuts

The Department of Workplace and Pensions (DWP) of the UK Government administers the Access to Work Scheme, which covers the costs of accommodations for people in the workplace. Since 2010, due to UK Government public sector funding cuts, British Sign Language interpreter pay rates have fallen by 12% (NUBSLI, 2014), and restrictions have been placed on the number of hours for which deaf people can employ sign language interpreters in the workplace. There has been pressure to employ unqualified interpreters who charge lower rates, or to reduce working conditions (e.g. employ one rather than two interpreters for all-day events). A website has been established to support deaf sign language users to make complaints, and representative bodies such as the British Deaf Association and the Association of Sign Language Interpreters UK have held meetings with DWP representatives to lobby for recognition of the importance of professional sign language interpreter provision to support deaf people in the workplace. (www. nubsli.com/about-us.php; www.theguardian.com/society/2015/jan/20/disabled-people-lose-jobs-access-to-work; www.disabilitynow.org.uk/article/access-work-deaf-employees-fear-future; www.deafatw.com)

6.2.2   Sign language interpreting practice

Now that we have established the importance of sign language interpreting as a *practice profession* (Dean & Pollard, 2004, 2013), let us consider the *professional practice* of sign language interpreters from an applied linguistics perspective. In their editorial for the re-launch of the Journal of Applied Linguistics as the *Journal of Applied Linguistics and Professional Practice*, Sarangi and Candlin (2010, p. 2) note the 'complexity of seeking to describe, interpret and explain the institutional and interactional orders of *what it is that is going on* in crucial communicative sites and at critical moments in those sites'. This observation is pertinent to the study of interpreting in that it is possible to examine 'what is going on' at critical moments in sites of interpreter-mediated interaction; thus, sign language interpreting can be placed 'within the wider context of interpreting as an applied linguistic activity' (Napier, 2013b, p. 85).

Quote 6.11   Interpreting studies: a field in its own right

Interpreting studies is a rich field of enquiry for applied linguists. The last three decades have seen the emergence of a growing body of research defining the field as a discipline in its own right rather than an off-shoot of translation studies ... Applied linguistics has contributed to this field and the understanding of what it is that interpreters do through discourse-based research of interpreter-mediated communication. Analysis of the pragmatic features of mediated cross-cultural communication, for example, has informed notions of accuracy in interpreting. Studies of the discourse of interpreter-mediated communication in a range of institutional settings have challenged accepted notions of the interpreter's role. This body of research is significant in marking a clear departure from earlier psycholinguistic and text-based approaches to researching interpreting. (Napier, Rohan & Slatyer, 2005, p. 186)

Sign language interpreting research has been dominated by work from researchers in the United States (Grbić, 2007; Metzger, 2006; Roy & Napier, 2015), but since 2005 there has been an explosion of sign language interpreting studies from other countries (Napier, 2011a). Research on sign language interpreting practice is interdisciplinary (Napier & Leeson, 2015) and covers a spectrum of topics from preparation strategies (e.g. Nicodemus, Swabey & Taylor, 2014) to equivalence and interpreting strategies (e.g. Leeson & Foley-Cave, 2007; Napier, 2002; Sheridan, 2009) to occupational stress or burnout (e.g. Hetherington, 2010; Madden, 2005). Here, we focus our discussion on sign language interpreting practice that draws specifically on research with an applied linguistics focus and that relates to other topics that we have interrogated thus far in relation to sign language in action, including modality, bilingualism, native-ness and discourse.

The practice of sign language interpreting differs from spoken language interpreting in that the typical default practice is to use the simultaneous, rather than the consecutive, interpreting technique (see Quote 6.12) as sign language interpreters do not have to contend with acoustic overlap from the vocalisation of two languages (Leeson, 2005a; Napier, 2015).

Quote 6.12   Modes of interpreting

... interpreters can utilize different interpreting techniques and modes. The choice of mode depends on the situation and the setting, the degree of formality, the length of the speech (segments) that is (are) to be interpreted, and the availability of the technical equipment necessary for certain interpreting modes. On the basis of their processing characteristics in general and the time flow of the source and target text presentation in particular, consecutive interpreting and simultaneous interpreting are the most general modes which can be distinguished. All other types of interpreting with their specific techniques fall into one of these two categories. Hybrid modes combine consecutive and simultaneous processing specificities. Also in signed language interpreting, the alternation of simultaneously and consecutively rendered segments can be observed, e.g. spoken into sign language (simultaneous mode) and vice versa (consecutive mode). ...

> In [consecutive interpreting], the speaker delivers his or her speech in the source language. The interpreter listens and analyzes the incoming text, memorizes its message, partly through memory, and partly by taking notes. When the speaker finishes or pauses, the interpreter takes over and renders the message in the target language by retrieving the memorized information from his or her memory and notes. ...
> [In simultaneous interpreting] the interpreter listens and speaks at the same time, i.e. the target text in SI is an immediate rendering of the source text message. (Ahrens, 2013, pp. 1–2)

However, the examination of sign language interpreting practice has revealed that (1) consecutive interpreting can actually be a more effective technique to ensure accuracy (Russell, 2002), and (2) sign language interpreters can also work in blended mode, shifting along a continuum between consecutive and simultaneous mode (see Quote 6.13).

Quote 6.13   Blending interpreting modes

For many dialogic interactions, consecutive interpretation is the most appropriate mode. These include medical appointments, Video Relay Service (VRS) calls, and interviews. Many interpreters use [consecutive interpreting] when interpreting for children, seniors, and foreign sign language users, or situations in which the interpreter lacks contextual knowledge or does not know the participants well. In some of these situations, a combination of consecutive and simultaneous interpreting can be most effective. (Russell, Shaw & Malcolm, 2010, p. 117)

One of the most interesting linguistic things about sign language interpreting practice is that it is bimodal (Brennan & Brown, 1997; Napier, 2011a, 2015; Nicodemus & Emmorey, 2012). Spoken language interpreters work between languages that are produced and perceived in the same modality, that is, auditory-verbal. In contrast, sign language interpreters work between two languages, a spoken and a signed language, that are produced and perceived in different modalities: auditory-verbal and visual-spatial. Thus spoken language interpreters (and, indeed, deaf interpreters working between two sign languages) can be referred to as *unimodal* interpreters (Napier, 2015; Nicodemus & Emmorey, 2012); sign language interpreters could also be referred to as *intermodal* interpreters (Metzger & Müller de Quadros, 2012). Due to the bimodality of sign language–spoken language interpreting, Padden (2000) argues that interpreters can operate more effectively in one mode at a time, and so should consider working consecutively more often; otherwise, an extra cognitive load is placed on interpreters working in two modalities simultaneously.

The realities of bimodal interpreting 'inevitably change the dynamics of live interactions' between deaf and hearing interlocutors (Brennan & Brown, 1997, p. 125) in that sign language interpreters always need to be seen; they cannot be hidden away in an interpreting booth at the back of the room (which is the norm in conference settings). Another issue is that in dialogic communication, people typically look at the person who is talking. In sign language interpreter-mediated interaction, when the deaf person makes a contribution, he or she is silent. The voice (literally) comes from someone else – the sign language interpreter – who is rendering the signed utterance into a spoken one. Thus, the hearing person who is relying on the 'voice-over' will often look at the person speaking (the interpreter) rather than the deaf person.

Another challenging aspect of bimodal interpreting for sign language interpreters is the fact that sign languages inherently encode 'real-world' visual information into the language (Johnston, 2013; Leeson, Saeed, Shaffer & Janzen., 2013; Liddell, 2003; Napoli & Leeson, in prep; Shaffer, Janzen & Leeson, 2012; Sutton-Spence & Woll, 1998; Wilcox, 2004b). This presents a challenge for interpreters in determining the most appropriate way to inter-pret the message in either language so that it is idiomatic (Brennan & Brown, 1997; Napier, 2011a, 2015). If visual real-world information is encoded into a BSL sentence and the interpreter renders that information literally into English, it would seem a little peculiar to the listener (see Example 6.6). In reverse, if an interpreter hears a superordinate term such as *murder* spoken in English, he or she will need to know how the person was murdered in order to accurately convey the information in BSL – for example, was the person stabbed, strangled, shot, hit over the head with a heavy object, etc. – because there is no one established sign for *murder* in BSL (Brennan, 1999a).

Example 6.6   What to encode when working from a sign language?

BSL sentence: I opened the door, ran across the room and up the stairs.

Literal English translation: I opened the door (which slid from left to right), ran across the room (from the left corner of the room to the far right corner of the room) and up the (spiral) staircase.

Sign languages have rich productive lexicons that draw on the use of spatial metaphors to create new signs in context (Brennan, 1990; Leeson & Saeed, 2012a), so not only is visual encoding challenging for interpreters to know how to depict or represent visual information, but also the fact that signers may create new visually rich, metaphorical signs 'on the spot' presents a further complexity to the work of interpreters (see Chapter 3 for discussion of signed languages as embodied languages). Thus, in practice, sign language interpreters face the challenge of constantly having to visualise what they hear in a linear form; or, when providing a 'voice-over', create sequential meaning from a visual picture. This factor adds an extra dimension to the interpreting process, as the interpreters have to create meaning in two different modalities. This is especially challenging for interpreters who are providing a voice-over for someone using International Sign (Best, Napier, Carmichael & Pouliot, in press) as it has a very small established lexicon, so it relies on signers exploiting visual metaphors even more than would be expected of someone using a national sign language (see Chapters 3 and 4).

Another interesting aspect of sign language interpreting within the context of applied sign linguistics is directionality. Directionality in interpreting describes the use of an interpreter's two languages when interpreting in the simultaneous or long consecutive mode, that is, when the source language discourse is monologic. It is a well-established precedent that spoken language conference interpreters work simultaneously in one language direction, typically from their 'B' (i.e. second) into their 'A' (i.e. first/native) language (Seleskovitch, 1978), but increasingly market demands necessitate that they also work into their 'B' language (Donovan, 2004). Interpreters can also be described as a 'double A' when they have native-like proficiency in two of their languages (Pöchhacker, 2004). Opinion about directionality is divided, with teachers of interpreting in the West supporting the view that an interpreter works best into their 'A' language because of the native-like quality of the target language production, whereas the Russian tradition supports the view that enhanced comprehension of the source language produces more accurate interpreting, and therefore interpreters should work out of their 'A' language (Gile, 2005). Many survey studies have concentrated on interpreters' feelings about directionality. Professional spoken language interpreters typically prefer, and feel more proficient in, L2-to-L1 interpreting and perceive L1-to-L2 interpreting to be more stressful and tiring (Bartłomiejczyk, 2004; Donovan, 2004; Lim, 2005; Nicodemus & Emmorey, 2012).

For sign language interpreters, however, it is typically the reverse. Unless a sign language interpreter has been exposed to a sign language from a very young age through parents or siblings, it is unlikely that he or she will acquire a sign language as a first language. Given the inherent dominance of spoken language use in phonocentric society, interpreters are typically present at communication events where information is being communicated in orally and thus requires interpretation into a signed language (e.g. lectures, training events, information sessions). Therefore, the interpreters are more likely to be working *into* their second language.

Both anecdotal reports and empirical studies confirm that sign language interpreters perceive that it is more difficult to interpret from a signed language (L2) into a spoken language (L1) than vice versa because they have fewer opportunities to work in this language direction (Napier, Rohan & Slatyer, 2005; Padden, 2000; Van Dijk, Christoffels, Postma & Hermans, 2012 Xiao & Yu, 2009; see Case study 6.3). In a survey of ASL interpreters, Nicodemus and Emmorey (2012) found that they not only preferred, but also felt more proficient in, working from their L1 (English) into L2 (ASL); novice interpreters expressed a stronger preference for interpreting from L1 into L2 than the expert interpreters, suggesting that considerable interpreting experience may reduce directionality preferences. Furthermore, Nicodemus and Emmorey (2012) found that sign language interpreters who were native signers largely expressed no directionality preferences, indicating that balanced bilingual proficiency may mitigate directionality preferences.

However, a statement of directionality preference may not match an interpreter's actual interpreting proficiency. Nicodemus and Emmorey (2015) investigated directionality effects on simultaneous interpreting performance of 32 expert and novice ASL interpreters, all of whom had learned ASL as second language in adulthood (elective bilinguals). They found no significant directionality effects on the accuracy, fluency, speed or prosody of the experts' simultaneous interpreting performance. The novices scored significantly higher in terms of accuracy, speed and prosody when simultaneously interpreting from ASL into English (L2-to-L1) than in the reverse language direction; however, the novices scored significantly lower in terms of fluency when simultaneously interpreting from ASL into English (L2-to-L1) than vice versa. Although novices typically expressed a strong preference for interpreting from English into ASL (L1-to-L2; Nicodemus & Emmorey, 2012), the results of Nicodemus and Emmorey (2015) demonstrated that novices actually performed significantly better when interpreting from ASL into English (L2-to-L1).

However, a similar study by Van Dijk et al. (2012) found the opposite. In their study of the effects of directionality and age of signed language acquisition on simultaneous interpreting performance of 25 experienced Sign Language of the Netherlands (SLN) interpreters who were a mixed group of native and non-native signers, Van Dijk et al. found that the native signers' Dutch-to-SLN simultaneous interpreting performance was significantly better than their SLN-to-Dutch simultaneous interpreting performance. Van Dijk et al. also noted that the non-native signers' Dutch-to-SLN simultaneous interpreting performance was significantly superior to their SLN-to-Dutch simultaneous interpreting performance; that is, the non-native signers interpreted significantly better from L1 into L2 than vice versa. Van Dijk et al. attributed the participants' inferior performance on SLN-to-Dutch interpreting to the following 2 reasons: (1) the participants had less practice interpreting in this language direction and (2) the participants may have encountered SLN comprehension problems due to linguistic variation in SLN. Working with a group of deaf raters, McDermid (2014a) found evidence of a 'hearing' dialect of ASL in elective

ASL bilingual interpreters when they were interpreting from English into ASL, which would indicate that although interpreters may feel comfortable working into their L2, the quality of the output may not be suitably idiomatic; this is confirmed by studies that found that deaf individuals do not comprehend as much from sign language interpreting due to a lack of interpreters' signing proficiency (Ortiz, 2007; Xiao, Chen & Palmer, 2015). In a separate study, McDermid (2014b) found that more experienced interpreters produced significantly more fluent and cohesive English-to-ASL interpretations, showing that native signing status is not the only factor that influences directionality effects. Stauffer (2011) suggests that if we teach interpreting students the skills of self-assessment, then they should be well placed to assess their sign language capabilities and evaluate their interpreting work, including their competence at working in each language direction.

Case study 6.3   Bilingualism and directionality in sign language interpreting

Two separate studies conducted with Auslan interpreters investigated the issue of directionality in sign language interpreting.

Napier, Rohan and Slatyer (2005) conducted a small-scale study of 56 Auslan interpreters' perceptions of their bilingual status in comparison with their preferences for working into Auslan or English. The impetus for the study came from discussions with interpreter educators, researchers and practitioners in which it was asked 'how bilingual' an interpreter must be in order to interpret effectively. Interpreters are assumed to have a high level of proficiency in both their languages and traditionally interpret into their dominant language. An e-mail survey was administered to accredited Auslan interpreters asking a range of questions about their perceptions of their bilingual status, their language fluency and how they acquired or learned their languages as well as which language direction they prefer when interpreting. The results showed that for many of the interpreters, their perceived bilingual status contradicted their preferred language direction when interpreting and also contravened established conference interpreting practice that interpreters work into their 'A' language, with the majority of interpreters preferring to interpret into their non-dominant language (i.e. Auslan). The results also showed that Auslan interpreters have differing opinions of their level of bilingualism depending on their level of experience, and many less experienced interpreters were not confident in their level of bilingualism.

In a later mixed-methods study, Wang and Napier (in press) investigated the effects of directionality and age of signed language acquisition on the simultaneous interpreting performance of professional Auslan interpreters, who comprised native signers and non-native signers. Each participant interpreted presentations simultaneously from English into Auslan and vice versa, with each task followed by a brief semi-structured interview. There were no significant differences between the native signers' English-to-Auslan simultaneous interpreting performance and their Auslan-to-English simultaneous interpreting performance, suggesting that balanced bilingual sign language interpreters are free from the rule of directionality. Although this finding held true for the non-native signers, results indicate a need for the non-native signers to continue to enhance their sign language (L2) competence. Furthermore, although the native signers were similar to the non-native signers in overall simultaneous interpreting performance in each language direction, the native signers were significantly superior to the non-native signers in both the target text features and the delivery features of English-to-Auslan simultaneous interpreting performance. These findings also suggest that the non-native signers need to further improve their sign language (L2) proficiency. Nevertheless, an analysis of the qualitative interview data reveals that the professional interpreters perceived distinct challenges that were unique to each language direction.

Either way, these studies reveal that directionality is a complex issue in the professional practice of sign language interpreters, and more research is needed to investigate this issue further. This has implications for the quality of interpreting practice and whether deaf people can confidently present information in sign language and know that it will be accurately interpreted. There is extensive discussion in the sign language interpreting literature concerning the difficulties of producing a 'voice-over' (e.g. Finton, 2005; Hema, 2002; Martinez, 2007; Zimmer, 1992). Authors have identified particular challenges for non-native sign language users in their sign language comprehension, especially in relation to the comprehension of fingerspelling, which involves morphological micro-movements of the hands and fingers (either one- or two-handed, depending on the sign language) to spell out names of people, places or key terms (Patrie, 2009).

Yet voice-over presents challenges not just at a lexical or morphological level but also at a discourse level. In the first interactional sociolinguistic analysis of a voice-over interpretation, Roy (1987) conducted an analysis of the discourse style and paralinguistic features in an authentic ASL-to-English interpretation of a lecture. She also played the recording of the voice-over to a group of hearing non-signers and asked them to comment on what they heard (see Quote 6.14). Her analysis found that although the interpreter had provided an accurate interpretation in terms of matching the propositional content, she had not adequately represented the register or matched the affect of the sign language lecture, and this was as a result of inappropriate use of intonation, rhythm, stress marking and pitch. More recently, Fitzmaurice and Purdy (2015) found that disfluent pausing (i.e. pausing in the wrong places or for too long when speaking in English) has a negative effect on listener judgements of ASL-to-English interpretations.

Feyne (in press) takes a similar approach, exploring the impact of the discursive practices of signed language interpreters on non-signers' perceptions of the identity of signing deaf museum educators. She explores variation in the perceptions of competence and professionalism of a deaf educator as constructed by one target recipient, a museum evaluator who relied upon the interpretations in making her assessments, reporting that the decisions made by interpreters contribute to the perceptions of the situated identity of interpreted presenters as professionals in their sphere of practice.

Napier (2007a) utilised a similar interactional sociolinguistics analytical approach to that used by Roy (1987) to analyse an authentic Auslan-to-English interpretation with a focus on positive cooperation strategies rather than the discourse style (see Case study 6.4). Her findings showed the importance of the deaf presenter and the interpreters working together to achieve a voice-over that matched the mood and intent of the presenter. The perceptions of deaf people about the quality of interpretations in either language direction are discussed further in Section 6.3.

Quote 6.14   'The stickleback fish and its mating habits'

The interpretation into English included the important content or the facts: a propositional analysis revealed that, out of 39 propositions in the original talk, the interpreter deleted only 2. When the monolingual observers were asked for a title of the talk they had just heard, they correctly identified it as 'The stickleback fish and its mating habits'. They were also able to provide many of the relevant details. However, when asked who the speaker was talking to, the unanimous answer was 'children'. Eleven people commented that the talk was like telling a story to a child.

This must be viewed as a communicative breakdown. While those who were listening seem to have acquired the information being presented, it is far from being what we would think of as a successful interpretation. Given that the intended audience was young adults, the speaker in the interpretation sounded condescending and foolish, and appeared to be a poor communicator. If how something is said gets in the way of what is said, we have a communication breakdown. (Roy, 1987, p. 140)

Case study 6.4   Cooperation in interpreter-mediated monologic talk

Drawing on a framework of interactional sociolinguistics, Napier (2007a) analysed naturalistic data from a monologic seminar presentation and presented a case study of a deaf presenter using Auslan and the cooperation strategies used by the presenter and two sign language interpreters to render the presentation from Auslan into spoken English. The analysis focussed on the use of pauses, nods and eye contact as contextualisation cues in the interpreter-mediated event.

Napier found that the three participants used these cues deliberately and strategically for signalling comprehension, marking episodes, clarification and controlling the pace of the presentation. The strategies were also used to draw on frames and establish the footing of the presenter. Thus Napier suggested a cooperative principle for monologic interpretation from a signed to a spoken language based on 6 linguistic, communicative and attitudinal maxims: (1) trust, (2) preparation, (3) negotiation, (4) eye contact, (5) turn-taking and (6) visual cues.

6.2.3   Sign language translation as an emerging practice

A more recent development, made possible by advances in technological capabilities to record and edit signed languages on video, is the emergence of sign language translation (SLT) as a distinct professional practice from sign language interpreting. Researchers in the field of applied sign linguistics have pushed the boundaries of thinking in translation and interpreting studies in redefining translation and interpreting practice.

Previous assumptions that sign language interpreters do not do what is traditionally known as translation work (see Quote 6.15) have been challenged by researchers who have critiqued previous definitions of translation (Banna, 2004; Gresswell, 2001; Turner & Pollitt, 2002).

Quote 6.15   Outdated definition of sign language translation

Interpreters who work between a spoken and signed language tend not to engage in the task of written translation because signed languages are visual-gestural languages with no standard written orthography. (Napier, 2002, pp. xi–xii)

Typically, the term *translation* refers to the general process of rendering the message in one language into another language, or it is used to specifically refer to the process of reformulating a written text in one language into a written text in another language. The term *interpreting* was traditionally used to refer to that same reformulation process but from one 'oral' language into another 'oral' language. Sign language interpreter researchers had already challenged the tradition definition of interpreting, so it has been reframed to focus on the 'live', real-time, spontaneous rendering of a message from one language into another, without the opportunity for review or correction (Leneham, 2005).

Furthermore, discussions of SLT have demanded that we extend our more traditional understanding of translation as text-to-text to focus less on the medium, and more on the process that allows for preparation, development, review, revision and polishing of the translation; the length of time that it takes for the audience to 'receive' the translation and the fact that the target text is captured for posterity (Leneham, 2007; Wurm, 2014), as depicted in Figure 6.1.

Leneham (2007) documents 6 sign language translation processes that can be considered as separate from sign language interpreting:

- Signed source text (ST; video) → spoken target text (TT; audio); e.g. voice-over for deaf TV programmes
- Signed ST (video) → signed TT (video); e.g. translation of a signed narrative into a different sign language on video

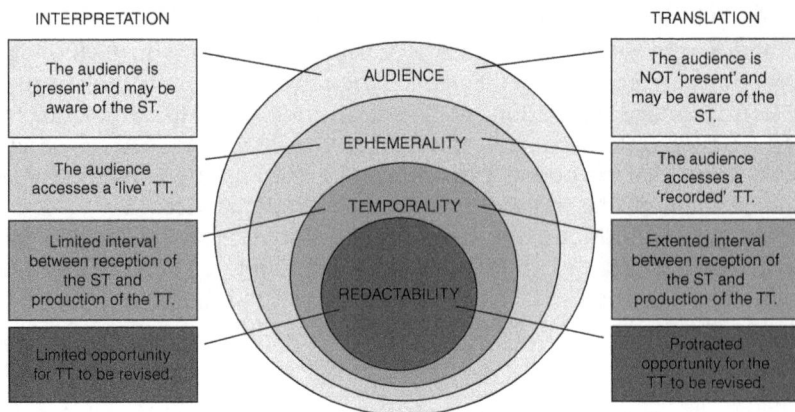

Figure 6.1   Definitions of translation and interpreting
Source: Leneham (2011).

- Spoken ST (audio) → signed TT (live or video); e.g. translation of a song, such as the national anthem or a hymn
- Written ST → signed TT (live); e.g. sight translations of social services leaflets or educational exam papers; translation of auto-cue into a signed language for news broadcasts
- Written ST → signed TT (video); e.g. translation of publications such as children's books, the Bible; psychometric or educational assessment tools; government legislation and policy
- Signed ST (live or video) → written TT; e.g. witness testimony, conference paper or journal article; TV captions

Although Adam, Carty and Stone (2011) argue that the practice of SLT has been evident informally among deaf people in signing communities for many years (see Section 6.1.2), there is no doubt that technological developments enabling the easier recording and editing of sign language translations has played a major part in the advent of SLT. However, sociocultural developments have also had an influence on the demand for this practice (Wurm, 2014). With deaf people now working in a range of professional contexts (see Chapter 5, Section 5.4) and various legislatures requiring information to be made available in a range of languages, there is greater need for the translation of various 'texts' into sign language (e.g. websites). Deaf people may also choose to present information in sign language and have it translated into a written text, such as journal articles (see e.g. Heaton & Fowler, 1997, presented in BSL and translated into English by Kyra Pollitt), or dictation of letters (e.g. Cragg, 2002) or the translation of historical narratives originated in sign language to make them accessible for the wider community (Padden, 2004).

Alternatively, there are also many more examples of translations of various assessment tools from written English into sign language, including educational tools (Tate et al. 2003), psychiatric and other mental health assessment tools (Cornes, Rohan, Napier & Rey, 2006; Montoya et al., 2004; Rogers et al., 2013a, 2013b), translation of academic texts for deaf university students (Wurm, 2014) and the translation of books into sign languages for the purposes of providing bilingual resources for deaf children to develop literacy skills (see Case study 6.5).

Case study 6.5 Translation of children's books

Conlon & Napier (2004) documented the process of translating resources (books) from written English to Auslan as part of the pilot Auslan Resources project, under the auspices of the Thomas Pattison School Bilingual Program and Renwick College in Sydney. The brief of the project was to produce translations of various books targeted at children of K–2 reading level (5–7 years old) for parents and teachers to use as a resource in reading books with children of this age group. They proposed that an effective translation process should follow various stages in order to develop effective deaf-culturally appropriate translations, with consideration given to the goal of each translation and through the adoption of a *functional approach* to translation (cf. Hatim & Mason, 1990, 1997), giving consideration to the purpose, intention and function of a translation (cf. Nord, 1997; Vermeer, 1989). These stages included a clear translation brief, appropriate selection of texts to be translated to fit the purpose of the brief, basic gloss of a translation from English into Auslan on paper, consultation with sign linguists, a videotaped draft Auslan version, a forward and backward approach to translation (see Quote 6.16) including consultation with various stakeholders and finalisation of translation. The study highlights the significance of the application of translation theory to, and the process of consultation in, producing effective Auslan translations of books.

Quote 6.16 Forward and backward translation

...as the translations are produced, these perspectives [i.e. issues of comparability and validity] are operating in tandem if bilinguals are involved in the process. Discussion of how to translate...goes forward and backward in creating a translation into the target language: forward in the sense that the source language version is already decided upon, and backward in the sense that discussion about the target language version often involves reference back to what the source language version is actually asking. (Tate, Collins & Tymms, 2003, p. 19)

Further research is needed in the area of SLT, to follow on from the work of Stone (2007, 2009), based on his comparison of deaf translators and hearing interpreters rendering spoken English broadcast news into BSL and his determination that hearing interpreters should follow a 'translation norm' for sign language translation established by deaf translators, which is less marked in sign language. In their analyses of the way that deaf people translate medical instructions or medical interview questions from English into ASL, Nicodemus, Swabey and Moreland (2014) and Swabey, Nicodemus and Moreland (2014) confirmed that deaf sign language–using medical experts adopt a different approach to translating the information as compared to professional hearing interpreters.

Another area of interest for SLT research is in the area of theatre interpreting. It has been suggested that the interpreting provided for theatre productions can be considered a hybrid between community interpreting and literary translation (Turner & Pollitt, 2002) and also a hybrid between translation and interpreting (Horwitz, 2014; Leneham, 2005). Theatre interpreting ranges across different genres (Horwitz, 2014), from classics such as Shakespeare (Llewellyn-Jones, 2004) to experimental multimedia productions (Turner & Pollitt, 2002), including musicals and children's theatre, and requires extensive amounts of preparation, although the final 'translation product' is delivered live (as an interpretation). A sign language translator can draw on approaches to translation (Banna, 2004; Rocks, 2011) and prepare by reading a script, watching pre-recorded footage of the play/musical or rehearsals and watching a play/musical or rehearsal live. Sign language translators can 'edit' their translation by videoing their 'drafts', watching them back and then revising the translation. The final translation, though, is performed live in real time, and thus can be considered as an interpretation as the translator will be influenced by what happens spontaneously; for example, if an actor stumbles over their lines, the translator may change the prepared translation accordingly. Another hybrid form is 'sign singing', where a performer can read and listen to the lyrics of a song in order to prepare a translation before performing it live in front of an audience (e.g. either as part of a stage production or a social karaoke night).

6.3   The relationship between sign language users and interpreters

---

Quote 6.17 Symbiosis

Interpreters have a symbiotic relationship with the Deaf community, since each depends on the other for certain benefits. Deaf people need interpreters to communicate with hearing people who can't sign, in a wide range of public and private situations. Interpreters need the Deaf community, first, to acquire the linguistic and cultural knowledge which underpins their professional skills, and ultimately for opportunities to earn a living and maintain professional status in society. (Napier, McKee & Goswell, 2010, p. 9)

Since the shift to professional interpreting services, the connection between deaf sign language users and interpreters has been redefined as a consumer–service provider relationship, and several studies have been conducted to explore sign language users' perceptions of interpreters. Discussions have ranged from what makes a good interpreter and why (e.g. Bienvenu, 1987; Corker, 1997; Forestal, 2005; Heaton & Fowler, 1997; Kurz & Langer, 2004; Stratiy, 2005) to discussions of interpreter 'quality' (McKee, 2008). Grbić (2008) explores quality as a social construct and asserts that perceptions of quality are relative to the context in which the concept is being discussed – namely training, professional practice and interpreting research.

As noted in Chapter 3, one of the key issues for hearing sign language interpreters is that because they can hear, they could be considered 'outsiders'. For this reason, the notion of trust between interpreters and sign language users is crucial but is often implicit in the relationship. The attitude that an interpreter has towards his or her work can affect the rapport that sign language users have with him or her (see Quote 6.9), which can have a significant impact on the outcome of the interpreted event.

Case study 6.6   Deaf consumer perceptions of sign language interpreters

Napier and Barker (2004) conducted a focus group with Australian deaf university students from diverse linguistic and educational backgrounds and asked them to provide insights into their perceptions of sign language interpreting provision in university lectures. They commented on their interpreting preferences after viewing two videotaped segments of university lecture interpretation, one demonstrating a predominantly free approach and the other a predominantly literal approach. Expectations of the deaf students were explored in relation to the educational backgrounds and qualifications of university interpreters and the students' perceived comprehension of interpreters. The results suggest that the university students preferred interpreters to combine both interpretation styles, switching between literal and free approaches when appropriate. In doing so, the students felt they could access lecture content in Auslan while accessing subject-specific terminology or academic language in English. In terms of qualifications, the students advocated for interpreters to have a university qualification in general, especially if they are working in a university context.

Napier and Rohan (2007) asked deaf Australians to keep a diary to reflect on and evaluate their experiences of working with interpreters over a 6-week period, in order to assess levels of satisfaction with interpreters. They explored perceptions of what makes some interpreters more understandable than others, identified what factors make Auslan interpreters 'comfortable' to watch and considered the question of what makes an ideal interpreter. Using a survey template, 31 deaf people kept a diary of their interpreting experiences. Ten deaf people then participated in focus groups so that further qualitative data could be collected to enhance the diary study results. Each of these data collection techniques provided evaluations of deaf people's experiences of working with interpreters. It was found that general satisfaction levels were high – although deaf people seem to receive little choice in the interpreters they access – with clear ideas on what makes an ideal interpreter: understanding of the consumer and context, professionalism and attitude are key factors to comfort in working with interpreters. The study also highlighted the need for interpreters and deaf people to work closely together.

Napier (2011b) returned to the focus group data used in Napier and Rohan's (2007) study, to conduct thematic and content analyses of discussions held by deaf people and to compare findings with discussions of hearing people who work with interpreters (but are not interpreters themselves) and sign language interpreters. Six focus groups yielded 8 hours of data, which was analysed to identify themes that emerged about participants' perceptions of sign language interpreters and interpreting in Australia. In particular, Napier (2011b) focussed on how the participants view the sign language interpreting profession and discussed the expectations of all parties of sign language interpreter-mediated encounters by analysing key themes that were evident from the most frequently used words/signs. Deaf participants covered 6 themes, including attitude, knowledge, understanding, needs, professionalism and language. Hearing participants concentrated on 4 issues of knowledge, needs, professionalism, and language. Interpreters talked about the most themes, including attitude, knowledge, challenges, trust, understanding, needs, professionalism and language. Only 5 topics were discussed by all the participants: attitude, knowledge, needs, professionalism and language. The content analysis focussed on those lexical items that were most frequently mentioned (*understand, need, professional, language* and *attitude*), and it was found that each stakeholder group talked about these things in different ways. The in-depth analysis of how deaf and hearing consumers and interpreters talk about interpreting exposed the fact that perceptions are more complex than would initially seem from summarised lists of key items of discussion (as is common in some studies).

In applied linguistics terms, a body of research has established that '[i]ssues surrounding trust are foundational to people's lives in contemporary societies ... more pervasively and ever-presently in the formation and maintenance of relationships' (Candlin & Crichton, 2013, p. 1). This is clearly evident in the relationship between signing communities and (hearing) interpreters. Trust is developed as deaf people see the level of interpreters' social engagement within the signing community and when they feel they are treated with respect and interpreters behave professionally and appropriately. In particular, deaf consumers evaluate interpreters' signing skills, as well as their ability to voice-over for them and represent them effectively, and may choose different interpreters for different contexts to match their needs (Bontempo et al., in prep; De Wit & Sluis, 2014). Thus, borrowing from Candlin and Crichton's (2013) 5 characteristics of the discursive practices of trust, we can see that:

1. Trust in the [signing] social world is *discursively constructed*;
2. The discourses of trust [between deaf people and interpreters] are *situated and bound by context*;

3. Trust as a practice is both a *form* and a *condition* of social [sign language in] action;
4. The meanings of trust are *continuously negotiated in* [sign language] *interaction*; and
5. Trust-building (and trust loss) is the basis for the formation of broader [signing] *community/institutional/social contexts* and *meanings*.

Regardless, though, of the scrutiny or 'deaf criticism' (Kent, 2012) that interpreters face, they are highly valued in the signing community because of the access that they provide to a world of information, as illustrated in Quote 6.18.

Quote 6.18 'We are nothing without a sign language interpreter'

Growing up I had to either try and understand by lipreading or rely on my mother to re-mouth someone's comment. I never really grasped at how much I did really missed.

I thought I could 'lipread' everything and that I missed nothing. Even there was countless times when I stood there baffled *'That doesn't make sense...'* but I thought I was just plain dumb and I had to learn more.

Lipreading is the most hardest thing ever... I was so tired every single day, I was tired before I had morning tea... my eyes watered so much, my mouth stayed open, dried all the time because I had to focused and focused. My mind, so often would wandered away half way lipreading then I am lost and cannot get back into the pattern again.

One eye would shut closed for a few minutes then I would switched to the other eye while trying to stay awake and keep the information in my head. So often I am tapped roughly on my arm *Rebekah, LISTEN!* ... Only if they knew I was just lipreading and not 'listening' I pretend to understand, I used the 'Deaf Nod' all the time and followed others to what we were supposed to do, most of the time I did the wrong thing.

[...]

Then...

When I was 17, I had my first encounter with a signing interpreter. I remembered watching in awe, I had no idea what were signing interpreters. I honestly thought there was no such thing as a signing interpreter. I didn't know they exist. I remembered standing at Deaf Club and watched the interpreters socialising with deaf people. I used to think 'Only if I can sign like that and they are my friends'. I remembered imagining I was buddies with the high profile Deaf people because they knew so much about life and they are friends with everyone.

I used to be ashamed of myself as an oral deaf person. I didn't like that I was taken away from my signing world and put into an oral, verbal and auditory world. I didn't like that I was deprived of communication.

I was never proud that I assumedly could 'hear' a lot and have brilliant speech...

However today I have learnt to accept the difference and no longer resent that. Then I discovered Theatre of the Deaf and I was so immersed in their creative style and language, I was so in love with ATOD. Every show I would go with glee and watched with pride. I would watch the interpreters introducing and voicing for the actors. I thought 'wow that's amazing'.

I learnt how to use an interpreter when I was in my mid 20s. I wished I knew I could access them years before that … I had a baby when I was 21 and my baby was born with a heart defect. She needed major surgery and stayed in hospital for a long time. I relied on my mother to 'interpret' for me …

I wished I knew my rights as a Deaf person then.

But interpreters were not common that time … it was a new thing.

When I first had an interpreter for a mental health appointment, I realised how much I understood and how I could express my emotions. It was the most fulfilling appointment I ever had.

Then I was taught that I am allowed to have interpreters and encouraged to use them.

From that moment onwards, I made sure I had interpreters all the time. I learnt so much more than I ever learnt by lipreading. I gained all these wisdoms, knowledges, skills, feelings, social awarenesses and so much more … things that I thought I would never thought I could obtained.

I was able to go for job interviews, get a job, go to TAFE and University, attend to workshops and conferences, have appointments with specialists, see a dentist without fear, have surgeries with full knowledge, give birth in the way I want and with confidence, attend to weddings and funerals, participate in playgroup and mother's groups, interact with my children's school, attend to Church and so much more.

I gained confidence, my identity and became sure of who I am as a person.

I stood up for myself. I was able to represented myself as a career woman with a passion for human rights and access for the Deaf Community. I was able to presented at many presentations because I had the ability to use interpreters to share my knowledge and express in my language.

That's a gift I wanted for so long and I no longer had to try hard … all I do is just be myself as I am.

Once I was told by somebody *You do not have any rights to sign language interpreters.*

I hate using the national relay service because they are nosy and it none of their business.

Rebekah, you do not need to use an interpreter with me, you can perfectly understand me clearly.

But you speak so well, surely you can hear me and understand what I am saying, don't you?

It's only a ten minutes meeting, it's a waste of time so just read the minutes.

It's not your funeral or *It's not your wedding.*

You can imagine how I felt … Thankfully I had a passion for teaching. I started to teach and encouraged every student I met to be a member of the Deaf Community.

I encouraged those with a potential to become an interpreter or to be a member of the Deaf Community.

I did some volunteering for a university to help with their training and research for interpreters. Often I would take on a newbie and help them develop their skills while interpreting for me.

I became so passionate about interpreters and wanted to be their supporter, not just for me but for the future of deaf people.

When my children were born I booked interpreters for them. I exposed them to interpreters from birth.

Over the years I have been privileged to see more and more interpreters within our community and better access for Deaf people. Interpreters are now taking part in community events, media, conferences, expos, government settings, schools and much more.

I went to my first comedy night two years ago and I laughed so hard, I was in tears. It was the most brilliant and funniest show I have ever seen ... I never thought I would attend to a comedy show by a non-deaf person ... I had an interpreter.

I went to see *Wicked Witch of the East, Chitty Chitty Bang Bang* and other performances and it was interpreted ... the music came alive! Oh how I loved music ... to understand 'music' and to 'sing' it was like Heaven opened it's doors and the ray of lights beamed down.

Lately TV emergency natural disaster situations are being interpreted. I watched with deep concern and took the warnings seriously ... Knowing my community is fully aware of the warnings because it is interpreted. How wonderful it is to access that? ...

I feel sad for those who mock interpreters because they do not have the rich life experiences like I do, nor have the understanding of real human beings ... and unfortunately they are small minded red necks.

However we have learnt from them because they give us the fire and the desire to continue fighting for our interpreters. I used to think that I know all the interpreters but now I don't know many of them ... many new faces ... I am so fortunate for those I have met on my journey. There are TAFE and university courses for interpreters ... And there is a NAATI level 4 accreditation ... BUT we need to keep fighting for them to cared for and fight for fundings so they can continue to develop the skills they need.

I have a favourite interpreter ... that is every single signing interpreter there is in the world.

I studied to become a Deaf Interpreter because I want to share the passion and give back to my community.

I am a member of ASLIA – Australian Sign Language Interpreters Association because I want to support my peers.

I had interpreters who sacrificed their time for me at a period of time I needed them and knowing they expected nothing in return.

I have been so inspired by interpreters and those who educated interpreters.

I have upmost respect every interpreter and have learnt to empathise with them ... because their job is not always a bed of roses.

With pride, I am proud to say that today, I have and worked with many amazing wonderful interpreters, I am proud to see them being acknowledged for their work.

We need to show that we appreciated interpreters by letting the Australian Government, Queensland's Premier, Deaf Organisations, Interpreters and Media know how grateful we are to have this access to OUR language.

It is time that we all take a bow to every single signing interpreter who follows the policies and ethics whether they are NAATI accredited or not and show how much they are valued to us and our people.

For we cannot survive in this world without them ... impossible ... honestly, it is impossible. (Rebekah Rose Mundy, deaf Auslan user and interpreter; http://darling-becky.me/2015/02/21/we-are-nothing-without-a-sign-language-interpreter/)

In Napier's (2011b) study of stakeholders' perceptions of interpreters and interpreting (see Case study 6.6), participants revealed their attitudes towards interpreters and interpreting in their linguistic choices. The study revealed that each participant group agreed on the fundamental aspects of interpreting in relation to the need for interpreters to be linguistically competent, professional, adaptable and considerate of the context and consumer needs, but the priorities given to interactant needs differed between the three stakeholder groups. Of particular interest was the amount of time dedicated by deaf participants and interpreters to talking about interpreters needing to have a 'good attitude', when this was not touched on at all by hearing (non-interpreter) participants. This implies an implicit trait of interpreters that is culturally valued within the signing community that it is essential for sign language interpreters to be aware of and embrace. When deaf and interpreter participants in Napier's study referred to interpreters having a 'good attitude', they typically referred to behavioural aspects of interpreters in making people feel comfortable and to the fact that interpreters were flexible and willing to 'give something' to the community.

In the field of applied linguistics, the study of language attitudes is prevalent (see e.g. Garret, Williams & Coupland, 2003). We discussed attitudes to sign languages and attitudes within signing communities in Chapter 3. People have attitudes, feelings and beliefs about language use in general and about people who use their own or other languages. Attitudes cannot be observed directly but are demonstrated through behaviour; for example, how people treat speakers of other languages or in their desire (or not) to learn another language. Thus, the notion of attitude would seem to be central in minority communities, which may explain why it is frequently mentioned by deaf sign language users in relation to interpreters: how they are treated by interpreters, how fluent interpreters are in using sign language, whether interpreters demonstrate that they value the goals of the signing community (see Case study 6.7) and why interpreters having a good attitude is central to the positive relationship between deaf people and interpreters.

Case study 6.7   Analysis of interpreter attitude

In an attempt to construct what is meant that sign language interpreters have a 'good attitude', Napier (2007b) drew on *appraisal theory* (Martin & Rose, 2003), which is a system of interpersonal meanings to identify how people convey their attitude and values in their linguistic choices. Appraisal theory can code for explicit, implicit, positive or negative attitude by analysing affect/emotion, judgement (character/behaviour) and appreciation (value of things). Returning to previous diary study data (Napier & Rohan, 2007) and previous focus group data (Napier, 2011b; see Case study 6.6), Napier (2007) found clear examples of appraisal of interpreter attitude in the way that deaf people and interpreters talk about interpreters, which is epitomised in the following dialogue:

Deaf participant: There are one or two, some who are good...
Napier: Why are they good?
Deaf participant: They are soft.
Napier: What do you mean by 'soft'?
Deaf participant: Their attitude. They make sure the person understands.

It was also clear from the interpreters' talk that they had clear perceptions of how they are appraised by deaf and hearing people, which can be categorised according to the three elements of attitude: affect/emotion, judgement (character/behaviour), and appreciation (value of things).

6.4 Sign language interpreter identity

Hearing people who are sign language users occupy an interesting position in the signing community, as discussed in Chapter 3. When we consider hearing sign language users in general, their identity in the community is dictated by their role in the signing community, how they came to learn sign language, when and where they use sign language, and who they interact with and in what contexts. Their perceived status is often directly related to their sign language fluency (Kent, 2012, as discussed in Chapter 4 and Section 6.3); as well as to their attitude towards deaf people and signed languages. These parameters also apply to professional (hearing) sign language interpreters.

In exploring the identity of interpreters in general, Hale (2005) argues that all interpreters face pressures and competing demands from the *institutional sphere*, the *professional sphere* and the *interpersonal sphere*. The interpersonal demands are particularly pertinent to the relationship between sign language interpreters and their deaf consumers and to the identities of sign language interpreters.

Various surveys conducted over the years have confirmed that sign language interpreters are typically white, female, self-employed and working part-time, and the most common age is 30–40 years old. Studies carried out among Auslan interpreters in Australia (Bontempo & Napier, 2007; Napier & Barker, 2003) and BSL interpreters in the UK (Brien, Brown & Collins, 2002; Mapson, 2013) found that only a small minority (around 10–15%) are native signers (PDFs), confirming that more people from 'outside' the deaf community are being drawn to learn a sign language and thus enter the sign language interpreting profession (Stone, 2012). The identity of hearing sign language interpreters is socially constructed according to the values of signing communities, with emphasis on interpreters having the right attitude (cultural identity) and being involved in their signing local community (social identity), which is valued more than sign language fluency (McDermid, 2009). It is recognised that interpreters have to negotiate multiple identities: as hearing individuals, as interpreters, as 'good citizens in an unfamiliar culture' (McDermid, 2009, p. 126); hearing PDF interpreters also have the additional identity of growing up hearing in a deaf world (Napier, 2008). Interpreters are multi-seitic (Napier, 2008); their several identities are complicated by the fact that they are hearing and therefore not 'from the same ethnic group' as the community with whom they work (Napier, 2002).

The identity of (hearing) sign language interpreters is shaped by the way they are perceived by deaf sign language users (as discussed in Section 6.3). Mason (2005) and Wadensjö (1998) assert that we need to consider interpreter identity within a participation framework, and Metzger (1999) and Roy (2000) have highlighted the fact that sign language interpreters are participants in triadic interaction through their situational analyses of interpreter-mediated communication. There is little research, however, that gives voice to sign language interpreters' perceptions of their own constructed identities in relation to the interpreting profession or their position in signing communities.

The notion of 'voice' is associated with the framing of individual and collective identities, identifications, subjectivities and discursive subject positionings (Arnot & Reay, 2007), and most contemporary voice research 'recognises the power of research relationships and methods in framing particular voices, eliciting some and not others. Therefore ... there is not one authentic voice of a single social category' (Arnot & Reay, 2007, p. 313). In the context of translation, it has been recognized that the translator has a 'voice', in that the 'presence' of the translator can be felt when reading a translated text (Hermans, 1996; Simon, 1996), especially when back translation is used so translators have a voice with their clients (Ozolins, 2009). In giving a collective voice to sign language interpreters and to recognise their 'authentic voices', Pollitt (2011) analysed the collective biographies and discussions of a group of sign language interpreters working on translations of the British Sign Language corpus into English on a closed Facebook group. She asserted that it is important to understand professional practice through the perspective of the practitioners themselves and not just through academic research.

Research that has considered the 'voice' of interpreters has predominantly focussed on linguistic analyses of first- or third-person use by interpreters, such as in a corpus of courtroom data and whether an interpreter relays the stance of the interlocutor or inserts their own voice (e.g. for clarification; Angermeyer, 2009). One of the few studies of sign language interpreters' voice was conducted by Napier (2012a) in order to evaluate their perceptions of their identity in relation to their standing in the signing community (see Case study 6.8).

Case study 6.8   Collective voice of interpreters

Using adapted 'categories of talk' from Arnot and Reay (2007), Napier (2012a) sought to identify whether there was a collective voice among sign language interpreters through the analysis of a corpus of 12 hours of data from interviews and focus groups with interpreters throughout Australia over a 5-year period (2006–2011) from various projects. The qualitative analysis focussed on the voice of the interpreter by analysing what they say about their work. The categories of talk for content analysis included the following:

(1) *Deaf talk:* the styles of communication and language codes used by interpreters and deaf people
(2) *Subject talk:* making explicit the recognition and realisation rules of competence in interpreting
(3) *Identity talk:* reference to self and collective identity
(4) *Code talk:* interpreters' representations of the rules which govern interpreting practice and their impact

Napier (2012a) found clear patterns of talk which revealed a collective voice among Australian sign language interpreters, particularly in relation to their identity.

Summary of themes of deaf talk:

• Attitude
• Community membership
• Sign language features
• Fingerspelling
• Sign language choices

Examples of deaf talk:
... the Deaf people would warn you, 'Be careful of the deaf community basically because people will be sceptical'... And I have to say that I didn't get that. I feel really lucky that the Deaf community in [a city] was really welcoming and nice and kind and I never... There was one Deaf person who was asking lots of probing questions as to my motives, and I kind of felt I was doing a test, which I may not have passed. But other than that one person, everyone was really kind and generous.
In English though I'm more likely to use facial expression, role shift to indicate characters' emotions or local intonation or stuff like that. Usually I fingerspell terminology because they need to know not only concept but the terminology... If it comes up regularly enough, like 'differentiation' is such a horrid thing to spell, we just all shortened it to D-I-F-F.
Summary of themes of subject talk:

• Interpreting strategies – free/literal
• Attention getting
• Preparation
• Interpreter comprehension
• Experience
• Skills
• Knowledge

- Qualifications
- Decision making (when to interpret or not)

Examples of subject talk:

... knowing what to omit. I remember doing a job at the Art Gallery a couple of months ago. There was a mother there who had a deaf child and it was for an Aboriginal storyteller. He was telling a story and I thought I was doing a really good job of interpreting into Auslan. There was one part of the story where the Aboriginal girl climbed up a tree to get something and the Aboriginal storyteller said it was a blue gum tree. I just got rid of that, not important information. There were other more important bits of information. Afterwards the mother came up to me and was talking about a few things in my interpreting choices and [she] said, 'What did you sign for blue gum?' and I said, 'Well, didn't do that'. Her response was sort of like [indicated dissatisfaction] 'Oh ... right'...

In that case, that also comes back to most professionals have no idea that Auslan is its own language in itself, so they just assume well you can read. You know they don't understand anything about it.

I refer to the board more in maths and, like, in maths I refer to the board a lot and, and the teachers ... The teachers tend to write in colours, so I'll say, oh, the green, or the red, because they'll have a particular thing in a different colour for a different reason, so great.

Summary of themes of identity talk:

- Professionalism
- Presence/insertion/assertion of self
- Recognition by other professionals
- Professional solidarity
- Role/participation/action (actor/initiator)

Examples of identity talk:

We are there, and we are important and without us it wouldn't happen, but we're not meant to get all the glory. We're meant to be that person in the background who makes it all happen ...

If we do want to move towards becoming a profession, then we do need to have some kind of professional association who can lobby and protect interpreters' interests and where we can all support each other and learn together.

Sometimes when you go into a medical appointment, the health professional seems to think that perhaps you're the deaf person's carer because they don't understand why you, the interpreter – having told them that. And it's like, I'm the interpreter, I just met this client. But they seem to think you must have been to the other times and should know all about the health concerns and why as the interpreter have you not told the medical professional.

Summary of themes of code talk:

- Code of ethics
- Impartiality
- Role – boundaries
- Positioning

Examples of code talk:

So the other thing about how fast the conversation goes and things going over, sometimes it's the most fun, I mean you can do that, you know, it's not witness testimony, it

really is, you know, the message, the content and the overlapping is part of it, but it does
get to be too much and we do speak up when it does, you know.
   Most of the time I'm sitting in front of the students as close to the board as possible.
Well, you have to let the client [speak. Do not ever speak] for the client, so you can only
wait and hope that and keep facilitating that communication so you feel that you've done
the right job, that's all you can do ...
   The analysis revealed the strength and importance of the interpreters' 'voice'
and the need to recognise the position of the interpreter as participant and
the various identities that interpreters can assume. Napier (2012a) concluded
that the 'community of practice' framework is a useful framework for considering the collective identity of sign language interpreters, that language is one
of many social practices in which participants engage to assert their identity
and that the community of practice model accommodates the individuality
that is paramount without overlooking the strong community ties that unify
interpreters.

The identity of sign language interpreters has been in the media spotlight lately as they are more frequently present to provide access to deaf
viewers to TV emergency broadcasts in relation to flood, cyclone, earth-
quake or other natural disasters (McKee, 2014); or most recently the sign
language interpreter for the 2015 Eurovision 'song' contest who 'stole
the show'.[3] The majority of the media commentary has focussed on the
aspects of sign language use, and the animation or face 'mugging' that
viewers regard either as entertaining (or offensive). Commentary from
signing communities, however, has focussed on why the attention is given
to sign language interpreters rather than deaf people themselves, and the
fact that the attention might be misplaced (see Example 6.7). Nonetheless,
McKee (2014) notes that having sign language interpreters in the spotlight
can actually raise awareness of signing communities and sign language
(see Quote 6.19). Therefore, a 'fractious interdependence' appears to exist
between deaf people and sign language interpreters (Napier, 2002, p. 33),
which means that the identity of sign language interpreters is complex
and somewhat opaque.

Example 6.7 **'Another storm, another sign language interpreter goes viral'**

Are interpreters like #Signguy, who sign during public emergencies, going viral
for the right reasons? (20 February 2015)
   'Another storm, another sign language interpreter goes viral.'
   In Queensland, Australia, a sign language interpreter has appeared on TV alongside Premier Annastacia Palaszczuk to warn the public how to stay safe during a
category cyclone. The TV audience saw his signing and went crazy about it, and
now he's gone viral. His name is Mark Cave, but to Twitter users, he's now known
as #signguy.

Here's a few of the tweets he's attracted:

#Signguy delivers the most animated cyclone warning ever.
#TCMarcia bit.ly/17xDjdT
We muted and made up our own commentary. #Signguy made way more sense. Bring
on #signguy for all her public announcements, cyclone or not!!
This guy is magic #signguy #TCMarcia

We've seen this happen before, when ASL interpreter Lydia Callis went viral for her signing during Hurricane Sandy, or more recently, when a Deaf interpreter called Jonathan Lamberton went viral for signing during an Ebola news conference.

Each time this happens, the wider audience can't help but notice that these interpreters seem incredibly animated, almost as though they think they're performing, rather than simply giving their audience (deaf people) a vital message.

Now, the reason sign language interpreters are seen on TV screens during these emergencies is because that's the best way for the authorities to ensure that deaf people who use sign language get the message about how to stay safe. Sign language is not all about the movements of hands and arms but also body language and facial expression, which help give the signs their meaning.

One way to understand it is to compare it with how a non-deaf person might adjust the tone of their voice to add emphasis to what they're saying. So, why do these interpreters look so 'animated'? Well, if you're signing about a storm, and telling people that they really need to take the advice you're giving them, otherwise they might be injured or die, it's not enough just to tell them – you need to show them, visually, through your demeanour, just how serious this situation is, and how powerful the storm might be. And that's exactly what these interpreters are doing. Watching the video of Mark Cave in action, he's no more animated than he should be, and the information he gives is perfectly clear (although I don't use Auslan, it is very similar to British Sign Language, and it seems clear to me).

In some ways, the way these interpreters go viral every time a storm comes is a good thing, in terms of raising public awareness of Deaf people – who are often so hidden from wider view – and of the language we use. My concern, however, can be summed up by tweets like these below.

#signguy reminds me of the character from the movie Airplane:
Why, I can make a hat or a brooch or a pterodactyl...

What worries me is that some people think that the interpreters are doing something comical – which they aren't. These skilled interpreters aren't making fun of the situation, or giving people at home a cheap laugh. They're simply signing in the most expressive and powerful way they can in order to tell deaf people how they can remain safe.

They deserve credit for how well they do that. (Charlie Swinbourne, deaf BSL user & journalist; http://limpingchicken.com/2015/02/20/signguy/)

Quote 6.19   Media commentary and interpreter demands

Examining experience in unusual work contexts enriches perspective on the spectrum of interpreters' professional practice, and illustrates a range of strategies and qualities that they deploy when performing their role in challenging conditions. In civil emergency media settings, there is little physical, psychological or temporal space in which to manage concurrent demands in the interpreting task. The experiences ... indicate the need in such situations for a small, consistent team of seasoned interpreters who possess: (i) strong cognitive and emotional resilience; (ii) sufficient contextual and audience knowledge to confidently make rapid decisions about effective message transfer; (iii) a repertoire of process management techniques in order to 'get the information out' within the interactional constraints; and (iv) the ethical maturity to recognise and manage one's role as an involved participant, accepting the likelihood that one will become an ambassador for sign language and the profession.

The amount of public and reflexive media comment (whether positive or negative) generated about the interpreters' presence signals that public and government awareness of sign language users within the general population was advanced during these events. (McKee, 2014, pp. 126–127)

In considering the non-professional practice of sign language language brokering and the professional practice of sign language interpreting and translation, it is worthwhile considering current changing practices.

6.5   Changing practices

There are evident challenges for sign language interpreters in dealing with the evolution and change in sign language use across the world, including increasing language contact between spoken and signed languages influenced by consumers who are deaf late learners of sign language (see Chapter 4); language contact between signed languages influenced by the internationalisation of the world signing community (Adam, 2012a) and travel patterns of deaf scholars and politicians who attend multilingual events (De Wit, 2010; Supalla, Clark, Neumann Solow & Müller de Quadros, 2010); dealing with sociolinguistic variation within their own countries (Leeson, 2005b; see Chapter 5); migration and refugee patterns so interpreters in one country have to interpret for deaf people who use a different sign language from another country (Ramsey & Peña, 2010); or working with indigenous deaf people who use a different sign language (Davis & McKay-Cody, 2010; McKee & Awheto, 2010).

Within the profession of sign language interpreting and translation, we now see two key areas where practices are changing to account for the updated perceptions of the status and identity of deaf sign language users, to capitalise on the new technologies available for sign language communication as well as the professionalisation of sign language interpreters and translators: (1) the emergence of deaf people working professionally in the field and (2) the provision of interpreting services through video remote technology. The advent of both of these practices is having an impact on sign language in professional practice in terms of the identity of sign language interpreters and the nature of sign language in action.

6.5.1   Deaf interpreters and translators

In recent times, there has been wider recognition of the role that deaf people have to play in brokering information between hearing and deaf people (see Quote 6.20). Adam, Carty and Stone (2011) have asserted that deaf sign language users have always functioned as interpreters and translators in a non-professional brokering role within signing communities. However, deaf people are now widely employed to work professionally in various contexts (Boudrealt, 2005; Collins & Walker, 2006), including on television (De Meulder & Heyerick, 2013; Duncan, 1997; Steiner, 1998; Stone, 2009).

This is a challenging concept, as it would never occur to the majority of non-deaf people that a sign language interpreter could be a deaf person (Turner, 2006). Even members of signing communities are not necessarily aware of how or why deaf people work as interpreters, because historically interpreters have always been hearing and members of the signing community may not understand how the interpreting process will work, which can leave them feeling uncomfortable and suspicious (Boudreault, 2005).

Nevertheless, in recognition of the fact that deaf people come from within the signing community and thus have ingrained linguistic and cultural community experiences which can contribute to the interpretation process (see Quote 6.20), more deaf people have begun to work as interpreters and translators, although it is recommended that it is still essential for deaf interpreters to be suitably trained (Forestal, 2005; Mathers, 2009; Morgan & Adam, 2012); countries such as the U.S, the UK, Austria, Germany and Australia now offer qualifications and testing for deaf interpreters on a par with hearing sign language interpreters (see Case study 6.9).

Quote 6.20   Including deaf interpreters

The inclusion of deaf interpreters in an interpreting team has increasingly become a part of best-practice interpreting service provision. Deaf and hearing interpreters work together to achieve the best possible outcome for the consumers, both deaf and hearing, because their skills complement each other, including how deaf interpreters have lived experience as deaf people. This ensures a high standard of service delivery which brings together the differing linguistic, cultural and life experience of both the deaf and hearing practitioners. (Robert Adam, deaf multilingual sign language user, sign linguist and qualified interpreter and translator)

An interpreter who is deaf may be employed in contexts where the (typically non-native signing) hearing interpreter feels he or she needs extra assistance to understand the signing of a deaf person or accurately convey a message to a deaf person. In their 1997 Standard Practice Paper on working with certified Deaf interpreters, the U.S. Registry of Interpreters for the Deaf (RID) state that deaf and hearing interpreters may need to work together 'when the communication mode of a deaf consumer is so unique that it cannot be adequately accessed by interpreters who are hearing'. Deaf and hearing interpreters can be found working together in situations when the deaf client uses idiosyncratic signs or gestures that could be thought of as 'home signs' that are unique to a family; uses a foreign sign language; has minimal or limited communication skills; is deafblind or deaf with limited vision (requiring a tactile form of sign language); uses signs particular to a given region, ethnic or age group; or has characteristics reflective of deaf culture not familiar to hearing interpreters (McKee & Awheto, 2010).

Case study 6.9   Deaf interpreter certification

Between 2006 and 2008, the Australian sign language interpreting profession made a significant step towards better recognition of deaf interpreters' skills via the creation of a national deaf interpreter testing instrument and assessment process by the Australian Sign Language Interpreters Association. The Deaf Relay Interpreter Certification Project (DRICP) took place from 2006–2008 at a time when the deaf interpreting profession was developing and gaining recognition worldwide as an emerging professional sub-field of sign language interpreting. The project involved a needs analysis of where and how deaf interpreters work in Australia, an exploration and pilot of various testing formats and a roll-out of a testing programme that led to an initial cohort of certified deaf interpreters (Bontempo, Goswell, Levitzke-Gray, Napier & Warby, 2014). The process was not without its challenges as the deaf interpreting profession was in such a fledgling state in the country, and at the time, there was minimal research in the field worldwide, so there were few precedents to rely on. Nevertheless, it was the first stepping-stone towards adoption by the National Accreditation Authority for Translators and Interpreters in Australia, who established a nationwide recognition system for deaf interpreters in 2014.

Deaf interpreters working in community settings (e.g. medical, legal) will therefore typically work unimodally and intra-lingually *within* one sign language. Deaf people's experience of making themselves understood nonverbally, their first-hand knowledge of diverse communication and personal backgrounds in the signing community and their ability to conceptualise experiences and ideas through the eyes of a deaf sign language user can give them a repertoire of visual communication skills that hearing interpreters cannot necessarily emulate – something referred to as Deaf Extra-Linguistic Knowledge (DELK; Adam, Aro, Druetta, Dunne & af Klintberg, 2014). In these contexts, the deaf interpreter takes the message from a hearing interpreter, who is signing in an established sign language (such as BSL), and re-frames the message into a different form within the same sign language; for example, a doctor speaks in English → relayed from English into BSL by a hearing interpreter → interpreted from BSL into a more basic, visual form of BSL by the deaf interpreter for a deaf patient who has limited language skills. Occasionally, deaf interpreters may need to draw on other skills, such as gesturing, drawing, writing or using props (Adam, Carty & Stone, 2011; Adam et al., 2014; Boudrealt, 2005; Morgan & Adam, 2012); or they can relay from a signed presentation into another communication mode, such as deafblind tactile signing, by watching the presenter and interpreting in consecutive chunks (Sforza, 2014).

Despite the RID stating that deaf interpreters are utilised where the communication mode of the deaf client is unique, interpreters who are deaf are also now seen more frequently working as conference interpreters, so therefore are more present in using sign language in professional practice in 'everyday life'. This practice presents complex logistics in ensuring that the deaf interpreters can access the source text. There are two options: either they rely on another interpreter to provide them with the source text in a *pivot* sign language (Stone & Russell, 2014) – that is, the interpreter listens to the spoken text or watches the original signed text, then conveys the message to the deaf interpreter on the platform in a different sign language, and the deaf interpreter then renders the information into yet another national sign language or International Sign); or they read from an auto-cue live transcription of the spoken source text: the interpreter who is deaf is on the platform facing the audience, and the hearing interpreter or auto-cue machine is placed off-stage and within the direct eye gaze of the interpreter who is deaf.

The process of reading from an auto-cue and interpreting into sign language is the typical practice for deaf interpreters working in television (Stone, 2009), producing translations of websites or pre-prepared information such as government leaflets to ensure accessible content, and other forms of sign language translation (see Section 6.2.3).[4] Stone (2009) argues that deaf people establish a 'deaf translation norm', and there is an emerging body of research that explores the strategies and processes used by deaf interpreters and translators (Forestal, 2014; Müller de Quadros, de Souza &

Segala, 2012; Rogers et al., 2013b), how deaf and hearing interpreters work in teams (Bentley-Sassaman & Dawson, 2012; Nicodemus & Taylor, 2014; Stone & Russell, 2014), and how deaf interpreters work together as a team (Sforza, 2014). The growing practice of including deaf people as language professionals is therefore pushing the boundaries of the sign language interpreting and translation profession in terms of identity, practice and sign language norms (see Quote 6.21).

Quote 6.21   Problematising ideas about interpreting

The emergence of Deaf practitioners [DIs] thus problematises ideas about interpreting in several significant ways: it invites us to review fundamental analyses and definitions of language, interpreting and translation with reference to the working practices of DIs, or be prepared to consider calls to abandon them and accept economic or other exogenous accounts; it invites us to re-appraise the landscape of professionalism in the field, specifically with reference to frameworks of training, assessment and 'occupational standards' criteria; it invites us to re-think assumptions and emerging understandings of power relations between Deaf and non-Deaf (signing and non-signing) communities as experienced and expressed through linguistic and cultural mediation and mediators; and finally, it invites us in general to attend to the shifting of social identities throughout the field. (Turner, 2006, p. 292)

6.5.2   The impact of video technology

Although deaf and hearing interpreters and translators have featured on TV for some time (Steiner, 1998; Stone, 2009; see Section 6.5.1 and Chapter 7, Section 7.3), this discussion will focus on the impact of technologies on communication via sign language, how interlocutors adapt sign language production for the two-dimensional medium and the changing practice of sign language interpreter provision through video technology.

The advent of technology that allows for the easy recording of video can be seen to have a positive influence on sign language literacy now that it is easier to record, edit and share sign language footage for the purposes of teaching or research (Lucas, Mirus, Palmer, Roessler & Frost, 2013; Snoddon, 2010; Young & Temple, 2014). Furthermore, technological devices that allow for communication via video (e.g. smartphones, tablets, webcams, video conference facilities) provide sign language users with increasing opportunities to communicate directly with one another in sign language. This situation is giving rise to increasing language contact between sign languages and observations of fewer boundaries between which lexical items belong to which sign language (see Quote 6.22).

Quote 6.22   Technological impact on sign language

I see several impacts on sign language as a result of technology. The first is as a result of the advent of the webcam as a popular technological device that can be used by deaf people, we are seeing a greater influence on BSL [from other sign languages]. For example, I recently saw a renowned deaf leader in the British signing community, who is a fluent BSL user, use the ASL sign for KNOW instead of the BSL sign. I was surprised to see this. But it happened because this person has regular contact with deaf Americans via webcam, so he has taken on board some of their signs. Another example is with my own [deaf] son, who is involved at a European level networking with other [deaf] students and young people throughout Europe [via webcam]. He is exposed to various sign languages, so sometimes I see his sign language use shifting to accommodate what he has seen elsewhere. We can see that signs from all over the world are now borrowed *into* BSL. This situation doesn't concern me, though. I think it's a positive shift; it gives sign language users the flexibility to choose how they want to sign and what signs they want to use...The second impact that I've noticed is that other European sign languages are borrowing signs *from* BSL. I recently saw a deaf Spanish man use several BSL lexical signs while I was watching him present. I think the younger generation are more flexible in their sign language use, and more open to adopting signs from other languages. In the same way that you can play with the English language by borrowing from other languages, for example, using Latin quotes, you can now do the same in sign language – bringing in signs from elsewhere to be creative in your sign language use...Language is dynamic, it cannot remain static...This is the nature of sign language use among the younger generation, and I think that is a positive thing for the signing community. (Jeff McWhinney, deaf multilingual sign language user, entrepreneur and founder of SignVideo)

A growing body of research has focussed on the way that sign language production is changing to accommodate for communication via technological interfaces, and as with spoken languages, it can be seen that technological and sign language innovation 'flow in concert with one another' (Schneider, Kozak, Santiago & Stephen, 2012, p. 368). For example, Young, Morris and Langdon (2012) found that the use of constructed dialogue, including eye gaze and body (posture) shifts, is influenced by the interface mode. Specifically, they found that eye-gaze shifts were less frequent in video blog monologues and even less common in videophone interactions. Keating and Mirus (2003) and Keating, Terra and Mirus (2008) have also discussed the way that deaf signers invent new communication behaviours and pragmatically adapt to communicating directly through video technology. They found that ASL users make accommodations in the way that they sign when communicating via videoconference in order to cope with the interference from video communication and to allow for proximity to the webcam lens. Accommodations particularly included adapting sign language production by slowing down the rate of fingerspelling and using clearer mouthing of words. This adaptation of sign language production was also found in a study involving deaf Auslan users and Auslan interpreters when interpreting was provided via videoconference in court (see Case study 6.10).

Sign language interpreter-mediated interaction is increasingly occurring via video technology, and interpreters are therefore required to be involved in (1) video conference interpreting (VCI), where there are two locations and the interpreter is in either one; or (2) remote interpreting (RI), where all participants are together in one location and the interpreter is in a separate, remote location. In both of these situations, the communication between locations takes place via videoconference (Braun & Taylor, 2011). In the sign language interpreting sector, there is also the potential for three different locations – where participants are in two different locations and an interpreter is in a third remote location – particularly through video relay services (Alley, 2012). Thus, to avoid any confusion between the differences, we will use a more generic overarching term to refer to any of the above combinations: *video remote interpreting* (VRI).

Case study 6.10   Sign language accommodation and clarification through VRI

In Australia, a study was conducted to investigate the effectiveness of sign language VRI in New South Wales' courts. The provision of services was tested in venues across five simulated scenarios. The aim of the original project was to assess the integrity of the interpreting process when interpreters or deaf people were in different locations and the stakeholder perceptions of interpreted interactions experienced remotely. One aspect of the study focussed on an analysis of three of the cases and the accommodation and clarification devices used.

The findings revealed that the video remote aspect of the legal proceedings had a pragmatic effect on the devices used by interpreters and deaf people: they slowed down their signing, mouthed more clearly and also oriented their palm towards the screen when fingerspelling. All of the interpreter and deaf participants reported the challenges of communicating via a video screen but acknowledged that when accommodations were made, it was possible to communicate clearly. However, the interpreters who were based remotely found that not knowing who was in the courtroom affected their sign language production in terms of spatial referents. As sign languages actively recruit visual information about location of people in a space, when the interpreters could not see that information, they could not incorporate it into their signed utterances. They also found that it was difficult to get the attention of deaf signers in the courtroom in order to seek clarification of a signed utterance if the deaf person was not looking directly at the videoconference screen.

The data from this study also supported findings from other studies (Berk-Seligson, 1990; Hale, 2004) that interpreters find it difficult to interrupt in the

> courtroom. This study revealed that Auslan interpreters found it even more difficult to interrupt when needing to seek clarification via video, and therefore they tended to request repetition or confirmation in only one language. (Napier, 2013b)

VRI services are utilised in order to make phone calls, participate in short meetings and access court proceedings and conferences, and the provision varies from country to country (Napier et al., submitted). It has been identified as an effective solution to providing increased access for deaf people to sign language interpreters, especially for those in regional or rural areas, but the perceptions of the VRI varies. Deaf sign language users and interpreters report that although VRI is an effective solution for providing timely access to information or mediated interaction in sign language, there is often a feeling of disconnect due to lack of proximity, so face-to-face interpreting is still preferred (Napier, 2012b).

From an applied sign linguistics perspective, one particularly interesting aspect of the impact of VRI on signing communities is the potential influence on sign language standardisation. Palmer, Reynolds and Minor (2012) suggest that because the spread of VRI has allowed deaf people to be more connected with other deaf people and interpreters across the U.S., and VRI therefore enables signers to be more exposed to regional sign variation, that awareness of regional variation and the skill level of VRI interpreters are possible factors that may encourage deaf consumers to limit usage of local or regional variants, replacing them with more standard forms. They also suggest that the exposure also has had an impact on sign language attitudes in the evaluation of 'correct' or 'incorrect' signs, which may further affect the standardisation of ASL.

Furthermore, VRI technology affects interpreting practice itself in several ways, including the need to adapt signing style to account for the two-dimensional medium and the difficulties of getting a deaf person's attention if the interpreter is in a different location (as demonstrated in Case study 6.10), difficulties in 'reading' micro-movements of fingerspelling and grammatical facial expressions through the video technology, limited options for interpreters to assess a deaf client's language needs, less opportunity for interpreters to brief with either party to ascertain the communicative goals of the interaction or develop rapport and greater number of turns in VRI interaction (compared to interpreter-mediated face-to-face interaction), meaning that interaction is slower (Brunson, 2011; Napier, McKee & Goswell, 2010; Taylor, 2005, 2009; Wilson, 2010) and more effortful (Brunson, 2011).

Providing interpreting through video technology is also changing the nature of interpreters' communicative management practice. It is well established that sign language interpreters utilise various footing shifts for the purposes of interactional management in a shared physical space, for example, indicating who is speaking (source attribution), asking an interlocutor to wait (turn management) or attention getting (Marks, 2012; Metzger, 1999). In her analysis of footing shifts in simulated phone calls using VRI, Marks (2015) found that in addition to using the same footing shifts as would be expected in face-to-face interaction, the interpreters also explicitly managed turns in the phone calls by outlining how the call would take place and took the floor in order to manage the technological issues, thus providing further evidence for the fact that interpreters are actively engaged in managing interpreted discourse (as discussed by Roy, 2000; Wadensjö, 1998; and others).

6.6   Sign language in (professional) practice: concluding comments

This chapter has examined how sign language is used in non-professional and professional practice, with consideration given to the role of deaf and hearing people as language brokers and also as language professionals (i.e. interpreters and translators). We have identified particular issues that are pertinent from an applied linguistic perspective in relation to sign language interpreting as a practice profession, sign language interpreting *in* practice and also changing practices. Another important aspect we have addressed is the relationship between (hearing) sign language interpreters and members of the core signing community (i.e. deaf people) and the consequent impact on sign language interpreter identity. It is clear that the study of sign language in (professional) practice has the potential to dominate in applied sign linguistics, given the need for deaf people to communicate with members of wider society through interpreters or to access information through translation. Thus, we would propose that applied linguistics and interpreting studies scholars work together more closely to investigate this area further.

Further reading

Ball, C. (2013). *Legacies and legends: History of interpreter education from 1800 to the 21st century*. Edmonton, Canada: Interpreting Consolidated.

Bontempo, K. (2015). Signed language interpreting. In H. Mikkelson & R. Jourdanais (Eds), *Routledge Handbook on Interpreting*. New York, NY: Routledge.

Brunson, J. (2011). *Video relay service interpreters: Intricacies of sign language access*. Washingon, DC: Gallaudet University Press.

Janzen, T. (Ed.). (2005). *Topics in signed language interpreting*. Amsterdam, the Netherlands: John Benjamins.

Leeson, L., Wurm, S., & Vermeerbergen, M. (2011). *Signed language interpreting: Preparation, practice and performance*. London, UK: Routledge.

Napier, J. (Ed.). (2009). *International perspectives on sign language interpreter education*. Washington, DC: Gallaudet University Press.

Napier, J. (2015). Comparing signed and spoken language interpreting. In H. Mikkelson & R. Jourdanais (Eds), *Routledge Handbook on Interpreting*. New York, NY: Routledge.

Napier, J., McKee, R., & Goswell, D. (2010). *Sign language interpreting: Theory and practice in Australia and New Zealand* (2nd ed.). Sydney, Australia: Federation Press.

Roy, C. B., & Napier, J. (Eds). (2015). *The sign language interpreting studies reader.* Amsterdam, the Netherlands: John Benjamins.

Part III

Research into Applied Sign Linguistics

7
Conducting Research in Applied Sign Linguistics

'[We] are interested in how researchers can work best with Deaf people, Deaf schools, Deaf children and families, and other professionals who work in the area of deafness... [There are] important considerations when embarking on studies that involve Deaf people and their sign languages. This is not just a philosophical question anymore; increasingly research funding agencies are expecting ethical compliance, good quality dissemination, and knowledge exchange, as well as evidence of how research is actually making an impact on the everyday lives of the participants and on wider society. We argue that sign language research that is **with** rather than **on** Deaf people will both be superior in scientific terms and will achieve more societal impact'. (Singleton et al., 2015, p. 8; emphasis in original)

In this final content chapter, we discuss the various steps involved in carrying out a research project in applied sign linguistics, focusing on the considerations needed in terms of research design and participant recruitment as well as analysis. Although the approaches utilised in applied sign linguistics research are the same as applied linguistics research in general, we highlight specific issues for consideration when investigating sign language in action. For more guidance on research methods in complementary fields of sign linguistics, Deaf Studies and interpreting studies, we recommend readers refer to books such as Hale and Napier (2013); Orfanidou, Woll and Morgan (2015); Pfau, Steinbach and Woll (2012) and Young and Temple (2014) – see Further Readings at the end of the chapter for more details.

The first part of the chapter (Section 7.1) provides a clear step-by-step approach to conducting practical, sign language–based research. We then give an overview of various research topics in applied sign linguistics with examples from existing research and conclude with suggestions for research project ideas.

Quote 7.1   Contested issues in sign language research

...to be deaf is to stand at multiple intersections of language, culture, disability, society, politics, ethics and the body. Consequently, research incursions into this complexity have to deal with the consequences of such issues as the contested nature of identity, bilingual and bimodal effects, definitionally unstable populations, relationship between epistemology and language, alternative and multiple ontologies or ways of being, socially constructed hierarchies of sameness and difference, not to mention the influence of who exactly is doing the looking and telling. (Young & Temple, 2014, p. 2)

7.1   Steps to conducting research

For applied linguists, Candlin and Crichton (2011) suggest a 5-perspective model of interdiscursivity with multiple possible entry points for research and analysis: the text perspective, the participant perspective, the social and institutional perspective, the social action perspective and the analyst's perspective. When we apply these lenses to the study of applied sign linguistics, we can consider the following:

1. *Text perspective:* exploration of signed languages as discursive texts within signing communities and 'across boundaries' to wider non-deaf communities; what is the status of sign language texts, how they are produced, understood and valued and how they are shared
2. *Participant perspective:* discussion of perspectives of deaf and non-deaf signers, native and non-native sign language users and other stakeholders who engage with deaf sign language users in everyday life either through professional practice or social circumstances (such as teachers, parents or service providers); how the use of sign language has an impact on identity and how that identity is conveyed
3. *Social and institutional perspective:* analysis of the interdependent nature of social institutions, communities of practice and sign language in use (e.g. deaf clubs, deaf sporting events) and societal institutions that affect sign language policy, planning and practice (e.g., deaf schools); the power ascribed to the use of sign language in society
4. *Social action perspective:* examination of signing communities and smaller sub-groups within signing communities; the actions carried out by signing individuals to which those individuals attach meaning (e.g., lobbying for the legal recognition of sign languages); intentions behind those actions
5. *Analyst's perspective:* presenting the 'voice' of the analysts, based on their expertise, their position as deaf or hearing researchers in signing

communities, their own epistemological and ontological positions as researchers; their insights into the data

Young and Temple (2014, p. 29) assert that it is important for researchers to consider how they *'represent* what it means to be d/Deaf in their research' (their emphasis), which means not only defining the nature of the community that is involved in the research but acknowledging their objectivity or subjectivity as researchers. There are many approaches to conducting research with signing communities, which will be influenced by the nature of the study, what exactly is being studied, who is involved in the project and what the desired outcomes are.

Hall (2002), Hale (2007) and others have described how an appropriate approach to conducting research with languages is to consider research steps as part of a cycle rather than a linear process, particularly so that findings can be applied in practice – which is, essentially, what lies at the heart of applied linguistics research. Depending on how the research was initiated (see Section 7.1.1), therefore, the research cycle may evolve as a research-practice-research cycle (Candlin, 2001), or a practice-research-practice cycle (Hatim, 2013). Key elements of any research project are important at different stages of either type of research cycle so that the research is systematic and so that it may be iterative. The remainder of Section 7.1 highlights these elements for researchers to consider with respect to their own applied sign linguistics projects.

7.1.1 Interest in a topic and defining research questions

Researchers in applied sign linguistics have different motivations for selecting topics to study, which may be influenced by whether they are deaf or hearing themselves and how and when they were exposed to sign language. In addition to being deaf sign language users themselves, researchers may have been exposed to sign language from an early age through family members, neighbours, or from living in a neighbourhood near a deaf school, for example. Other researchers discover the benefits of studying sign languages through their general work as linguists or applied linguists; still others come into contact with sign language through deaf work colleagues, which leads their interest into studying sign languages.

Investigators who explore sign language in action often come from a background of professional practice, perhaps as sign language teachers, interpreters or translators or teachers of the deaf, or through their involvement in signing communities in other professional capacities that piques their interest in sign language description or use. Quote 7.2 was written by applied sign linguist Graham H. Turner with respect to sign language interpreting and translation studies, but it epitomises the diversity of backgrounds of applied sign linguists.

Quote 7.2 Authentic co-operation

It is arguable that one of the successes of [applied sign linguistics studies] to date has been the authentic co-operation among many who arrive at this field of enquiry from different points of departure. Let us not pretend that everyone works closely with everyone else all the time; but there are numerous instances of collaborative activity, which demonstrate a genuine sense of mutual respect for the differing contributions to be made by a range of participants. Published work in our field is by no means dominated by career academics of the 'ivory tower' persuasion who pronounce from on high to and for some imagined 'lesser mortals'. Those who have shaped the field into its present state have been employed in institutes of higher and further education; they have been involved in the delivery of research-based and vocational education; their academic roots have been in education and psychology, social work and policy, languages and linguistics, and other areas; they have been salaried and freelance language-mediation practitioners; they have been service designers, managers, promoters, consumers and evaluators; they have been lifetime members of minority language communities (Deaf people and the hearing children of Deaf parents) and long-term participants in family networks and socio-cultural activities, and they have been adult entrants to the relevant groups and social processes. This can be seen as a reflection of the relatively small size of the participant groups, combined with the feeling of urgency to create change in contexts where the sense of injustice has become undeniable and intolerable: it has not been possible to wait for individuals to emerge with all of the relevant skills and qualities to undertake this work, and so combinations of people have combined and re-combined, and different perspectives have been elicited and expressed so that a healthy diversity of 'voices' has been recorded and acknowledged in the emergence of the sub-discipline. (Turner, 2007, p. 1)

Regardless of the circumstances that bring researchers to applied sign linguistics, the key is to ensure that the topic is of relevance to signing communities and has involvement from deaf sign language users – that is, the research is conducted *with* deaf people and not *on* deaf people (Singleton, Martin & Morgan, 2015; Sutherland & Young, 2014; Turner & Harrington, 2000; see Section 7.1.4), and researchers should specify their epistemological stance: 'what they view as valid knowledge claims, who can make such claims, and the status of the research they are producing' (Young & Temple, 2014, p. 6). Furthermore, the dynamics of deaf-hearing research teams need to be acknowledged in terms of assumed epistemologies and the potential impact on data collection and analysis (Young & Ackerman, 2001).

Quote 7.3 Deaf 'ways of knowing'

Deaf 'ways of knowing' [should be] at the heart of the interpretative process involved in the research, particularly with regard to data analysis...although an increasing number of research studies have been conducted with both Deaf and hearing researchers on the team, there is often scant information about the extent of the Deaf researcher's involvement. Although it is often reported that the Deaf researcher collected the data in sign language, little further information is supplied about his or her role ... it [is] vital that the Deaf researcher occupy a central role. (Young & Ackerman, 2001, p. 182)

As the field of applied sign linguistics is still relatively new, there are many topics and research questions still to be explored. Researchers can consider stages of the life cycle where sign language is seen in action – from birth, childhood, through school years, to work and everyday life, family and ageing – and the inherent questions that can be explored at each stage in order to focus their attention on topics to explore. Here we provide some suggestions:

1. *Young children's acquisition, development and use of sign languages:* How and where do deaf and non-deaf young children acquire sign language? How do deaf and non-deaf children develop sign language fluency? How and where do these children use sign language in everyday life? What are the characteristics of child sign language discourse? How does a given stage of sign language acquisition affect the sign language identity of these children? What is the language capacity of a bimodal-bilingual child?
2. *Sign language in families:* How is sign language used in family communication, and how does it differ amongst deaf-hearing family combinations? How, when and where does sign brokering occur in deaf families? How do hearing parents feel about acquiring sign language in order to communicate with their deaf children? How do deaf children feel about their status in their family? What is the relationship between sign language bilingualism and family dynamics? To what extent does 'home sign' evolve and function across the life of a deaf person in a hearing family? What are the characteristics of family sign language discourse? How does sign language storytelling feature in family discourse?
3. *Sign language in education:* How is sign language used in education with deaf children? How is sign bilingualism implemented in deaf education? What is the relationship between sign language literacy and sign language identity? What is the relationship between sign language literacy and educational outcomes? How is sign language used in teacher-student interaction? What are the characteristics of educational/academic sign language discourse? What are the experiences of deaf students in accessing their education directly in sign language or indirectly via interpreter mediation? What is the relationship between sign bilingualism and vocational or higher education qualifications and experiences? How does one 'perform' expertise in a sign language?

4. *Second language learners of sign languages:* Who chooses to learn a sign language as a second language and why? How and where do (deaf and non-deaf) young people and adults learn a sign language? What are the challenges of learning sign language as a second language as compared to spoken foreign languages? How and where do second language learners use sign language in everyday life? What are the characteristics of second language learner sign language discourse? How does the stage of sign language acquisition affect the sign language identity of these second language learners? What is the experience of (deaf and non-deaf) second language learners as 'new speakers' of sign language? What milestones and 'threshold competencies' apply in the learning of sign languages as second or subsequent languages? Are these the same or different when the learner already knows another sign language (L2, M2 vs. L2, M1)?

5. *Sign language curricula, teaching methodology and assessment:* What are the key elements of sign language teaching curricula? What methods can be used to assess or test sign language learning and practice for formative, summative and professional practice purposes? How can technology be applied in sign language teaching and assessment? How and where is sign language for specific purposes taught? How and where is sign language for academic purposes taught? How should sign language teachers be trained? What are the discourse features of sign language teaching classrooms? How do sign language learners develop metalinguistic awareness? What is the relationship between cultural awareness, community engagement and language learning motivation?

6. *Sign language in the workplace:* How is sign language used in different workplaces? How is subject-specific terminology developed in a sign language? How is expertise 'performed' in a sign language? What is the relationship between sign language bilingualism and employment status? How is sign language used in workplace interaction? What are other communicative strategies used by deaf people in workplace settings? What are the characteristics of workplace sign language discourse? What are the experiences of deaf employees in accessing workplace communication directly in sign language or indirectly via interpreter mediation?

7. *Sign language in everyday life:* How is sign language used in different contexts? What are the characteristics of sign language discourse in formal and informal settings, at sites of public service delivery and in social institutions? What are the experiences of deaf people in relying on sign language interpretation throughout their lives? What texts are typically accessed through sign language translation? How do deaf people 'read' sign language translations? What sign language policies are in existence, and what impact do they have on sign language planning? At what sites does language contact occur between spoken, written and signed languages? How is sociolinguistic variation evident in signing

communities: what are the differences between country, region, race, gender, education, employment, sign language acquisition and family circumstances?
8. *Ageing signing populations*: What are the features of elderly sign language discourse? How and where do elderly deaf people use sign language in everyday life? How do stages of sign language acquisition and type of education affect the sign language identity of these elderly people? How does their deaf/hearing family dynamic influence the nature of their sign language use? What are the social networks of deaf elderly sign language users? How do elderly sign language users perceive the role of sign language users? How do elderly sign language users navigate access to information in sign language through technology? How does storytelling feature as a form of elderly sign language discourse? How prevalent is tactise signing among older deaf populations?

7.1.2 Conducting a literature review

In considering relevant literature to review for applied sign linguistics projects, it is important to remind researchers to draw on a wide range of relevant literature from the broader field of linguistics: generative linguistics, functional linguistics, cognitive linguistics, applied linguistics, corpus linguistics, translation and interpreting studies, bilingualism studies, discourse studies, psycholinguistics, sociolinguistics and educational linguistics as well as sign linguistics, anthropological linguistics and Deaf Studies.

A review of wider literature will enable researchers to identify where there may be gaps in the study of applied sign linguistics, what questions there are still to be asked and how existing studies of spoken languages could be replicated with signed languages. The results of applied sign linguistics research have been published in a wide range of journals, including *Medical Anthropology, Applied Linguistics, Disability and Society, Cognitive Linguistics, Qualitative Inquiry, Human Studies, Metaphor and Symbol, International Journal of the Sociology of Language, Discourse and Communication* and the discipline-specific journals listed in Chapter 8, Section 8.2.1.

Key databases that can be searched using key words such as *deaf, sign language, sign language interpreting, sign bilingualism* and *sign language acquisition* include Applied Social Sciences Index and Abstracts, Arts and Humanities Citation Index, British Humanities Index, Directory of Open Access Journals, EBSCOhost, ERIC, Google Scholar, Ingenta Connect, International Bibliography of the Social Sciences, Linguistics and Language Behaviour Abstracts, Project MUSE, ProQuest Theses and Dissertation Abstracts, ProQuest: Literature and Language, ProQuest: Social Sciences, ProQuest: The Arts, Psychology and Behavioural Sciences Collection, Science Direct, Social Science Citation Index, Sociological Abstracts, Translation Studies Abstracts and Bibliography of Translation Studies and Web of Knowledge.

7.1.3   Data collection and participant recruitment

Once the topic has been decided and the research questions confirmed, typically following from a review of the relevant literature (though we note that approaches like Grounded Theory take a different starting point; see Glaser, 2001, 2003, 2005), researchers must select the most appropriate methodological approach, the sources of data to be collected and how to recruit participants. The most appropriate method should be selected in order to answer the research question(s) rather than drawing up the questions to fit the methodology.

Sign linguists use various data elicitation methods to describe signed languages, depending on whether it is naturalistic or elicited data (Perniss, 2015), including recording natural sign language use in context, free and guided composition, role play and simulation games, communication games, story retelling, video clip and picture description, elicited translation or imitation, completion tasks and other structured exercises (Vermeerbergen & Van Herreweghe, 2012).

But more broadly, all research methods that are utilised in applied linguistics research generally are equally applicable to applied sign linguistics research, including ethnographic (fieldwork) observations, linguistic/discourse analysis of simulated and/or authentic sign language data, action research, experimental methods, interviews, focus groups, surveys and questionnaires, case studies, narrative inquiry and mixed methods (Dörnyei, 2007; Partridge & Phakiti, 2015). More details can be found in the other books in the Palgrave Research and Practice in Applied Linguistics series (e.g., Hale, 2007; Spencer-Oatey & Franklin, 2009). Here instead we focus on issues specific to data collection and participant recruitment in sign language research.

Vermeerbergen and Van Herreweghe (2012) assert that before embarking on any form of sign language data collection, researchers need to consider not only where on the continuum between qualitative and quantitative methodologies their research is situated, but also, importantly, they need to pay attention to the process for selecting informants. As not all deaf people are native sign language users, researchers need to be careful to define the criteria used for recruitment of participants. Furthermore, other sociolinguistic issues may need to be taken into account to determine the ideal demographics of research participants; for example, whether they attended a deaf school, if they use sign language at home, if they have deaf or hearing children or whether they have completed a university education. These factors may not be crucial in all applied sign linguistics research, depending on the nature and goal of the study, but they may be vital considerations as they may affect the results.

Considering the background of potential participants is important not only from the researcher perspective but also from the participant perspective in terms of matching their language preferences in data collection (Young & Hunt, 2011). For example, if participants are not bilingual, they might not feel comfortable reading information about the project; even if a participant is a signer, they might not be a fluent user if they are a late learner. It is highly recommended that research materials are created, adapted or translated into sign language to ensure that participants can suitably access information about the project or the data elicitation method itself and also that written forms of information are made available if need be.

Another aspect to consider in collecting sign language data is the use of technology. Technological developments have had a major impact on the how data can be generated with sign language users and have changed the scope of research questions that can be asked (Lucas, Mirus, Palmer, Roessler & Frost, 2013; Perniss, 2015; Young & Temple, 2014). It is now easier to capture, record and store sign language data on various small (but powerful) devices which are less intrusive and which are therefore less likely to affect the data collection process and/or the quality of the data elicited. For example, Metzger and Roy (2011) note that their attempts to collect samples of authentic sign language interpreter-mediated interactions were negatively impacted by having a camera and tripod in the room and the researcher present to operate the camera. Other sign language interpreting researchers, such as Major (2013), however, have noted that small, discreet cameras can be placed in different parts of the room and the researcher can switch them on, then leave, meaning there is no observer's paradox (Labov, 1972) from having the researcher present. And because the cameras are less obvious, participants are more likely to forget they are there and behave as normal. Even still, it can be difficult to get all participants into shot in order to record every aspect of the interaction (Metzger & Roy, 2011), or a participant may move out of shot (Major, 2013).

In order to capture sign language data effectively and ensure that it is of a suitable quality for analysis, it is necessary to ensure that recording conditions are optimal: that participants are framed in shot; the participants' clothing, the background and the lighting minimise distractions, glare or interference with the video signal; and that, ideally, multiple cameras are used in different positions to capture all aspects of the data (Perniss, 2015; Vermeerbergen & Van Herreweghe, 2012). Perniss (2015) and Nyst (2015) also suggest creating metadata for all video recordings as soon as possible after recording, so that information can be used to archive the data appropriately.

Lucas et al. (2013, p. 548) note that because of technology's impact on sign language research, researchers can utilise 'face-to-face video chatting and user-generated video sharing' technologies to record sign language dialogues and monologues using video phones, mobile and desktop applications, video sharing websites, and social media. This means that sign language data can be more easily sourced, for example, through vlogs or public Facebook sites, or researchers can easily capture naturalistic or elicited data. Furthermore, online survey tools now allow for the uploading of video clips, which means that questionnaire instruments that have been traditionally written can now be delivered online and designed to embed questions presented in sign language video clips. Figure 7.1 shows an example from a survey of European deaf sign language users' perceptions of video remote interpreting as part of the INSIGN project, funded by the European Commission Directorate for Justice (Skinner, Turner & Napier, in press). This form of delivering questionnaires means that researchers can rely less on face-to-face interviews, which was previously the case to ensure that deaf sign language users could participate in research *in* sign language (Lucas et al., 2013). A similar approach was taken in the PRO-Signs Project questionnaire, circulated in 2012 (as outlined in Chapter 4, Section 4.4.1).

Lucas et al. (2013) have identified how technology has impacted on sign language research in other ways:

(1) *Participant recruitment:* Previously, researchers would rely on deaf people to source participants through their local community networks, but now researchers can recruit online and send out calls for research participation expressions of interest in sign language through websites and social media networks.
(2) *Minimal travel:* Data collection can conducted remotely via video, which minimises the extent of travel required either by the researchers or the informants.

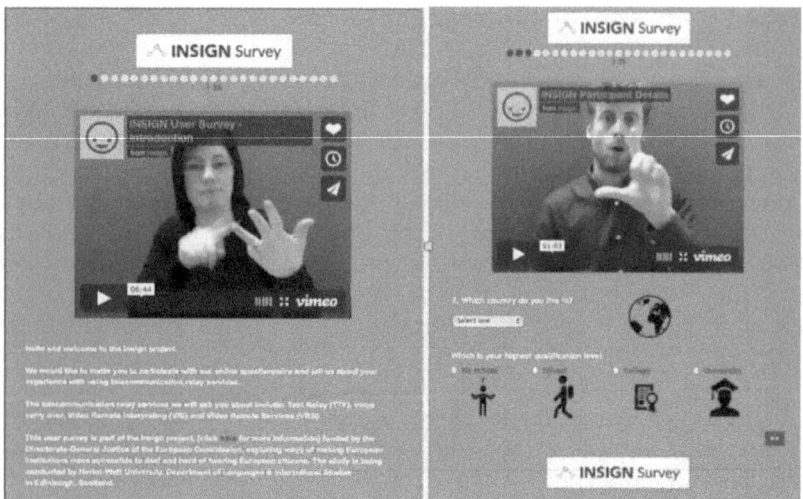

Figure 7.1 Example of online questionnaire using embedded sign language

(3) *Available technologies:* Data can be recorded through various means and not just using traditional camera equipment, which can expedite data collection and storing.

(4) *Informed consent:* Information and consent forms, as well as permissions to film and use sign language data collected, can be created in or translated into sign language and presented to research participants through websites, social media or DVDs prior to data collection.

(5) *Less conflict of interest:* Remote participant recruitment or data collection can minimise the amount of direct interaction that researchers need to have within signing communities in order to carry out research, which means that they may experience less conflict in having to socialise or interact with sign language users in the community outside of the research context.

7.1.4 Conducting ethical research

Processes for conducting research ethically with 'human subjects' in social and behavioural studies are now well established (Diener & Crandall, 1978), with clear guidelines, policies or recommendations for ethical practice from governmental bodies, such as the U.S. National Bioethics Advisory Commission Report on ethical and policy issues in human research (NBAC, 2001); research funding bodies, such as the UK Economics and Social Research Council Framework on Research Ethics (ESRC, 2010); and research institutions, such as the University of Manchester's (n.d.) code of practice for investigating concerns about the conduct of research. Researchers need to apply to relevant bodies to get ethical clearance after they have demonstrated that the research will be conducted responsibly and will have no undue negative impact on participants, that participants will have given informed consent to be involved but will have the opportunity to withdraw without consequence, that participants will remain anonymous in reporting of the data unless they specifically give permission otherwise, and that the data will be protected.

There is a history of criticism of the ethical conduct of researchers who have worked across cultures, with issues concerning exploitation, community damage, inaccurate findings and a lack of recognition of power dynamics, as well as the nature of consent, research processes, research design, data ownership and uses of data (Marshall & Batten, 2004). Although adherence to ethical clearance processes should be able to alleviate some of these issues, conducting cross-cultural research still has ethical and methodological challenges, primarily in relation to language issues and cultural sensitivities (Liamputtong, 2008, 2010), and failure to acknowledge the language and cultural issues may affect the rigour and reliability of the research (Hennink, 2008).

There is evidence that the rigour of research conducted with minority language groups is enhanced when researchers share the language and culture of that group; that is, they are 'insiders' (Irvine, Roberts & Bradbury-Jones, 2008). When this is not possible, measures can be taken to ensure the research is still rigorous (e.g., using inter-rater reliability checks), but sensitivity to the language and cultural issues is still necessary when considering how to capture and record data (Irvine, Roberts & Bradbury-Jones, 2008).

One strategy is to involve interpreters or translators in cross-cultural research as 'cultural brokers' (Hennink, 2008) when researchers do not use the language of the participants fluently enough to communicate directly, but this needs to be considered carefully (Edwards, 1998; Temple, 2002). Rather than just bringing in interpreters to mediate data collection between two different languages, Temple and Young (2004) suggest that interpreters should be involved as co-researchers, an approach that will make them more visible in the research process. Failing to treat interpreters or translators as co-researchers can affect the lead researcher's understanding of the research process and the data itself (Temple & Edwards, 2002).

Temple and Young (2004) assert that insider/outsider identities and boundaries cannot be so easily drawn when it comes to cross-cultural research, and this is especially pertinent to applied sign linguistics research. As we have discussed at length in Chapter 3, there are ongoing debates as to the identity of hearing people in signing communities, who are judged on their level of sign language fluency. But some hearing people may not be regarded as 'outsiders' necessarily. So, when it comes to conducting research ethically with signing communities, researchers need to employ a level of critical reflexivity about their position in the signing community, the academic discipline of sign language research generally and their position within any specific sign language–related research project. Sutton-Spence and West (2011) began a debate on this very issue in examining their position in sign language research as hearing people, and they suggested that as more deaf people become active researchers, hearing people (like themselves) should shift from being in the majority to being in the minority. As we have noted earlier in this volume, their article was subsequently critiqued by two deaf researchers, O'Brien and Emery (2013), who argued that Sutton-Spence and West still did not grasp the complexities of their true power and 'capital' as hearing researchers in a 'deaf space'.

Turner and Harrington (2000) consider power dynamics in applied sign linguistics research with respect specifically to sign language interpreting research, and they note the importance of managing power relations with all key stakeholders, including sign language interpreters themselves, who may give their time to researchers and therefore need to be acknowledged. They highlight that research should be 'on, for and with' all stakeholders (i.e. those whom the research affects or who have a vested interest in the outcome), that participants should be treated with respect, that informants may bring their own agendas when agreeing to participate in the research and that it is important to share research findings with all stakeholders.

Robert Pollard, a hearing researcher who is fluent in ASL and specialises in health-related research with deaf sign language users, began the discussion of cross-cultural ethics in the conduct of research with signing communities more than 20 years ago (Pollard, 1994, 1996, 1998, 2002). Key ethical issues for consideration include the need to understand and respond to population-specific concerns, to culturally mediate fundamental ethical principles, to provide access to informed consent in sign language and seek informed consent on both a collective community level and an individual participant level and to explore issues of ownership of the research and data (Young & Temple, 2014).

These suggestions have led to several recent publications that discuss how to conduct research ethically with signing communities that are driven by deaf researchers themselves, but often in partnership with hearing researchers (see Harris, Holmes & Mertens, 2009; Hochgesang, Villanueva, Mathur & Lillo-Martin, 2010; Ladd, Gulliver & Batterbury, 2003; Mertens, Harris & Holmes, 2009; Singleton, Jones & Hanumantha, 2012; Singleton, Martin & Morgan, 2015).

The clear message that emerges from all of these discussions is that deaf sign language users must have an integral role in research with sign language communities and projects should ideally be deaf-led (see Quote 7.4); Harris et al. (2009) suggest that sign language communities stand to benefit by building on the work of members of indigenous communities because of their shared concerns related to language, culture and historically differential positions in the societal hierarchy.

Quote 7.4 Deaf researchers as cultural mediators

D/deaf researchers [should] lead research projects within sign language communities as a cultural group since they possess the necessary cultural understanding and knowledge of the community members. If D/deaf researchers conducted studies within their own cultural community, their work would have a profound impact on the members' lives. (Harris et al., 2009, p. 124)

Another ethical aspect of applied sign linguistics research is not only to have involvement from deaf sign language users as researchers but also to adopt a community participatory approach (Cornwall & Jewkes, 1995) in order to build and maintain trust between communities and researchers (Christopher, Watts, McCormick & Young, 2008). (See Chapter 5, Case study 5.8, for an example of a community participatory-based approach to investigating access to health care information in the Australian signing community.)

As a result of a focus group study with deaf members of the American signing community and deaf researchers, Singleton et al. (2012) identified that there was a lack of trust and some resentment towards hearing researchers in particular and concerns about confidentiality. The lack of trust from community members is to be expected if deaf sign language users have served as research informants or sign language models for hearing researchers without then receiving any acknowledgement in subsequent publications or presentations (Lucas et al., 2013). Similarly, the lack of trust from deaf researchers relates to perceptions that their level of involvement in research has been tokenistic, that they have been exploited by hearing researchers and that they have not received adequate credit for their contributions to the research (Singleton et al., 2012).

The issue of confidentiality has also been noted by other researchers such as Hill (2015) with respect to the fact that signing communities are small, so it may be easy for other community members to figure out who has participated in research, or people may be easily identifiable if participant samples are described in publications. Typically, research participants are provided with assurances that they will remain anonymous in any presentation of the data, but anonymity is also difficult to preserve in sign language research, given the visual nature of the language and the fact that participants are easily identifiable (Hill, 2015; Vermeerbergen & Van Herreweghe, 2012). Now that available technology allows for easy editing of video clips, it is tempting for researchers to demonstrate sign language data in conference presentations or even as pictures in printed publications. Young and Temple (2014) question whether anonymity of sign language research participants could be considered a further form of oppression rather than protection, and they suggest that enabling deaf people in particular to have their sign language shared gives them a greater 'voice'. Such acknowledgement can, in some instances, form part of the unwritten contract of trust that we mentioned earlier. For example, it was a bid to ensure that the 'voice' of contributors to the Signs of Ireland corpus was recognised that led Leeson and Saeed (2012a) to formally (and with participants' permission) acknowledge all 40 of their participants in the volume and name each explicitly at their book launch, to which all of the corpus participants were invited.

But (hearing) sign language researchers cannot expect to walk into a signing community and just start filming (Lucas et al., 2013). They need to develop trust with the community. Even deaf sign language researchers working with vulnerable sub-groups or underprivileged members of signing communities, for example in developing countries, need to consider how to conduct sign language fieldwork so that data is collected sensitively and with respect for local contexts and cultural sensitivities (Nyst, 2015;

Singleton et al., 2015). Regardless of whether researchers are deaf or hearing, researchers in small communities often have dual relationships: they may be a member of the community as well as a researcher, or they may also function in another role such as an interpreter, so that dynamic needs to be managed carefully (Young & Temple, 2014).

Based on the results of her research, Jennifer Singleton and her colleagues have suggested key points for consideration in conducting ethical sign language research (Singleton et al., 2012; Singleton et al., 2015):

(1) Ensure the informed consent information is accessible in sign language.
(2) Be aware of 'over-testing' and risks of confidentiality, and avoid convenience samples as signing communities may become research-saturated or fatigued.
(3) Reciprocate with signing communities by ensuring that they receive the information about research results, and disseminate findings in sign language.
(4) Consider the dynamics of deaf-hearing research teams and when and how sign language interpreters will be involved.

With respect to attaining informed consent from sign language research participants, one key aspect to consider is that simply generating a consent form in sign language or translating a standard form into sign language may not be enough (Young & Hunt, 2011; Young & Temple, 2014). Researchers should not assume what 'fund of knowledge' (Pollard, 1998) deaf participants have, so the basic concept of consent may need to be spelled out; but neither should researchers assume that deaf people will not understand, so judgements should be made carefully about how to deliver this information (Young & Temple, 2014). Researchers 'need to anticipate potential sources of misunderstanding about the nature of the research and how to resolve them' (Singleton et al., 2015, p. 13). Furthermore, given that data is typically collected on video, it may need to be explained in detail what the video content will be used for and how it will be used: will it be used only for educational purposes, will it be shown at conferences, or will screen grabs be featured in written publications? How will the data be shown? Will faces be blurred out, or will people be identifiable? Will the video data be made available for further research? And can participants choose for the data to be shown in some contexts but not others (Metzger & Roy, 2011)?

In order to account for the complexities of conducting research ethically with signing communities, Harris et al. (2009) adapted the Indigenous Terms of Reference for academic research and publications and proposed a Sign Language Communities' Terms of Reference (SLCTR), which includes the following 6 principles:

(1) The authority for the construction of meanings and knowledge within the sign language community rests with the community's members.

(2) Investigators should acknowledge that sign language community members have the right to have those things that they value to be fully considered in all interactions.

(3) Investigators should take into account the worldviews of the sign language community in all negotiations or dealings that impact on the community's members.

(4) In the application of sign language communities' terms of reference, investigators should recognise the diverse experiences, understandings, and way of life (in sign language societies) that reflect their contemporary cultures.

(5) Investigators should ensure that the views and perceptions of the critical reference group (the sign language group) is reflected in any process of validating and evaluating the extent to which sign language communities' terms of reference have been taken into account.

(6) Investigators should negotiate within and amongst sign language groups to establish appropriate processes to consider and determine the criteria for deciding how to meet cultural imperatives, social needs, and priorities.

An ethics statement has since been adopted in 2014 by international sign language researchers and endorsed by the Sign Language Linguistics Society (SLLS; Singleton et al., 2015), which outlines key principles of ethical sign language research: (1) responsibility to individual consultants, (2) responsibility to deaf communities and (3) responsibility to scholarship and the public (SLLS, 2014).

7.1.5   Data annotation and analysis

As noted earlier with approaches to data collection, broadly speaking, any approach to data analysis that is used in applied linguistics research can be generally drawn on for applied sign linguistics research, and depending on whether it the study in question is a quantitative or qualitative study. Analytical approaches can include linguistic description and corpus approaches, descriptive and inferential statistics, discourse analysis and other qualitative analyses, such as thematic or narrative analysis.

Depending on the type of sign language data collected, researchers will need to consider the transcription and annotation methods to be used, given that sign languages do not have a written form and therefore cannot be easily transcribed (Crasborn, 2015). Many aspects of signed languages are found in spoken languages (and vice versa); however, there appear to be modality-specific properties that can only happen in signed languages (visual-gestural) or spoken languages (oral-auditory) – that is, there are certain things that only occur in languages that are visual, and others that only occur in languages that are spoken. So, one thing for sign language researchers to consider is their research 'philosophy' with regards to sign language analysis, in terms of whether theories, categories and terminology from spoken language research are appropriate to be applied to the analysis of signed languages, or whether a 'sign language differential' model should be adopted, which assumes that sign language structures are unique and so sign language description should not be modelled on spoken languages (Vermeerbergen & Van Herreweghe, 2012). If the former approach is adopted, then researchers can borrow from established spoken language transcription methods, such as conversation analysis (Sacks, Schegloff & Jefferson, 1974). One good example is the work of Cynthia Roy (1992, 1996, 2000), who used conventions for analysing turn-taking in conversation to examine turn-taking in sign language interpreter-mediated discourse. Further collaborative work is ongoing to discuss the potential for developing common protocols for annotating sign language corpora (Digging into Signs Workshop[1]).

Regardless of which approach is adopted, researchers still need to decide what they are going to annotate or code and devise a suitable method (Perniss, 2015), as sign language annotation is not yet standardised (Crasborn, 2015; Frishberg, Hoiting & Slobin, 2012). The nature of annotation will be influenced by the level of detail of analysis required: For sign language description purposes, is the sign language being analysed at a discourse, syntactical, morphological or phonological level? For sign language interaction analysis, what is of interest – the turn-taking, communication management, overlaps or interruptions? For sign language interpreting or translation analysis, is the focus on a lexical, semantic or discourse level? For sign language data that has been captured as part of interviews or focus groups to explore participants' perceptions of particular experiences, will content, thematic, discourse or narrative analysis be used? Given the strong collective 'oral' storytelling culture that is embedded within signing communities, narrative analysis is recommended as a particularly suitable approach for analysing deaf people's talk (Young & Temple, 2014).

If annotating sign language data for description purposes, a phonological/ phonetic transcription to identify the micro-movements involved in the production of sign language – for example, handshape, orientation of the palm, location and movement of the hands(s), non-manual features on the face – may need to be developed (Crasborn, 2015). In addition to phonological transcription, linguists may also want to annotate morphological aspects of manual signs, non-manual devices, and meaning (Frishberg et al., 2012). At a lexical level, it is possible to use 'ID-Glossing', where words that most closely represent signed lexical items are selected as unique identifiers of sign types (Johnston, 2001), and thus make it possible to search sign language databases by lexical items. Johnston (2010) asserts that researchers should prioritise annotation of ID-Glosses above detailed levels of transcription in order to create sign language corpora.

Various systems have been developed to annotate different aspects of sign language, including Stokoe Notation, Sign Font, Sign Writing, the Hamburg Notation System (HamNoSys) and the Berkley Transcription System (Frishberg et al., 2012). All these analytical techniques were developed prior to the video capturing and editing capabilities now available to sign language researchers and were attempts to represent layers of sign language articulation in a written form. However, by the very fact that sign languages are visual-gestural languages, these annotation systems cannot possibly capture all the nuances of sign language use in written form.

Other transcription systems used to annotate direct sign language conversation or sign language interpreter-mediated interaction capture the interaction as it unfolds, for example, by using a musical score format, as proposed by Metzger and Roy (2011). Figure 7.2 shows an example from Metzger and Roy (2011, p. 72) of how they transcribed data of interpreter-mediated interaction with periods of silence. This form of transcription, however, is still paper-based.

Researchers can now make use of technology to code or analyse sign language data so that video clips can be uploaded into a digital annotation tool, thus preserving the visual-gestural elements of the language being analysed. The two most common annotation tools are SignStream[2] and ELAN[3] (Frishberg et al., 2012). SignStream was developed specifically for sign language research, whereas ELAN was developed initially at the Max Planck Institute for Psycholinguistics for gesture research. The use of ELAN is becoming more popular for the annotation of sign language data and is widely used by sign linguists (Johnston & Schembri, 2005; Leeson & Saeed 2012; Perniss, 2015). ELAN allows for the synchronisation of up to 4 videos so multiple cameras can be used to capture different angles and the data can

Participants	Time					
	0:21:24:00	0:21:25:00	0:21:26:00	0:21:27:00	0:21:28:00	0:21:29:00
Deaf person: ASL			THUMBS-UP	[f-handshape (GOOD)] THUMBS-UP	THUMBS-UP	THUMBS-UP
Interpreter: English			[to hygienist] You're welcome,	You can do it just like	That. INDEX to deaf person	Yes, just like that
Hygienist B: English						Like this? [imitates interpreter's INDEX]
Interpreter: ASL		W-E-L-C-O-M-E	KNOW THANK YOU INDEX to Deaf person		INDEX to Deaf person	INDEX to Deaf person

Figure 7.2 Sample of musical score transcription of sign language interpreter-mediated interaction

be aligned. ELAN also utilises tiers for different levels of annotation. Tiers can represent different linguistic features, for example, articulation or movement of the left hand or right hand, or constructed action (CA; see Figure 7.3 for an example of an ELAN window with tiers from Johnston, 2013).

Applied sign linguists use ELAN to effectively analyse sign language interaction data (see Figure 7.4 for an example of an ELAN window with annotation of utterances between a hearing child and deaf parent from Chen Pichler, Hochgesang, Lillo-Martin & Müller de Quadros, 2010) for the purposes of examining bilingual-bimodal language acquisition. Furthermore, sign language interpreting researchers use ELAN to analyse sign language interpreter-mediated interaction data (see Figure 7.5 for an example of an ELAN window with annotation of CA, or role shift, in sign language interpretation from Goswell, 2011, 2012). ELAN is being increasingly used to annotate sign language interpreter-mediated interaction; for example, to analyse footing shifts and turn-taking in academic meetings and video remote interpreting (Marks, 2012, 2015), accuracy and clarification requests in healthcare interaction (Major & Napier, 2012; Major, 2014) and in International Sign conference interpreting (Stone & Russell, in press).

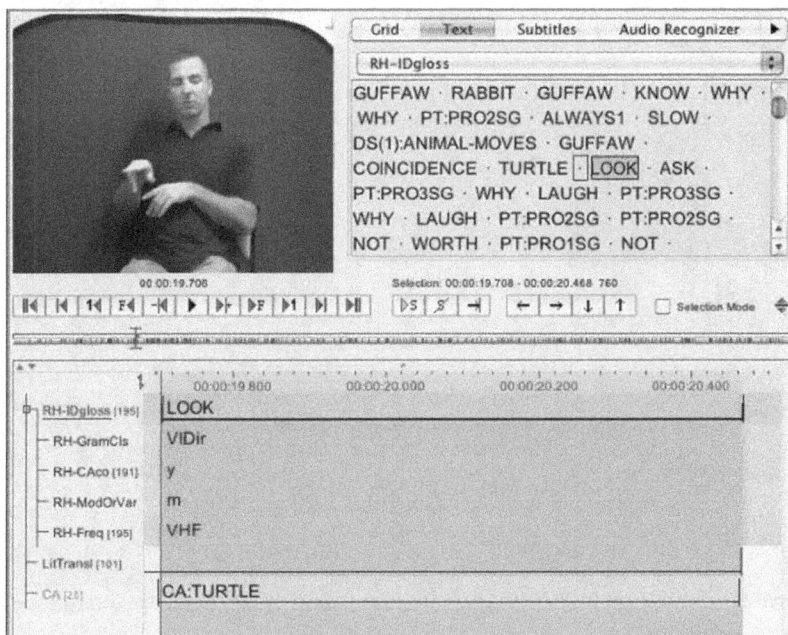

Figure 7.3   Example of ELAN window with tiers
Source: Johnston (2013).

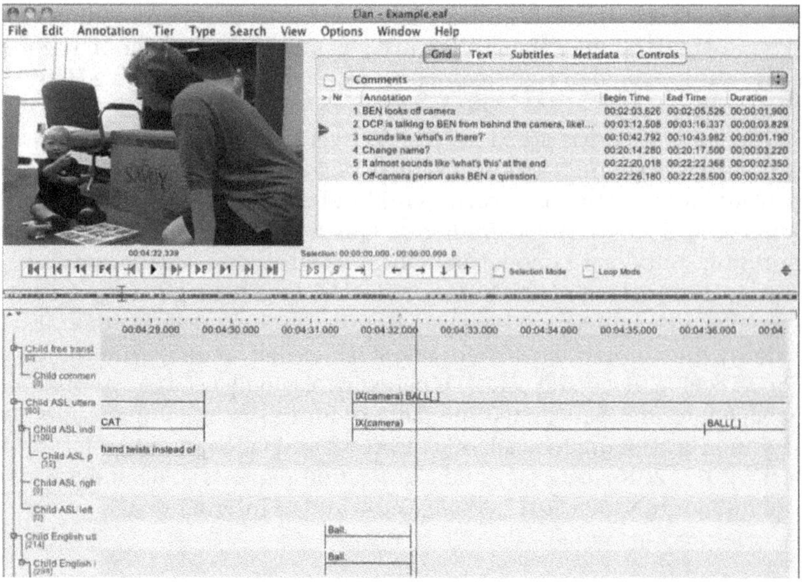

Figure 7.4   Example of ELAN window with annotation of sign language interaction
Source: Chen Pichler et al. (2010).

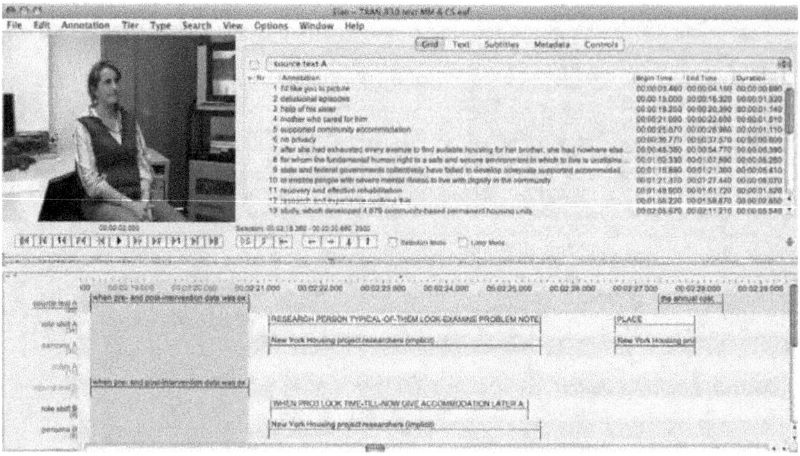

Figure 7.5   Example of ELAN window with annotation of sign language interpretation
Source: Goswell (2012).

ELAN can also be used to annotate video recorded interviews conducted in sign language (e.g. Napier, Sabolcec et al., 2014; see Figure 7.6) by using tiers to insert guide translations of sign language discourse, thematic coding and meta-commentary (observations of data). NVivo discourse analysis software can also be effectively used to code and search for themes in sign language data (Young & Temple, 2014).

It should be noted, however, that there are limitations in translating sign language text for the purposes of analysis, as subtle aspects of the original sign language discourse may not be adequately captured in a written translation (Napier, Sabolcec et al., 2014; Pizzutto & Pietandrea, 2001; Stone & West, 2012). In fact, Young and Temple (2014) argue that sign language data does not necessarily need to be translated or transcribed at all in some forms of research (particularly social research) because of the technologies now available for data capture, annotation and analysis. Sign language data can now be preserved in its original form so as to avoid any potential corruption or misinterpretation of the data through translation. In these instances, the sign language data would be annotated for key themes, and then only illustrative quotes would be translated for the purposes of written publication. So, rather than translating the sign language data and then coding the written translation, the coding would focus on the sign language data itself. This suggested approach reflects the debate in cross-cultural research on whether to transcribe data in the original language of interviews so as to preserve cultural subtleties (Liamputtong, 2010; Temple, 2002).

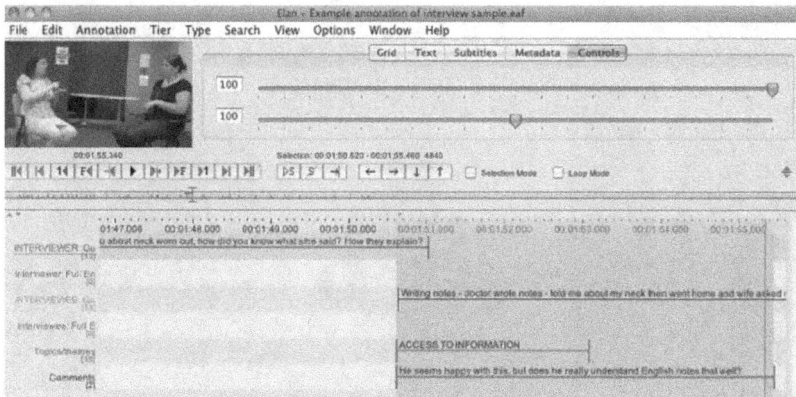

Figure 7.6 Example of ELAN window with annotation of sign language interview
Source: Napier, Sabolcec et al. (2014).

7.1.6   Dissemination of results

Dissemination of applied sign linguistics research can occur through traditional means of writing and publication of books and journal articles in discipline-specific book series and journals (see Chapter 8). There are also particular merits in publishing in journals from different disciplines in order to target audiences that might benefit from knowing about sign language in action in various contexts (see Napier, 2011c).

It is also possible to publish academically *in* sign language. Published books can be translated into sign language and made available on DVD or through web streaming; for example Steve Emery's PhD and subsequent book on *Citizenship in Deaf Communities* has been translated into BSL,[4] and sign language–related conference proceedings have been made available on DVD in sign language (Young & Temple, 2014).

There is also the *Deaf Studies Digital Journal* (*DSDJ*),[5] published by Gallaudet University, which features articles that are created in sign languages with visual graphics, captions and accompanying written text (see Figure 7.7 for the layout of a *DSDJ* signed academic article). The articles are predominantly presented in ASL, but there are some that feature other sign languages, and there are a range of deaf and hearing researchers.

Typical dissemination also includes presentations at discipline-specific or discipline-related conferences (see Chapter 8, Section 8.2.5), which are given in spoken or signed languages, depending on the preferred language of the presenter and whether they are deaf or hearing. Presenters work with sign

Figure 7.7   Screenshot of layout, *DSDJ* signed academic article

language interpreters to ensure that presentations are accessible to the wider audience (see Chapter 5). One specific cross-disciplinary conference that has taken place approximately every two years since 2002 is the International Deaf Academics and Researchers Conference.[6] This conference provides a space for deaf academics to present in International Sign (see Chapter 6, Section 6.2.2) to an audience of deaf academics directly, without any interpreter mediation. While the presentations often focus on discussing, defining and problematising issues related to being a deaf academic in academia, the conference also provides deaf researchers with the opportunity to disseminate their research findings in sign language. Research-based presentations draw on a range of disciplines, particularly Deaf Studies, sociology, anthropology, psychology, education and linguistics.

The key to the success of this conference, and to emerging opportunities to publish in sign language, is that dissemination of research is occurring in the language of the signing community and not the language of academia. Adam (2015) notes that in the current academic climate, where research knowledge transfer and research impact are highly valued, it is important to ensure that research knowledge transfer to signing communities occurs. He asserts that because research on deaf culture and sign language would not be possible without the participation of deaf sign language users themselves, researchers need to ensure that their work has an impact on the community (i.e. they learn and benefit from it) and that the information should be provided in an accessible way (i.e. in sign language). Thus, researchers need to participate in public engagement with signing communities to disseminate research findings; for example, through workshops and information events that include presentations, hands-on interactive sessions and posters, which could be combined with cultural events featuring deaf-specific performances (e.g. signed poetry or storytelling). Adam (2015) also suggests that researchers can further engage with, and empower, signing communities by working with deaf children in schools. However, in practice, and despite the desire to present academic work in sign languages, some deaf academics have reported that career-wise, the pressure to publish in English – and the status associated with peer-reviewed publications in English – means that they tend to privilege publication in English over those in a sign language (Leeson, Sheikh & Vermeerbergen, 2015).

7.2 Research topics in applied sign linguistics

Now that we have provided an overview of conducting research in applied sign linguistics, in this section we run through some key research areas, referring back to some of the list of suggested topics and questions from Section 7.1.1, and provide examples of research that has already been conducted on these topics. In Section 7.3, we provide suggestions for future research topics that need to be explored.

7.2.1   Young children's acquisition, development and use of sign languages

The study of sign language acquisition represents a fairly large body of literature in applied sign linguistics (see Chapter 4) and includes studies on a range of sign languages, including BSL, ASL, Auslan, Brazilian Sign Language (Libras), Japanese Sign Language, Sign Language of the Netherlands and German Sign Language, although the literature is dominated by studies of ASL. Chen Pichler (2012) provides a selective overview of the existing literature on sign language acquisition, with a focus on early acquisition of sign language as a first language up to the age of 4, and claims that early sign language acquisition research focused on drawing parallels between acquisition of spoken languages by hearing children and signed languages by deaf children in order to demonstrate 'the underlying similarities in acquisition regardless of modality' (pp. 647–648). Various acquisition studies have analysed how the phonological, lexical, morphological, syntactic and discourse properties of sign languages are acquired by deaf and hearing children.

Studies have focused, for example, on the relationship between how deaf children use gesture and acquisition of signs (Cheek, Cormier, Repp & Meier, 2001; Goldin-Meadow, 2003), the relationship between modality and stages of language acquisition or grammaticalisation (Masataka, 2000; Pfau & Steinbach, 2006), age constraints on first versus second language acquisition (Mayberry & Locke, 2003) and bilingual signed and spoken language acquisition from birth (Petitto et al., 2000).

Other studies have examined young children's acquisition of specific sign language parameters, such as syntax (Bellugi, van Hock, Lillo-Martin & O'Grady, 1988; Boudreault & Mayberry, 2006; Hanel, 2005; Lillo-Martin & Müller de Quadros, 2011), handshape (Boyes Braem, 1990; Chen Pichler, 2011; Conlin, Mirus, Mauk & Meier, 2000), location of signs (Bonvillian & Siedlecki, 1996), phonological features (Karnopp, 2002), grammatical development (Morford, 2003; Schick, 2002), verbs (De Beuzeville, 2006; Hoiting, 2006), sign (word) order and combinations (Chen Pichler, 2010; Torigoe & Takei, 2001) and the development of narrative discourse skills (Morgan, 2006; Rathmann, Mann & Morgan, 2007).

In order to assess the sign language development of deaf children, various sign language assessment instruments have been designed and created in sign languages to assess receptive and productive skills (Haug, 2005); for example in BSL (Herman, 1998b; Herman & Roy, 2006), Auslan (Johnston, 2004c; Schembri et al., 2002), Sign Language of the Netherlands (Hermans, Knoors & Verhoeven, 2009), ASL (Enns & Herman, 2011) and German Sign Language (Haug, 2011b).

7.2.2   Sign language in families

Sign language communication in families can be multilayered, depending on which members of the family are deaf and whether they are adults or children, and thus can involve various blends of spoken, written and signed communication and bimodal- bilinguality. Much of the research that has been conducted within an applied linguistics framework has focused on the interactions that take place primarily between deaf mothers and their deaf babies or young children in order to support both the argument for early interventions in sign language with deaf children who are born to hearing parents and the benefits of introducing visual language strategies early on for the purposes of bilingual language development.

For example, studies have explored joint picture book reading using sign language and the interaction patterns and eye gaze that are used by deaf mothers (Van der Lem & Timmerman, 1990), the role of parents in developing visual turn-taking in their young deaf children (Swisher, 1992), affect and language in ASL motherese (Reilly & Bellugi, 1996), the use of gesturing and 'home signs' in mother-child interaction between deaf children and hearing mothers who do not use an established sign language (Goldin-Meadow, 2012; Iverson, Capirci, Longobardi & Caselli, 1999), attentional behaviour in deaf children with deaf and hearing mothers (Harris & Mohay, 1997), sign language use of deaf children in communication with their hearing family members (Lindert, 2001), deaf mothers' strategies for making language visually accessible to deaf children (Mohay, 2000) and fingerspelling interaction between deaf parents and deaf children (Blumenthal-Kelly, 1995).

Other studies have concentrated on how deaf parents communicate with their hearing children in order to better understand sign language discourse in general, to explore communication patterns, and the role of the hearing child in deaf family communicative experiences with the wider (hearing) community (Singleton & Tittle, 2000). Analyses have covered the types of interactions between deaf parents and their infants (Maestas, 1980), how 'sight triangles' are established and maintained in conversations between deaf parents and hearing toddlers (Mather, Rodriguez-Fraticelli, Andrews & Rodriguez, 2006), child-directed signing in ASL (Holzrichter & Meier, 2000), attention interchanges between deaf parents and their deaf and hearing children in the same interaction (Cramér-Wolrath, 2011) and code-mixing in mother-child interaction (Van den Bogaerde & Baker, 2005).

There are surprisingly few studies of intergenerational sign language interaction or variation, aside from discussions on how difficult it is for sign language to be passed between generations because the majority of deaf children are born to hearing parents (e.g. Compton, 2014). Mallory, Zingle and Schein (1993) studied the communication modes between hearing children, their deaf parents and hearing grandchildren, and Lucas and Schatz (2003) studied the nature of communication between deaf adults and their hearing family members as compared to their deaf and hearing friends. Both studies found that deaf people tend to use speech and written language with their hearing family members, and Lucas and Schatz (2003) found that deaf signers reported using ASL with their (predominantly deaf) friends.

7.2.3 Sign language in education

The establishment of deaf schools has been of critical importance in the development of signing communities and their sign languages (Plaza-Pust & Main, 2012), and Brennan (1999b) has suggested that deaf children face linguistic exclusion if they are integrated into mainstream schools. We have discussed sign language in school and tertiary education in Chapter 4, so here we focus on providing an overview of research that has been conducted specifically on the use of sign language in education, either in relation to bilingual pedagogical practices or on a discourse level.

Residential deaf schools are a 'crucible' for sign language acquisition (Lucas & Schatz, 2003), and this is where intergenerational sign language transmission *actually* predominantly occurs – between peers rather than family members (Compton, 2014; Fenlon & Wilkinson, 2015; Senghas, 2003). Research has shown that there is a strong relationship amongst where deaf people are educated, the educational approach used and their sign language use. For example, in Dublin, Ireland, girls and boys attended different segregated schools, and this is evidenced through the lexical differences in their signing (Fitzgerald, 2014; Grehan, 2008; Leeson, 2005b; LeMaster, 2003; Mohr-Militzer 2011). Quinn's (2010) study of regional variation in BSL suggests that regional variation is more closely tied to where the deaf residential schools were located in the UK rather than just where people live. Also, various sociolinguistic variation studies have noted that the higher incidence of fingerspelling in the signing of older deaf people could reflect their educational experiences, in that they were instructed at a time when fingerspelling usage was emphasised (Schembri & Johnston, 2007, 2012; Sutton-Spence, Woll & Allsop, 1990).

Even with the current existence of sign bilingual policies, which state that sign language should be promoted as a first language and also as the primary language of instruction in deaf education, these policies can be difficult to operationalise if there are not directly equivalent learning materials available in sign language (Johnston, Leigh & Foreman, 2002). Thus, various projects have focused on the translation of educational materials into sign language, either for educational assessment instruments (Cawthon, Winton, Garberoglio & Gobble, 2010; Tate, Collins & Tymms, 2003) or to translate books into sign language for the purposes of bilingual literacy development (Conlon & Napier, 2004).

There is an interesting body of work that has focused on sign language discourse in the classroom and the interactions that take place between deaf students and their teachers: Smith and Sutton-Spence (2005) explored attention-getting strategies and interaction between adults and deaf children in a BSL nursery; Ramsey and Padden (1998) studied communication practices in the classroom and revealed that language contact is used as a pedagogical tool; Mugnier (2006) analysed the bilingual communication dynamics in classrooms taught by deaf or hearing teachers and found that while the deaf teacher in their study validated the children's responses through both spoken and signed language, the hearing teacher only confirmed the correctness of spoken responses, and that when deaf children were being taught by a hearing teacher, they often had parallel conversations in sign language that were not dealt with by the teacher. Using ethnographic methods, Mather has observed and documented patterns of eye gaze and communication in a deaf classroom (Mather, 1987), the visually oriented teaching strategies used with deaf preschool children (Mather, 1989) and how classroom interaction is regulated visually by teachers and sign language interpreters (Mather, 2005). Keating and Mirus (2003) studied the cross-modal interactions between deaf and hearing students outside the classroom in mainstream school settings, and they noted that the deaf children were more adept at communicating with their hearing peers than vice versa. Contributors to a new volume on teaching and learning in bilingual classrooms (Mulrooney, 2015) engaged in research to explore the strategies used in classrooms at Gallaudet University that utilise both ASL and written English to enhance the learner experience.

Few studies have examined deaf students' perceptions of their educational experiences in relation to sign language use: Morales-López (2008) interviewed deaf children in mainstream schools about their preferences for interpreters or tutors in the classroom to enable their access to information in sign language; Sutherland and Young (2014) used innovative visual methods (video diaries, photography, peer interviewing, drawing, poster making) in a 6-year longitudinal study to explore deaf children's perceptions and experiences of sign bilingual education.

There is a significant amount of research on educational interpreting with deaf children that has been reviewed by Napier (2010). Many studies focus on talking to interpreters about their perceptions of their role and the additional tasks/roles that they take on inside and outside the classroom that would not typically be expected of interpreters in other contexts; either tutoring, teaching sign language, clerical work or being a 'friend' to the deaf students (e.g. Jones, Clark & Soltz, 1997). This is obviously still an ongoing issue, as Smith (2013) noted similar behaviours in her non-participant observations of interpreter-student interactions in a range of schools in the U.S. Swift (2012) identified that interpreters working in South African post-secondary education also take on various roles. Winston (2004) and others have begun to question the effectiveness of interpreting for children's education and challenge the assumption that placing a sign language interpreter in a mainstream classroom will ensure access to learning for deaf students when the students are accessing information indirectly through mediated communication rather than direct instruction. Various research has suggested that only experiencing teaching indirectly through interpreters may hinder deaf children's access to cognitive development and learning

(Schick, 2004); that deaf children may not really be able to equally partici-pate in inclusive education via interpreters, which creates a power differen-tial (Thoutenhoofd, 2005); that interpreters may not have been adequately trained to interpret in a register suitable for deaf children, that is, they may not know how to understand and produce child sign language discourse (Kluwin & Stewart, 2001) or to interpret 'teacher speak', the discourse strate-gies used by teachers which are very specific to controlling the classroom environment (Schick, 2001); that interpreters may not always adequately convey teacher footing shifts, discourse markers, questioning strategies or communication and classroom management strategies (Goswell, Leigh, Carty & Napier, 2013; Grimes & Cameron, 2005; LaBue, 1998; Ramsey, 1996, 2001; Russell, 2008a); and that interpreters who demonstrate higher-order cognitive thinking skills and attend to teacher intent and student language preferences provide more effective interpretations than interpreters who focus primarily on linguistic choices and interpreting decisions (Russell & Winston, 2014). An evidence-based testing instrument is now available in the U.S. specifically to assess educational interpreter performance (Schick & Williams, 2004).

Regardless of whether they are working in schools with children or in universities with undergraduate or postgraduate students, research has confirmed that interpreters face the challenge of interpreting subject-specific terminology (Leeson & Foley-Cave, 2007; Napier, 2002; Tabak, 2014). Further research that focuses on university interpreting has found that there is potential for miscommunication between hearing and deaf people in university classrooms when the deaf student has to attend to the signing of the interpreter as well as visually presented information (Johnson, 1991); there are various communicative strategies used by lecturers, deaf students, hearing students, and interpreters to fulfil their roles in the university learning process (Harrington, 2005).

7.2.4   Second language learners of sign languages: curricula and assessment

The study of second language learning, teaching and assessment of sign languages is an emerging area of research in applied sign linguistics (see Chapter 4), evidenced by the recent publication of the first edited volume dedicated to sign language teaching and learning (McKee, Rosen & McKee, 2014). Linguists have primarily focused on ascertaining the difference between acquiring sign language as an L1 or L2, particularly in relation to modality (Mayberry, 2006).

However, increasing attention is being paid to what to teach, and how sign language is taught as a second language to hearing (adult) learners, with the literature still dominated by research on ASL. Studies have explored, for example, how to implement an acculturation model for sign language learners (Kemp, 1998); the challenges for hearing adults learning sign language as a second language, such as their production errors (Rosen, 2004); how to teach signed discourse cohesion (Cresdee, 2006); what needs to be taught specifically to hearing parents with deaf children (Harder & Meijer, 1995; Napier, Leigh & Nann, 2007; Snoddon, 2014); using sign language corpora to inform the teaching of sign language as a second language (Cresdee & Johnston, 2014; Leeson, 2008); strategies for teaching sign language vocabulary (Rosen, DeLouise, Boyle & Daley, 2014); implementation of formative assessment for L2 sign language learning (Smith & Davis, 2014); effective strategies for teaching sign language to high school students (Rosen, 2015); and how to train sign language teachers (McKee & Woodward, 2014; Quinn & Turner, 2014).

Although the bulk of sign language teaching is directed at hearing students who may go on to use sign language in professional practice, applied sign linguists are now beginning to consider other learners, such as deaf children, adults with cochlear implants, hard-of-hearing adolescents or adults who choose to learn to sign (Nilsson & Schönström, 2014), who could be considered 'new speakers' because they choose to learn a minority language to use on a daily basis (O'Rourke, Pujolar & Ramallo, 2015). Others have experimented with teaching a sign language as a second sign language to deaf sign language users who already have a first sign language (Hessmann & Pyfers, 2014).

Another emerging area in this domain relates to sign language interpreter pedagogy. Although there are many publications on interpreter training featured, for instance, in proceedings of conventions of the *Conference of Interpreter Trainers* and in the Interpreter Education series published by Gallaudet University Press, which provide descriptions of teaching methods and curricula, the systematic and empirical investigation of sign language interpreter teaching and assessment is still relatively recent (Napier, 2009a). Examples of research-based investigations of sign language interpreter teaching and assessment include embedding the teaching of discourse within the curriculum (Napier, 2006a), comparison of interpreter education programme outcomes (Petronio & Hale, 2009), scaffolding of deliberate practice to develop expertise (Schafer, 2011), evaluation of programme admission screening tests (Bontempo & Napier, 2009), the development and validation of interpreter tests (Leeson, 2011; Napier 2013a; Russell & Malcolm, 2009), the testing of deaf interpreters (Bontempo, Goswell, Levitzke-Gray, Napier & Warby, 2014) and examining learner autonomy (Pivac, 2014).

7.2.5 Sign language in the workplace

There are very few studies to report on with respect to research on sign language in the workplace. Hersh (2012) has described communicative practices in the workplace (i.e. that deaf people need accommodations through interpreters or other technical support) and the benefits to employers of employing deaf people, but to date, there have been no observations or analyses of sign language discourse at work (e.g. use of humour, gendered talk, meeting talk, power dynamics, politeness, negotiation) that could be compared with research to date on spoken language use at work (see Cameron, 2008; Holmes, 2006; Holmes & Marra, 2002; Holmes & Stubbe, 2015; Tannen, 1994). This is likely because there are very few workplaces where interactions would be conducted solely in sign language, although there have been explorations of working relationships between deaf and hearing professionals in workplaces that are signing environments (Young & Ackerman, 2001; Young, Ackerman & Kyle, 2000).

The only research that could be considered under the banner of applied sign linguistics has focused on sign language *interpreting* in the workplace. For example, Van Herreweghe (2002) analysed turn-taking mechanisms and active participation in meetings with deaf and hearing participants, and Dickinson (2014) explored working relationships and boundaries in the workplace, the complexity of interpreters' task and how interpreters manage their role.

One book has been dedicated to interpreting in the workplace and proposed a framework for a 'deaf professional-designated interpreter model' (Hauser, Finch & Hauser, 2008, as discussed in Chapter 4, Section 4.4.6). The book features empirical and descriptive accounts of various aspects of the ways in which interpreters work with deaf people when the deaf person is in a professional role. Those of most interest in applied linguistics terms discuss the cooperative discourse markers used by a deaf presenter and interpreters to ensure that the message has the most impact on the audience (Napier, 2007a; Napier, Carmichael & Wiltshire, 2008); the importance of interpreters enabling social networking in work contexts, the appropriate register to use and effective communication management strategies (Clark & Finch, 2008); powerful and powerless language and gendered communicative styles at work, and the fact that female sign language interpreters may inadvertently misrepresent a male conversational style (and vice versa) so interpreters should think carefully about their language choices (Bontempo et al., 2014; Morgan, 2008).

7.2.6 Sign language in everyday life

For the purposes of this book, when we discuss sign language in everyday life, we take this to mean sign language in everyday communicative interaction. There is very little research on this form of sign language in action (Baker & van den Bogaerde, 2012), and the majority that exists focuses on ASL, but some of the earliest studies date back to the 1970s. Here, we give an overview of research on how people use sign language in conversation or other communicative events (i.e. sign language discourse) and how people use sign language differently (i.e. sign language variation).

There are analytical studies of several aspects of everyday sign language discourse between deaf people, including turn-taking (Baker, 1977; Coates

& Sutton-Spence, 2001), narrative and story structure (Gee & Kegl, 1983), conversational repairs and etiquette (Dively, 1998; Hall, 1989), politeness (Hoza, 2007, 2011; Mapson, 2014; Pietrosemoli, 2001), discourse features (Davis, 2011; McKee & Wallingford, 2011; Roy, 1989b), use of constructed action and dialogue (Metzger, 1995; Thumann, 2011) and register and genre (Russo, 2004; Stone, 2011; Zimmer, 1989).

One particular area of focus is on the way that deaf and hearing signers bring different features of spoken and signed languages together in different contexts through various forms of language contact (Davis, 1989; Lucas & Valli, 1992; Napier, 2006a) by predominantly borrowing from a spoken language into a signed language through mouthing and fingerspelling; the incidence of bimodal code-blending amongst hearing signers, where they incorporate aspects of sign language into speech or vice versa (Bishop, 2010; Bishop & Hicks, 2005, 2008; Emmorey, Borinstein & Thompson, 2005; Emmorey, Borinstein, Thompson & Gollan, 2008); and the contact that occurs between two different signed languages through borrowing of lexical items (Adam, 2012a, 2012b; Meir & Sandler, 2008; Quinto-Pozos, 2008).

Much work remains to be carried out to better understand sociolinguistic variation in signing communities (Schembri & Johnston, 2012). Nevertheless, there is a growing body of work in this area that has documented various forms of variation across a range of signed languages, including ASL, Auslan, BSL, Flemish Sign Language, ISL, NZSL, and Sign Language of the Netherlands. These studies have revealed differences in phonological, lexical, numeral and regional variation (Bayley, Lucas & Rose, 2000; McKee, McKee & Major, 2011; Schembri et al., 2009; Schermer, 2004; van Hecke & De Weerdt, 2004); variation according to race (Aramburo, 1989; Lucas, Bayley, Reed & Wulf, 2001; McCaskill, Lucas, Bayley & Hill, 2011), gender (Leeson & Grehan, 2004; LeMaster & Dwyer, 1991; Mansfield, 1993); Fitzgerald, 2014; and sexuality (Beck & Hesselberg, 1995; Kleinfeld & Warner, 1997; Michaels, 2008, 2010; Rudner & Butowsky, 1981); and historical variation between older and younger signers, for example in relation to the use of fingerspelling (Frishberg, 1975; Kelly, 1991; Schembri & Johnston, 2007; Sutton-Spence, Woll & Allsop, 1990).

7.3 Suggested research projects in applied sign linguistics

As can be seen from Section 7.2, applied sign linguistics is still an emerging field of research, so there is great need for the exploration of new ideas – but there is also the need for expansion of existing research and replication of applied linguistics studies with spoken languages in the context of sign language in action. Applied sign linguistics research is often interdisciplinary, and research findings can typically be applied in the professional practice of deaf and hearing people working with signing communities.

As there are so many possibilities for research in this area, we cannot supply an exhaustive list of what is needed, but we would like to make some suggestions for what we see as key topics that perhaps need to be explored more urgently. In order to provide a list of suggested topics for future research, we have categorised ideas according to key concepts that have been raised throughout the book: Deaf Studies and deaf education; sign language teaching, learning and assessment; sign language in everyday life; and sign language interpreting and translation.

7.3.1   Deaf Studies and deaf education

- Deaf Gain: how is it experienced by deaf people? By hearing people working with signing communities in educational contexts?
- Bilingual education: Do we have evidence for what works?
- Deaf pedagogies: What is it that deaf teachers do? What do they bring to the classroom?

7.3.2   Sign language teaching, learning and assessment

- How can digital resources be maximised for sign language teaching, learning and assessment?
- How can sign language be taught and learned effectively through online and/or blended delivery?
- What are the milestones for L2 M2 acquisition? How do they compare with L2 M1 acquisition?
- What are the barriers to L2 sign language acquisition?
- Interpreter education: How do we teach cultural sensitivity?
- How can sign language testing instruments be standardised?
- How can we ensure that high-stakes tests are appropriately criterion-referenced and 'fit for purpose'?

7.3.3   Sign language discourse

- How does intercultural negotiation occur between deaf and hearing people?
- How do deaf and hearing signers co-construct shared concepts and vocabulary?
- How is sign language used in the workplace in deaf-dominated work spaces?
- What does political discourse look like in sign language?
- What is funny in sign language?
- How is professionalism 'performed' in sign languages in mediated and unmediated settings?
- Intergenerational variation: What does sign language use look like between different members of the same deaf families?
- How are generational gaps bridged in contemporary signing communities?

- How does temporary or permanent visual impairment (e.g. as the result of an eye testing procedure or disease) affect the use of sign language over time?

7.3.4 Sign language interpreting and translation

- What interpreting and communication management strategies do interpreters use in institutional settings?
- What interpreting and communication management strategies do interpreters use in video remote interpreting?
- What are deaf individuals' ontological experiences of being translated (interpreting across the life cycle)?
- How does educational interpreting function inside and outside the classroom?
- How can corpus-based approaches to research be applied in sign language interpreting and translation research?
- How do we distinguish between the linguistic and cultural experiences that deaf and hearing interpreters and translators bring to their work?
- How and when do deaf cochlear implant users work with interpreters? What are their experiences of same? How do they compare/contrast with the experiences of non-cochlear implanted deaf sign language using deaf people?
- How do signing communities perceive and respond to deaf interpreters?

One thing we would like to reiterate is that no applied sign linguistics research should happen in a vacuum. All researchers must be conscious of adopting a community participatory approach and must ensure that deaf sign language users are involved in all stages of the research process and that research has a positive impact on signing communities. In this way, research can be meaningful and answer questions that deaf signing communities feel deserve attention rather than simply serving institutional or individual academic agendas.

7.4 Conducting research in applied sign linguistics: concluding comments

In this final content chapter, the focus has been on conducting research in applied sign linguistics. We have given a detailed breakdown of steps to conducting research with sign language users and in signing communities by giving consideration to the following: how research questions can be defined and developed; various literature that can be considered to frame the research; issues to be mindful of in relation to data collection, participant recruitment and adopting an ethical research approach; suggestions for the analysis of data; and strategies for dissemination of research results. We have also provided examples of existing published research on applied sign linguistics, which we categorised into topics that cover the life cycle: young children's acquisition and use of sign languages, sign language in families, sign language in education, second language learners of sign languages, sign language in the workplace and sign language in everyday life. The last part of the chapter provided suggestions for future applied sign linguistics studies according to key concepts that have come up throughout the book.

The goal of this book is to bring various aspects of sign language research under the umbrella of applied linguistics, and thus provide a stronger grounding for the recognition of applied sign linguistics. We have done this by exploring various key themes that can be found in applied linguistics and by showcasing the range of research, concepts and debates in the intersecting fields of Deaf Studies, sign linguistics, sign language teaching and sign language interpreting studies.

As we said in the introductory chapter, it is our hope that anyone who may have an interest in languages can get some insight into the research and language practices of the signing community through reading this book, and we also hope that anyone considering sign language research will take away the strong message that researchers must work *with* the signing community and must engage in reflexive practice to examine their own position in the signing community.

Further reading

Hale, S., & Napier, J. (2013). *Interpreting research methods: A practical resource.* London, UK: Bloomsbury.

Orfanidou, E., Woll, B., & Morgan, G. (Eds). (2015). *Research methods in sign language studies: A practical guide.* London, UK: Wiley Blackwell.

Pfau, R., Steinbach, M., & Woll, B. (Eds). (2012). *Sign Language: An International Handbook.* Berlin, Germany: De Gruyter Mouton.

Young, A., & Temple, B. (2014). *Approaches to social research: The case of Deaf Studies.* New York, NY: Oxford University Press.

Part IV

Further Resources in Applied Sign Linguistics

8
Key Resources

8.1 Recommended readings

At the end of each chapter, we have provided readers with a few suggestions for further reading. In this section, we list books that we would particularly recommend for anyone wishing to pursue research in the area of applied sign linguistics.

Bauman, H. D. L. (Ed.). (2008). *Open your eyes: Deaf Studies talking*. Minneapolis, MN: University of Minnesota Press.

Bauman, H. D. L., & Murray, J. (Eds). (2014). *Deaf Gain: Raising the stakes for human diversity*. Minneapolis, MN: University of Minnesota Press.

Bragg, L. (Ed.). (2001). *Deaf world: A historical reader and primary sourcebook*. New York, NY: New York University Press.

Cooper, A. C., & Khadijat, K. R. (Eds). (2015). *Citizenship, politics, difference: Perspectives from Sub-Saharan Signed Language communities*. Washington, DC: Gallaudet University Press.

Hale, S., & Napier, J. (2013). Interpreting research methods: A practical resource. London, UK: Bloomsbury.

Hill, J. C. (2012). *Language attitudes in the American Deaf community*. Washington, DC: Gallaudet University Press.

Jepsen, J., De Clerck, G., Lutalo-Kling, S., & McGregor, W. (2015). *Sign languages of the world: A comparative handbook*. Nijmegen, The Netherlands: De Gruyter Mouton and Ishara Press.

Johnston, T., & Schembri, A. (2007). *Australian Sign Language (Auslan): An introduction to sign linguistics*. Cambridge, UK: Cambridge University Press.

Knoors, H., & Marschark, M. (2014). *Teaching deaf learners: Psychological and developmental foundations*. New York, NY: Oxford University Press.

Kusters, A. (2015). *Deaf space in Adamorobe: An ethnographic study in a village in Ghana*. Washington, DC: Gallaudet University Press.

Ladd, P. (2003). *Deafhood: In search of Deaf culture*. Clevedon, UK: Multilingual Matters.

Leigh, I. W. (2009). *A lens on deaf identities*. New York, NY: Oxford University Press.

Leeson, L., & Saeed, J. (2012). *Irish Sign Language: A cognitive linguistic approach*. Edinburgh, UK: Edinburgh University Press.

Leeson, L. & Vermeerbergen, M. (eds) (2015). *Working with the Deaf Community: Education, Mental Health and Interpreting*. Dublin: Interesource Publishing Ltd. (2nd edition).

Leeson, L., Wurm, S., & Vermeerbergen, M. (2011). *Signed language interpreting: Preparation, practice and performance*. London, UK: Routledge.

Lucas, C. (Ed.). (1995). *Sociolinguistics in Deaf communities*. Washington, DC: Gallaudet University Press.

Lucas, C. (Ed.). (2001). *Multicultural aspects of sociolinguistics in Deaf communities*. Washington, DC: Gallaudet University Press.

Lucas, C. (Ed.). (2002). *Turn-taking, fingerspelling and contact in signed languages*. Washington, DC: Gallaudet University Press.

Lucas, C. (Ed.). (2003). *Language and the law in Deaf communities*. Washington, DC: Gallaudet University Press.

Lucas, C. (Ed.). (2007). *Multilingualism and sign languages: From the Great Plains to Australia*. Washington, DC: Gallaudet University Press.

Marschark, M., Peterson, R., & Winston, E. A. (2005). *Sign language interpreting and interpreter education: Directions for research and practice*. New York, NY: Oxford University Press.

Marschark, M., & Spencer, P. (2003). *Oxford Handbook of Deaf Studies, language and education*. New York, NY: Oxford University Press.

Marschark, M., Tang, G., & Knoors, H. (Eds). (2014). *Bilingualism and bilingual deaf education*. New York, NY: Oxford University Press.

Meurant, L., Sinte, A., Van Herreweghe, M., & Vermeerbergen, M. (Eds). (2013). *Sign language research uses and practices: Crossing views on theoretical and applied sign language linguistics*. Nijmegen, The Netherlands: De Gruyter Mouton and Ishara Press.

McKee, D., Rosen, R., & McKee, R. (Eds). (2014). *Teaching and learning signed languages: International perspectives and practices*. Basingstoke, UK: Palgrave Macmillan.

Metzger, M. (Ed.). (2000). *Bilingualism and identity in Deaf communities*. Washington, DC: Gallaudet University Press.

Mindess, A. (2014). *Reading between the signs: Intercultural communication for sign language interpreters* (3rd ed.). Yarmouth, ME: Intercultural Press.

Mulrooney, K. (Ed.). (2015). *Teaching and learning in bilingual classrooms: New scholarship*. Washington, DC: Gallaudet University Press.

Orfanidou, E., Woll, B., & Morgan, G. (Eds). (2015). *Research methods in sign language studies: A practical guide*. London, UK: Wiley Blackwell.

Padden, C., & Humphries, T. (2005). *Inside Deaf Culture*. New York, NY: Harvard University Press.

Pabsch, A. (Ed.). (2014). *UNCRPD Implementation in Europe – A Deaf Perspective. Article 29: Participation in Political and Public Life*. Brussels, Belgium: European Union of the Deaf.

Parasnis, I. (Ed.). (1998). *Cultural and language diversity and the deaf experience.* New York, NY: Cambridge University Press.

Pfau, R., Steinbach, M., & Woll, B. (Eds). (2012). *Sign language: An international handbook.* Berlin, Germany: De Gruyter Mouton.

Quinto-Pozos, D. (Ed.). (2007). *Sign languages in contact.* Washington, DC: Gallaudet University Press.

Quinto-Pozos, D. (Ed.). (2014). *Multilingual aspects of signed language communication and disorder.* Bristol, UK: Multilingual Matters.

Ramsey, C. (1997). *Deaf children in public schools: Placement, context, and consequences.* Washington, DC: Gallaudet University Press.

Reagan, T. (2010). *Language policy and planning for sign languages.* Washington, DC: Gallaudet University Press.

Rosen, R. (2015). *Learning American Sign Language in high school: Motivation, strategies, and achievement.* Washington, DC: Gallaudet University Press.

Roy, C. (Ed.). (2011). *Discourse in signed languages.* Washington, DC: Gallaudet University Press.

Roy, C., & Napier, J. (Eds). (2015). *The sign language interpreting studies reader.* Amsterdam, The Netherlands: John Benjamins.

Schembri, A. & Lucas, C. (Ed.). (2015). *The sociolinguistics of sign languages* (2nd ed.). Cambridge, UK: Cambridge University Press.

Supalla, T., & Clark, P. (2015). *Sign language archaeology: Understanding the historical roots of American Sign Language.* Washington, DC: Gallaudet University Press.

Sutton-Spence, R., & Woll, B. (1998). *The linguistics of British Sign Language.* Cambridge, UK: Cambridge University Press.

Valli, C., Lucas, C., Mulrooney, K., & Villanueva, M. (2011). *Linguistics of American Sign Language: An introduction* (5th ed.). Washington, DC: Gallaudet University Press.

Van Herreweghe, M., & Vermeerbergen, M. (Eds). (2004). *To the lexicon and beyond: Sociolinguistics in European Deaf communities.* Washington, DC: Gallaudet University Press.

Winston, E. A. (Ed.). (1999). *Storytelling and conversation: Discourse in Deaf communities.* Washington, DC: Gallaudet University Press.

Wheatley, M., & Pabsch, A. (2012). *Sign language legislation in the European Union: Edition II.* Brussels, Belgium: European Union of the Deaf.

Young, A., & Temple, B. (2014). *Approaches to social research: The case of Deaf Studies.* New York, NY: Oxford University Press.

8.2 Resources

Given the broad nature of applied sign linguistics, any resources drawing from applied linguistics, sign linguistics, translation and interpreting studies, intercultural communication, deaf studies and bilingualism are all very relevant and often feature articles on applied sign linguistics related research (see References). In this section, we focus on suggesting specific resources (e.g. journals and book series) that strictly fall within the applied sign linguistics framework: drawing on sign linguistics, deaf studies, sign language teaching and learning, sign language interpreting and translation and deaf education literature and web-based resources.

8.2.1   Journals

- *American Annals of the Deaf* (Gallaudet University Press)
  http://gupress.gallaudet.edu/annals/
- *Deaf Studies Digital Journal* (Gallaudet University)
  http://dsdj.gallaudet.edu
- *Deafness & Education International* (Maney Publishing)
  www.maneyonline.com/loi/dei
- *Journal of Deaf Studies and Deaf Education* (Oxford University Press)
  http://jdsde.oxfordjournals.org
- *Journal of Interpretation* (Registry of Interpreters for the Deaf)
  http://digitalcommons.unf.edu/joi/
- *Sign Language & Linguistics* (John Benjamins)
  https://benjamins.com/#catalog/journals/sll/main
- *Sign Language Studies* (Gallaudet University Press)
  http://gupress.gallaudet.edu/SLS.html

8.2.2   Book series

- Gallaudet University Press Interpreter Education series (Editor: Cynthia Roy)
  http://gupress.gallaudet.edu/interpreter-ed.html
- Gallaudet University Press Sociolinguistics in Deaf communities series (Editor: Ceil Lucas)
  http://gupress.gallaudet.edu/socio-series.html
- Gallaudet University Press Studies of Interpretation series (Editor: Melanie Metzger)
  http://gupress.gallaudet.edu/studies-in-interpretation.html
- Oxford Perspectives on Deafness series (Editor: Marc Marschark)
  http://ukcatalogue.oup.com/category/academic/series/pn/pd.do

8.2.3   Research centres

Here we suggest a list of established research centres or groups that focus their research on aspects of applied sign linguistics and that have a web-based 'identity'. Others are still developing in many universities that have only one or two researchers; therefore, this list is only indicative at press time.

- Catalan Sign Language Lab (Universitat Pompeu Fabra, Spain): http://
  parles.upf.edu/en/content/josep-quer-0
- Center for the Advancement of Interpreting and Translation Research
  (Gallaudet University, U.S.): www.gallaudet.edu/interpretation/center_
  for_the_advancement_of_interpreting_and_translation_research_(caitr).
  html
- Center for Sign Language Research (Basel, Switzerland): www.fzgresearch.
  org
- Centre for Deaf Studies (Trinity College, Dublin, Ireland): www.tcd.ie/
  slscs/cds; www.deafstudies.eu/
- Centre for Sign Language & Communication with the Deaf (University of
  Klagenfurt, Austria): www.uni-klu.ac.at/zgh/inhalt/1.htm
- Centre for Translation & Interpreting Studies in Scotland (Heriot-Watt
  University, UK): http://ctiss.hw.ac.uk
- Centre for Sign Linguistics & Deaf Studies (Chinese University of Hong
  Kong): www.cslds.org/v3/
- Centre for Education Research Group on Deaf Studies (University of
  Applied Sciences, Utrecht, The Netherlands): www.research.hu.nl/
  Kenniscentra/Educatie/Dovenstudies.aspx
- Deaf Studies Research Unit (Victoria University of Wellington, New
  Zealand): www.victoria.ac.nz/lals/centres-and-institutes/dsru
- Deaf Studies Unit (University of Patras, Greece): www.deaf.elemedu.
  upatras.gr
- Deafness Cognition and Language Research Centre (University College
  London, UK): www.ucl.ac.uk/dcal
- Department of Languages Finnish Sign Language section (University of
  Jyväskylä, Finland): www.jyu.fi/hum/laitokset/kielet/oppiaineet_kls/
  viittomakieli/en
- Department of South African Sign Language (University of the Free State,
  South Africa): http://humanities.ufs.ac.za/content.aspx?DCode=157
- Flemish Sign Language Centre (Belgium): www.vgtc.be/en/node/81
- Institute of German Sign Language and Communication of the Deaf
  (University of Hamburg, Germany): www.sign-lang.uni-hamburg.de/
  english.html
- International Institute for Sign Language and Deaf Studies (University
  of Central Lancashire, UK): www.uclan.ac.uk/research/explore/groups/
  islands.php
- Institute of Czech Language and Theory of Communication (Charles
  University in Prague, Czech Republic): www.ff.cuni.cz/FF-7886-version1-
  Research_Profile_of_the_Institute_of_Czech_Language_and_Theory_of_
  Communication.pdf
- Japan Institute for Sign Language Studies (Japan Federation of the Deaf):
  http://kamei.aacore.jp/jisls-e.html

- Laboratory for Language and Cognitive Neuroscience (San Diego State University, USA): http://slhs.sdsu.edu/llcn/
- National Center for Deaf Health Research (University of Rochester, U.S.): www.urmc.rochester.edu/Ncdhr/
- Research Group for Quebecoise Sign Language and Deaf Bilingualism (Université du Québec à Montréal, Canada): www.unites.uqam.ca/surdite/
- Section for Sign Linguistics in the Faculty of Polish Studies (University of Warsaw, Poland): www.plm.uw.edu.pl/en/about
- Social Research with Deaf People programme (University of Manchester, UK): www.nursing.manchester.ac.uk/research/researchgroups/socialcare-andpopulationhealth/sord/
- South African Sign Language Section, School of Literature, Language and Media (University of the Witwatersrand, South Africa): www.wits.ac.za/sllm/sasl
- Sign Language Lab (University of Göttingen, Germany): www.uni-goettingen.de/en/news/154157.html
- Sign Language Research Center (University of Rochester, U.S.): www.rochester.edu/College/slrc/
- Sign Language Research Lab (Center for Brain Plasticity and Recovery, Georgetown University, U.S.): https://cbpr.georgetown.edu/researchlabs/slrl
- Sign Language Research Lab (University of Haifa, Israel) - http://sandler-signlab.haifa.ac.il
- Sign Language Section, Department of Linguistics (Stockholm University, Sweden): www.ling.su.se/english/sign-language-section
- Sign Linguistics and Language Acquisition Laboratory (University of Connecticut, U.S.): http://homepages.uconn.edu/~dcl02005/DLM/Lab.html
- Sign Linguistics Group at the Centre for Language Studies (Radboud University, Nijmegen, The Netherlands): www.ru.nl/cls/
- Visual Language and Visual Learning Research Center (Gallaudet University, U.S.): http://vl2.gallaudet.edu
- Western Canadian Centre for Deaf Studies (University of Alberta, Canada): www.wccds.ualberta.ca

8.2.4 Associations and organisations

Below are listed key organisations relevant to sign language in action, sign language in everyday life and sign language in professional practice.

- CODA International: www.coda-international.org
- Conference of Interpreter Trainers: www.cit-asl.org/new/
- Deaf History International: www.deafhistoryinternational.com
- DeafAcademics.org: http://www.deafacademics.org/about_us/index.php

- European Forum of Sign Language Interpreters: http://efsli.org
- European Society for Mental Health and Deafness: www.esmhd.org/eu/
- European Society of Students of Sign Language Interpreting: http://whz-cms-10.zw.fh-zwickau.de/els100oh/
- European Union of the Deaf: www.eud.eu
- Interpreter Trainers' Network: http://itn.aslia.com.au/Interpreter_Trainers_Network/Welcome.html
- Sign Health: www.signhealth.org.uk
- Sign Language Linguistics Society: http://slls.eu
- World Association of Sign Language Interpreters: http://wasli.org
- World Federation of the Deaf: http://wfdeaf.org

8.2.5 Conferences

The conferences listed here are those organised by the organisations above on a regular basis, and they regularly feature research-based papers on applied sign linguistics topics such as bilingualism, sign language teaching and learning, sign language interpreting and translation and sign language identity.

- Conference of the European Forum of Sign Language Interpreters (every year)
- Conference of the World Association of Sign Language Interpreters (every 4 years)
- Convention of the Conference of Interpreter Trainers (every 2 years)
- Deaf Academics Conference (every 2 years)
- International Congress of Educators of the Deaf (every 5 years)
- Theoretical Issues in Sign Language Research conference (every 3 years)
- World Congress of the World Federation of the Deaf (every 4 years)
- World Congress on Mental Health and Deafness (every 3 years)

8.2.6 Websites

Anyone typing the words *deaf* or *sign language* into a search engine will come across thousands of sites dedicated to discussion, presentation or analysis of related topics. Here we suggested various websites that we feel are most pertinent to applied sign linguistics researchers.

Deaf Studies

- Deaf Citizenship: http://deafcitizenship.com
- Deaf Scientists: http://deafscientists.com
- Deaf Studies in Ireland: www.deafstudies.eu/
- Gallaudet Deaf History project: www.gallaudet.edu/history_through_deaf_eyes.html
- Signall 3 (Working with the Deaf Community): www.signall3.com
- Signall II (Perspectives on Deafness): www.signallproject.eu

- The Deafhood Foundation: http://deafhoodfoundation.org/Deafhood/Home.html

Language Teaching, Learning and Assessment

- Deaf Learners: www.deaflearners.org
- Dsigns: www.dsigns-online.eu
- PRO-Sign: www.ecml.at/F5/tabid/867/Default.aspx
- Sign Language Assessment: www.signlang-assessment.info
- Sign World: www.signworldlearn.com
- Signs2Go: www.signs2go.eu
- SignTeach: www.signteach.eu

Translation and Interpreting

- Discover Interpreting: www.discoverinterpreting.com
- Interpreter Trainers' Network: http://itn.aslia.com.au
- Justisigns Project: www.justisigns.com
- Medisigns Project: www.medisignsproject.eu
- National Consortium of Interpreter Education Centers: www.interpretereducation.org
- Street Leverage: www.streetleverage.com

Linguistics and Terminology

- Asian Signbank: www.cslds.org/asiansignbank/
- BSL Corpus Project: www.bslcorpusproject.org
- BSL Signbank: http://bslsignbank.ucl.ac.uk
- Corpus NGT: www.ru.nl/corpusngten/
- DGS-Corpus: www.sign-lang.uni-hamburg.de/dgs-korpus/
- ELAN – The Language Archive: https://tla.mpi.nl/tools/tla-tools/elan/
- Hand Talk: American Indian Sign Language: http://pislresearch.com
- NGT Corpus: http://www.ru.nl/corpusngtuk/
- Medical Signbank: www.auslan.org.au/about/medicalsignbank/
- Sign Linguistics: http://signlinguistics.com

Sign Language and the Deaf Community

- Deaf Nation: http://deafnation.com
- Deaf TV: http://deaftv.com
- H3 TV: http://h3world.tv
- Limping Chicken Deaf News and Blogs: http://limpingchicken.com
- Signstation: www.signstation.org
- UNCRPD (in BSL): www.youtube.com/watch?v=upqDI8EzJWU
- UNCRPD (in English): www.un.org/disabilities/default.asp?navid=12&pid=150

Notes

1 Introduction

1. See video clip presented in American Sign Language (with captions) comparing hearing privilege with white privilege: https://www.youtube.com/watch?v=P071B5sPCvg

2 Understanding Applied Sign Linguistics

1. www.who.int/mediacentre/factsheets/fs300/en/
2. www.ifhoh.org
3. http://wfdeaf.org/whoarewe/mission-and-objectives
4. http://edl.ecml.at/FAQ/FAQsonsignlanguage/tabid/2741/Default.aspx
5. European Union of the Deaf (2014).
6. See: www.un.org/disabilities/countries.asp?id=166
7. A separate study by Vermeerbergen and Leeson (2011) reports that analysis of European publications from the 1980s and early 1990s reveals two different traditions in approaching sign language research. Following Karlsson (1984), they label these the 'oral language compatibility view' and the 'sign language differential view', which map onto Woll's 'modern' and 'postmodern' phases.
8. Bergman, Brita. 1973. Teckenspråkets lingvistiska status. In von der Lieth (ed.), Lars. Psykologisk skriftserie nr 4. Köpenhamns universitet, 211–215.

3 Sign Language in Action

1. See: www.deafhoodfoundation.org
2. See: www.gallaudet.edu/about_gallaudet/mission_and_goals.html
3. See: http://limpingchicken.com/2014/05/09/why-jim-cromwell-argues-hearing-people-should-sign-for-themselves-even-when-interpreters-are-present/
4. See for example, British deaf man John Walker's blog 'Deaf Capital': http://deaf-capital.blog.com/2013/02/11/my-journey-to-capital-deaf/
5. See, for example: www.alldeaf.com/deaf-education/30217-making-plans-nigel-erosion-identity-mainstreaming-dr-paddy-ladd.html
6. See, for example: www.sciencesigns.ac.uk
7. www.wfdeaf.org/wp-content/uploads/2011/04/Statement-on-the-Unification-of-Arab-Sign-Languages-FINAL-091.pdf

4 Learning and Teaching Sign Languages

1. See also "Children create new sign language": http://news.bbc.co.uk/1/hi/sci/tech/3662928.stm
2. See: www.unm.edu/~wilcox/UNM/univlist.html
3. See: www.coe.int/t/cm/home_en.asp
4. www.signature.org.uk

5. http://dsps.wi.gov/LicensesPermitsRegistrations/Credentialing-Division-Home-Page/Health-Professions/Sign-Language-Interpreter/Sign-Language-Interpreter-License-Information
6. www.cdhh.state.nm.us/Licensure.aspx
7. www.kbi.ky.gov/Pages/default.aspx
8. www.enpsit.eu
9. www.nrcpd.org.uk

5 Sign Language in Everyday Life

1. See: www.uclan.ac.uk/courses/ba_hons_british_sign_language_and_deaf_studies.php
2. See:www.wlv.ac.uk/about-us/our-schools-and-institutes/faculty-of-social-sciences/school-of-social-historical-and-political-studies/undergraduate-subject-areas/interpreting-and-deaf-studies/deaf-studies/
3. See: www.deafacademics.org/about_us/index.php
4. See these blog posts: https://lifeinlincs.wordpress.com/2013/09/24/sign-language-research-deaf-hearing-involvement-and-research-ethics/, https://tiger-deafie.wordpress.com/?s=academic&submit=Search
5. See, for example: www.mirror.co.uk/news/world-news/edward-connors-homeless-deaf-drug-5218679
6. www.bbc.co.uk/aboutthebbc/insidethebbc/howwework/policiesandguidelines/subtitles.html
7. http://stakeholders.ofcom.org.uk/broadcasting/broadcast-codes/tv-access-services/code-tv-access-services-2013/
8. www.sfgate.com/news/article/CNN-sued-over-lack-of-closed-captioning-on-website-3002228.php
9. http://flashinglights.co.uk
10. See http://h3world.tv
11. www.eud.eu/Insign_Project-i-716.html

6 Sign Language in (Professional) Practice

1. See: www.mirror.co.uk/3am/celebrity-news/nelson-mandela-fake-sign-language-2921028
2. See: http://terpatron9000.com/the-spectacle-of-sign-language-interpreting/
3. See: www.3aw.com.au/news/eurovision-sign-language-interpreter-steals-the-show-20150317–1m1mif.html
4. See, for example: www.signpostbsl.com

7 Conducting Research in Applied Sign Linguistics

1. See: www.bslcorpusproject.org/events/digging-workshop/
2. See: www.bu.edu/asllrp/SignStream/
3. See: https://tla.mpi.nl/tools/tla-tools/elan/
4. See: http://deafcitizenship.com
5. See: http://dsdj.gallaudet.edu
6. See: www.deafacademics.org/conferences/index.php

References

Adam, R. (2012a). Language contact and borrowing. In R. Pfau, M. Steinbach, & B. Woll (Eds), *Sign language: An international handbook* (pp. 841–861). Berlin: De Gruyter Mouton.

Adam, R. (2012b). *Unimodal bilingualism in the Deaf community: Contact between dialects of BSL and ISL in Australia and the United Kingdom* (Unpublished doctoral dissertation). University College London.

Adam, R. (2015). Dissemination and transfer of knowledge to the Deaf community. In E. Orfanidou, B. Woll, & G. Morgan (Eds), *Research methods in sign language studies: A practical guide* (pp. 41–52). London: Wiley Blackwell.

Adam, R., Aro, M., Druetta, J. C., Dunne, S., & af Klintberg, J. (2014). Deaf interpreters: An introduction. In R. Adam, C. Stone, S. D. Collins, & M. Metzger (Eds), *Deaf interpreters at work: International insights* (pp. 1–18). Washington, DC: Gallaudet University Press.

Adam, R., Carty, B., & Stone, C. (2011). Ghostwriting: Deaf translators within the Deaf community. *Babel, 57*(4), 375–393.

Adams, S. (2008). Characteristics of the Coda experience in 21st century contemporary culture. In M. Bishop & S. Hicks (Eds), *Hearing, Mother Father deaf: Hearing people in Deaf families* (pp. 261–292). Washington, DC: Gallaudet University Press.

Ahrbeck, B. (1995). *Problems of Identity Development of Deaf Children.* Paper presented at the 18th International Congress on Education of the Deaf, Tel Aviv, Israel, 16–20 July 1995. Available: http://files.eric.ed.gov/fulltext/ED391330.pdf

Ahrens, B. (2013). Interpreting techniques and modes. In C. A Chapelle (Ed.), *The encyclopedia of applied linguistics.* doi:10.1002/9781405198431.wbeal0570

Al-Fityani, K. (2010). *Deaf people, modernity, and a contentious effort to unify Arab Sign Languages* (Unpublished doctoral dissertation). University of California, San Diego.

Allen, C. (2013). *Equality for Deaf people: How do we get there?* Centre for Deaf Studies Occasional Lecture Series, Trinity College, Dublin.

Allen, T. E., & Enns, C. (2013). Psychometric study of the ASL Receptive Skills Test when administered to deaf 3-, 4-, and 5-year-old children. *Sign Language Studies, 14*(1), 58–79.

Alley, E. (2012). Exploring remote interpretation. *International Journal of Interpreter Education, 4*(1), 111–119.

Americans with Disabilities Act of 1990. Pub. L. No. 101–336, § 2, 104 Stat. 328 (1991).

Angelelli, C. (2010). A professional ideology in the making: Bilingual youngsters interpreting for the communities and the notion of (no) choice. *Translation and Interpreting Studies, 5*(1), 94–108.

Ann, J. (2001). Bilingualism and language contact. In C. Lucas (Ed.), *The sociolinguistics of sign languages* (pp. 33–60). Cambridge: Cambridge University Press.

Antonini, R., & Torresi, I. (2012). *Italian child language brokers' perspectives on ad-hoc interpreting.* Paper presented to the International Association of Translation & Intercultural Studies conference, Belfast, July 2012.

Aramburo, A. (1989). Sociolinguistic aspects of the Black Deaf community. In C. Lucas (Ed.), *The sociolinguistics of the Deaf community* (pp. 103–21). San Diego, CA: Academic Press.

Armstrong, D. (1983). Iconicity, arbitrariness, and duality of patterning in signed and spoken language: Perspectives on language evolution. *Sign Language Studies, 38* (Spring 1983), 51–83.

Armstrong, D. (1988). Review article: The world turned inside out. *Sign Language Studies, 61,* 419–428.

Armstrong, D. F., Stokoe, W. C., & Wilcox, S. (1995). *Gesture and the nature of language.* Cambridge: Cambridge University Press.

Arnot, M., & Reay, D. (2007). A sociology of pedagogic voice: Power, inequality and pupil consultation, *Discourse: Studies in the Cultural Politics of Education, 28*(3), 311–325.

Atkinson, J. (2006). The perceptual characteristics of voice-hallucinations in deaf people: Insights into the nature of subvocal thought and sensory feedback loops. *Schizophrenia Bulletin, 32*(4), 701–708.

Atherton, M., Turner, G. H., & Russell, D. (2000). *Deaf united: A history of football in the British Deaf community.* Coleford: Douglas McLean.

Bahan, B. (1997, July). *Developing the Deaf Nation.* Keynote paper presented to the Deaf Nation Symposium at the University of Central Lancashire, Preston, UK.

Bahan, B. (2008). Upon the formation of the visual variety of the human race. In H.-D. L. Bauman (Ed.), *Open your eyes: Deaf Studies talking* (pp. 83–99). Minneapolis, MN: University of Minnesota Press.

Bahan, B., & Nash, J. (1995). The formation of signing communities. In J. Mann (Ed.), *Deaf Studies IV conference proceedings* (pp. 1–16). Washington, DC: Gallaudet University College of Continuing Education.

Bailey, R. (2007). Black studies in historical perspective. In N. Normont Jr. (Ed.), *The African American Studies reader* (2nd ed., pp. 302–310). Durham, NC: Carolina Academic Press.

Baker, A., & Van den Bogaerde, B. (2005). *Eye gaze in turntaking in sign language interaction.* Paper presented at the 10th International Congress for Study of Child Language, Berlin, July 2005.

Baker, A., & Van den Boegarde, B. (2012). Communicative interaction. In R. Pfau, M. Steinbach, & B. Woll (Eds), *Sign language: An international handbook* (pp. 489–512). Berlin: De Gruyter Mouton.

Baker, A., & Van den Bogaerde, B. (2014). KODAS: A special form of bilingualism. In D. Quinto-Pozos (Ed.), *Multilingual aspects of signed language communication and disorder* (pp. 211–234). Bristol, UK: Multilingual Matters.

Baker, C. (1977). Regulators and turn-taking in American Sign Language discourse. In L. Friedman (Ed.), *On the other hand* (pp. 218–236). New York: Academic Press.

Baker, C. (2006). *Foundations of bilingual education and bilingualism* (5th ed.). Clevedon, England: Multilingual Matters.

Baker, C. (2011). *Foundations of bilingual education and bilingualism* (5th ed.). Bristol, UK: Multilingual Matters.

Ball, C. (2013). *Legacies and legends: History of interpreter education from 1800 to the 21st century.* Edmonton, Canada: Interpreting Consolidated.

Banna, K. (2004). Auslan interpreting: What can we learn from translation theory? *Deaf Worlds, 20*(2), 100–119.

Barnes, L. (2006). Formal qualifications for language tutors in higher education: A case for discussion. *Deafness Education International, 8*(3), 106–124.

Barnett, S. (2002). Cross-cultural communication with patients who use American Sign Language. *Family Medicine, 34*(5), 376–382.

Bartha, C. (2003). Language ideologies, discriminatory practices and the Deaf community in Hungary. In *Proceedings of the Fourth International Symposium on Bilingualism* (pp. 210–222). Arizona: Arizona State University.

Bartłomiejczyk, M. (2004). Simultaneous interpreting A-B vs. B-A from the interpreters' standpoint. In G. Hansen, K. Malmkjaer, & D. Gile (Eds), *Claims, changes and challenges in translation studies: Selected contributions from the Est Congress, Copenhagen 2001* (pp. 239–249). Amsterdam: John Benjamins.

Bat-Chava, Y. (2000). Diversity of deaf identities. *American Annals of the Deaf, 145*(5), 420–427.

Batterbury, S. (2012). Language justice for sign language peoples: The UN Convention on the Rights of People with Disabilities. *Language Policy, 11*, 253–272.

Batterbury, S., Ladd, P., & Gulliver, M. (2007). Sign Language Peoples as indigenous minorities: Implications for research and policy. *Environment and Planning, 39*(12), 2899–2915.

Battisson, R., & Carter, S. M. (1981). *The academic status of sign language.* Paper presented at the Third National Symposium on Sign Language Research and Teaching, Silver Spring, MD.

Bauman, H-D. L., & Murray, J. (2009). Reframing: From hearing loss to Deaf Gain. *Deaf Studies Digital Journal, 1*(1). Available: http://dsdj.gallaudet.edu/

Bauman, H-D. L., & Murray, J. (2010). Deaf studies in the 21st century: "Deaf-gain" and the future of human diversity. In M. Marschark & P. E. Spencer (Eds), *The Oxford Handbook of deaf studies, language and education, Vol. 2.* DOI: 10.1093/oxfordhb/9780195390032.013.0014

Bauman, H-D. L. (Ed.). (2008). *Open your eyes: Deaf Studies talking.* Minneapolis, MN: University of Minnesota Press.

Bayley, R., Lucas, C., & Rose, M. (2000). Variation in American Sign Language: The case of DEAF. *Journal of Sociolinguistics, 4*, 81–107.

Baynton, D. C. (1998). *Forbidden signs: American culture and the campaign against sign language.* Chicago: University of Chicago Press.

Beck, H., & Hesselberg, S. (1995, July). *Culture and membership of the gay male Deaf community: Gay male variation in British Sign Language.* Paper presented at the XII World Congress of the World Federation of the Deaf, Vienna.

Behares, L. E., Brovetto, C., & Crespi, L. P. (2012). Language policies in Uruguay and Uruguayan Sign Language (LSU). *Sign Language Studies, 12*(4), 519–542.

Bellugi, U., Van Hoek, K., Lillo-Martin, D., & O'Grady, L. (1988). The acquisition of syntax and space in young deaf signers. In D. Bishop & K. Mogford (Eds), *Language development in exceptional circumstances* (pp. 132–149). Edinburgh: Churchill Livingstone.

Bentley-Sassaman, J., & Dawson, C. (2012). Deaf-hearing interpreter teams: A teamwork approach. *Journal of Interpretation, 22*(1), Article 2. Available: http://digital-commons.unf.edu/joi/vol22/iss1/2

Berk-Seligson, S. (1990). *The bilingual courtroom: Court Interpreters in the judicial process.* Chicago: University of Chicago Press.

Bernd, M., Birte, P., & Kliche, O. Family interpreters in hospitals: Good reasons for bad practice? *MediAzioni, 10*, 297–324.

Best, B., Napier, J., Carmichael, A., & Pouliot, O. (in press). From a koine to gestalt: Critical points and interpreter strategies in interpretation from International

Sign into spoken English. In R. Rosenstock & J. Napier (Eds), *International Sign*. Washington, DC: Gallaudet University Press.

Bienvenu, M. J. (1987). Third culture: Working together. *Journal of Interpretation, 4*, 1–12.

Bienvenu, M. J. (2014). Bilingualism: Are sign language interpreters bilinguals? Paper presented at Street Leverage Live, Austin TX, 3 May 2014. Available: http://www.streetleverage.com/2015/05/bilingualism-are-sign-language-interpreters-bilinguals/

Bishop, M. (2010). Happen can't hear: An analysis of code-blends in hearing, native signers of American Sign Language. *Sign Language Studies, 11*, 205–240.

Bishop, M., & Hicks, S. (2005). Orange eyes: Bimodal bilingualism in hearing adults from deaf families. *Sign Language Studies, 5*, 188–230.

Bishop, M., & Hicks, S. (2008a). Introduction. In M. Bishop & S. Hicks (Eds), *Hearing, Mother Father deaf: Hearing people in Deaf families* (pp. xv–xxxviii). Washington, DC: Gallaudet University Press.

Bishop, M., & Hicks, S. (2008b). Coda talk: Bimodal discourse among hearing, native signers. In M. Bishop & S. Hicks (Eds), *Hearing, Mother Father deaf: Hearing people in Deaf families* (pp. 54–98). Washington, DC: Gallaudet University Press.

Blume, S. (2010). *The artificial ear: Cochlear implants and the culture of deafness*. New Brunswick, NJ: Rutgers University Press.

Blumenthal-Kelly, A. (1995). Fingerspelling interaction: A set of deaf parents and their deaf daughter. In C. Lucas (Ed.), *Sociolinguistics in deaf communities* (pp. 62–73). Washington, DC: Gallaudet University

Bontempo, K. (2015). Signed language interpreting. In H. Mikkelson & R. Jourdanais (Eds), *Routledge Handbook on Interpreting*. New York, NY: Routledge.

Bontempo, K., Goswell, D., Levitzke-Gray, P., Napier, J., & Warby, L. (2014). Testing times: Toward the professionalization of deaf interpreters in Australia. In R. Adam, C. Stone, S. D. Collins, & M. Metzger (Eds), *Deaf interpreters at work: International insights* (pp. 51–89). Washington, DC: Gallaudet University Press.

Bontempo, K., Haug, T., Leeson, L., Napier, J., Nicodemus, B., Van den Boegaerde, B., & Vermeerbergen, M. (in prep). Insights on interpreting from Deaf leaders on three continents. For submission to *Across Languages and Cultures*.

Bontempo, K., Haug, T., Leeson, L., Napier, J., Van den Bogaerde, B., & Vermeerbergen, M. (2014, March). *Deaf consumers' perceptions of signed to spoken language interpretation in eight signed languages*. Paper presented at the Inaugural International Interpreting Research Symposium, Gallaudet University, Washington DC.

Bontempo, K., & Napier, J. (2007). Mind the gap! A skills analysis of sign language interpreters. *The Sign Language Translator & Interpreter, 1*(2), 275–299.

Bontempo, K., & Napier, J. (2009). Getting it right from the start: Program admission testing of signed language interpreters. In C. Angelelli & H. Jacobson (Eds), *Testing and assessment in translation and interpreting studies: A call for dialogue between research and practice* (pp. 247–295). Amsterdam: John Benjamins.

Bonvillian, J., & Siedlecki, T. (1996). Young children's acquisition of the location aspect of American Sign Language signs: Parental report findings. *Journal of Communication Disorders, 29*, 13–35.

Bornstein, H., Saulnier, K., & Hamilton, L. (1980). Signed English: A first evaluation. *American Annals of the Deaf, 125*, 467–481.

Boudreault, P. (2005). Deaf interpreters. In T. Janzen (Ed.), *Topics in signed language interpreting* (pp. 323–356). Philadelphia: John Benjamins.

Boudreault, P., & Mayberry, R. I. (2006). Grammatical processing in American Sign Language: Age of first-language acquisition effects in relation to syntactic structure. *Language and Cognitive Processes, 21,* 608–635.

Bourdieu, P. (1977). *Outline of a theory of practice.* Cambridge: Cambridge University Press.

Bourdieu, P. (1997). The forms of capital. In A. H. Halsey, H. Lauder, P. Brown, & A. S. Wells (Eds), *Education: Culture, economy and society* (pp. 46–58). Oxford, UK: Oxford University Press.

Boyes Braem, P. (1990). Acquisition of the handshape in American Sign Language: A preliminary analysis. In V. Volterra & C. Erting (Eds), *From gesture to language in hearing and deaf children* (pp. 107–127). Washington, DC: Gallaudet University Press.

Braun, S., & Taylor, J. L. (2011). Video-mediated interpreting: an overview of current practice and research. In S. Braun & J. L. Taylor (Eds), *Videoconference and remote interpreting in criminal proceedings* (pp. 145–185). Guildford: University of Surrey Press.

Breivik, J. (2005). *Deaf identities in the making: Local lives, transnational connections.* Washington, DC: Gallaudet University Press.

Breivik, J. (2006). Deaf identities: Visible culture, hidden dilemmas and scattered belonging. In H. G. Sicakkan & Y.G. Lithman (Eds), *What happens when a society is diverse: Exploring multidimensional identities* (pp. 75–104). Lewiston, NY: Edwin Mellen Press.

Brennan, M. (1990). *Word Formation in British Sign Language.* Stockholm: University of Stockholm Press.

Brennan, M. (1992). The visual world of BSL: An introduction. In D. Brien (Ed.), *Dictionary of British Sign Language/English* (pp. 1–133). London: Faber & Faber.

Brennan, M. (1999a). Signs of injustice. *The Translator, 5*(2), 221–246.

Brennan, M. (1999b). Challenging linguistic exclusion in deaf education. *Deaf Worlds, 15*(1), 2–10.

Brennan, M. (2005). Conjoining word and image in British Sign Language (BSL): An exploration of metaphorical signs in BSL. *Sign Language Studies, 5*(3), 360–382.

Brennan, M., & Brown, R. (1997). *Equality before the law: Deaf people's access to justice.* Durham, NC: Deaf Studies Research Unit, University of Durham.

Brien, D., Brown, R., & Collins, J. (2002). *The organisation and provision of British Sign Language/English interpreters in England, Scotland and Wales.* London: Department for Work and Pensions.

Bristoll, S. (2009). "But we booked an interpreter!" The glass ceiling and deaf people: Do interpreting practices contribute? *The Sign Language Translator & Interpreter, 3*(2), 117–140.

British Deaf Association. (2014). BSL Heritage Project. *British Deaf News, July 2014,* 19–20.

Brophy, J. E., & Good, T. L. (1970). Teacher-child dyadic interaction: A manual for coding classroom behaviour. in A. Simon and E. G. Boyer (Eds), *Mirrors for behavior: An anthology of classroom observation instruments.* Philadelphia: Research for Better Schools.

Brophy, J. E., & Good, T. L. (1974). *Teacher-student relationships: Causes and consequences.* New York: Holt, Rinehart and Winston.

Brown, J. D. (2004). *Language assessment: Principles and classroom practices.* White Plains, NY: Pearson Education.

Brown, J. D., & Hudson, T. (2002). *Criterion-referenced language testing.* Cambridge: Cambridge University Press.

Brück, P., Hemmel, A., Hessmann, J., Meinicke, B., Rode, J., & Unruh, D. (2014). Difficult patients and demigods in white? Sign language interpreters as observers and managers of doctor-patient relations. In B. Nicodemus & M. Metzger (Eds), *Investigations in healthcare interpreting.* Washington, DC: Gallaudet University Press.

Brueggemann, B. J. (2009). *Deaf subjects: Between identities and places.* New York: New York University Press.

Brumfit, C. (1995). Teacher professionalism and research. In G. Cook & B. Sedlhofer (Eds), *Principle and practice in applied linguistics* (pp. 27–42). Oxford: Oxford University Press.

Brunson, J. (2007). Your case will now be heard: Sign language interpreters as problematic accommodations in legal interactions. *Journal of Deaf Studies & Deaf Education.* doi:10.1093/deafed/enm032

Brunson, J. (2011). *Video relay service interpreters: Intricacies of sign language access.* Washington, DC: Gallaudet University Press.

Buchino, M.A. (1993). Perceptions of the oldest hearing child of Deaf parents: On interpreting, communication, feelings and role reversal. *American Annals of the Deaf 138,* 40–45.

Burke, T. (2006). Comments on W(h)ither the Deaf community? *Sign Language Studies, 6,* 174–180.

Burns, S., Matthews, P., & Nolan-Conroy, E. (2001). Language attitudes. In C. Lucas (Ed.), *The sociolinguistics of sign languages* (pp. 181–216). Cambridge: Cambridge University Press.

Buxton, D. (2014). Being a local council representative: Challenges and opportunities. In A. Pabsch (Ed.), *UNCRPD implementation in Europe – a deaf perspective: Article 29: Participation in Political and Public Life.* (pp. 119–123). Brussels: European Union of the Deaf.

Bybee, J. (1985). Diagrammatic iconicity in stem-inflection relations. In J. Haiman (Ed.), *Iconicity in syntax* (pp. 11–47). Amsterdam: John Benjamins.

Cameron, D. (2008). Talk from the top down. *Language & Communication, 28*(2), 143–155.

Cameron, D., Frazer, E., Harvey, P., Rampton, B., & Richardson, K. (1992). *Researching language: Issues of power and method.* London: Routledge.

Campbell, L., Rohan, M., & Woodcock, K. (2008). Academic and educational interpreting from the other side of the classroom: Working with deaf academics. In P. Hauser, K. Finch, & A. Hauser (Eds), *Deaf professionals and designated interpreters: A new paradigm* (pp. 81–105). Washington, DC: Gallaudet University Press.

Candlin, C. (2001). Medical discourse as professional and institutional action: Challenges to teaching and researching language for specific purposes. In M. Bax & J. W. Zwart (Eds), *Reflections on language and language learning* (pp. 185–208). Amsterdam: John Benjamins.

Candlin, C., & Candlin, S. (2003). Healthcare communication as a problematic site for applied linguistic research. *Annual Review of Applied Linguistics, 23,* 134–154.

Candlin, C. N., & Crichton, J. (2011). Emergent themes and research challenges: Reconceptualising LSP. In M. Petersen & J. Engberg (Eds), *Current trends in LSP research: Aims and methods* (pp. 277–316). Bern: Peter Lang.

Candlin, C. N., & Crichton, J. (2013). From ontology to methodology: Exploring the discursive landscape of trust. In C. Candlin & J. Crichton (Eds), *Discourses of trust* (pp. 1–20). Basingstoke, UK: Palgrave Macmillan.

Candlin, C., & Sarangi, S. (2004a). Editorial: Making applied linguistics matter. *Journal of Applied Linguistics & Professional Practice, 1*(1), 1–8.

Candlin, C., & Sarangi, S. (2004b). Editorial: Making inter-relationality matter in applied linguistics. *Journal of Applied Linguistics & Professional Practice, 1*(3), 225–228.

Carty, B. (2000). John Carmichael: Australian deaf pioneer. In A. Schembri & J. Napier (Eds), *Deaf studies, Sydney, 1998: Selected papers from the Australasian Deaf Studies Research Symposium, Renwick College, August 22–23, 1998*. Sydney: North Rocks Press.

Carty, B. (2006). Comments on W(h)ither the Deaf community? *Sign Language Studies, 6*, 181–189.

Cawthon, S., Winton, S., Garberoglio, C., & Gobble, M. (2010). The effects of American Sign Language as an assessment accommodation for students who are deaf or hard of hearing. *Journal of Deaf Studies & Deaf Education*. doi:10.1093/deafed/enq053

Cheek, A., Cormier, K., Repp, A., & Meier, R. (2001). Prelinguistic gesture predicts mastery and error in the production of first signs. *Language, 77*, 292–323.

Chen Pichler, D. (2010). Using early ASL word order to shed light on word order variability in sign language. In M. Anderssen, K. Bentzen, & M. Westergaard (Eds), *Variation in the input: Studies in theoretical psycholinguistics* (Vol. 39, pp. 157–77). Dordrecht: Springer.

Chen Pichler, D. (2011). Sources of handshape error in first-time signers of ASL. In D. J. Napoli & G. Mathur (Eds), *Deaf around the world: The impact of language* (pp. 96–121). Oxford: Oxford University Press.

Chen Pichler, D. (2012). Acquisition. In R. Pfau, M. Steinbach, & B. Woll (Eds), *Sign language: An international handbook* (pp. 647–686). Berlin: De Gruyter Mouton.

Chen Pichler, D., Hochgesang, J., Lillo-Martin, D., & Müller de Quadros, R. (2010). Conventions for sign and speech transcription of child bimodal bilingual corpora in ELAN. *LIA, 1*(1), 11–40. Available: www.ncbi.nlm.nih.gov/pmc/articles/PMC3102315/

Chin, N. B., & Wigglesworth, G. (2007). *Bilingualism: An advanced resource book*. London: Routledge.

Christian, M. (2006). Black studies in the 21st century: Longevity has its place. *Journal of Black Studies, 36*(5), 698–719.

Christiansen, J., & Leigh, I. (2002). *Cochlear implants in children: Ethics and choices*. Washington, DC: Gallaudet University Press.

Christie, K., Wilkins, D. M., McDonald, B. H., Neuroth-Gimbrone, C. (1999). GET-TO-THE-POINT: Academic bilingualism and discourse in American Sign Language and Written English. In E. Winston (Ed.), *Storytelling and conversation: Discourse in Deaf communities* (pp.162–189). Washington, D.C: Gallaudet University Press

Chomsky, N. (1957). *Syntactic structures*. The Hague: Mouton & Co.

Chomsky, N. (1965). *Aspects of the theory of syntax*. Special technical report / Massachusetts Institute of Technology. Research Laboratory of Electronics, No. 11. Cambridge, Mass: MIT Press.

Christopher, S., Watts, V., McCormick, A., & Young, S. (2008). Building and maintaining trust in a community-based participatory research partnership. *American Journal of Public Health, 98*, 1398–1406.

CILT. (2006). *National occupational standards in interpreting*. London: CILT, the National Centre for Languages.

CILT. (2010). *UK occupational language standards (revised)*. London: CILT, the National Centre for Languages.

Cirillo, L., Torresi, I., & Valentini, I. (2010). Institutional perceptions of child language brokering in Emilia Romagna. *MediAzioni, 10,* 269–296.

Clark, P., & Finch, K. (2008). Interpreting in the work-related social setting: How not to trump your partner's ace. In P. Hauser, K. Finch, & A. Hauser (Eds), *Deaf professionals and designated interpreters: A new paradigm* (pp. 58–65). Washington, DC: Gallaudet University Press.

Cline, T., Crafter, S., O'Dell, L., & De Abreu, G. (2011). Young people's representations of language brokering. *Journal of Multilingual and Multicultural Development, 32*(3), 207–220.

Cline, T., Crafter, S., & Prokopiou, E. (in press). Child language brokering in schools: a discussion of selected findings from a survey of teachers and ex-students. *Education and Psychology.*

Coates, J., & Sutton-Spence, R. (2001). Turn-taking patterns in Deaf conversation. *Journal of Sociolinguistics, 5,* 507–529.

Cokely, D. (2005). Shifting positionality: A critical examination of the turning point in the relationship of interpreters and the Deaf community. In M. Marschark, R. Peterson, & E. A. Winston (Eds), *Interpreting and interpreting education: Directions for research and practice* (pp. 3–28). New York: Oxford University Press.

Collins, J., & Walker, J. (2006). What is a Deaf interpreter? In R. McKee (Ed.), *Proceedings of the inaugural conference of the World Association of Sign Language Interpreters* (pp. 79–90). Coleford, UK: Douglas McLean.

Colonomos, B. (2014). *Sign language interpreters and the quest for a deaf heart.* Available: www.streetleverage.com/2013/02/sign-language-interpreters-and-the-quest-for-a-deaf-heart/

Compton, S. (2014). American Sign Language as a heritage language. In T. Wiler, J. Peyton, D. Christian, S. Moore, & N. Liu (Eds), *Handbook of heritage, community, and Native American languages in the United States: Research, policy and educational practice* (pp. 272–283). New York: Routledge.

Conama, J.B., & Grehan, C. (2002). *Is there Poverty in the Deaf Community?* Dublin: Irish Deaf Society and Combat Poverty Agency.

Conlin, K., Mirus, G., Mauk, C., Meier, R. (2000). The acquisition of first signs: Place, handshape, and movement. In C. Chamberlain, J. Morford, & R. Mayberry (Eds), *Language acquisition by eye* (pp. 51–69). Mahwah, NJ: Lawrence Erlbaum.

Conlon, C., & Napier, J. (2004). Developing Auslan educational resources: A process of effective translation of children's books. *Deaf Worlds, 20*(2), 141–161.

Conrad, R. (1979). *The deaf school child: Language and cognitive function.* London: Harper & Row.

Conroy, P. (2006). *Signing in and signing out: The education and employment experiences of Deaf people in Ireland: A study of inequality and Deaf people in Ireland.* Dublin: Irish Deaf Society.

Corfmat, P. (1990). *Please sign here: Insights into the world of the Deaf.* Worthing, UK: Churchman Publishing.

Corina, D., & Singleton, J. (2009). Developmental social cognitive neuroscience: Insights from deafness. *Child Development, 80,* 952–967.

Corker, M. (1996). *Deaf Transitions: Images and origins of deaf families, deaf communities and deaf identities.* London: Jessica Kingsley Publishers.

Corker, M. (1997). Deaf people and interpreting: The struggle in language. *Deaf Worlds, 13*(3), 13–20.

Corker, M. (1998). *Deaf and disabled or deafness disabled?* Buckingham: Open University Press.

Cornes, A., Rohan, M., Napier, J., & Rey, J. (2006). Reading the signs: Impact of signed vs. written questionnaires on the prevalence of psychopathology among deaf adolescents. *Australia & New Zealand Journal of Psychiatry, 40*(8), 665–673.

Cornwall, A., & Jewkes, R. (1995). What is participatory research? *Social Science & Medicine, 41*(12), 1667–1676.

Costello, B., Fernández, J., & Landa, A. (2008). The non-(existent) native signer: Sign language research in a small deaf population. In R. Müller de Quadros (Ed.), *Sign languages: Spinning and unraveling the past, present and future* (pp. 77–94). Florianapolis, Brazil: Editora Arara Azul.

Costello, E. (2014). Best practice example: Citizen's Hour Dublin. In A. Pabsch (Ed.), *UNCRPD implementation in Europe – a deaf perspective: Article 29: Participation in Political and Public Life* (pp. 124–129). Brussels: European Union of the Deaf.

Coulmas, F. (1980). *The handbook of sociolinguistics*. Oxford: Blackwell.

Council of Europe. (1992). *European charter for regional or minority languages*. Strasburg: Council of Europe.

Council of Europe. (2001). *Common European framework of reference for languages: Learning, teaching, assessment*. Cambridge: Cambridge University Press.

Council of Europe. (2014). *The importance of competences in the language(s) of schooling for equity and quality in education and for educational success*. Strasburg: Council of Europe.

Cowlishaw, S. (2012, July 26). Sick toddler phones her own ambulance. Available: www.stuff.co.nz/national/7349847/Sick-toddler-phones-her-own-ambulance

Crafter, S., De Abreu, G., Cline, T., & O'Dell, L. (2015). Using vignette methodology as a tool for exploring cultural identity positions of language brokers. *Journal of Constructivist Psychology, 28*(1), 83–96.

Cragg, S. (2002). Peeling back the skins of an onion. *Deaf Worlds, 18*(2), 56–61.

Cramér-Wolrath, E. (2011). Attention interchanges at story-time: A case study from a deaf and hearing twin pair acquiring Swedish Sign Language in their deaf family. *Journal of Deaf Studies & Deaf Education*. doi:10.1093/deafed/enr029

Crasborn, O. (2001). *Phonetic implementation of phonological categories in Sign Language of the Netherlands* (Unpublished doctoral dissertation). University of Utrecht, Utrecht.

Crasborn, O. (2015). Transcription and notation methods. In E. Orfanidou, B. Woll, & G. Morgan (Eds), *Research methods in sign language studies: A practical guide* (pp. 74–88). London: Wiley Blackwell.

Crenshaw, K. (1991). Mapping the margins: Intersectionality, identity politics, and violence against women of color. *Stanford Law Review, 43*(6), 1241–1299.

Cresdee, D. (2006). *A study of the way(s) to teach signed discourse cohesion, particularly reference, within a story context* (Unpublished doctoral dissertation). Charles Darwin University, Darwin, Australia.

Cresdee, D., & Johnston, T. (2014). Using corpus-based research to inform the teaching of Auslan (Australian Sign Language) as a second language. In D. McKee, R. Rosen, & R. McKee (Eds), *Teaching and learning signed languages: International perspectives and practices* (pp. 85–110). London: Palgrave Macmillan.

Cromwell, J. (2014). *Dr Jim's Little Red Book*. Unpublished monograph.

Crystal, D. (2002). *The English language* (2nd ed.). London: Penguin.

Cummins, J., & Swain, M. (1986). *Bilingualism in education: Aspects of theory, research and practice*. London: Longman.

Czubek, T., & Greenwald, J. (2005). Understanding Harry Potter: Parallels to the Deaf World. *Journal of Deaf Studies & Deaf Education*. doi:10.1093/deafed/eni041

Davie, C. (1993). *Passport without a country* [DVD]. Australia.

Davies, A., Brown, A. D., Elder, C., Hill, K., Lumley, T., & McNamara, T. F. (1999). *Dictionary of language testing*. Cambridge: Cambridge University Press.

Davis, J. (1989). Distinguishing language contact phenomena in ASL interpretation. In C. Lucas (Ed.), *The sociolinguistics of the Deaf community* (pp. 85–102). San Diego, CA: Academic Press.

Davis, J. (2011). Discourse features of American Indian Sign Language. In C. B. Roy (Ed.), *Discourse in signed languages* (pp. 179–218). Washington, DC: Gallaudet University Press.

Davis, J., & McKay-Cody, M. (2010). Signed languages of American Indian Communities: Considerations for interpreting work and research. In R. L. McKee & J. Davis (Eds), *Interpreting in multilingual, multicultural contexts* (pp. 119–157). Washington, DC: Gallaudet University.

Dean, R. K. (2014). Condemned to repetition? An analysis of *problem-setting* and *problem-solving* in sign language interpreting ethics. *International Journal for Translation & Interpreting Research, 6*(1), 60–75.

Dean, R. K. (2015). *Sign language interpreters' ethical discourse and moral reasoning patterns* (Unpublished doctoral dissertation). Heriot-Watt University, Edinburgh.

Dean, R. K., & Pollard, R. Q. (2004, October). A practice-profession model of ethical reasoning. *VIEWS, 21*(9), 1, 28–29.

Dean, R. K., & Pollard, R. Q. (2005). Consumers and service effectiveness in interpreting work: A practice profession perspective. In M. Marschark, R. Peterson, & E. Winston (Eds), *Interpreting and interpreter education: Directions for research and practice*. New York: Oxford University Press.

Dean, R. K., & Pollard, R. Q. (2013). *The demand control schema: Interpreting as a practice profession*. North Charleston, SC: CreateSpace.

De Beuzeville, L. (2006). *Visual and linguistic representation in the acquisition of depicting verbs: A study of native signing deaf children of Auslan* (Unpublished doctoral dissertation). University of Newcastle, Australia.

Degener, J.L. (2010). "'Sometimes my mother does not understand, then I need to translate'. Child and Youth Language Brokering in Berlin-Neukölln (Germany)", *mediAzioni, 10*, 346–367.

De Lacerda, C. B. F., & Belém, L. J. M. (2012). The work of Brazilian Sign Language interpreter in high schools. In R. Müller de Quadros & M. Metzger (Eds), *Signed language interpreting in Brazil* (pp. 77–95). Washington, DC: Gallaudet University Press.

De Meulder, M., & Heyerick, I. (2013). (Deaf) Interpreters on television: Challenging power and responsibility. In L. Meurant, A. Sinte, M. Van Herreweghe, & M. Vermeerbergen (Eds), *Sign language research uses and practices: Crossing views on theoretical and applied sign language linguistics* (pp. 111–316). Nijmegen, The Netherlands: De Gruyter Mouton and Ishara Press.

Del Torto, L. M. (2008). Once a broker, always a broker: Non-professional interpreting as identity accomplishment in multigenerational Italian English bilingual family interaction. *Multilingua – Journal of Cross-Cultural and Interlanguage Communication, 27*(1–2), 77–97.

Del Torto, L. M. (2010). Child language brokers all grown up: Interpreting in multigenerational Italian-Canadian family interaction. *MediAzioni, 10*, 147–181.

Department of Education (1972) *The education of children who are handicapped by impaired hearing*. Dublin: Government Publications.

Deuchar, M. (1983). Is British Sign Language an SVO language? In J. G. Kyle & B. Woll (Eds), *Language in sign: An international perspective on sign language* (pp. 69–76). London: Croom Helm.

De Wit, M. (2010). The complexity of interpreting in multilingual international settings. In R. L. McKee & J. Davis (Eds), *Interpreting in multilingual, multicultural contexts* (pp. 226–242). Washington, DC: Gallaudet University Press.

De Wit, M., Salami, M., & Hema, Z. (2012). Educating sign language interpreters in healthcare settings: A European perspective. In L. Swabey & K. Malcolm (Eds), *In our hands: Educating healthcare interpreters* (pp. 229–260). Washington DC: Gallaudet University Press, 2012.

De Wit, M., & Sluis, I. (2014). Sign language interpreter quality: The perspective of deaf sign language users in the Netherlands. *The Interpreter's Newsletter, 19*, 63–85.

Dickinson, J. (2010). *Interpreting in a community of practice: A sociolinguistic study of the signed language interpreter's role in workplace discourse* (Unpublished doctoral dissertation). Heriot-Watt University, Edinburgh.

Dickinson, J. (2014). *Sign language interpreting in the workplace.* Coleford: Douglas McLean.

Dickinson, J., & Turner, G. H. (2008). Sign language interpreters and role conflict in the workplace. In C. Valero-Garces & A. Martin (Eds), *Crossing borders in community interpreting: Definitions and dilemmas* (pp. 231–244). Amsterdam : John Benjamins.

Diener, E., & Crandall, R. (1978). *Ethics in social and behavioral research.* Oxford: University of Chicago Press.

Dively, V. (1998). Conversational repairs in ASL. In C. Lucas (Ed.), *Pinky extension and eye gaze: Language use in Deaf communities* (pp. 137–169). Washington, DC: Gallaudet University Press.

Donovan, C. (2004). European Masters Project Group: Teaching simultaneous interpretation into a B language. *Interpreting, 6*(2), 205–216.

Dorner, L., Orellana, M. F., & Jimenez, R. (2008). "It's one of those things that you do to help the family": Language brokering and the development of immigrant adolescents. *Journal of Adolescent Research, 23*(5), 515–543.

Dörnyei, Z. (2007). *Research methods in applied linguistics: Quantitative, qualitative, and mixed methodologies.* Oxford: Oxford University Press.

Drolsbaugh, M. (2008). *Deaf again.* Springhouse, PA: Handwave Publications.

Dudis, P. (2004). Body partitioning and real-space blends. *Cognitive Linguistics, 15*, 223–238.

Du Feu, M., & Chovaz, C. (2014). *Mental health and deafness.* Oxford: Oxford University Press.

Du Feu, M., & McKenna, P. (1999). Prelingually profoundly deaf schizophrenic patients who hear voices: A phenomenological analysis. *Acta Psychiatrica Scandinavica, 99*(6), 453–459.

Duff, P. (2015). Transnationalism, multilingualism, and identity. *Annual Review of Applied Linguistics, 35*, 57–80.

Duncan, B. (1997). Deaf people interpreting on television. *Deaf Worlds, 13*(3), 35–39.

Earhart, A., & Hauser, A. (2008). The other side of the curtain. In P. Hauser, K. Finch, & A. Hauser (Eds), *Deaf professionals and designated interpreters: A new paradigm* (pp. 143–164). Washington, DC: Gallaudet University Press.

Eckert, R. C. (2010). Toward a theory of deaf ethnos: Deafnicity – D/deaf (Ho´maemon-Homo´glosson-Homo´threskon). *Journal of Deaf Studies & Deaf Education, 15*(4), 317–333.

Edwards, R. (1998). A critical examination of the use of interpreters in qualitative research. *Journal of Ethnic and Migration Studies, 24*(1), 197–208.

Eggly, S. (2002). Physician-patient co-construction of illness narratives in the medical interview. *Health Communication, 14*(3), 339–360.

Ehrlich, S., & Napier, J. (2015). (Eds). *Interpreter education in the digital age.* Washington, DC: Gallaudet Univeristy Press.

Eichmann, H. (2009). Planning sign languages: promoting hearing hegemony? Conceptualizing sign language standardization. *Current Issues in Language Planning, 10*(3), 293–307.

Emerton, R. G., Foster, S., & Gravitz, J. (1996). Deaf people in today's workplace: Use of the ADA and mediation processes in resolving barriers to participation. In P. C. Higgins & J. E. Nash (Eds), *Understanding deafness socially: Continuities in research and theory* (pp. 44–59). Springfield, IL: Charles C. Thomas.

Emery, S. (2006). *Citizenship and the Deaf community* (Unpublished doctoral dissertation). University of Central Lancashire, Preston, UK.

Emery, S. (2007). Citizenship and sign bilingualism: '... There is nothing wrong with being bilingual...it's a positive and fantastic thing!' *Deafness and Education International, 9*(4), 173–186.

Emery, S. (2009). In space no one can see you waving your hands: Making citizenship meaningful to Deaf worlds. *Citizenship Studies, 13*(1), 31–44.

Emery, S. (2011). *Citizenship and the Deaf community.* Nijmegen: Ishara Press.

Emery, S., Middleton, A. & Turner, G. H. (2010). Whose Deaf genes are they anyway?: The Deaf community's challenge to legislation on embryo selection. *Sign Language Studies, 10*(2), 155–169.

Emmorey, K. (2002). *Language, cognition, and the brain: Insights from sign language research.* Mahwah, NJ: Lawrence Erlbaum Associates.

Emmorey, K., Borinstein, H., & Thompson, R. (2005). Bimodal bilingualism: Code-blending between spoken English and American Sign Language. In J. Cohen, T. McAlister, K. Rolstad, & J. MacSwan (Eds), *ISB4: Proceedings of the Fourth International Symposium on Bilingualism* (pp. 663–673). Somerville, MA: Cascadilla Press.

Emmorey, K., Borinstein, H., Thompson, R., & Gollan, T. (2008). Bimodal bilingualism. *Bilingualism: Language and Cognition, 11*, 43–61.

Emmorey, K., & Reilly, J. (Eds). (1995). *Language, gesture, and space: Fourth International conference on theoretical issues in sign language research: Papers.* Hillsdale: Lawrence Erlbaum.

Engberg-Pederson, E. (1993). *Space in Danish Sign Language: The semantics and morphosyntax of the use of space in a visual language.* Hamburg: Signum Verlag.

Enns, C., & Herman, R. (2011). Adapting the assessing British Sign Language Development: Receptive skills test into American Sign Language. *Journal of Deaf Studies and Deaf Education.* doi:10.1093/deafed/enr004

Enright, S. (1999). The deaf juror and the thirteenth man. *New Law Journal, 1720.*

Erting, C., Johnson, R., Smith, D., & Snider, B. (Eds) (1994). *The Deaf way: Perspectives from the international conference on Deaf culture.* Washington, D.C: Gallaudet University Press.

Esmail, J. (2008). The power of Deaf poetry: The exhibition of literacy and nineteenth century sign language debates. *Sign Language Studies, 8*(4), 348–368.

ESRC (2010). Framework for Research Ethics. Available: www.esrc.ac.uk/_images/framework-for-research-ethics-09–12_tcm8–4586.pdf

European Union of the Deaf. (2001). *EUD update, special edition: Update on the status of sign languages in the European Union.* Brussels: European Union of the Deaf.

European Union of the Deaf. (2013). *2013 UNCRPD Report*. Brussels: European Union of the Deaf.

Evans, V., & Green, M. (2006). *Cognitive linguistics: An introduction*. Edinburgh: Edinburgh University Press.

Fauconnier, G. (1985). *Mental spaces: Aspects of meaning construction in natural language*. Cambridge, MA: MIT Press.

Faulks, K. (2002). Citizenship. In G. Blakely & V. Bryson (Eds), *Contemporary political concepts: A critical introduction* (pp. 35–50). London: Pluto Press.

Fayd'herbe, K., & Teuma, R. (2010). Interpreting for Indigenous Australian deaf clients in Far North Queensland Australia within the legal context. In R. L. McKee & J. Davis (Eds), *Interpreting in multilingual, multicultural contexts* (pp. 158–194). Washington, DC: Gallaudet University.

Fehrmann, G., Huber, W., Jäger, L., Sieprath, H., & Werth, I. (1995a). *Linguistische Konzeption des Aachener Tests zur Basiskompetenz in Deutscher Gebärdensprache (ATG)* [Linguistic conception of the Aachen test of basic competence of German Sign Language (ATG)]. Unpublished manuscript. RWTH-Aachen, Germanistisches Institut & Neurologische Klinik, Projekt DESIRE.

Fehrmann, G., Huber, W., Jäger, L., Sieprath, H., & Werth, I. (1995b). *Aufbau des Aachener Tests zur Basiskompetenz in Deutscher Gebärdensprache (ATG)* [Design of the Aachen test of basic competence of German Sign Language (ATG)]. Unpublished manuscript. RWTH-Aachen, Germanitisches Institut & Neurologische Klinik, Projekt DESIRE.

Fenlon, J., & Wilkinson, E. (2015). Sign languages in the world. In A. Schembri & C. Lucas (Eds), *Sociolinguistics and Deaf communities* (pp. 5–28). Cambridge: Cambridge University Press.

Feyne, S. (in press). Variation in perceptions of the identity of interpreted Deaf lecturers. In C. Stone & L. Leeson (Eds), *Interpreting and the politics of recognition*. London: Routledge.

Finton, L. (2005). Compression strategies: ASL to English interpreting. *Journal of Interpretation*, 49–64.

Fischer, R., & Lane, H. (Eds). (1993). *Looking back: A reader on the history of Deaf communities and their sign languages*. Hamburg: Signum.

Fischer, R., & Muller, A. (2014). eLCA – An e-learning unit for acquiring constructed action. In D. McKee, R. S. Rosen, & R. McKee (Eds), *Teaching and learning of signed language: International perspectives* (pp. 111–128). London: Palgrave Macmillan.

Fischer, S. (1975). Influences on word order change in ASL. In C. Li (Ed.), *Word order and word order change* (pp. 1–25). Austin: University of Texas Press.

Fitzgerald, A. (2014). *A cognitive account of mouthings and mouth gestures in Irish Sign Language* (Unpublished doctoral dissertation). Trinity College, Dublin.

Fitzmaurice, S., & Purdy, K. (2015). Disfluent pausing effects on listener judgments of an ASL-English interpretation. *Journal of Interpretation, 24*(1), Article 3. Available: http://digitalcommons.unf.edu/joi/vol24/iss1/3

FLAC. (2010). *Judge rules Deaf man can sit on jury*. Free Legal Aid Centre (FLAC). Avalable: www.flac.ie/news/2010/11/29/judge-rules-deaf-man-can-sit-on-jury/

Frishberg, N. (1975). Arbitrariness and iconicity: Historical change in American Sign Language. *Language, 51*, 696–719.

Forestal, E. (2005). The emerging professionals: Deaf interpreters and their views and experiences on training. In M. Marschark, R. Peterson, & E. A. Winston (Eds), *Interpreting and interpreting education: Directions for research and practice* (pp. 235–258). New York: Oxford University Press.

Forestal, E. (2014). Deaf interpreters: The dynamics of their interpreting processes. In R. Adam, C. Stone, S. D. Collins, & M. Metzger (Eds), *Deaf interpreters at work: International insights* (pp. 29–50). Washington, DC: Gallaudet University Press.

Freel, B., Clark, M. D., Anderson, M., Gilbert, G., Musyoka, M., & Hauser, P. (2011). Deaf individuals' bilingual abilities: American Sign Language proficiency, reading skills and family characteristics. *Psychology, 2*(1), 18–23.

Friedman, L.A. (1976). Subject, object and topic in American Sign Language. In C. Li, *Subject and Topic* (pp. 125–148). New York: Academic Press.

Frishberg, N., Hoiting, N., & Slobin, D. (2012). Transcription. In R. Pfau, M. Steinbach, & B. Woll (Eds). *Sign language: An international handbook* (pp. 1045–1075). Berlin: De Gruyter Mouton.

Gahir, M., O'Rourke, S., Monteiro, B., & Reed, R. (2011). The unmet needs of deaf prisoners: A survey of prisons in England and Wales. *International Journal on Mental Health & Deafness, 1*(1), 58–63.

García Sánchez, I. M. (2010). (Re)shaping practices in translation: How Moroccan immigrant children and families navigate continuity and change. *MediAzioni, 10*, 182–214.

Garret, P., Williams, A., & Coupland, N. (2003). *Investigating language attitudes: Social meanings of dialect, ethnicity and performance*. Cardiff: University of Wales Press.

Gast, R., & Nachtrab, M. (2014). Inclusive state parliaments: Live streaming on the Internet as an instrument for transparency and accessibility. In A. Pabsch (Ed.), *UNCRPD Implementation in Europe – a Deaf Perspective: Article 29: Participation in Political and Public Life*. (pp. 130–142). Brussels: European Union of the Deaf.

Gee, J. P., & Kegl, J. (1983). Narrative/story structure, pausing and American Sign Language. *Discourse Processes, 6*, 243–258.

Geraci, C. (2012). Language policy and planning: The case of Italian Sign Language. *Sign Language Studies, 12*(4), 494–518.

Gesser, A. (2007). Learning about hearing people in the land of the deaf: An ethnographic account. *Sign Language Studies, 7*(3), 269–283.

Gile, D. (1994). Opening up in interpretation studies. In M. Snell-Hornby, F. Pöchhacker, & K. Kaindl (Eds), *Translation Studies: An Interdiscipline* (pp. 149–58). Amsterdam: John Benjamins.

Gile, D. (2005). Directionality in conference interpreting: A cognitive view. *Communication and Cognition, 38*(1–2), 9–26.

Givón, T. (1991). Isomorphism in the grammatical code: Cognitive and biological considerations. *Studies in Language, 15*(1), 85–114.

Glaser, B. G. (2001). *The Grounded Theory Perspective I: Conceptualization contrasted with description*. Mill Valley, CA: Sociology Press.

Glaser, B. G. (2003). *The Grounded Theory Perspective II: Description's remodeling of Grounded Theory*. Mill Valley, CA: Sociology Press.

Glaser, B. G. (2005). *The Grounded Theory Perspective III: Theoretical coding*. Mill Valley, CA: Sociology Press.

Glaser, B. G. (2007). Constructivist grounded theory? (Reprinted from FQS-Forum Qualitative Sozialforschung, Vol. 6). *Historical Social Research-Historische Sozialforschung*, 93–105.

Glickman, N. (1993). Deaf identity development: Construction and validation of a theoretical model. Unpublished doctoral dissertation, University of Massachusetts, Amhurst.

Glickman, N., & Crump, C. (2013). Sign language dysfluency in some deaf persons: Implications for interpreters and clinicians working in mental health settings. In N. Glickman (Ed.), *Deaf mental health care* (pp. 107–132). London: Routledge.

Glickman, N., & Harvey, M. (Eds) (2013). *Culturally affirmative therapy with deaf persons*. Mahwah, NJ: Lawrence Erlbaum Associates.

Goffman, E. (1974). *Frame analysis: an essay on the organization of experience*. London: Harper & Row.

Goldin-Meadow, S. (2003). *The resilience of language: What gesture creation in deaf children can tell us about how all children learn language*. New York: Psychology Press.

Goldin-Meadow, S. (2012). Homesign: Gesture to language. In R. Pfau, M. Steinbach, & B. Woll (Eds), *Sign language: An international handbook* (pp. 601–625). Berlin: De Gruyter Mouton.

Gold Brunson, J., Molner, J., & Lerner, M. N. (2008). Hearts, minds, hands: A dream team for mental health. In P. Hauser, K. Finch, & A. Hauser (Eds), *Deaf professionals and designated interpreters: A new paradigm* (pp. 180–195). Washington, DC: Gallaudet University Press.

Goodstein, H., & Brown, L. (Eds) (1994). *Deaf Way 2: An international celebration*. Washington, D.C: Gallaudet University Press.

Goswell, D. (2011). Being there: Role shift in English to Auslan interpreting. In L. Leeson, S. Wurm, & M. Vermeerbergen (Eds), *Signed language interpreting: Preparation, practice and performance* (pp. 61–86). Manchester: St. Jerome.

Goswell, D. (2012). Do you see what I see? Using ELAN for self-analysis and reflection. *International Journal of Interpreter Education, 4*(1), 73–82.

Goswell, D., Leigh, G., Carty, B., & Napier, J. (2013, October). *The myth of equality for deaf students in interpreted mainstream classrooms: Whose responsibility is it to ensure equality?* Paper presented to the Conference of the World Federation of the Deaf, Sydney.

Graham, B., & Sharp-Pucci, M. (1994). The special challenge of late-deafened adults: Another Deaf Way. In C. Erting, R. Johnson, D. Smith, & B. Snider (Eds), *The Deaf Way: Perspectives from the International Conference on Deaf culture* (pp. 504–515). Washington, DC: Gallaudet University Press.

Graybill, P., Aggas, J., Dean, R. K., Demers, S., Finigan, E., & Pollard, R. Q. (2010). A community participatory approach to adapting survey items for Deaf individuals and American Sign Language. *Field Methods, 22*(4), 429–448.

Grehan, C. (2008). *Communication islands: The Impact of segregation on attitudes to ISL among a sample of graduates of St. Mary's School for Deaf Girls* (Unpublished M.Phil dissertation). Trinity College, Dublin.

Grbić, N. (2007). Where do we come from? What are we? Where are we going? A bibliometrical analysis of writings and research on sign language interpreting. *The Sign Language Translator & Interpreter, 1*(1), 15–51.

Grbić, N. (2008). Constructing interpreting quality. *Interpreting, 10*, 232–257.

Gresswell, E. (2001). How applicable to BSL are contemporary approaches to translation? *Deaf Worlds, 17*(2), 50–62.

Grimes, M., & Cameron, A. (2005). *Inclusion of Deaf pupils in Scotland: Achievements, strategies and services*. Paper given at Inclusive and Supporting Education Congress, International Special Education Conference, Inclusion: Celebrating Diversity? Glasgow.

Groce, N. E. (1985). *Everyone here spoke sign language: Hereditary deafness in Martha's Vineyard*. Cambridge: Harvard University Press.

Grosjean, F. (1997). The bilingual individual. *Interpreting, 2*(1–2), 163–188.

Grosjean, F. (2001). The right of the deaf child to grow up bilingual. *Sign Language Studies, 1*(2), 110–114.

Grosjean, F. (2011). Life as a bilingual: The reality of living with two (or more) languages. *Psychology Today*. Available: www.psychologytoday.com/blog/life-bilingual/201109/those-incredible-interpreters

Gulliver, M. (2005). *Deaf geographies: Spaces of ownership and other real and imaginary places* (Unpublished monograph). Centre for Deaf Studies, University of Bristol.

Gulliver, M. (2006). *Introduction to DEAF space*. Unpublished paper. Available: www.academia.edu/197254/Introduction_to_DEAF_space

Gulliver, M. (2015). Book review. Approaches to social research: The case of Deaf Studies. *Disability & Society, 30*(2), 314–16.

Guiora, A. (1982). Language, personality and culture. *TESOL 81,* 169–177.

Guske, I. (2010). Familial and institutional dependence on bilingual and bicultural go-betweens – effects on minority children. *mediAzioni, 10,* 325–345.

Haiman, J. (Ed.). (1985). *Iconicity in syntax*. Amsterdam: John Benjamins.

Hale, S. (2004) *The discourse of court interpreting: discourse practices of the law, the witness, and the interpreter*. Amsterdam, The Netherlands & Philadelphia: John Benjamins.

Hale, S. (2005). The interpreter's identity crisis. In J. House, M. R. M. Ruano, & N. Baumgarten (Eds), *Translation and construction of identity* (pp. 14–29). Seoul: IATIS.

Hale, S. (2007). *Community interpreting*. London: Palgrave Macmillan.

Hale, S., & Napier, J. (2013). *Interpreting research methods: A practical resource*. London, UK: Bloomsbury.

Hall, C. J., O'Brien, D., & the LIdIA Policy Forum (2015). *Making higher education more Deaf-friendly: LIdIA Position Statement and Position Paper 01*. York: York St John University. Available: www.yorksj.ac.uk/lidia/policy

Hall, J. K. (2002). *Teaching and researching language and culture*. London: Longman Pearson.

Hall, N. (2004). The child in the middle: Agency and diplomacy in language brokering events. In G. Hansen, K. G. Malmkaer, & D. Gile (Eds), *Claims, changes and challenges in translation studies* (pp. 285–296). Philadelphia: John Benjamins.

Hall, N., & Guery, F. (2010). Child language brokering: Some considerations. *Mediazioni, 10,* 24–46.

Hall, N., & Sham, S. (2007). Language brokering as young people's work: Evidence from Chinese adolescents in England. *Language and Education, 21*(1), 16–30. doi:10.2167/le645.0

Hall, S. (1989). TRAIN-GONE-SORRY: The etiquette of social conversations in American Sign Language. In S. Wilcox (Ed.), *American Deaf culture: An anthology* (pp. 89–102). Burtonsville, MD: Linstok Press.

Halliday, M. A. K. (1978). *Language as social semiotic: The social interpretation of language and meaning*. Baltimore: University Park Press.

Hamers, J. F., & Blanc, M. H. A. (2000). *Bilinguality and bilingualism* (2nd ed.). New York: Cambridge University Press.

Hanel, B. (2005). The acquisition of agreement in DGS: Early steps into a spatially expressed syntax. In H. Leuninger & D. Happ (Eds), *Gebärdensprachen: Struktur, Erwerb, Verwendung: Linguistische Berichte, Special Issue 15* (pp. 201–232). Hamburg: Buske.

Harder, R., & Meijer, E. (1995). Sign language courses for hearing parents of deaf children in the Netherlands. In H. Bos, F. Schermer & M. Gertrude (Eds), *Sign Language Research 1994: Proceedings of the Fourth European Congress on Sign Language Research, Munich, September 1–3, 1994* (pp. 273–284). Hamburg: Signum.

Harold, G. (2012). *Deafness, difference and the city: Geographies of urban difference and the right to the Deaf city* (Unpublished doctoral dissertation). National University of Ireland, Cork.

Harris, J. (1995). Boiled eggs and baked beans: A personal account of a hearing researcher's journey through Deaf culture. *Disability & Society, 10*(3), 295–308.

Harrington, F. (2005). A study of the complex nature of interpreting with deaf students in higher education. In M. Metzger & E. Fleetwood (Eds), *Attitudes, innuendo and regulators: Challenges in interpretation* (pp. 162–187). Washington, DC: Gallaudet University Press.

Harris, M., & Mohay, H. (1997). Learning to look in the right place: A comparison of attentional behaviour in deaf children with deaf and hearing mothers. *Journal of Deaf Studies and Deaf Education, 2,* 95–103.

Harris, R., Holmes, H., & Mertens, D. (2009). Research ethics in signing communities. *Sign Language Studies, 9*(2), 104–131.

Harrison, D. (2010). *The last speakers: The quest to save the world's most endangered languages.* Washington, DC: National Geographic.

Hatim, B. (2013). *Teaching and researching translation* (2nd ed.). New York: Routledge.

Hatim, B., & Mason, I. (1990). *Discourse and the translator.* London: Longman.

Hatim, B., & Mason, I. (1997). *Translator as communicator.* London: Routledge.

Haug, T. (2005). Review of sign language assessment instruments. *Sign Language & Linguistics, 8,* 61–98.

Haug, T. (2011a). Approaching sign language test construction: Adaptation of the German Sign Language Receptive Skills Test. *Journal of Deaf Studies and Deaf Education.* doi:10.1093/deafed/enq06

Haug, T. (2011b). *Adaptation and evaluation of a German Sign Language test: A computer-based receptive skills test for deaf children ages 4–8 years.* Hamburg, Germany: Hamburg University Press.

Haualand, H. (2009). Sign language interpreting: A human rights issue. *International Journal of Interpreter Education, 1,* 95–110.

Haualand, H., & Allen, C. (2009). *Deaf people and human rights.* Helsinki, Finland: World Federation of the Deaf. Available at: http://www.wfdeaf.org/pdf/Deaf%20People%20and%20Human%20Rights%20Report%20-%2023%20Feb%2009%20Version.pdf (Accessed on 29 June 2009).

Hauser, A., & Hauser, P. (2008). The deaf professional-designated interpreter model. In P. Hauser, K. Finch, & A. Hauser (Eds), *Deaf professionals and designated interpreters: A new paradigm* (pp. 3–21). Washington, DC: Gallaudet University Press.

Hauser, P., Finch, K., & Hauser, A. (Eds). (2008). *Deaf professionals and designated interpreters: A new paradigm.* Washington, DC: Gallaudet University Press.

Hauser, P., O'Hearn, A., McKee, M., Steider, A., & Thew, D. (2010). Deaf epistemology: Deafhood and deafness. *American Annals of the Deaf, 154*(5), 486–492.

Heaton, M., & Fowler, D. (1997). Aches, aspirins and aspirations: A Deaf perspective on interpreting service delivery. *Deaf Worlds, 13*(3), 3–8.

Helmberger, J. L. (2006). Language and ethnicity: Multiple literacies in context, language education in Guatemala. *Bilingual Research Journal, 30*(1), 65–86.

Herlighy, S. (2012, March). *Teaching through Irish Sign Language.* Paper presented at AHEAD Conference 2012: Access to Teacher Training for Students With Disabilities, Dublin.

Hema, Z. (2002). Dialogism. *Deaf Worlds, 18*(2), 62–65.

Hennink, M. (2008). Language and communication in cross-cultural qualitative research. In P. Liamputtong (Ed.), *Doing cross-cultural research: Ethical and methodological perspectives* (pp. 21–33). London: Springer.

Herman, R. (1998a). The need for an assessment of deaf children's signing skills. *Deafness & Education, 4,* 3–8.

Herman, R. (1998b). Issues in designing an assessment of British Sign Language development. In *Proceedings of the Conference of the Royal College of Speech and Language Therapists* (pp. 332–337). Liverpool, UK.

Herman, R., Grove, N., Holmes, S., Morgan, Gary Sutherland, H., & Woll, B. (2004). *Assessing BSL development: Production test (narrative skills)*. London: City University Publication.

Herman, R., Holmes, S., & Woll, B. (1999). *Assessing BSL development: Receptive Skills Test*. Coleford, UK: Forest Books.

Herman, R., & Roy, P. (2006). Evidence from the wider use of the BSL receptive skills test. *Deafness and Education International, 8*, 33–47.

Hermans, D., Knoors, H., & Verhoeven, L. (2009). Assessment of sign language development: The case of deaf children in the Netherlands. *Journal of Deaf Studies and Deaf Education*. doi:10.1093/deafed/enp030

Hermans, T. (1996). The translator's voice in translated narrative. *Target, 8*(1), 23–48.

Hersh, M. (2012). Deaf people in the workplace. In G. Moss (Ed.), *Lessons on profiting from diversity* (pp. 213–238). London: Palgrave Macmillan.

Hessmann, J., & Pyfers, L. (2014). Teaching British Sign Language as a second language to deaf sign language users: Insights from the Signs2Go online course. In D. McKee, R. Rosen, & R. McKee (Eds), *Teaching and learning signed languages: International perspectives and practices* (pp. 35–64). London: Palgrave.

Hetherington, A. (2010). A magical profession? Causes and management of occupational stress in the signed language interpreting profession. In L. Leeson, S. Wurm, & M. Vermeerbergen (Eds), *Signed language interpreting: Preparation, practice and performance* (pp. 138–159). Manchester: St Jerome.

Heyerick, I., & Vermeerbergen, M. (2012). Sign language interpreting in educational settings in Flanders, Belgium. In L. Leeson & M. Vermeerbergen (Eds), *Interpreting with the Deaf community: Mental health, education and interpreting* (n.p.). Dublin: Interesource Group Publishing.

Higgins, P. (1980). *Outsiders in a hearing world: A sociology of deafness*. London: Sage Publications.

Hill, J. (2013a). Language ideologies, policies, and attitudes toward signed languages. In R. Bayley & C. Lucas (Eds), *The Oxford handbook of sociolinguistics*. New York: Oxford University Press.

Hill, J. (2013b). *Language attitudes in the American Deaf community*. Washington, DC: Gallaudet University Press.

Hill, J. (2015). Data collection in sociolinguistics. In E. Orfanidou, B. Woll, & G. Morgan (Eds), *Research methods in sign language studies: A practical guide* (pp. 193–206). London: Wiley Blackwell.

Hindley, P. (2005). Mental health problems in deaf children. *Current Paediatrics, 15*, 114–119.

Hochgesang, J., Villanueva, P., Mathur, G., & Lillo-Martin, D. (2010). *Building a database while considering research ethics in sign language communities* (Unpublished report). Available: http://homepages.uconn.edu/~dcl02005/DLM/Publications_files/Hochgesang_et_al_2010_LREC.pdf

Hodge, G., Schembri, A., & Rogers, I. (2014). *The Auslan (Australian Sign Language) Production Skills Test: Responding to challenges in the assessment of deaf children's sign language proficiency*. Paper presented at the Fourth Australasian Deaf Studies Research Symposium: RIDBC Renwick Centre and La Trobe University, Australia.

Hoffman, C. (1991). *An introduction to bilingualism*. London: Longman.

Hoffmeister, R. (1985). Families with deaf parents: A functional perspective. In S. K. Thurman (Ed.), *Children of handicapped parents: Research and clinical perspectives* (pp. 111–130). Orlando, FL: Academic Press.

Hoiting, N. (2006). Deaf children are verb attenders: Early sign language acquisition in Dutch toddlers. In B. Schick, M. Marschark, & P. Spencer (Eds), *Advances in sign language development by deaf children* (pp. 161–188). New York: Oxford University Press.

Holmes, J. (2006). *Gendered talk at work: Constructing social identity through workplace interaction.* London: Blackwell.

Holmes, J. (2008). *An introduction to sociolinguistics* (3rd ed.). Harlow: Pearson Education.

Holmes, J., & Major, G. (2003). Talking to patients: The complexity of communication on the ward. *Vision: A Journal of Nursing, 11*(17), 4–9.

Holmes, J., & Marra, M. (2002). Having a laugh at work: How humour contributes to workplace culture. *Journal of Pragmatics, 34*(12), 1683–1710.

Holmes, J., & Stubbe, M. (2015). *Power and politeness in the workplace: A sociolinguistic analysis of talk at work* (2nd ed.). London: Routledge.

Holzrichter, A., & Meier, R. (2000). Child-directed signing in American Sign Language. In C. Chamberlain, J. Morford, & R. Mayberry (Eds), *Language acquisition by eye* (pp. 25–40). Mahwah, NJ: Lawrence Erlbaum.

Horwitz, M. (2014). Demands and strategies of interpreting a theatrical performance into American Sign Language. *Journal of Interpretation, 23*(1). Available: http://digitalcommons.unf.edu/joi/vol23/iss1/4

Hoza, J. (2007). *It's not what you sign, it's how you sign it: Politeness in American Sign Language.* Washington, DC: Gallaudet University Press.

Hoza, J. (2011). The discourse and politeness functions of HEY and WELL in American Sign Language. In C. B. Roy (Ed.), *Discourse in signed languages* (pp. 69–95). Washington, DC: Gallaudet University Press.

Hult, F., & Compton, S. (2012). Deaf education policy as language policy: A comparative analysis of Sweden and the United States. *Sign Language Studies, 12*(4), 602–620.

Humphries, T. (1977). Communicating across cultures (deaf-hearing) and language learning. Unpublished doctoral dissertation. Union Institute and University.

Humphries, T., & Humphries, J. (2010). Deaf in the time of the cochlea. *Journal of Deaf Studies and Deaf Education.* doi:10.1093/deafed/enq054

Humphries, T., Kushalnagar, P., Mathur, G., Napoli, D. J., Padden, C. A., Rathmann, C., & Smith, S. R. (2012). Language acquisition for deaf children: Reducing the harms of zero tolerance to the use of alternative approaches. *Harm Reduction Journal, 9*(16). Available: www.harmreductionjournal.com/content/9/1/16

Hurwitz, A., Weisel, A., Parasnis, I., DeCaro, J., & Savir, H. (1997/1998). Attitudes of teachers, parents and Deaf adults in Israel toward career advice to deaf and hearing people. *Journal of the American Deafness and Rehabilitation Association, 31*(2&3), 23–31.

Hyde, M., Power, D., & Lloyd, K. (2006). Comments on W(h)ither the Deaf community? *Sign Language Studies, 6,* 190–201.

Hymes, D. (1971). Competence and performance in linguistic theory. In R. Huxley & E. Ingram (Eds), *Language acquisition: Models and methods* (pp. 3–18). London: Academic Press.

Irvine, F., Roberts, G., & Bradbury-Jones, C. (2008). The researcher as insider versus the researcher as outsider: Enhancing rigour through language and cultural sensitivity. In P. Liamputtong (Ed.), *Doing cross-cultural research: Ethical and methodological perspectives* (pp. 35–48). London: Springer.

ISO International Standards. (2014), Interpreting – Guidelines for community interpreting. 13611:2014(E). Geneva, Switzerland: ISO. Available: http://www.iso.org/iso/catalogue_detail.htm?csnumber=54082

Isham, W. (1995). Memory for form after simultaneous interpretation: Comparisons of language, modality and process. In *A confluence of diverse relationships: Proceedings of the 13th National Convention of the Registry of Interpreters for the Deaf, August 10–14, 1993* (pp. 60–69). Silver Spring, MD: RID Publications.

Iverson, J., Capirci, O., Longobardi, E., & Caselli, C. (1999). Gesturing in mother-child interaction. *Cognitive Development, 14,* 57–75.

Janzen, T. (Ed.) (2005). *Topics in signed language interpreting.* Amsterdam, the Netherlands: John Benjamins.

Janzen, T. (2010, November). *Pragmatics as start point; discourse as end point.* Keynote paper presented at the High Desert Linguistics Conference. University of New Mexico, Albuquerque.

Janzen, T. D., Leeson, L., & Shaffer, B. (2012, July). *Motivations underlying pronoun location in two signed languages.* Paper presented at Language, Culture and Mind V, University of Lisbon, Portugal.

Janzen, T. D., O'Dea, B., & Shaffer, B. (2001). The construal of events: Passives in American Sign Language. *Sign Language Studies, 1*(3), 281–310.

Janzen, T., & Shaffer, B. (2002). Gesture as the substrate in the process of ASL grammaticalization. In R. Meier, D. Quinto-Pozos, & K. Cormier (Eds), *Modality and structure in signed and spoken languages* (pp. 199–223). Cambridge: Cambridge University Press.

Janzen, T., & Shaffer, B. (2008). Intersubjectivity in interpreted interactions: The Interpreter's role in co-constructing meaning. In J. Zlatev, T. P. Racine, C. Sinha, & E. Itkonen (Eds), *The shared mind* (pp. 333–355). Amsterdam: John Benjamins.

Johnson, K. (1991). Miscommunication in interpreted classroom interaction. *Sign Language Studies, 70,* 1–34.

Johnson, M. (1987). *The body in the mind: The bodily basis of meaning, imagination, and reason.* Chicago: University of Chicago Press.

Johnston, J. (2007). Assessment of language learning in English-speaking children. In *Encyclopedia of language and literacy development* (p. 109). London, Canada: Canadian Language and Literacy Research Network.

Johnston, R. E., Liddell, S. K., & Erting, C. (1989). *Unlocking the curriculum: Principles for achieving access in deaf education.* Gallaudet Research Institute Working Paper 89–3. Washington DC: Department of Linguistics and Interpreting and the Gallaudet Research Institute.

Johnston, T. (1989). *Auslan dictionary: A dictionary of the sign language of the Australian Deaf community.* Maryborough, VIC: Deafness Resources Australia.

Johnston, T. (2001). The lexical database of Auslan (Australian Sign Language). *Sign Language & Linguistics, 4*(1–2), 145–169.

Johnston, T. (2003). BSL, Auslan and NZSL: Three signed languages or one? In A. Baker, B. Van den Bogaerde, & O. Crasborn (Eds), *Cross-linguistic perspectives in sign language research: Selected papers from TISLR 2000* (pp. 47–69). Hamburg: Signum Verlag.

Johnston, T. (2004). Sign bilingual education programs and the need for language resources. *Australian Journal of Education of the Deaf, 10,* 26–34.

Johnston, T. (2004c). The assessment and achievement of proficiency in a native sign language within a sign bilingual program: The pilot Auslan receptive skills test. *Deafness and Education International, 6,* 57–81.

Johnston, T. (2006). W(h)ither the Deaf community? Population, genetics, and the future of Australian Sign Language. *Sign Language Studies, 6,* 137–173.

Johnston, T. (2010). From archive to corpus: Transcription and annotation in the creation of signed language corpora. *International Journal of Corpus Linguistics, 15*(1), 106–131.

Johnston, T. (2013). *Auslan corpus annotation guidelines*. Sydney: Centre for Language Sciences, Department of Linguistics, Macquarie University. Available: http://media.auslan.org.au/attachments/AuslanCorpusAnnotationGuidelines_Johnston.pdf

Johnston, T. (2013). Formational and functional characteristics of pointing signs in a corpus of Auslan (Australian sign language): Are the data sufficient to posit a grammatical class of 'pronouns' in Auslan? *Corpus Linguistics and Linguistic Theory, 9*(1), 109–159.

Johnston, T., & Crasborn, O. (2006). The use of ELAN annotation software in the creation of signed language corpora. In *Proceedings of the EMELD'06 Workshop on Digital Language Documentation: Tools and Standards: The State of the Art*. Lansing, MI: EMELD. Available: http://emeld.org/workshop/2006/papers/johnston-crasborn.pdf

Johnston, T., Leigh, G., & Foreman, P. (2002). The implementation of the principles of sign bilingualism in a self-described sign bilingual program: Implications for the evaluation of language outcomes. *Australian Journal of Education of the Deaf, 8*, 38–46.

Johnston, T. & Napier, J. (2010). Medical Signbank-bringing deaf people and linguists together in the process of language development. *Sign Language Studies, 10*(2), 258–275.

Johnston, T., & Schembri, S. (2005). *The use of ELAN annotation software in the Auslan Archive/Corpus Project*. Ethnographic Research Annotation Conference. University of Melbourne, Australia.

Johnston, T., Vermeerbergen, M., Schembri, A. & Leeson, L. (2007). 'Real Data are Messy': On the cross-linguistic analysis of constituent ordering in Australian Sign Language, Vlaamse Gebarentaal (Flemish Sign Language) and Irish Sign Language (pp. 163–205). In P. Perniss, R. Pfau & B. Woll (Eds), *Sign languages: A cross-linguistic perspective*. Berlin: Mouton de Gruyter.

Jokinen, M. (2001). The Sign Language Person – a term to describe us and our future more clearly? In L. Leeson (Ed.), *Looking forward: EUD in the 3rd millennium – the deaf citizen in the 21st century* (pp. 50–63). Coleford: Douglas Maclean.

Jones, B. E., Clark, G., & Soltz, D. (1997). Characteristics and practices of sign language interpreters in inclusive education programs. *Exceptional Children, 63*(2), 257–268.

Jones, C. J., & Trickett, E. J. (2005). Immigrant adolescents behaving as culture brokers: A study of families from the former Soviet Union. *Journal of Social Psychology, 145*(4), 405–427.

Jones, E., Strom, R., & Daniels, S. (1989). Evaluating the success of deaf parents. *American Annals of the Deaf, 134*, 312–316.

Jordan, I. K. (1993). Quoted in S. Gillespie & M. Miller-Nomeland, *Kendall Demonstration Elementary School: Deaf curriculum guide*. Washington DC: Pre-College Programs, Gallaudet University.

Karlsson, F. (1984). Structure and iconicity in sign language. In F. Loncke, P. Boyes-Braem, & Y. Lebrun (Eds), *Recent research on European sign languages* (pp. 149–155). Lisse: Swets and Zeitlinger.

Karnopp, L. B. (2002). Phonology acquisition in Brazilian Sign Language. In G. Morgan & B. Woll (Eds), *Directions in sign language acquisition* (pp. 29–53). Amsterdam: John Benjamins.

Kaul, T., Griebel, R., & Kaufmann, E. (2014). Transcription as a tool for increasing metalinguistic awareness in learners of German Sign Language as a second language. In D. McKee, R. Rosen, & R. McKee (Eds), *Teaching and learning of signed language: International perspectives* (pp. 129–144). London: Palgrave Macmillan.

Kauppinen, L. (2013). An Interview with Liisa Kauppinen (in conversation with Dr. John Bosco Conama) on the occasion of her conferral with an honorary doctorate by Trinity College Dublin. Dublin: Deaf Village Ireland.

Keating, E., & Mirus, G. (2003). American Sign Language in virtual space: Interactions between deaf users of computer-mediated video communication and the impact of technology on language practices. *Language in Society, 32*, 693–714.

Keating, E., Terra, E., & Mirus, G. (2008). Cybersign: Impacts of new communication technologies on space and language. *Journal of Pragmatics, 40*(6), 1067–1081.

Kelly, A. (1991). Fingerspelling use among the Deaf senior citizens of Baltimore. In E. Winston (Ed.), *Communication forum* (pp. 90–98). Washington, DC: Gallaudet University.

Kemp, M. (1998). An acculturation model for learners of ASL. In C. Lucas (Ed.), *Pinky extension and eye gaze: Language use in Deaf communities* (pp. 213–230). Washington DC: Gallaudet University Press.

Kent, S. J. (2012). Deaf voice and the invention of community interpreting. *Journal of Interpretation, 22*(1). Available: http://digitalcommons.unf.edu/joi/vol22/iss1/3

Kermit, P., Mjøen, O. M., & Olsen, T. (2014). Safe in the hands of the interpreter? A qualitative study investigating the legal protection of Deaf people facing the criminal justice system in Norway. *Disability Studies Quarterly, 31*(4). Available: http://dsq-sds.org/article/view/1714/1762

Kerridge, M. (2011). *CODAs: The rebuttal.* Available: http://the-rebuttal.com/?s=Codas

Kisch, S. (2008). Deaf discourse: The social construction of deafness in a Bedouin community. *Medical Anthropology: Cross-Cultural Studies in Health and Illness, 27*(3), 283–313.

Klein, H. (2000). *Sign language in mental health: Deaf professionals in mental health.* Coleford: Douglas McLean.

Kleinfeld, M., & Warner, N. (1997). Lexical variation in the Deaf community relating to gay, lesbian, and bisexual signs. In A. Livia & K. Hall (Eds), *Queerly phrased: Language, gender, and sexuality* (pp. 58–84). New York: Oxford University Press.

Kluwin, T., & Stewart, D. (2001). Interpreting in schools: A look at research. *Odyssey: Directions in Deaf Education, 2*(2), 15–17.

Kósa, A. (2014). Exercising the Right to Stand as Candidates in Elections to the European Parliament (Article 20 Tefu). In A. Pabsch (Ed.), *UNRCPD Implementation in Europe – a Deaf Perspective: Article 29: Participation in Political and Public Life* (pp. 85–88). Brussels: European Union of the Deaf.

Krausneker, V. (2000). Sign languages and the minority language policy of the European Union. In M. Metzger (Ed.), *Bilingualism and identity in Deaf communities* (pp. 142–158). Washington DC: Gallaudet University Press.

Krausneker, V. (2009). On the legal status of sign languages: A commented compilation of resources. *Current Issues in Language Planning, 10*(3), 351–354.

Krentz, C. (2006). The camera as printing press: How film has infuenced ASL literature. In H.-D. L. Bauman, J. Nelson, & H. Rose (Eds), *Signing the body poetic* (pp. 51–70). Berkeley, CA: University of California Press.

Kuntze, M. (2000). Codeswitching in ASL and written English contact. In K. Emmorey & H. Lane (Eds), *The signs of language revisited: An anthology to honor Ursula Bellugi and Edward Klima* (pp. 287–302). Mahwah, NJ: Lawrence Erlbaum.

Kuntze, M. (2008). Turning literacy inside out. In H.-D. L. Bauman (Ed.), *Open your eyes: Deaf Studies talking* (pp. 146–157). Minneapolis: University of Minnesota Press.

Kurlander, K. W. (2008). "Walking the Fine Line." In P. C. Hauser, K. L. Finch & A. B. Hauser (Eds), *Deaf professionals and designated interpreters: A new paradigm* (pp. 106–128). Washington, DC: Gallaudet University Press.

Kurz, K.B. & E.C. Langer (2004) Student perspectives on educational interpreting: Twenty deaf and hard of hearing students offer insights and suggestions. In E.A. Winston (Ed.), *Educational Interpreting: How it can succeed* (pp. 9–47). Washington, DC: Gallaudet University Press.

Kusters, A. (2010). Deaf utopias? Reviewing the sociocultural literature on the world's 'Martha's Vineyard Situations'. *Journal of Deaf Studies & Deaf Education, 15*(1). doi:10.1093/deafed/enp026

Kyle, J. G. (2007). *Sign on television: Analysis of data based on projects carried out by the Deaf Studies Trust 1993–2005.* Bristol, UK: Deaf Studies Trust.

Kyle, J. G. (2012). He's just not normal: Services, families and Deaf identity. In L. Leeson & M. Vermeerbergen (Eds), *Working with the Deaf community: Mental health, education and interpreting* (pp. 201–216). Dublin: Interesource Group Publishing.

Kyle, J., & Allsop, L. (1997). *Sign on Europe: A study of Deaf people and sign language in the European Union.* Bristol: University of Bristol, Centre for Deaf Studies.

Kyle, J., Sutherland, H., & Stockley, S. (2012). *Legal Choices – Silent Process: Engaging legal services when you do not hear.* Research report, Deaf Studies Trust. Available: http://www.deafstudiestrust.org/files/pdf/reports/Legal%20Choices%20Final-sml. pdf

Kyle, J., Sutherland, H., Allsop, L., Ridd, M., & Emond, A. (2013). *Deaf Health: A UK collaborative study into the health of Deaf people.* Research report, Deaf Studies Trust. Available: http://www.deafstudiestrust.org/files/pdf/reports/Deaf%20Health-exec-final.pdf

Labov, W. (1972). *Sociolinguistic patterns.* Philadelphia: University of Pennsylvania Press.

LaBue, M. A. (1998). *Interpreted education: A study of deaf students' access to the content and form of literacy instruction in a mainstreamed high school English class* (Unpublished doctoral dissertation). Harvard University, Cambridge, MA.

Ladd, P. (2003). *Understanding Deaf culture: In search of Deafhood.* Clevedon, UK: Multilingual Matters.

Ladd, P., & Gonçalves, J. C. (2012). A final frontier? How Deaf cultures and Deaf pedagogies can revolutionize Deaf education. In L. Leeson & M. Vermeerbergen (Eds), *Working with the Deaf community: Deaf education, mental health and interpreting* (n.p.). Dublin: Interesource Group Ireland Limited.

Ladd, P., Gulliver, M., & Batterbury, S. (2003). Reassessing minority language empowerment from a Deaf perspective: The other 32 languages. *Deaf Worlds, 19*(2), 6–32.

Ladd, P., & Lane, H. (2013). Deaf ethnicity, Deafhood, and their relationship. *Sign Language Studies, 13*(4), 565–579.

Laffon de Ladébat, A. D. (1815). *Recueil des définitions et réponses les plus remarquables de Massieu et Clerc, sourds-muets, aux diverses questions qui leur ont été faites dans les séances publiques [Definitions and Answers of Massieu and Clerc].* London: Cox and Baylis.

Lakoff, G. (1987). *Women, fire, and dangerous things: What categories reveal about the mind.* Chicago: University of Chicago Press.

Lakoff, G., & Johnson, M. (2003). *Metaphors we live by.* Chicago: University of Chicago Press.

Lamb, L. & Wilcox, P. (1998). Acceptance of American Sign Language at the University of New Mexico: The history of a process. *Sign Language Studies, 69*, 213–219.

Lane, H. (1984). *When the mind hears: A history of the Deaf* (1st ed.). New York: Random House.

Lane, H. (1992). *The mask of benevolence*. New York: Alfred A. Knopf.

Lane, H. (2005). Ethnicity, ethics, and the Deaf-World. *Journal of Deaf Studies and Deaf Education, 10*(3), 291–310.

Lane, H. (2008). Do Deaf people have a disability? In H.-D. L. Bauman (Ed.), *Open your eyes: Deaf Studies talking* (pp. 277–292). Minneapolis: University of Minnesota Press.

Lane, H., Hoffmeister, R., & Bahan, B. (1996). *A journey into the Deaf World*. San Diego, CA: Dawn Sign Press.

Lane, H., Pillard, R., & Hedberg, U. (2011). *The people of the eye: Deaf ethnicity and ancestry*. New York: Oxford University Press.

Lang, H. (2000). Higher education for deaf students: Research priorities in the new millennium. *Journal of Deaf Studies & Deaf Education, 7*(4), 267–280.

Langacker, R. (1981). Observations and speculations on subjectivity. In J. Haiman (Ed.), *Iconicity in syntax* (pp. 109–150). Amsterdam: John Benjamins.

Larsen-Freeman, D., & Long, M. (1991).. *An introduction to second language acquisition research*. New York: Longman.

Lawrence, S. (2007). Expansion and compression. *Views: A Monthly Publication of the Registry of Interpreters for the Deaf, 1*, 15–16.

Leder, G. (1987). Teacher-student interaction: A case study. *Educational Studies in Mathematics, 18*(3), 255–271.

Leeson, L. (2001). *Aspects of verbal valency in Irish Sign Language* (Unpublished doctoral dissertation). Trinity College, Dublin.

Leeson, L. (2004). Signs of Change in Europe: Current European Perspectives in the Status of Sign Languages. In P. McDonnell (Ed.), *Deaf Studies in Ireland: An Introduction* (pp. 172–197). Gloustershire, UK: Douglas McLean.

Leeson, L. (2005a). Making the effort in simultaneous interpreting: Some considerations for signed language interpreters. In T. Janzen (Ed.), *Topics in signed language interpreting* (pp. 51–68). Amsterdam: John Benjamins.

Leeson, L. (2005b). Vying with variation: Interpreting language contact, gender variation and generational difference. In T. Janzen (Ed.), *Topics in signed language interpreting* (pp. 251–292). Amsterdam: John Benjamins.

Leeson, L. (2006). *Signed Languages in Education in Europe – a preliminary exploration*. (Preliminary Study. Languages of Education). Strasbourg: Council of Europe Language Policy Division.

Leeson, L. (2007). *Seeing is learning: A review of education for deaf and hard of hearing people in Ireland*. Unpublished report submitted to the National Council for Special Education, Trim, Ireland.

Leeson, L. (2008). Quantum leap: Leveraging the Signs of Ireland Digital Corpus in Irish Sign Language/English interpreter training. *The Sign Language Translator and Interpreter, 2*(2), 149–176.

Leeson, L. (2010, October). *Exploring discourse in Irish Sign Language*. Paper presented at the Department of Linguistics, University of Manitoba, Winnipeg.

Leeson, L. (2011). "Mark my words": The linguistic, social, and political significance of the assessment of signed language interpreters. In B. Nicodemus & L. Swabey (Eds), *Advances in interpreting research: Inquiry in action* (pp. 153–176). Amsterdam: John Benjamins.

Leeson, L. (2012). Interpreters in tertiary education. In L. Leeson & M. Vermeerbergen (Eds), *Working with the Deaf community: Mental health, education and interpreting* (pp. 157–182). Dublin: Interesource Group Publishing.

Leeson, L. (2014, March). *Tell the truth and shame the devil.* Keynote paper presented at the Inaugural International Symposium on Sign Language Interpreting Research, Gallaudet University, Washington DC.

Leeson, L. (2015, April). *Intersectional identity matters: Constructing and performing identity in interpreted settings.* Paper presented at GURIEC, Gallaudet University, Washington, DC.

Leeson, L., Bown, S., & Calles, L. (2013). *Assessment guidelines for sign language interpreting training programmes.* Brussels: European Forum of Sign Language Interpreting.

Leeson, L., & Byrne-Dunne, D. (2009). Applying the Common European Reference Framework to the teaching, learning and assessment of signed languages. *D-Signs: Distance online training in sign language* (UK/08/LLP-LdV/TOI/163_141). Dublin: Trinity College, Dublin.

Leeson, L., & Calles, L. (2013). *Learning outcomes for graduates of a three-year sign language interpreting programme.* Brussels: European Forum of Sign Language Interpreters.

Leeson, L., & Foley-Cave, S. (2007). Deep and meaningful conversation: Challenging interpreter impartiality in the semantics and pragmatics classroom. In M. Metzger & E. Fleetwood (Eds), *Translation, sociolinguistic, and consumer issues in interpreting* (pp. 45–70). Washington, DC: Gallaudet University Press.

Leeson, L., & Grehan, C. (2004). To the lexicon and beyond: The effect of gender on variation in Irish Sign Language. In M. Van Herreweghe & M. Vermeerbergen (Eds), *To the lexicon and beyond: Sociolinguistics in European Deaf communities* (pp. 39–73). Washington, DC: Gallaudet University Press.

Leeson, L., & Saeed, J. (2007). Conceptual Blending and the Windowing of Attention in Irish Sign Language. In M. Vermeerbergen, L. Leeson, & O. Crasborn (Eds), *Simultaneity in Signed Languages,* (pp. 55–73). Amsterdam and Philadelphia: John Benjamins.

Leeson, L., & Saeed, J. (2012a). *Irish Sign Language.* Edinburgh: Edinburgh University Press.

Leeson, L., & Saeed, J. (2012b). Word order. In R. Pfau, M. Steinbach, & B. Woll (Eds), *Sign language: An international handbook* (pp. 245–264). Berlin: De Gruyter Mouton.

Leeson, L., & Saeed, J. I. (in press). Embodiment in passives in Irish Sign Language. In T. D. Janzen, S. Wilcox, & B. Shaffer (Eds), *Cognitive sign linguistics.* Berlin: De Gruyter Mouton.

Leeson, L., Saeed, J., Shaffer, B., & Janzen, T. D. (2013, July). *An embodied view of pragmatic inferencing in signed language discourse.* Paper presented at Theoretical Issues in Sign Language Research (TISLR), University College, London.

Leeson, L., & Sheikh, H. (2010). *Experiencing deafhood: Snapshots from 5 nations (Ireland, Czech Republic, Finland, Poland and the UK).* SIGNALL II Project. Dublin: Interesource Group Ireland.

Leeson, L., Sheikh, A., Rozanes, I., Grehan, C., & Matthews, P. (2014). Critical care required: Access to interpreted healthcare in Ireland. In B. Nicodemus & M. Metzger (Eds), *Investigations in healthcare interpreting* (pp. 185–232). Washington, DC: Gallaudet University Press.

Leeson, L., Sheikh, H., & Vermeerbergen, M. (2015). The superhighway or the slow lane? Evaluating challenges in creating new learning spaces for interpreters. In S. Ehrlich & J. Napier (Eds), *Digital education in interpreter education: Fostering innovation, change and community engagement* (pp. 153–206.), Washington DC: Gallaudet University Press.

Leeson, L., Stewart, M., Ferrara, C., Drexel, I., Nilsson, P., & Cooper, M. (in press). "A President for all of the Irish": Performing Irishness in an interpreted Inaugural Presidential Speech. In C. Stone & L. Leeson (Eds), *Interpreting and the politics of recognition*. London: Routledge.

Leigh, I. (2009). *A lens on deaf identities*. New York: Oxford University Press.

Leigh, I., & Christiansen, J. (2006). The dilemma of pediatric cochlear implants. In H. Goodstein (Ed.), *The Deaf Way 2 reader: Perspectives from the 2nd International Conference on Deaf Culture* (pp. 363–369). Washington, DC: Gallaudet University Press.

Lemass, E. (1988). *Plenary Address to the European Parliament on the occasion of the adoption of the Resolution on Sign Languages (B4–0985/98)*, Brussels, June 17, 1988.

LeMaster, B. (1990). *The maintenance and loss of female and male signs in the Dublin Deaf community* (Unpublished doctoral dissertation). University of California.

LeMaster, B. (1999). Reappropriation of gendered Irish Sign Language in one family. *Visual Anthropology Review, 15*(2), 1–15.

LeMaster, B. (2002). What difference does difference make?: Negotiating gender and generation in Irish Sign Language. In S. Benor, M. Rose, D. Sharma, J. Sweetland, & Q. Zhang (Eds), *Gendered practices in language* (pp. 309–338). Stanford, CA: CSLI Press.

LeMaster, B. (2003). School language and shifts in Irish identity. In L. Monaghan, C. Schmaling, K. Nakamura, & G. H. Turner (Eds), *Many ways to be Deaf: International variation in Deaf communities* (pp. 153–172). Washington, DC: Gallaudet University Press.

LeMaster, B., & Dwyer, J. (1991). Knowing and using female and male signs in Dublin. *Sign Language Studies, 73*, 361–369.

Leneham, M. (2005). The sign language interpreter as translator: Challenging traditional definitions of translation and interpreting. *Deaf Worlds, 21*(1), 79–101.

Leneham, M. (2007). Exploring power and ethnocentrism in sign language translation. *Babel: Journal of the AFMLTA, 41*(3), 4–12.

Leneham, M. (2011). *Re-defining the nexus between translation and interpretation: Lessons from sign language research* (Unpublished lecture presentation). Macquarie University Translation & Interpreting programme, Sydney.

Liamputtong, P. (2008). Doing research in a cross-cultural context: Methodological and ethical challenges. In P. Liamputtong (Ed.), *Doing cross-cultural research: Ethical and methodological perspectives* (pp. 3–20). London: Springer.

Liamputtong, P. (2010). *Performing qualitative cross-cultural research*. New York: Cambridge University Press.

Liddell, S. K. (1977). Non-manual signals in ASL: A many layered system. In W. Stokoe (Ed.), *Proceedings of the First National Symposium on Sign Language Research and Training* (pp. 193–228). Chicago: National Association of the Deaf.

Liddell, S. K. (2003). *Grammar, gesture, and meaning in American Sign Language*. Cambridge: Cambridge University Press.

Liddell, S., & Metzger, M. (1998). Gesture in sign language discourse. *Journal of Pragmatics, 30*, 65717697.

Lillo-Martin, D., & Müller de Quadros, R. (2011). Acquisition of the syntax-discourse interface: The expression of point of view. *Lingua, 121*(4), 623–636.

Lim, H.-O. (2005). Working into the B language: The condoned taboo? *Meta, 50*(4). doi:10.7202/019870ar

Lindert, R. (2001). *Hearing families with deaf children: Linguistic and communicative aspects of American Sign Language development* (Unpublished doctoral dissertation). University of California, Berkeley.

Little, D. G., & Ushioda, E. (1998). *Institution-wide language programmes: A research-and-development approach to their design, implementation and evaluation.* Dublin: Trinity College, Dublin, Centre for Language and Communication Studies.

Littleton, P. (2000). Early development of conversational skills in a signed language: Protoconversations in Australian Sign Language (Auslan). In A. Schembri, J. Napier, R. Beattie, & G. Leigh (Eds), *Proceedings of the Australasian Deaf Studies Research Symposium, Renwick College, Sydney, August 22–23, 1998.* (pp. 53–66). Sydney: North Rocks Press.

Llewellyn-Jones, P. (2004). Interpreting Shakespeare's plays into British Sign Language. In T. Hoenselaars (Ed.), *Shakespeare and the language of translation* (pp. 199–213). London: Thomson.

Llewellyn-Jones, P., & Lee, R. (2013). Getting to the core of role: Defining interpreters' role-space. *International Journal of Interpreter Education, 5*(2), 54–72.

Lo Bianco, J. (2004). Language planning as applied linguistics. In A. Davies & C. Elder (Eds), *The handbook of applied linguistics* (pp. 738–762). Oxford: Blackwell.

Lubinksi, R., & Hudson, M. W. (2013). *Professional issues in speech language pathology and audiology* (4th ed.). Clifton Park, NY: Delmar CENGAGE Learning.

Lucas, C., & Bayley, R. (2010). Variation in American Sign Language. In D. Brentari (Ed.), *Sign languages* (pp. 451–476). Cambridge: Cambridge University Press.

Lucas, C., Bayley, R., Reed, R., & Wulf, A. (2001). Lexical variation in African American and White signing. *American Speech, 76*, 339–360.

Lucas, C., Mirus, G., Palmer, J., Roessler, N., & Frost, A. (2013). The effect of new technologies on sign language research. *Sign Language Studies, 13*(4), 541–564.

Lucas, C., & Schatz, S. (2003). Sociolinguistic dynamics in American Deaf communities: Peer groups versus families. In L. Monaghan, C. Schmaling, K. Nakamura, & G. H. Turner (Eds), *Many ways to be Deaf: International variation in Deaf communities* (pp. 141–152). Washington, DC: Gallaudet University Press.

Lucas, C., & Valli, C. (1992). *Language contact in the American Deaf community.* San Diego, CA: Academic Press.

Lucas, C., & Valli, C. (1991). ASL or contact signing: Issues of judgment. *Language in Society, 20*, 201–216.

MacSweeney, M., Woll, B., Campbell, R., Calvert, G. A., McGuire, P. K., David, A. S., Simmons, A., & Brammer M. J. (2002). Neural correlates of British Sign Language comprehension: Spatial processing demands of topographic language. *Journal of Cognitive Neuroscience, 14*(7), 1064–1075.

Madden, M. (2005). The prevalence of occupational overuse syndrome in signed language interpreters in Australia – What a pain! In M. Metzger & E. Fleetwood (Eds), *Attitudes, innuendo, and regulators: Challenges of interpretation* (pp. 3–70). Washington, DC: Gallaudet University Press.

Maestas, J. M. (1980). Early linguistic environment: Interaction with deaf parents and their infants. *Sign Language Studies, 25*, 1–13.

Mahshie, S. N. (1995). *Educating Deaf children bilingually.* Washington DC: Gallaudet University Press.

Major, G. (2013). *Healthcare interpreting as relational practice* (Unpublished doctoral dissertation). Macquarie University, Sydney.

Major, G. (2014). "Sorry, could you explain that?" Clarification requests in interpreter-mediated healthcare interaction. In B. Nicodemus & M. Metzger (Eds), *Investigations in healthcare interpreting* (pp. 32–69). Washington, DC: Gallaudet University Press.

Major, G., & Napier, J. (2012). Interpreting and knowledge mediation in the healthcare setting: What do we really mean by 'accuracy'? In V. Montalt & M. Shuttleworth (Eds), *Linguistica Antiverpiesa: Translation and knowledge mediation in medical and health settings*. Antwerp: Artesius University College, 207–226.

Major, G., Napier, J., Ferrara, L., & Johnston, T. (2012). Exploring lexical gaps in Australian Sign Language for the purposes of health communication. *Communication and Medicine, 9*(1), 37–47.

Major, G., Napier, J., & Stubbe, M. (2012). 'What happens truly, not text book!': Using authentic interactions in discourse training for healthcare interpreters. In K. Malcolm & L. Swabey (Eds), *In our hands: Educating healthcare interpreters* (pp. 27–53). Washington DC: Gallaudet University Press.

Maller, S. J., Singleton, J. L., Supalla, S. J., & Wix, T. (1999). The development and psychometric properties of the American Sign Language Proficiency Assessment (ASL-PA). *Journal of Deaf Studies and Deaf Education, 4*(4), 249–269.

Mallory, B., Zingle, H., & Schein, J. (1993). Intergenerational communication modes in deaf-parented families. *Sign Language Studies, 78*, 73–92.

Mansfield, D. (1993). Gender differences in ASL: A sociolinguistic study of sign choices by Deaf native signers. In E. Winston (Ed.), *Communication forum* (pp. 86–98). Washington, DC: Gallaudet University Press.

Mapson, R. (2013). Who are we? *NEWSLI: Magazine of the Association of Sign Language Interpreters UK.*

Mapson, R. (2014). Polite appearances: how non-manual features convey politeness in British Sign Language. *Journal of Politeness Research: Language, Behaviour, Culture, 10*(2), 157–184.

Marks, A. (2012). Participation framework and footing shifts in an interpreted academic meeting. *Journal of Interpretation, 22*(1), Article 4. Available: http://digitalcommons.unf.edu/joi/vol22/iss1/4

Marks, A. (2015). Investigating footing shifts in video relay service interpreted interaction. In B. Nicodemus & K. Cagle (Eds), *Selected papers from the International Symposium on Signed Language Interpretation and Translation Research* (Vol. 1). Washington, DC: Gallaudet University Press.

Marschark, M. (2007). *Raising and educating a Deaf child: A comprehensive guide to the choices, controversies, and decisions faced by parents and educators* (2nd ed.). Oxford: Oxford University Press.

Marschark, M., & Humphries, T. (2010). Deaf Studies by any other name? *Journal of Deaf Studies and Deaf Education, 15*(1), 1–2.

Marschark, M., Sapere, P., Convertino, C., & Seewagen, R. (2005). Access to postsecondary education through sign language interpreting. *Journal of Deaf Studies and Deaf Education 10*, 38–50.

Marschark, M., Sapere, P., Convertino, C., Seewagen, R., & Maltzen, H. (2004). Comprehension of sign language interpreting: Deciphering a complex task situation. *Sign Language Studies, 4*(4), 345–368.

Marschark, M., Schick, B., & Spencer, P. (2006). Understanding sign language development. In B. Schick, M. Marschark, & P. Spencer (Eds), *Advances in sign language development by deaf children* (pp. 3–19). New York: Oxford University Press.

Marschark, M., & Spencer, P. E. (2003). *Oxford handbook of Deaf Studies, language, and education*. Oxford: Oxford University Press.

Marschark, M., & Spencer, P. (2009). *Evidence of best practice models and outcomes in the education of deaf and hard of hearing children: An international review*. Trim, Ireland: National Council for Special Education.

Marshall, A., & Batten, S. (2004). Researching across cultures: Issues of ethics and power. *Forum: Qualitative Social Research, 5*(3). Available: www.qualitative-research. net/index.php/fqs/article/view/572/1241

Martin, J., & Rose, D. (2003). *Working with discourse: Meaning beyond the clause*. London: Bloomsbury.

Martinez, L. (1995). Turn-taking and eye gaze in sign conversations between Deaf Filipinos. In C. Lucas (Ed.), *Sociolinguistics in Deaf communities* (pp. 272–306). Washington, DC: Gallaudet University Press.

Martinez, L. (2007). Initial observations on code-switching in the voice interpretations of two Filipino interpreters. In M. Metzger & E. Fleetwood (Eds), *Translation, sociolinguistic, and consumer issues in interpreting* (pp. 71–102). Washington, DC: Gallaudet University Press.

Mason, I. (2005). Projected and perceived identities in dialogue interpreting. In J. House, R. M. Ruano, & N. Baumgarten (Eds), *Translation and the construction of identity* (pp. 30–52). Seoul: International Association for Translation and Intercultural Studies.

Masataka, N. (2000). The role of modality and input in the earliest stage of language acquisition: Studies of Japanese Sign Language. In C. Chamberlain, J. Morford, & R. Mayberry (Eds), *Language acquisition by eye* (pp. 3–24). Mahwah, NJ: Lawrence Erlbaum.

Mather, S. (1987). Eye gaze and communication in a Deaf classroom. *Sign Language Studies, 54*, 11–30.

Mather, S. (1989). Visually oriented teaching strategies with Deaf preschool children. In C. Lucas (Ed.), *The sociolinguistics of the Deaf community* (pp. 165–187). New York: Academic Press.

Mather, S. (2005). Ethnographic research on the use of visually based regulators for teachers and interpreters. In M. Metzger & E. Fleetwood (Eds), *Attitudes, innuendos and regulators: Challenges of interpretation* (pp. 136–161). Washington, DC: Gallaudet University Press.

Mather, S., Rodriguez-Fraticelli, Y., Andrews, J., & Rodriguez, J. (2006). Establishing and maintaining sight triangles: Conversations between deaf parents and hearing toddlers in Puerto Rico. In C. Lucas (Ed.), *Multilingualism and sign languages* (pp. 159–187). Washington, DC: Gallaudet University Press.

Mathers, C. (2006). *Sign language interpreters in court: Understanding best practices*. Bloomington, IN: AuthorHouse.

Mathers, C. (2009). Modifying instruction in the Deaf interpreting model. *International Journal of Interpreter Education, 1*, 68–76.

Mathews, E. (2011). *Mainstreaming of Deaf education in the Republic of Ireland: Language, power, and resistance* (Unpublished doctoral dissertation). National University of Ireland, Maynooth.

Mathews, E. (2012). 'We got nothing…a big fat zero': Levels of awareness theory and the lived experiences of Irish mothers of Deaf children. In L. Leeson & M. Vermeerbergen (Eds), *Working with the Deaf community: Mental health, education and interpreting* (pp. 93–102). Dublin: Interesource Group Publishing.

Mathur, G., & Rathmann, C. (2006). Variability in verbal agreement forms across four sign languages. In L. Goldstein, D. Whalen, & C. Best (Eds), *Laboratory phonology 8* (pp. 289–316). Berlin: De Gruyter Mouton.

Maxwell-McCaw, D., & Zea, M. (2011). The Deaf Acculturation Scale (DAS): Development and validation of a 58-item measure. *Journal of Deaf Studies & Deaf Education.* doi:10.1093/deafed/enq061

Mayberry, R. (2006). *Learning sign language as a second language* (pp. 743–746). In B. Woll (Ed.), *Sign language.* Vol. 6., Encyclopedia of Language & Linguistics, 2nd edition. Ed. Keith Brown (pp. 739–743). Oxford: Elsevier.

Mayberry, R. (2007). When timing is everything: Age of first language acquisition effects on second-language teaching. *Applied Psycholinguistics, 28,* 537–549.

Mayberry, R., & Locke, E. (2003). Age constraints on first versus second language acquisition: Evidence for linguistic plasticity and epigenesis. *Brain and Language, 87,* 369–383.

Mayer, C., & Akamatsu, T. (1999). Bilingual-bicultural models of literacy education for deaf students: Considering the claims. *Journal of Deaf Studies & Deaf Education, 4*(1), 1–8.

McBurney, S. (2012). History of sign languages and sign language linguistics. In R. Pfau, M. Steinberg, & B. Woll (Eds), *Sign language: An international handbook* (pp. 909–948). Zurich: De Gruyter Mouton.

McCaskill, C., Lucas, C., Bayley, R., & Hill, J. (2011). *The hidden treasure of black ASL: Its history and structure.* Washington, DC: Gallaudet University Press.

McDonnell, P. (2001). Deep Structures' in Deaf Education: Implications for policy. In L. Leeson (Ed.) *Looking forward: the EUD in the 3rd Millennium – the Deaf Citizen in the 21st Century* Douglas McLean, Coleford, UK.

McDonnell, P., & Saunders, H. (1993). Sit on your hands: Strategies to prevent signing. In R. Fischer & H. Lane (Eds), *Looking back: A reader on the history of Deaf communities and their sign languages,* (pp. 255–260). Hamburg: Signum.

McDermid, C. (2009). The social construction of American Sign Language–English interpreters. *Journal of Deaf Studies & Deaf Education, 14*(1), 105–130.

McDermid, C. (2014a). Evidence of a "hearing" dialect of ASL while interpreting. *Journal of Interpretation, 23*(1), Article 2. Available at: http://digitalcommons.unf.edu/joi/vol23/iss1/2

McDermid, C. (2014b). Cohesion in English to ASL interpreting. *International Journal of Translation & Interpreting Research, 6*(1), 76–101.

McIlroy, G., & Storbeck, C. (2011). Development of Deaf identity: An ethnographic study. *Journal of Deaf Studies & Deaf Education.* doi:10.1093/deafed/enr017

McIntosh, P. (1989, July/August). White privilege: Unpacking the invisible knapsack. *Peace & Freedom.* Available: http://wh.agh.edu.pl/other/materialy/663_2014_03_04_15_03_55_WhitePrivilegeUnpackingtheInvisibleKnapsack.pdf

McKee, D., McKee, R., & Major, G. (2011). Numeral variation in New Zealand Sign Language. *Sign Language Studies, 12,* 72–97.

McKee, D., Rosen, R., & McKee, R. (Eds). (2014). *Teaching and learning of signed languages: International perspectives.* London, UK: Palgrave.

McKee, D., & Woodward, J. (2014). Developing Deaf communities through sign language teacher training. In D. McKee, R. Rosen, & R. McKee (Eds), *Teaching and learning signed languages: International perspectives and practices* (pp. 35–64). London: Palgrave.

McKee, R. (2001). *People of the eye: Stories from the Deaf World.* Wellington, NZ: Bridget Williams Books.

McKee, R. L. (2008). Quality in interpreting: A survey of practitioner perspectives. *The Sign Language Translator & Interpreter, 2*(1), 1–14.

McKee, R. L. (2011). Action pending: Four years on from the New Zealand Sign Language Act 2006. *Victoria University of Wellington Law Review, 42*(2), 277–298.

McKee, R. L. (2014). Breaking news: Sign language interpreters on television during natural disasters. *Interpreting, 16*(1), 107–130.

McKee, R. L., & Awheto, S. (2010). Constructing roles in a Māori deaf trilingual context. In R. L. McKee & J. Davis (Eds), *Interpreting in multilingual, multicultural contexts* (pp. 85–118). Washington, DC: Gallaudet University.

McKee, R. L., & Wallingford, S. (2011). 'So, well, whatever': Discourse functions of palm-up in New Zealand Sign Language. *Sign Language & Linguistics, 14*(2), 213–247.

McNamara, T. F. (2000). *Language testing.* Oxford: Oxford University Press.

McNeill, D. (1992). *Hand and mind: What gestures reveal about thought.* Chicago: University of Chicago Press.

McQuillan, J., & Tse, L. (1995). Child language brokering in linguistic minority communities: Effects on cultural interaction, cognition, and literacy. *Language and Education, 9*, 195–215.

Meier, R. (2012). Language and modality. In R. Pfau, M. Steinberg, & B. Woll (Eds), *Sign language: An international handbook* (pp. 574–601). Zurich: De Gruyter Mouton.

Meir, I., & Sandler, W. (2008). *A language in space: The story of Israeli Sign Language.* New York: Lawrence Erlbaum.

Mertens, D. (2010). Transformative mixed-methods research. *Qualitative Inquiry.* doi:10.1177/1077800410364612

Mertens, D., Harris, R., & Holmes, H. (2009). Transformative research ethics. In D. M. Mertens & P. Ginsberg (Eds), *Handbook of social research ethics* (pp. 85–102). Thousand Oaks, CA: Sage.

Metzger, M. (1995). Constructed dialogue and constructed action in American Sign Language. In C. Lucas (Ed.), *Sociolinguistics of Deaf communities* (pp. 255–271). Washington, DC: Gallaudet University Press.

Metzger, M. (1999). *Sign language interpreting: Deconstructing the myth of neutrality.* Washington, DC: Gallaudet University Press.

Metzger, M. (Ed.). (2000). *Bilingualism and identity in Deaf communities.* Washington DC: Gallaudet University Press.

Metzger, M. (2006). Salient studies of signed language interpreting in the context of community interpreting scholarship. In E. Hertog & B. Van der Veer (Eds), *Taking stock: Research and methodology in community interpreting (Linguistica Antverpiensia,* Vol. 5). Antwerpen: Hogeschool Antwerpen, Hoger Instituut voor Vertalers en Tolken.

Metzger, M., & Bahan, B. (2001). Discourse analysis. In C. Lucas (Ed.), *Sociolinguistics of sign languages* (pp. 112–144). Cambridge: Cambridge University Press.

Metzger, M., & Müller de Quadros, R. (2012). Cognitive control in intermodal bilingual interpreters. In R. Müller de Quadros & M. Metzger (Eds), *Signed language interpreting in Brazil* (pp. 43–57). Washington, DC: Gallaudet University Press.

Metzger, M. & Roy, C.B. (2011). The first three years of a three-year grant: When a research plan doesn't go as planned. In B. Nicodemus & L. Swabey (Eds), *Advances in Interpreting Research: Inquiry in action,* (pp. 59–84). Washington DC: Gallaudet University Press.

Meurant, L., Sinte, A., Van Herreweghe, M., & Vermeerbergen, M. (Eds). (2013). *Sign language research, uses and practices: Crossing views on theoretical and applied sign language linguistics.* Berlin: De Gruyter Mouton.

Meyer, B., Pawlack, B., & Kliche, O. (2010). Family interpreters in hospitals: Good reasons for bad practice? *mediAzioni, 10*, 297–324.

Michaels, P. (2008). *The cultural and linguistic study of gay sign variation in the Deaf gay community* (Unpublished master's dissertation). Durham University, Durham, NC.

Michaels, P. (2010). A study of GSV. *Newsli, 74*, 12–14.

Miller, C. (1994). Simultaneous constructions in Quebec Sign Language. In M. Brennan and G. H. Turner (Eds), *Word order issues in sign language: Working papers* (pp. 89–112). Durham, NC: International Sign Linguistics Association.

Miller, K. (2001). Access to sign language interpreters in the criminal justice system. *American Annals of the Deaf, 146*(4), 328–330.

Miller, K. (2003). Signs of prison life: Linguistic adaptations of deaf inmates. *Journal of Interpretation*, 129–142.

Miller, K. R., & Vernon, M. (2001). Linguistic diversity in Deaf defendants and due process rights. *Journal of Deaf Studies and Deaf Education, 6*(3), 226–234.

Mindess, A. (1999). *Reading between the signs: Intercultural communication for sign language interpreters*. Yarmouth, ME: Intercultural Press.

Mirus, G., Rathmann, C., & Meier, R. (2001). Proximalisation and distalisation of sign movement in adult learners. In V. Dively, M. Metzger, S. Taub, & A. M. Baer (Eds), *Signed languages: Discoveries from international research* (pp. 103–19). Washington DC: Gallaudet University Press.

Mitchell, R. (2006). Comments on W(h)ither the Deaf community? A normalisation juggernaut? *Sign Language Studies, 6*, 210–219.

Mitchell, R., & Karchmer, M. (2004). Chasing the mythical 10%: Parental hearing status of Deaf and hard of hearing students in the United States. *Sign Language Studies, 4*, 138–163.

Mohay, H. (2000). Language in sight: Mothers' strategies for making language visually accessible to deaf children. In P. E. Spencer, C. J. Erting, & M. Marshark (Eds), *The Deaf child in the family and at school: Essays in honor of Kathryn P. Meadow-Orlans* (pp. 151–166). Mahwah, NJ: Lawrence Erlbaum.

Mohr-Militzer, S. (2011). *Mouth actions in Irish Sign Language: Their system and functions* (Unpublished doctoral dissertation). Cologne, Germany: University of Cologne.

Montoya, L. A., Egnatovitch, R., Eckhardt, E., Goldstein, M., Goldstein, R. A., & Steinberg, A. (2004). Translation challenges and strategies: The ASL translation of a computer-based psychiatric diagnostic interview. *Sign Language Studies, 4*(4) 314–344.

Moores, D. (2006). Comments on W(h)ither the Deaf community? *Sign Language Studies, 6*, 202–209.

Morales-López, E. (2008). Sign bilingualism in Spanish Deaf education. In C. Plaza-Pust & L. Morales-López (Eds), *Sign bilingualism: Language development, interaction, and maintenance in Sign Language Contact Situations* (pp. 223–276). Amsterdam: Benjamins.

Moreland, C., Latimore, D., Sen, A. Arato, N., & Zazove, P. (2013). Deafness among physicians and trainees: A national survey. *Academic Medicine, 88*(2), 224–232.

Morford, J. (2003). Grammatical development in adolescent first-language learners. *Linguistics, 41*(4), 681–721.

Morgan, E. (2008). Interpreters, conversational style, and gender at work. In P. Hauser, K. Finch, & A. Hauser (Eds), *Deaf professionals and designated interpreters: A new paradigm* (pp. 66–80). Washington, DC: Gallaudet University Press.

Morgan, G. (2002). Children's encoding of simultaneity in British Sign Language narratives. *Sign Language and Linguistics, 5*(2), 131–165.

Morgan, G. (2006). The development of narrative skills in British Sign Language. In B. Schick, M. Marschark, & P. Spencer (Eds), *Advances in sign language development by deaf children* (pp. 314–343). New York: Oxford University Press.

Morgan, P., & Adam, R. (2012). Deaf interpreters in mental health settings: Some reflections on and thoughts about deaf interpreter education. In K. Malcolm & L. Swabey (Eds), *In our hands: Educating healthcare interpreters* (pp. 190–208). Washington DC: Gallaudet University Press.

Most, T., Wiesel, A., & Blitzer, T. (2007). Identity and attitudes towards cochlear implant among deaf and hard of hearing adolescents. *Deafness and Education International, 9*(2), 68–82.

Mudgett-DeCaro, P. (1996). On being both hearing and Deaf: My bilingual-bicultural experience. In I. Paranis (Ed.), *Cultural and language diversity: The Deaf experience.* York: Cambridge University Press.

Mugnier, S. (2006). Le bilinguisme des enfants sourds: De quelques freins aux possibles moteurs. GLOTTOPOL.Revue de sociolinguistique en ligne. Retrived from: http: www.univ-rouen.fr/dyalang/glottopol

Müller de Quadros, R. M., De Souza, S. X., & Segala, R. R. (2012). Brazilian Sign Language deaf-translation performance: Descriptive concepts and approaches to procedures led by deaf translator-actors. In R. Müller de Quadros, E. Fleetwood, & M. Metzger (Eds), *Signed language interpreting in Brazil* (pp. 21–42). Washington, DC: Gallaudet Univeristy Press.

Mulrooney, K. (Ed.). (2015). *Teaching and learning in bilingual classrooms: New scholarship.* Washington, DC: Gallaudet University Press.

Murray, J. (2007). Coequality and transnational studies: Understanding Deaf lives. In H.-D. L. Bauman (Ed.), *Open your eyes: Deaf studies talking.* Minneapolis: University of Minnesota Press.

Myers-Scotton, C. (2006). *Multiple voices: An introduction to bilingualism.* Malden, MA: Blackwell.

Myers-Scotton, C. (2008). Code-switching. In F. Coulmas (Ed.), *The handbook of sociolinguistics* Blackwell Reference Online 28 December 2007. http://www.blackwellreference.com Oxford: Blackwell Publishers.

Myers, S. S., & Fernandes, J. K. (2010). Deaf Studies: A critique of the predominant U.S. theoretical direction. *Journal of Deaf Studies & Deaf Education, 15*(1), 30–49.

Napier, J. (2002). *Sign language interpreting: Linguistic coping strategies.* Coleford: Douglas McLean.

Napier, J. (2004). Sign language interpreter training, testing, and accreditation: An international comparison. *American Annals of the Deaf, 149*(4), 350–359.

Napier, J. (2006a). Effectively teaching discourse to sign language interpreting students. *Language, Culture and Curriculum, 19*(3), 252–265.

Napier, J. (2006b). The D/deaf-H/hearing Debate. *Sign Language Studies, 2*(2), 141–149.

Napier, J. (2007a). Cooperation in interpreter-mediated monologic talk. *Discourse & Communication, 1*(1), 407–431.

Napier, J. (2007b, April). *What are our expectations? A discourse analysis of practitioner and consumer attitudes towards signed language interpreting in the community.* Paper presented at the Critical Link 5: Interpreting in the Community Conference, Sydney.

Napier, J. (2008). Exploring linguistic and cultural identity: My personal experience. In M. Bishop & S. Hicks (Eds), *Hearing, Mother Father deaf: Hearing people in Deaf families* (pp. 219–243). Washington, DC: Gallaudet University Press.

Napier, J. (Ed.). (2009a). *International perspectives on sign language interpreter education.* Washington, DC: Gallaudet University Press.

Napier, J. (2009b). Editorial: The real voyage of discovery. *International Journal of Interpreter Education, 1,* 1–6.

Napier, J. (2010). An historical overview of signed language interpreting research: Featuring highlights of personal research. *Cadernos de Tradução,* 63–97.

Napier, J. (2011a). "It's not what they say but the way they say it": A content analysis of interpreter and consumer perceptions of signed language interpreting in Australia. *International Journal of the Sociology of Language, 207,* 59–87.

Napier, J. (2011b). Signed language interpreting. In K. Windle & K. Malmkjaer (Eds), *The Oxford handbook of translation studies* (pp. 353–372). Oxford: Oxford University Press.

Napier, J. (2011c). If a tree falls in the forest, does it make a noise? The merits of publishing interpreting research. In B. Nicodemus & L. Swabey (Eds), *Advances in interpreting research: Inquiry in action* (pp. 121–152). Philadelphia: John Benjamins.

Napier, J. (2012a, July). *The interpreters' 'voice': A sociological analysis.* Paper presented to the International Association of Translation & Intercultural Studies Conference, Queens University, Belfast.

Napier, J. (2012b). Exploring themes in stakeholder perspectives of video remote interpreting in court. In C. J. Kellett (Ed.), *Interpreting across genres: Multiple research perspectives* (pp. 219–254). Trieste, Italy: EUT Edizioni Università di Trieste.

Napier, J. (2012c). *"Please just translate word-for-word and let me interpret the meaning": Understanding linguistic and role issues for courtroom interpreters.* Keynote presentation to the Institute of Legal Interpreting conference, April 2012, Westminster, Colorado.

Napier, J. (2013a, 20 December). Sign language brokering experiences in the deaf community [Weblog post]. Available: http://lifeinlincs.org/2013/12/20/sign-language-brokering-experiences-in-the-deaf-community/

Napier, J. (2013b). "You get that vibe": A pragmatic analysis of clarification and communicative accommodation in legal video remote interpreting. In L. Meurant, A. Sinte, M. Van Herreweghe, & M. Vermeerbergen (Eds), *Sign language research uses and practices: Crossing views on theoretical and applied sign language linguistics* (pp. 85–110). Nijmegen, The Netherlands: De Gruyter Mouton and Ishara Press.

Napier, J. (2013c). Legal interpreting, Deaf people, and jury service: A happy union? *Newsli: Magazine of the Association of Sign Language Interpreters of the UK, December issue,* 6–12.

Napier, J. (2014a). Review of the book *Approaches to social research: The case of Deaf Studies,* by A. Young & B. Temple. *International Journal of Social Research Methodology.* doi:10.1080/13645579.2014.957043

Napier, J. (2014b, 28 October). *What's in a name?* [Weblog post]. Available: http://lifeinlincs.org/2014/10/28/whats-in-a-name/

Napier, J. (2015). Comparing spoken and signed language interpreting. In H. Mikkelson & R. Jourdanais (Eds), *The Routledge handbook of interpreting.* New York: Routledge.

Napier, J. (in preparation). "It's a catch-22": Sign language brokering experiences in the Deaf community. For submission to *Sign Language Studies.*

Napier, J. (in press). Not just child's play: Exploring bilingualism and language brokering as a precursor to the development of expertise as a professional signed language interpreter. In R. Antonini (Ed.), *Non-professional interpreting and trans-*

lation: *State of the art and future of an emerging field of research.* Amsterdam: John Benjamins.

Napier, J., & Barker, R. (2003). A demographic survey of Australian Sign Language interpreters. *Australian Journal of Education of the Deaf, 9,* 19–32.

Napier, J., & Barker, R. (2004). Accessing university education: Perceptions, preferences, and expectations for interpreting by Deaf students. *Journal of Deaf Studies & Deaf Education, 9*(2), 228–238.

Napier, J., Carmichael, A., & Wiltshire, A. (2008). LOOK-PAUSE-NOD: A linguistic case study of a deaf professional and interpreters working together. In P. Hauser, K. Finch, & A. Hauser (Eds), *Deaf professionals and designated interpreters: A new paradigm* (pp. 22–42). Washington, DC: Gallaudet University Press.

Napier, J., & Cornes, A. (2004). The dynamic roles of interpreters and therapists. In S. Austen & S. Crocker (Eds), *Deafness in mind: Working psychologically with deaf people across the lifespan* (pp. 161–179). London: Whurr Publishers.

Napier, J., Goswell, D., Leigh, G., & Carty, B. (2012, December). *Exploring cross-boundary collaboration between teacher and signed language interpreter in the inclusive classroom.* Paper presented at the Applied Linguistics and Professional Practice Conference, Sydney.

Napier, J., & Haug, T. (2014). *Justisigns: A European overview of sign language interpreting provision in legal settings* (Unpublished research report).

Napier, J., & Kidd, M. (2013). English literacy as a barrier to health care information for deaf people who use Auslan. *Australian Family Physician, 42*(12), 896–899.

Napier, J., & Leeson, L. (2015). Signed language interpreting. In F. Pöchhacker (Ed.), *Routledge encyclopedia of interpreting studies.* New York: Routledge.

Napier, J., Leigh, G., & Nann, S. (2007). Teaching sign language to parents of deaf children: An action research process. *Deafness Education International, 9*(2), 83–100.

Napier, J., Major, G., & Ferrara, L. (2011). Medical Signbank: A cure-all for the aches and pains of medical signed language interpreting? In L. Leeson, S. Wurm, & M. Vermeerbergen (Eds), *Signed language interpreting: Preparation, practice and performance* (pp. 110–137). Manchester: St. Jerome.

Napier, J., Major, G., Ferrara, L., & Johnston, T. (2014). Medical Signbank as a model for sign language planning? A review of community engagement. *Current Issues in Language Planning.* http://dx.doi.org/10.1080/14664208.2014.972536

Napier, J., & McEwin, A. (2015). Do Deaf people have the right to serve as jurors in Australia? *Alternative Law Journal, 40*(1), 23–27.

Napier, J., McKee, R., & Goswell, D. (2010). *Sign language interpreting: Theory and practice in Australia and New Zealand* (2nd ed.). Sydney, Australia: Federation Press.

Napier, J., & Rohan, M. (2007). An invitation to dance: Deaf consumers' perceptions of signed language interpreters and interpreting. In M. Metzger & E. Fleetwood (Eds), *Translation, Sociolinguistic, and Consumer Issues in Interpreting* (pp. 159–203). Washington, DC: Gallaudet University Press.

Napier, J., Rohan, M., & Slatyer, H. (2005). Perceptions of bilingual competence compared to preferred language direction in the case of Auslan/English interpreters. *Journal of Applied Linguistics, 2*(2), 185–218.

Napier, J., Sabolcec, J., Hodgetts, J., Linder, S., Mundy, G., Turcinov, M., & Warby, L. (2014). Direct, interpreter-mediated or translated? A qualitative study of access to preventive and ongoing healthcare information for Australian Deaf people. In B. Nicodemus & M. Metzger (Eds), *Investigations in healthcare interpreting* (pp. 233–276). Washington, DC: Gallaudet University Press.

Napier, J., & Spencer, D. (2008). Guilty or not guilty? An investigation of deaf jurors' access to court proceedings via sign language interpreting. In D. Russell & S. Hale (Eds), *Interpreting in Legal Settings* (pp. 72–122). Washington DC: Gallaudet University Press.

Napoli, D. J., & Leeson, L. (in prep). A visual account of reference in sign languages.

National Accreditation Authority for Translators and Interpreters Ltd. (2014). *Accreditation in Auslan/English interpreting information booklet.* Canberra: Author.

National Bioethics Advisory Commission. (2001). *Ethical and policy issues in research involving human participants: Report and recommendations of the National Bioethics Advisory Commission* (Vol. 1). Rockville, MD: Author. Available: https://scholarworks.iupui.edu/handle/1805/25

National Council for Special Education. (2011). *The education of Deaf and hard of hearing children in Ireland.* Trim, Ireland: Author.

National Technical Institute for the Deaf. (1999). *Sign Language Proficiency Interview (SLPI) rating scale.* Rochester, NY: NTID, Rochester Institute of Technology. Available: www.rit.edu/ntid/slpi/system/files/RatingScale%20and%20Analyzing%20Function.pdf

Neves, J. (2007). Of pride and prejudice: The divide between subtitling and sign language interpreting on television. *The Sign Language Translator & Interpreter, 1*(2), 251–274.

Neville, H. J., Coffey, S. A., Lawson, D. S., Fischer, A., Emmorey, K., & Bellugi, U. (1997). Neural systems mediating American Sign Language: Effects of sensory experience and age of acquisition. *Brain and Language, 57,* 285–308.

Newell, W., Caccamise, F., Boardman, K., & Holcomb, B. R. (1983). Adaptation of the Language Proficiency Interview (LPI) for assessing sign communicative competence. *Sign Language Studies, 41,* 311–352.

Nicodemus, B., & Emmorey, K. (2012). Direction asymmetries in spoken and signed language interpreting. *Bilingualism: Language and Cognition.* doi:10.1017/S1366728912000521

Nicodemus, B., & Emmorey, K. (2015). Directionality in ASL–English interpreting: Accuracy and articulation quality in L1 and L2. *Interpreting, 17* (2), 145–166.

Nicodemus, B., Swabey, L., & Moreland, C. (2014). Conveying medication prescriptions in American Sign Language: Use of emphasis in translations by interpreters and deaf physicians. *International Journal of Translation & Interpreting Research, 6*(1). doi:ti.106201.2014.a01

Nicodemus, B., Swabey, L., & Taylor, M. (2014). Preparation strategies used by American Sign Language–English interpreters to render President Barack Obama's inaugural address. *The Interpreter's Newsletter, 19,* 27–44.

Nicodemus, B., & Taylor, M. (2014). Deaf and hearing interpreting team preparation: A study using conversation analysis. In R. Adam, C. Stone, S. D. Collins, & M. Metzger (Eds), *Deaf interpreters at work: International insights* (pp. 90–116). Washington, DC: Gallaudet University Press.

Nilsson, A-L. (2014). *Use of signing space in simultaneous sign language interpretation: marking discourse structure with the body.* Paper presented at the European Forum of Sign Language Interpreters (efsli) Annual Conference. Antwerp, Belgium, September 13–14, 2014.

Nilsson, A-L. (2010). *Studies in Swedish Sign Language: Reference, real space blending, and interpretation.* Unpublished doctoral dissertation, Stockholm University.

Nilsson, A.-L., & Schönström, K. (2014). Swedish Sign Language as a second language: Historical and contemporary perspectives In D. McKee, R. Rosen, & R. McKee (Eds),

Teaching and learning signed languages: International perspectives and practices (pp. 11–34). London: Palgrave.

Nilsson, A.-L., Turner, G. H., Sheikh, H., & Dean, R. (2013). *An overview of European healthcare provision for Deaf sign language users.* Dublin: Interesource Group (Ireland) Limited.

Noijons, J., Beresova, J., Breton, G., & Szabo, G. (2011). *Relating language examinations to the Common European Framework of References or Languages: Learning, teaching, assessment (CEFR): Highlights from the manual.* Graz, Austria: European Centre for Modern Languages and Council of Europe Publishing.

Nord, C. (1997). *Translating as a purposeful activity: Functionalist approaches explained.* Manchester: St Jerome Publishing.

Nyst, V. (2012). Shared sign languages. In R. Pfau, M. Steinbach, & B. Woll (Eds), *Sign language: An international handbook* (pp. 552–573). Berlin: De Gruyter Mouton.

Nyst, V. (2015). Sign language fieldwork. In E. Orfanidou, B. Woll, & G. Morgan (Eds), *Research methods in sign language studies: A practical guide* (pp. 107–122). London: Wiley Blackwell.

O'Brien, D., & Emery, S. (2013). The role of the intellectual in minority group studies: Reflections on Deaf Studies in social and political contexts. *Qualitative Inquiry, 20*(1), 27–36.

Ofcom. (2007). Signing on television: New arrangements for low audience channels (Unpublished report). London: Ofcom.

Ofcom. (2012). Code on Television Access Services. Available: http://stakeholders. ofcom.org.uk/broadcasting/broadcast-codes/tv-access-services/code-tv-access-services-2013/

Olesen, J., Baker, M.G.; Freund, T; di Luca, M.; Mendlewicz, J.; Ragan, I. & Westphal, M.; (2006) Sensory Systems and Autonomic Disturbances. Theme 3: From Deafness to Brain Mechanisms of Hearing. *Journal of Neurosurgical Psychiatry, 77* (Suppl I) i1--i49. Available: http://www.europeanbraincouncil.org/pdfs/Publications_/ Consensus%20Document%20-%20EBC%2006.pdf

Orellana, M. F. (2009). *Translating childhoods: Immigrant youth, language and culture.* New Brunswick, NJ: Rutgers University Press.

Orellana, M. F. (2010). From here to there: On the process of an ethnography of language brokering. *Mediazioni, 10,* 47–67.

Orellana, M. F., Dorner, L., & Pulido, L. (2003). Accessing assets: Immigrant youth's work as family translators or "para-phrasers". *Social Problems, 50*(4), 505–524.

Orfanidou, E., Woll, B., & Morgan, G. (Eds). (2015). *Research methods in sign language studies: A practical guide.* London: Wiley Blackwell.

O'Rourke, B., Pujolar, J., & Ramallo, F. (2015). New speakers of minority languages: The challenging opportunity. *International Journal of the Sociology of Language, 231,* 1–20.

Ortega, G., & Morgan, G. (2010). Comparing child and adult development of a visual phonological system. *Language, Interaction and Acquisition, 1,* 67–81.

Ortiz, I. R. R. (2007). Sign language comprehension: The case of Spanish Sign Language. *Journal of Deaf Studies & Deaf Education.* doi:10.1093/deafed/enm063

Ozolins, U. (2009). Back translation as a means of giving translators a voice. *International Journal of Translation & Interpreting Research, 1*(2), 1–13.

Pabsch, A. (2014a). Lessons from the 2013 EUD UNCRPD survey. In A. Pabsch (Ed.), *UNCRPD Implementation in Europe – a Deaf Perspective: Article 29: Participation in Political and Public Life* (pp. 76–84). Brussels: EUD.

Pabsch, A. (Ed.). (2014b). *UNCRPD Implementation in Europe – a Deaf Perspective: Article 29: Participation in Political and Public Life.* Brussels: EUD.

Padden, C. (1980). The Deaf community and the culture of Deaf people. In C. Baker & R. Battison (Eds), *Sign language and the Deaf community* (pp. 89–104). Silver Spring, MD: National Association of the Deaf.

Padden, C. (2000). Simultaneous interpreting across modalities. *Interpreting, 5*(2), 169–186.

Padden, C. (2004). Translating Veditz. *Sign Language Studies, 4*(3), 244–260.

Padden, C. (2014). Do sign language interpreter accents compromise comprehension? Paper presented at Street Leverage Live, Austin Texas, May 4, 2014. Available: http://www.streetleverage.com/#sthash.vCwVjjeP.dpuf

Padden, C., & Humphries, T. (1998). *Deaf in America: Voices from a culture.* Cambridge, MA: Harvard University Press.

Padden, C., & Humphries, T. (2005). *Inside Deaf culture.* Cambridge, MA: Harvard University Press.

Palmer, J. L., Reynolds, W., & Minor, R. (2012). "You want *what* on your PIZZA?!": Videophone and video-relay service as potential influences on the lexical standardization of American Sign Language. *Sign Language Studies, 12*(3), 371–397.

Parisot, A. M., & Rinfret, J. (2012). Recognition of Langue des Signes Québécoise in Eastern Canada. *Sign Language Studies, 12*(4), 583–601.

Partridge, B., & Phakiti, A. (Eds). (2015). *Research methods in applied linguistics: A practical resource.* London: Bloomsbury.

Patrie, C. (2009). *Fingerspelled names and introductions: A template building approach.* San Diego, CA: Dawn Sign Press.

Paul, P. V., & Moores, D. F. (2012). *Deaf epistemologies: Multiple perspectives on the acquisition of knowledge.* Washington, DC: Gallaudet University Press.

Pereira, M. C. P., & Fronza, C. A. (2010). The Prolibras test as an assessment of Brazilian Sign Language Interpreters proficiency: A critique. In L. Leeson, S. Wurm, & M. Vermeerbergen (Eds), *Signed language interpreting: Preparation, practice and performance.* Manchester: St Jerome.

Perniss, P. (2007). Locative functions of simultaneous perspective constructions in german Sign language narratives. In M. Vermeerbergen, L. Leeson, & O. Crasborn (Eds), *Simultaneity in Signed Languages,* (pp. 27–54.). Amsterdam and Philadelphia: John Benjamins.

Perniss, P. (2015). Collecting and analysing sign language data: Video requirements and use of annotation software. In E. Orfanidou, B. Woll, & G. Morgan (Eds), *Research methods in sign language studies: A practical guide* (pp. 55–73). London: Wiley Blackwell.

Perniss, P., Pfau, R., & Steinbach, M. (2007). *Visible variation: Comparative studies on sign language structure.* Berlin: De Gruyter Mouton.

Perniss, P., & Vigliocco, C. (2014). The bridge of iconicity: From a world of experience to the experience of language. *Philosophical Transactions of the Royal Society,* No. 369: 20130300.

Perrin-Wilcox, P. (2000). *Metaphor in American Sign Language.* Washington, DC: Gallaudet University Press.

Peterson, R. (2009). *The unlearning curve: Learning to learn American Sign Language.* Eden Prairie, MN: Harris Communications.

Petitto, L., Katerelos, M., Levy, B., Gauna, K., Trault, K., & Ferraro, V. (2001). Bilingual signed and spoken language acquisition from birth: Implications for the mechanisms underlying early bilingual language acquisition. *Journal of Child Language,* *28,* 453–496.

Petitto, L. A., & Marentette, P. F. (1991). Babbling in the manual mode: Evidence for the ontogeny of language. *Science, 252,* 1493–1496.

Petitto, L. A., Zatorre, R. J., Gauna, K., Nikelski, E. J., Dostie, D., & Evans, A. C. (2000). Speech-like cerebral activity in profoundly deaf people processing signed languages: Implications for the neural basis of human language. *Proceedings of the National Academy of Science, 97*(25), 13961–13966.

Petronio, L., & Hale, K. (2009). One interpreter education program, two sites: A comparison of factors and outcomes. *International Journal of Interpreter Education,* *1,* 45–61.

Pfau, R., & Steinbach, M. (2006). Modality-independent and modality-specific aspects of grammaticalization in sign languages. *Linguistics in Potsdam, 24,* 3–98.

Pfau, R., Steinbach, M., & Woll, B. (Eds). (2012). *Sign language: An international handbook.* Berlin, Germany: De Gruyter Mouton.

Piccardo, E., Berchoud, M., Cignatta, T., Mentz, O., & Pamula, M. (2011). *Pathways through assessing, learning and teaching in the CEFR.* Graz, Austria: European Centre for Modern Languages, Council of Europe Publishing.

Pietrosemoli, L. (2001). Politeness and Venezuelan Sign Language. In V. Dively, M. Metzger, S. Taub, & A. M. Baer (Eds), *Signed languages: Discoveries from international research* (pp.163–179). Washington DC: Gallaudet University Press.

Pivac, L. (2014). Learner autonomy in New Zealand Sign Language interpreting students. In D. McKee, R. Rosen, & R. McKee (Eds), *Teaching and learning signed languages: International perspectives and practices* (pp. 197–221). London: Palgrave.

Pizer, G. (2007). "It's like he can't' be bothered": Ideologies of effort in CODA family narratives. *Texas Linguistics Forum, 51,* 126–133.

Pizer, G., Walters, K., & Meier, R. P. (2012). "We communicated that way for a reason": Language practices and language ideologies among hearing adults whose parents are deaf. *Journal of Deaf Studies & Deaf Education.* doi:10.1093/deafed/ens031

Pizzutto, E., & Pietandrea, P. (2001). The notation of signed texts. *Sign Language and Linguistics, 4*(1–2), 29–45.

Plaza-Pust, C., & Main, F. A. (2012). Deaf education and bilingualism. In R. Pfau, M. Steinbach, & B. Woll (Eds), *Sign language: An international handbook* (pp. 949–979). Berlin: De Gruyter Mouton.

Pöchhacker, F. (2004). *Introducing interpreting studies.* London: Routledge.

Polich, L. G. (1998). *Social agency and Deaf communities: A Nicaraguan case study* (Unpublished doctoral dissertation). University of Texas, Austin.

Pollard, R. Q. (1994). Cross-cultural ethics in the conduct of deafness research. *Journal of the American Deafness and Rehabilitation Association, 27*(3), 29–41.

Pollard, R. Q. (1996). Professional psychology and deaf people: The emergence of a discipline. *American Psychologist, 51*(4), 389–396.

Pollard, R. (1998). Psychopathology. In M. Marschark & D. Clark (Eds), *Psychological perspectives on deafness* (Vol. 2, pp. 171–197). Mahwah, NJ: Lawrence Erlbaum.

Pollard, R. Q. (2002). Ethical conduct in research involving deaf people. In V. Gutman (Ed.), *Ethics in mental health and deafness* (pp. 162–178).Washington, DC: Gallaudet University Press.

Pollard, R. W., & Barnett, S. (2009). Health related vocabulary knowledge among deaf adults. *Rehabilitation Psychology, 54*(2), 182–185.

Pollitt, K. (2011) Towards a collective biography of spoken/written ~ sign language translating? Unpublished research paper. Available: http://www.kyrapollitt.com/

wp-content/uploads/2012/05/Edited-version-Towards-a-collective-biography-of-spoken.pdf. Accessed: 21 July 2014.

Pollitt, K. (2014). *(British) Sign Language Poetry as Gesamtkunstwerk* (Unpublished doctoral dissertation). University of Bristol.

Power, D., & Hyde, M. (2002). The characteristics and extent of participation of Deaf and hard-of-hearing students in regular classes in Australian schools. *Journal of Deaf Studies and Deaf Education, 7,* 302–311.

Powers, S., Gregory, S., & Thoutenhoofd, E. D. (1998). *The educational achievements of deaf children: A literature review* (Research report 65). London: Department for Education and Employment.

Preston, P. (1994). *Mother Father Deaf: Living between sound and silence.* Cambridge, MA: Harvard University Press.

Preston, P. (1996). Chameleon voices: Interpreting for deaf parents. *Social Science and Medicine, 42,* 1681–1690.

Pruss-Ramagosa, E. (2001). *Ei is not huevo: Bilingualism in two sign languages* (Unpublished doctoral dissertation). University of Hamburg.

Pyers, J., & Emmorey, K. (2008). The face of bimodal bilingualism: ASL Grammatical markers are produced when bilinguals speak to English monolinguals. In M. Bishop & S. Hicks (Eds), *Hearing, Mother Father deaf: Hearing people in Deaf families* (pp. 44–53). Washington, DC: Gallaudet University Press.

Quer, J. (2012). Legal pathways to recognition of sign languages: A comparison of the Catalan and Spanish sign language acts. *Sign Language Studies, 12*(4), 565–582.

Quinn, G. (2010). Schoolisation: An account of the origins of regional variation in British Sign Language. *Sign Language Studies, 10*(4), 476–501.

Quinn, G., & Turner, G. H. (2014). Educating the trainers of British Sign Language tutors: Documenting the educational experience. In D. McKee, R. Rosen, & R. McKee (Eds), *Teaching and learning signed languages: International perspectives and practices* (pp. 65–82). London: Palgrave.

Quinto-Pozos, D. (2007). Outlining considerations for the study of signed language contact. In D. Quinto-Pozos (Ed.), *Sign languages in contact* (pp. 1–30). Washington, DC: Gallaudet University Press.

Quinto-Pozos, D. (2008). Sign language contact and interference: ASL and LSM. *Language in Society, 37,* 161–189.

Quinto-Pozos, D. (2011). Teaching American Sign Language to hearing adult learners. *Annual Review of Applied Linguistics, 31,* 137–158.

Quinto-Pozos, D., Casanova de Canales, K., & Treviño, R. (2010). Trilingual video relay service (VRS) interpreting in the United States. In R. L. McKee & J. Davis (Eds), *Interpreting in multilingual, multicultural contexts.* Washington, DC: Gallaudet University Press.

Rainò, P. (2001) Mouthings and Mouth Gestures in Finnish Sign Language (FinSL). In Boyes Braem, P. & Sutton-Spence, R. (Eds) *The Hands are the Head of the Mouth: The Mouth as Articulator in Sign Languages,* (pp. 41–50). Hamburg: Signum Verlag.

Rainò, P., & Martikainen, L. (2013). Sisäkorvaistutteen saaneiden lasten kuntoutuksen ja tulkkauspalvelujen tarkoituksenmukaisuus ja tulevaisuuden tarve 2011–2012 [*The current and future needs of interpretation services and rehabilitation for children with a cochlear implant*] (Unpublished manuscript). Humak University of Applied Sciences.

Rampton, B., Tusting, K., Maybin, J., Barwell, R., Creese, A., & Lytra, V. (2004). *UK linguistic ethnography: A discussion paper* (Unpublished report). Available: http://uklef.ioe.ac.uk/documents/papers/ramptonetal2004.pdf

Ramsey, C. (1996). *Deaf children in public schools.* Washington, DC: Gallaudet University Press.

Ramsey, C. (2001). Beneath the surface: Theoretical frameworks shed light on educational interpreting. *Odyssey: Directions in Deaf Education, 2*(2), 19–24.

Ramsey, C., & Padden, C. (1998). Natives and newcomers: Gaining access to literacy in a classroom for Deaf children. *Anthropology & Education Quarterly, 29*(1), 5–24.

Ramsey, C., & Peña, S. (2010). Sign language interpreting at the border of the two Californias. In R. L. McKee & J. Davis (Eds), *Interpreting in multilingual, multicultural contexts* (pp. 3–27). Washington, DC: Gallaudet University.

Rathmann, C., Mann, W., & Morgan, G. (2007). Narrative structure and narrative development in deaf children. *Deafness Education International, 9*(4), 187–196.

Rayman, J. (2007). Visions of equality: Translating power in a deaf sermonette. *The Sign Language Translator & Interpreter, 1*(1), 73–114.

Reagan, T. (2010). *Language policy and planning for sign languages.* Washington, DC: Gallaudet University Press.

Reffell H., McKee R. L. (2009). Motives and outcomes of New Zealand Sign Language legislation: A comparative study between New Zealand and Finland. *Current Issues in Language Planning, 10*(3), 272–292.

Registry of Interpreters for the Deaf (RID) (1997). Standard Practice Paper: Use of a Certified Deaf Interpreter. SilverSpring, MD, Registry of Interpreters for the Deaf. https://drive.google.com/file/d/0B3DKvZMflFLdbXFLVVFsbmRzTVU/view

Reilly, C. (2014, 17 January). A message made loud and clear – deafness could kill. *Irish Medical Times.*

Reilly, J., & Bellugi, U. (1996). Competition on the face: Affect and language in ASL motherese. *Journal of Child Language, 23*(1), 219–239.

Richards, J. C. (2001). *Curriculum development in language teaching.* Cambridge: Cambridge University Press.

Richardson, J., Barnes, L., & Fleming, J. (2004). Approaches to studying and perceptions of academic quality in deaf and hearing students in higher education. *Deafness & Education International, 6*(2), 100–122.

Richardson, J., MacLeod-Gallinger, J., McKee, B., & Long, G. (2000). Approaches to studying in deaf and hearing students in higher education. *Journal of Deaf Studies & Deaf Education, 5*(2), 156–173.

Ringham, L. (2013). *Access all areas?* Research report, Access on Hearing Loss. Available: http://www.actiononhearingloss.org.uk/supporting-you/policy-research-and-influencing/research/access-all-areas.aspx

Risler, A. (2007). A cognitive linguistic view of simultaneity in process signs in French Sign Language. In M. Vermeerbergen, L.Leeson & O.Crasborn (Eds), *Simultaneity in Signed Languages,* (pp. 73–102.). Amsterdam and Philadelphia: John Benjamins.

Rocks, S. (2011). The theatre sign language interpreter and the competing visual narrative: The translation and interpretation of theatrical texts to British Sign Language. In R. Baines, C. Marinetti, & M. Perteghella (Eds), *Staging and performing translation.* New York: Palgrave Macmillan.

Rogers, K., & Young, A. (2012). Is there an association between Deaf children's mental health difficulties and their adult wellbeing? The state of the evidence. In L. Leeson & M. Vermeerbergen (Eds), *Working with the Deaf community: Mental health, education and interpreting* (pp. 183–200). Dublin: Interesource Group Publishing.

Rogers, K. D., Young, A., Lovell, K., Campbell, M., Scott, P. R., & Kendal, S. (2013a). The British Sign Language versions of the Patient Health Questionnaire, the

Generalized Anxiety Disorder 7-Item Scale, and the Work and Social Adjustment Scale. *Journal of Deaf Studies and Deaf Education, 18*(1), 110–122.

Rogers, K. D., Young, A., Lovell, K., & Evans, C. (2013b). The challenges of translating the clinical outcomes in Routine Evaluation Outcome Measure (CORE-OM) into British Sign Language. *Journal of Deaf Studies and Deaf Education, 18*(3), 287–298.

Romaine, S. (1995). *Bilingualism* (2nd ed.). Oxford: Blackwell.

Rosen, R. (2004). Beginning L2 production errors in ASL lexical phonology. *Sign Language Studies, 7,* 31–61.

Rolstad, K., Mahoney K., & Glass, G.V. (2005). The big picture: A meta- analysis of program effectiveness research on English language learners. *Educational Policy, 19* (4), 572–594.

Rosen, R. (2010). American Sign Language curricula: A review. *Sign Language Studies, 10*(3), 348–380.

Rosen, R. (2015). *Learning American Sign Language in high school: Motivation, strategies and achievement*. Washington, DC: Gallaudet University Press.

Rosen, R., DeLouise, M. K., Boyle, A. T., & Daley, K. (2014). Native language, target language, and the teaching and learning of American Sign Language vocabulary. In D. McKee, R. Rosen, & R. McKee (Eds), *Teaching and learning signed languages: International perspectives and practices* (pp. 145–174). London: Palgrave.

Roy, C. (1986). Who is a native speaker of ASL? *Journal of Interpretation, 3,* 63–66.

Roy, C. (1987). Evaluating performance: An interpreted lecture. In M. McIntire (Ed.), *New dimensions in interpreter education: Curriculum and instruction: Proceedings of the 6th National Convention of the Conference of Interpreter Trainers* (pp. 139–147). Alexandria, VA: RID Publications.

Roy, C. (1989a). *A sociolinguistic analysis of the interpreter's role in the turn exchanges of an interpreted event* (Unpublished doctoral dissertation). Georgetown University, Washington, DC.

Roy, C. (1989b). Features of discourse in an American Sign Language lecture. In C. Lucas (Ed.), *Sociolinguistics of the Deaf community* (pp. 231–251). San Diego, CA: Academic Press.

Roy, C. (1992). A sociolinguistic analysis of the interpreter's role in simultaneous talk in a face-to-face interpreted dialogue. *Sign Language Studies, 74,* 21–61.

Roy, C. (1993). The problem with definitions, descriptions and the role metaphors of interpreters. *Journal of Interpretation, 6,* 127–154.

Roy, C. (1996). An interactional sociolinguistic analysis of turntaking in an inter-preted event. *Interpreting, 1,* 39–68.

Roy, C. (2000). *Interpreting as a discourse process*. Oxford: Oxford University Press.

Roy, C., & Napier, J. (2015). Beginnings (1960s and early 1970s). In C. Roy & J. Napier (Eds), *The sign language interpreting studies reader* (pp. 1–50). Amsterdam: John Benjamins.

Royal National Institute for the Deaf. (2006). *Opportunity blocked: The employment experiences of deaf and hard of hearing people*. London: Author.

Rozanes, I. (2014). *Addressing the language barrier in healthcare: Developing a theory to understand the work of medical interpreters* (Unpublished doctoral dissertation). Trinity College, Dublin.

Rubin, J., & Thompson, I. (1994). *How to be a more successful language learner*. Boston: Heinle and Heinle.

Rudner, W., & Butowsky, R. (1981). Signs used in the Deaf gay community. *Sign Language Studies, 30,* 36–38.

Russell, D. (2002). *Interpreting in legal contexts: Consecutive and simultaneous interpreta-tion*. Burtonsville, MD: Sign Media.

Russell, D. (2008). Interpreter preparation conversations: Multiple perspectives. In D. Russell & S. Hale (Eds), *Interpreting in legal settings* (pp. 123–147). Washington DC: Gallaudet University Press.

Russell, D. (2010). *Illusion of inclusion: Realities and consequences.* Paper presented at the International Conference on Education and Deafness (ICED). June 2010, Vancouver, Canada.

Russell, D., & Hale, S. (Eds). (2008). *Interpreting in legal settings.* Washington DC: Gallaudet University Press.

Russell, D., & Malcolm, K. (2009). Assessing ASL–English interpreters: The Canadian model of national certification. In C. Angelelli & H. Jacobson (Eds), *Testing and assessment in translation and interpreting studies: A call for dialogue between research and practice* (pp. 331–376). Amsterdam: John Benjamins.

Russell, D., Shaw, R., & Malcolm, K. (2010). Effective strategies for teaching consecutive interpreting. *International Journal of Interpreter Education, 2,* 111–119.

Russell, D., & Winston, B. (2014). TAPing into the interpreting process: Using participant reports to inform the interpreting process. *International Journal of Translation & Interpreting Research, 6*(1). doi:ti.106201.2014.a07

Russo, T. (2004). Iconicity and productivity in sign language discourse: An analysis of three LIS discourse registers. *Sign Language Studies, 4*(2), 164–197.

Sacks, H., Schegloff, E. A., & Jefferson, G. (1974). Simplest systematics for the organisation of turn-taking for conversation. *Language, 50,* 696–735.

Sacks, O. (1989). *Seeing voices.* Berkeley: University of California Press.

Sadlier, L. (2009). Pandora's box: Lifting the lid on issues of testing: A case study of sign language interpreters training in Ireland. *The Sign Language Translator & Interpreter, 3*(2), 177–201.

Sadlier, L., Van den Bogaerde, B., & Oyserman, J. (2012). Preliminary collaborative steps in establishing CEFR sign language levels. In D. Tsagari & I. Csepes (Eds), *Collaboration in language testing and assessment* (pp. 185–199). Frankfurt: Peter Lang.

Sallandre, M. (2007). Simultaneity in French Sign Language Discourse. In M. Vermeerbergen, L.Leeson & O.Crasborn (Eds), *Simultaneity in Signed Languages,* (pp. 103–126). Amsterdam and Philadelphia: John Benjamins.

Sandler, W., & Lillo-Martin, D. (2006). *Sign language and linguistic universals.* Cambridge, NY: Cambridge University Press.

Sanheim, L. (2003). Turn exchange in an interpreted medical encounter. In M. Metzger, S. Collins, V. Dively, & R. Shaw (Eds), *From topic boundaries to omission* (pp. 27–54) Washington DC: Gallaudet University Press.

Sarangi, S., & Candlin, C. (2010). Applied linguistics and professional practice: Mapping a future agenda (Editorial). *Journal of Applied Linguistics & Professional Practice, 7*(1), 1–9.

Savvalidou, F. (2010). Interpreting (im)politeness strategies in a media political setting. In L. Leeson, S. Wurm, & M. Vermeerbergen (Eds), *Signed language interpreting: Preparation, practice and performance.* Manchester: St Jerome.

Schafer, T. (2011). Developing expertise through a deliberate practice project. *International Journal of Interpreter Education, 3,* 15–27.

Schein, J. (1989). *At home among strangers: Exploring the Deaf community in the United States.* Washington, DC: Gallaudet University Press.

Schembri, A., Cormier, K., Johnston, T., McKee, D., McKee, R., & Woll, B. (2010). Sociolinguistic variation in British, Australian and New Zealand Sign Languages. In D. Brentari (Ed.), *Sign languages* (pp. 476–498). Cambridge: Cambridge University Press.

Schembri, A., & Johnston, T. (2007). Sociolinguistic variation in the use of finger-spelling in Australian Sign Language (Auslan): A pilot study. *Sign Language Studies, 7,* 319–347.

Schembri, A., & Johnston, T. (2012). Sociolinguistic aspects of variation and change. In R. Pfau, M. Steinbach, & B. Woll (Eds), *Sign language: An international handbook* (pp. 788–816). Berlin: De Gruyter Mouton.

Schembri, A., Jones, C., & Burnham, D. (2005). Comparing action gestures and classifier verbs of motion: Evidence from Australian Sign Language, Taiwan Sign Language and non-signers' gestures without speech. *Journal of Deaf Studies and Deaf Education, 10*(3), 272–290.

Schembri, A., McKee, D., McKee, R., Johnston, T., Goswell, D., & Pivac, S. (2009). Phonological variation and change in Australian and New Zealand Sign Languages: The location variable. *Language Variation and Change, 21,* 193–231.

Schembri, A., Wigglesworth, G., Johnston, T., Leigh, G., Adam, R., & Barker, R. (2002). Issues in development of the test battery for Australian sign language morphology and syntax. *Journal of Deaf Studies and Deaf Education, 7,* 18–40.

Schermer, T. (2004). Lexical variation in the Netherlands. In M. Van Herreweghe & M. Vermeerbergen (Eds), *To the lexicon and beyond: Sociolinguistics in European Deaf communities* (pp. 91–110). Washington, DC: Gallaudet University Press.

Schermer, T. (2012a). Language planning. In R. Pfau, M. Steinbach, & B. Woll (Eds), *Sign language: An international handbook* (pp. 889–908). Berlin: De Gruyter Mouton.

Schermer, T. (2012b). Sign language planning in the Netherlands between 1980 and 2010. *Sign Language Studies, 12*(4), 467–493.

Schick, B. (2001). Interpreting for children: How it's different. *Odyssey: Directions in Deaf Education, 2*(2), 8–11.

Schick, B. (2002). The expression of grammatical relations by deaf toddlers learning ASL. In G. Morgan & B. Woll (Eds), *Directions in sign language acquisition* (pp. 143–158). Amsterdam: John Benjamins.

Schick, B. (2004). How might learning through an educational interpreter influence cognitive development? In E. A. Winston (Ed.), *Educational interpreting: How it can succeed* (pp. 73–88). Washington, DC: Gallaudet University Press.

Schick, B. (2008). A model of learning in an interpreted education. In M. Marschark & P. Hauser (Eds), *Deaf cognition: Foundations and outcomes* (pp. 351–386). Oxford: Oxford University Press.

Schick, B., & Williams, K. (2004). The educational interpreter performance assessment: Current structure and practices. In E. A. Winston (Ed.), *Educational interpreting: How it can succeed* (pp. 186–205). Washington, DC: Gallaudet University Press.

Schneider, E., Kozak, L., & Santiago, R., & Stephen, A. (2012). The effects of electronic communication on American Sign Language. *Sign Language Studies,* 12(3), 347–370.

Schönström, K., Dye, M., Leeson, L., & Mesch, J. (2015, July). *Building up L2 corpora in different signed languages – ASL, ISL and SSL.* Paper presented at ICSLA, Amsterdam.

Seleskovitch, D. (1978). *Interpreting for international conferences.* Washington, DC: Pen and Booth.

Senghas, A. (1995). *Children's contribution to the birth of Nicaraguan Sign Language* (Unpublished doctoral dissertation). Massachussets Institute of Technology, Boston.

Senghas, R. (1997). *An 'unspeakable, unwriteable' language: Deaf identity, language and personhood among the first cohorts of Nicaraguan signers* (Unpublished doctoral dissertation). University of Rochester, Rochester, NY.

Senghas, A. (2003). Intergenerational influence and ontogenetic development in the emergence of spatial grammar in Nicaraguan Sign Language. *Cognitive Development, 18*(4), 511–531.

Senghas, A., & Coppola, M. (2001). Children creating language: How Nicaraguan Sign Language acquired a spatial grammar. *American Psychological Society, 12*(4), 323–328.

Senghas, R. J., & Kegl, J. (1994). Social considerations in the emergence of Idioma de Signos Nicaragüense (Nicaraguan Sign Language). *Signpost, 7*(1), 40–46.

Senghas, R. J., & Monaghan, L. (2002). Signs of their times: Deaf communities and the culture of language. *Annual Review of Anthropology, 31*, 69–97.

Senghas, R. J., Senghas, A., & Pyers, J. E. (2004). The emergence of Nicaraguan Sign Language: Questions of development, acquisition and evolution. In J. Langer, S. T. Parker, & C. Milbrath (Eds), *Biology and knowledge revisited: From neurogenesis to psychogenesis* (pp. 287–306). Mahwah, NJ: Lawrence Erlbaum Associates.

Sforza, S. (2014). DI(2) = Team interpreting. In R. Adam, C. Stone, S. D. Collins, & M. Metzger (Eds), *Deaf interpreters at work: International insights* (pp. 19–28). Washington, DC: Gallaudet University Press.

Shaffer, B. (2014). Evolution of theory, evolution of role: How interpreting theory shapes interpreter role. In E. A. Winston & C. Monikowski (Eds), *Evolving paradigms in interpreter education: Impact of interpreting research on teaching interpreting* (pp. 128–150). Washington, DC: Gallaudet University Press.

Shaffer, B., Janzen, T. D., & Leeson, L. (2012). *Understanding pronoun location choice in signed language discourse: Grammar, semantics and pragmatics.* Paper presented at AVLIC 2012, University of Calgary, Calgary, Canada.

Sheridan, S. (2009). Translating idiomatic expressions from English to Irish Sign Language (ISL): Theory and practice. *The Sign Language Translator and Interpreter, 3*(1), 69–84.

Sherwood, B. (1987). Third culture: Making it work. *Journal of Interpretation, 4*, 13–24.

Shield, A., & Meier, R. (2014). The acquisition of sign language by deaf children with autism and spectrum disorder. In D. Quinto-Pozos (Ed.), *Multilingual aspects of signed language communication and disorder* (pp. 90–122). Bristol: Multilingual Matters.

Sidransky, R. (2006). *In silence: Growing up hearing in a deaf world.* New York: St Martins Press.

Siedlecki, T., Jr., & Bonvillian, J. (1993). Location, handshape and movement: Young children's acquisition of the formational aspects of American Sign Language. *Sign Language Studies, 78*, 31–52.

Sign Language Linguistics Society. (2014). SLLS ethics statement for sign language research. Available: http://slls.eu/slls-ethics-statement-for-discussion/

Simon, S. (1996). *Gender in translation: Cultural identity and the politics of transmission.* London: Routledge.

Singleton, J. L., & Tittle, M. D. (2000). Deaf parents and their hearing children. *Journal of Deaf Studies and Deaf Education, 5*(3), 221–236.

Singleton, J., Jones, G., & Hanumantha, S. (2012). Deaf friendly research? Toward ethical practice in research involving deaf participants. *Deaf Studies Digital Journal, 3.* Available: http://dsdj.gallaudet.edu/index.php?issue=4&section_id=2&entry_id=123

Singleton, J., Martin, A., & Morgan, G. (2015). Ethics, Deaf-Friendly Research, and good practice when studying sign languages. In E. Orfanidou, B. Woll, & G. Morgan (Eds), *Research methods in sign language studies: A practical guide* (pp. 7–20). London: Wiley Blackwell.

Skelton, T., & Valentine, G. (2003). 'It feels like being Deaf is normal': An exploration into the complexities of defining D/deafness and young D/deaf people's identities. *The Canadian Geographer, 47*(4), 451–466.

Skelton, T., & Valentine, G. (2010). "It's my umbilical cord to the world ... the Internet": D/deaf and hard of hearing people's information and communication practices. In V. Chouinard, E. Hall, & R. Wilton (Eds), *Towards enabling geographies: 'Disabled' bodies and minds in society and space* (pp. 85–106). Farnham, UK: Ashgate.

Skinner, B. F. (1953). *Science and human behavior.* New York: Macmillan.

Skinner, R., Turner, G. H., & Napier, J. (in press). Democracy, telecommunications and Deaf citizenship. *Journal of Deaf Studies and Deaf Education.*

Skutnabb-Kangas, T. (2000). *Linguistic genocide in education or worldwide diversity and human rights.* Mahwah, NJ: Lawrence Erlbaum Associates.

Sloman, L., Perry, A., & Frankenburg, F. (1987). Family therapy with deaf member families. *American Journal of Family Therapy, 15*, 242–252.

Small, A., & Cripps, J. (n.d.). *Attitude planning: Constructing a language planning framework towards empowerment in deaf education* (Unpublished manuscript). Toronto: Canadian Hearing Society.

Smeijers, A., & Pfau, R. (2009). Towards a treatment for treatment: On the communication between general practitioners and their Deaf patients. *The Sign Language Translator and Interpreter, 3*(1), 1–14.

Smeijers, A., Van den Bogaerde, B., Ens-Dokkum, M., & Oudesluys-Murphy, A. M. (2014). Scientific-based translation of standardised questionnaires into Sign Language of the Netherlands. In B. Nicodemus & M. Metzger (Eds), *Investigations in healthcare interpreting* (pp. 277–301). Washington, DC: Gallaudet University Press.

Smiler, K., & McKee, R. (2007). Perceptions of Māori Deaf identity. *Journal of Deaf Studies and Deaf Education, 12*(1), 99–111.

Smith, C., Lentz, E.M., & Mikos, K. (1988). *Signing Naturally Unit 1–6 Workbook.* San Diego, CA: Dawn Sign Press.

Smith, D., & Davis, J. (2014). Formative assessment for student progress and program improvement in sign language as L2 programs. In D. McKee, R. Rosen, & R. McKee (Eds), *Teaching and learning signed languages: International perspectives and practices* (pp. 253–280). London: Palgrave.

Smith, D. H., & Ramsey, C. (2004). Classroom discourse practices of a deaf teacher using American Sign Language. *Sign Language Studies, 5*(1), 39–62.

Smith, M. (2013). *More than meets the eye: Revealing the complexities of an interpreted education.* Washington, DC: Gallaudet University Press.

Smith, S., & Sutton-Spence, R. (2005). Adult-child interaction in a BSL nursery: Getting their attention! *Sign Language & Linguistics, 8*(1–2), 131–152.

Snoddon, K. (2010). Technology as a tool for learning ASL literacy. *Sign Language Studies, 10*(2). doi:10.1353/sls.0.0039

Snoddon, K. (2014). Hearing parents as plurilingual learners of ASL. In D. McKee, R. Rosen, & R. McKee (Eds), *Teaching and learning signed languages: International perspectives and practices* (pp. 175–196). London: Palgrave.

Spanjer, P., Fieret, M., & Baker, A. (2014). The influence of dementia on language in a signing population. In D. Quinto-Pozos (Ed.), *Multilingual aspects of signed language communication and disorder* (pp. 186–210). Bristol: Multilingual Matters.

Sparrow, R. (2005). Defending Deaf culture: The case of cochlear implants. *Journal of Political Philosophy, 13*(2), 135–152. doi:10.1111/j.1467–9760.2005.00217.x

Spencer-Oatey, H., & Franklin, P. (2009). *Intercultural interaction: A multidisciplinary approach to intercultural communication.* New York: Palgrave Macmillan.

Spencer, L., Tomblin, J. B., & Gantz, B. (2012). Growing up with a cochlear implant: Education, vocation, and affiliation. *Journal of Deaf Studies & Deaf Education, 17*(4). Doi: 10.1093/deafed/enso24/

Spencer, P., Bodran-Johnson, B., & Gutfreund, M. (1992). Interacting with infants with a hearing loss: What can we learn from mothers who are deaf? *Journal of Early Intervention, 16*(1), 64–78.

Stauffer, L. (2011). ASL students' ability to self-assess ASL competency. *Journal of Interpretation,* 80–95.

Steiner, B. (1998). Signs from the void: The comprehension and production of sign language on television. *Interpreting, 3*(2), 99–146.

Stevens, H. (2005, July). *Equal rights for Deaf people: From being a stranger in one's own country to full citizenship.* Paper presented at the International Conference on Deaf Education, Maastricht, the Netherlands.

Stevens, H. (2014). Effective participation as a Deaf sign language user in mainstream politics. In A. Pabsch (Ed.), *UNCRPD Implementation in Europe – a Deaf Perspective: Article 29: Participation in Political and Public Life* (pp. 112–118). Brussels: European Union of the Deaf.

Stokoe, W. C. (1960). *Sign language structure: An outline of the visual communication systems of the American Deaf* (Vol. 8). Silver Spring, MD: Linstok Press.

Stone, C. (2007). Deaf translators/interpreters' rendering processes. *The Sign Language Translator & Interpreter, 1*(1), 53–72.

Stone, C. (2009). *Toward a Deaf translation norm.* Washington, DC: Gallaudet University Press.

Stone, C. (2010). Access all areas: Sign language interpreting, is it that special? *Journal of Specialised Translation, 14,* 41–54.

Stone, C. (2011). Register, discourse, and genre in British Sign Language (BSL). In C. B. Roy (Ed.), *Discourse in signed languages* (pp. 121–154). Washington, DC: Gallaudet University Press.

Stone, C. (2012). Interpreting. In B. Woll, M. Steinbach, & R. Pfau (Eds), *International handbook of sign linguistics* In R. Pfau, M. Steinbach, & B. Woll (Eds), *Sign language: An international handbook* (pp. 980–998). Berlin: De Gruyter Mouton.

Stone, C., & Russell, D. (in press). Comparative analysis of depicting verbs in IS and natural sign languages. In R. Rosenstock & J. Napier (Eds), *International Sign.* Washington, DC: Gallaudet University Press.

Stone, C., & Russell, D. (2014). Conference interpreting and interpreting teams. In R. Adam, C. Stone, S. D. Collins, & M. Metzger (Eds), *Deaf interpreters at work: International insights* (pp. 140–156). Washington, DC: Gallaudet University Press.

Stone, C., & West, D. (2012). Translation, representation and the Deaf 'voice'. *Qualitative Research, 12,* 1–21.

Stone, C., & Woll, B. (2008). Dumb O Jemmy and others: Deaf people, interpreters and the London Courts in the 18th and 19th Centuries. *Sign Language Studies, 8*(3), 226–240.

Storme, S. (2014). Self-awareness: How sign language interpreters acknowledge privilege and oppression. *Street Leverage.* Available: http://www.streetleverage.com/2015/03/self-awareness-how-sign-language-interpreters-acknowledge-privilege-and-oppression/

Stratiy, A. (2005). Best practices in interpreting: A Deaf community perspective. In T. Janzen (Ed.), *Topics in signed language interpreting* (pp. 231–250). Amsterdam: John Benjamins.

Strong, M., & Prinz, P. (1997). A study of the relationship between ASL and English Literacy. *Journal of Deaf Studies and Deaf Education, 2*(1), 37–46.

Strong, M., & Prinz, P. (2000). Is American Sign Language skill related to English literacy? In C. Chamberlain, J. P. Morford, & R. Mayberry (Eds), *Language Acquisition by Eye* (pp. 131–142). Mahwah, NJ: Lawrence Erlbaum Associates.

Supalla, S. (2013). Some pitfalls of the focus on deafness as specialized knowledge. *Journal of Deaf Studies & Deaf Education, 18*(3), 425.

Supalla, S., Clark, P., Neumann Solow, S., & Müller de Quadros, R. (2010). Developing protocols for interpreting in multilingual international conferences. In R. L. McKee & J. Davis (Eds), *Interpreting in multilingual, multicultural contexts*. Washington, DC: Gallaudet University Press.

Suppalla, T. & Webb, R. (1995). The grammar of international sign: A new look at pidgin languages. In Emmorey, K. & Reilly, J. S (Eds), Language, Gesture & Space: International Conference on Theoretical Issues in Sign Language Research (pp. 333–352). Hillsdale, NJ: Erlbaum.

Sutherland, H., & Young, A. (2014). Research with Deaf children and not on them: A study of method and process. *Children & Society, 28*(5), 366–379.

Sutton-Spence, R. (2005). *Analysing sign language poetry*. Basingstoke: Palgrave.

Sutton-Spence, R. (2007). Mouthings and simultaneity in British Sign Language. In M. Vermeerbergen, L. Leeson & O. Crasborn (Eds), *Simultaneity in signed languages: Form and function* (pp. 147–162). Amsterdam: John Benjamins.

Sutton-Spence, R. (2011). Sign language narratives for Deaf children: Identity, culture and language. *Journal of Folklore Research, 47*(3), 265–305.

Sutton-Spence, R. (2012). Poetry. In R. Pfau, M. Steinbach, & B. Woll (Eds), *Sign language: An international handbook* (pp. 998–1021). Berlin: De Gruyter Mouton.

Sutton-Spence, R., & Müller de Quadros, R. (2014, March). *The role of the interpreter in performances of sign language poetry*. Paper presented to the First International Symposium on Signed Language Interpretation and Translation Research, Gallaudet University, Washington, DC.

Sutton-Spence, R., & West, D. (2011). Negotiating the legacy of hearingness. *Qualitative Inquiry, 17*(5), 422–432.

Sutton-Spence, R., & Woll, B. (1998). *The linguistics of British Sign Language*. Cambridge: Cambridge University Press.

Sutton-Spence, R., Woll, B., & Allsop, L. (1990). Variation and recent change in finger-spelling in British Sign Language. *Language Variation and Change, 2*, 313–330.

Swabey, L., & Malcolm, K. (2012). Introduction. In L. Swabey & K. Malcolm (Eds), *In our hands: Educating healthcare interpreters* (pp. ix–xv). Washington, DC: Gallaudet University Press.

Swabey, L., & Nicodemus, B. (2014). "Take one tablet twice a day": An examination of dosage statements translated in American Sign Language by deaf physicians and interpreters. In B. Nicodemus & M. Metzger (Eds), *Investigations in healthcare interpreting*. Washington, DC: Gallaudet University Press.

Swabey, L., Nicodemus, B., & Moreland, C. (2014). An examination of medical interview questions rendered in American Sign Language by deaf physicians and interpreters. In B. Nicodemus & M. Metzger (Eds), *Investigations in healthcare interpreting* (pp. 104–127). Washington, DC: Gallaudet University Press.

Swanwick, R., & Tsverik, I. (2007). The role of sign language for deaf children with cochlear implants: Good practicein sign bilingual settings. *Deafness & Education International, 9*(4), 214–231.

Swift, O. (2012). *The roles of signed language interpreters in post-secondary education settings in South Africa* (Unpublished master's dissertation). University of South Africa, Pretoria.

Swisher, M. V. (1992). The role of parents in developing visual turn-taking in their young deaf children. *American Annals of the Deaf, 137*, 92–100.

Tabak, J. (2014). What is higher mathematics? Why is it so hard to interpret? What can be done? *Journal of Interpretation, 23*(1), Article 5. Available: http://digitalcommons.unf.edu/joi/vol23/iss1/5

Takkinen, R. (2012). Two languages in the lives of children using a cochlear implant: A multiple case study. In L. Leeson & M. Vermeerbergen (Eds), *Working with the Deaf community: Deaf education, mental health and interpreting* (pp. 71–92). Dublin: Interesource Group Ireland Ltd.

Tannen, D. (1994). *Talking from 9 to 5: Women and men in the workplace: Language, sex and power*. New York: Avon Books.

Tapio, E., & Takkinen, R. (2012). When one of your languages is not recognized as a language at all. In J. Blommaert, S. Leppänen, P. Pahta, & T. Räisänen (Eds), *Dangerous multilingualism: Northern perspectives on order, purity and normality* (pp. 284–308). London: Palgrave.

Tate, G., Collins, J., & Tymms, P. (2003). Assessments using BSL: Issues of translation for performance indicators in primary schools. *Deaf Worlds, 19*(1), 6–35.

Tate, G. & Turner, G.H. (2002) The Code and the Culture. Sign Language Interpreting – in search of the new breed's ethics. In F. Pochhacker & M. Shlesinger (Eds), *The Interpreting Studies Reader*, (pp. 372–385). London: Routeledge.

Taub, S. F. (2001). *Language from the body: Iconicity and metaphor in American Sign Language*. Cambridge: Cambridge University Press.

Taylor, M. (2005). *Video relay service task analysis report* (Unpublished research report). Greeley, CO: Distance Opportunities for Interpreting Training Center, University of Northern Colorado.

Taylor, M. (2009). *Video relay services industry research: New demands on interpreters* (Unpublished research report). Sorenson Instituties, USA.

Tebble, H. (2014). Researching medical interpreting: An applied linguistics perspective. In E. Winston & C. Monikowski (Eds), *Evolving paradigms in interpreter education* (pp. 42–75). Washington DC: Gallaudet University Press.

Temple, B. (2002). Crossed wires: Interpreters, translators, and bilingual workers in cross-language research. *Qualitative Health Research, 12*(6), 844–854.

Temple, B., & Edwards, R. (2002). Interpreters/translators and cross-language research: Reflexivity and border crossings. *International Journal of Qualitative Methods, 1*(2), 1–12.

Temple, B., & Young, A. (2004). Qualitative research and translation dilemmas. *Qualitative Research, 4*(2), 161–178.

Tervoort, B. T. (1953). *Structurele analyse van visueel taalgebruik binnen een groep dove kinderen* [Structural analysis of visual language use within a group of deaf children] (Unpublished doctoral dissertation). University of Amsterdam.

Thoutenhoofd, E. (2000). Philosophy's Real-World Consequences for Deaf People: Thoughts on Iconicity, Sign Language and Being Deaf. *Human Studies, 23*, 261–279.

Thoutenhoofd, E. (2005). The sign language interpreter in inclusive education: Power of authority and limits of objectivism. *The Translator, 11*(2), 237–258.

Thumann, M. (2011). Identifying depiction: Constructed action and constructed dialogue in ASL presentations. In C. B. Roy (Ed.), *Discourse in signed languages* (pp. 46–68). Washington, DC: Gallaudet University Press.

The Irish Times (February 23, 2015). *Homeless man jailed for pushing man to his death under bus.*

The Mirror (February 23, 2015). *Homeless deaf drug addict who killed pal by pushing him under a bus jailed for seven years.*

Timmermans, N. (2005). *The Status of Sign Languages in Europe.* Strasbourg: Council of Europe.

Torigoe, T., & Takei, W. (2001). A descriptive analysis of early word combinations in deaf children's signed utterance. *Japanese Psychological Research, 43,* 249–250.

Trowler, P., & Turner, G. H. (2002). Exploring the hermeneutic foundations of university life: Deaf academics in a hybrid 'community of practice'. *Higher Education, 43*(2), 227–256.

Tse, L. (1995). Language brokering among Latino adolescents: Prevalence, attitudes, and school performance. *Hispanic Journal of Behavioral Sciences, 17*(2), 180–193.

Tse, L. (1996). Language brokering in linguistic minority communities: The case of Chinese- and Vietnamese-American students. *The Bilingual Research Journal, 20*(3–4), 485–498.

Turner, G. H. (1994). How is Deaf culture? Perspective on a fundamental concept. *Sign Language Studies, 83,* 103–126.

Turner, G. H. (2005). *Applied linguistics and sign languages: Pasts and futures.* Paper presented to the International Association of Applied Linguistics (AILA) conference, Madison, Wisconsin, July 10–15, 2015.

Turner, G. H. (2006). Re-thinking the sociology of sign language interpreting and translation: Some challenges posed by deaf practitioners. In M. Wolf (Ed.), *Übersetzen - translating - traduire: Towards a social turn?* (pp. 284–293). Berlin: LIT Verlag.

Turner, G. H. (2007). 37 Metres in 12 seconds: Sign language translation and interpreting leave "terra firma." *The Sign Language Translator and Interpreter, 1*(1), 1–14.

Turner, G. H. (2009). Sign language planning: Pragmatism, pessimism and principles. *Current Issues in Language Planning, 10*(3), 243–254.

Turner, G. H., & Harrington, F. (2000). Issues of power and method in interpreting research. In M. Olohan (Ed.), *Intercultural faultlines: Research models in translation studies I - Textual and cognitive aspects* (pp. 253–266). Manchester, UK: St Jerome.

Turner, G. H., & Napier, J. (2014). On the importance of professional sign language interpreting to political participation. In A. Pabsch (Ed.), *UNCRPD Series: Political Participation* (pp. 54–71). Brussels: European Union of the Deaf.

Turner, G. H., Skinner, R., & Napier, J. (under review). Democracy, telecommunications and deaf citizenship. *Journal of Deaf Studies & Deaf Education.*

Turner, G. H., & Pollitt, K. (2002). Community interpreting meets literary translation: English–BSL interpreting in the theatre. *The Translator, 8*(1), 25–48.

United Nations. (2006). *Convention on the Rights of Persons with Disabilities,* edited by Ad Hoc Committee on a Comprehensive and Integral International Convention and on the Protection and Promotion of the Rights and Dignity of Persons with Disabilities. New York: United Nations.

University of Manchester (n.d.). Code of practice for investigating concerns about the conduct of research. Available: www.manchester.ac.uk/research/environment/ethics/

Valdes, G., & Angelelli, C. (2003). Interpreters, interpreting, and the study of bilingualism. *Annual Review of Applied Linguistics, 23*, 58–78.

Valdes, G., Chavez, C., Angelelli, C., Enright, K., Garcia, D., & Gonzalez, M. (2003). *Expanding definitions of giftedness: The case of young interpreters from immigrant communities*. Mahwah, NJ: Lawrence Erlbaum Associates.

Van Cleve, J. V. (2007). *The Deaf history reader* (2nd ed.). Washington, DC: Gallaudet University Press.

Van Cleve, J. V., & Crouch, B. A. (1989). *A place of their own: Creating the Deaf community in America*. Washington, DC: Gallaudet University Press.

Van den Bogaerde, B., & Andrews, J. (2008). Bimodal language acquisition in Kodas. In M. Bishop & S. Hicks (Eds), *Hearing, Mother Father deaf: Hearing people in Deaf families* (pp. 99–131). Washington, DC: Gallaudet University Press.

Van den Bogaerde, B., & Baker, A. (2005). Code mixing in mother-child interaction in deaf families. In A. Baker & B. Woll (Eds), *Sign language acquisition* (pp. 141–163). Amsterdam: Benjamins.

Van den Bogaerde & De Lange, R. (2014). Healthcare accessibility and the role of sign language interpreters. In B. Nicodemus & M. Metzger (Eds), *Investigations in healthcare interpreting* (pp. 326–359). Washington, DC: Gallaudet University Press.

Van den Broek-Laven, A. (2014, September). *Characteristics of signed texts for sign language comprehension*. Paper presented at PRO-Signs Conference II - CEFR for Sign Languages, Hamburg University, Hamburg, Germany.

Van der Lem, T., & Timmerman, D. (1990). Joint picture book reading in signs: An interaction process between parent and child. In S. Prillwitz & T. Vollhaber (Eds), *Sign language research and application. Proceedings of the International Congress on Sign Language Research and Application, March 23–25, 1990, Hamburg* (pp. 77–88). Hamburg: Signum.

Van Dijk, R., Christoffels, I., Postma, A., & Hermans, D. (2012). The relation between the working memory skills of sign language interpreters and the quality of their interpretations. *Bilingualism: Language and Cognition, 15*(2), 340–350.

Van Hecke, E., & De Weerdt, K. (2004). Regional variation in Flemish Sign Language. In M. Van Herreweghe & M. Vermeerbergen (Eds), *To the lexicon and beyond: Sociolinguistics in European Deaf communities* (pp. 27–38). Washington, DC: Gallaudet University Press.

Van Herreweghe, M. (2002). Turn-taking mechanisms and active participation in meetings with Deaf and hearing participants in Flanders. In C. Lucas (Ed.), *Turntaking, fingerspelling, and contact in signed languages* (pp. 73–106). Washington, DC: Gallaudet University Press.

Van Herreweghe, M., & Vermeerbergen, M. (2009). Flemish Sign Language standardisation. *Current issues in language planning, 10*(3), 308–326.

Van Herreweghe, M., & Vermeerbergen, M. (2012). Data collection. In R. Pfau, M. Steinbach, & B. Woll (Eds), *Sign language: An international handbook* (pp. 1023–1045). Berlin: De Gruyter Mouton.

Vermeer, H. J. (1989). Skopos and commission in translational action. In L. Venuti (Ed.), *The translation studies reader* (pp. 221–232). London: Routledge.

Vermeerbergen, M., & Demey, E. (2007). Sign + gesture = speech + gesture? Comparing aspects of simultaneity in Flemish Sign Language to instances of concurrent speech and gesture. In M. Vermeerbergen, L. Leeson, & O. Crasborn (Eds), *Simultaneity in signed languages: Form and function* (pp. 257–282). Amsterdam: John Benjamins.

Vermeerbergen, M. & Leeson, L (2011). European Signed Languages – Towards a Typological Snapshot. In B. Kortmann & J. van der Auwera, Johan (Eds), *The Field of Linguistics* (pp. 269–287). Berlin: Mouton de Gruyter.

Vermeerbergen, M., Leeson, L., & Crasborn, O. (Eds). (2007). *Simultaneity in signed languages: Form and function*. Amsterdam: John Benjamins.

Vermeerbergen, M., & Van Herreweghe, M. (2012). Data collection. In R. Pfau, M. Steinbach, & B. Woll (Eds), *Sign language: An international handbook* (pp. 1023–1045). Berlin: De Gruyter Mouton.

Vermeerbergen, M., Van Herreweghe, M., Smessaert, I., & De Weerdt, D. (2012). "De eenzaamheid blijft": Mainstreamed Flemish Deaf pupils about wellbeing at school. In L. Leeson & M. Vermeerbergen (Eds), *Working with the Deaf community: Mental health, education and interpreting* (pp. 103–120). Dublin: Interesource Group Publishing.

Vonen, A. M. (2006). Comments on W(h)ither the Deaf community? A timely warning. *Sign Language Studies, 6*, 220–224.

Vernon, M. (2010). The horror of being deaf and being in prison. *American Annals of the Deaf, 155*(3), 311–321.

Vernon, M., & Miller, K. (2001). Linguistic incompetence to stand trial: A unique condition in some deaf defendants. *Journal of Interpretation*, 99–120.

Vernon, M., & Miller, K. (2005). Obstacles faced by deaf people in the criminal justice system. *American Annals of the Deaf, 150*(3), 283–291.

Vinson, D. P., Cormier, K., Denmark, T., Schembri, A., & Vigliocco, G. (2008). The British Sign Language (BSL) norms for age of acquisition, familiarity and iconicity. *Behavior Research Methods, 40*(4), 1079–1087.

Wadensjö, C. (1992). *Interpreting as interaction: On dialogue-interpreting in immigration hearings and medical encounters* (Unpublished doctoral dissertation). Linköping University, Linköping, Sweden.

Wadensjö, C. (1998). *Interpreting as interaction*. London: Longman.

Wang, J., & Napier, J. (in press). Directionality and signed language interpreting. *Meta*.

Wehmeyer, J. (2014). Eye-tracking Deaf and hearing viewing of sign language interpreted news broadcasts. *Journal of Eye Movement Research, 7*(1), 1–16.

Weir, C. J. (2003). A survey of the history of the Certificate of Proficiency in English (CPE) in the twentieth century. In C. J. Weir & M. Milanovic (Eds), *Continuity and innovation: The history of the CPE 1913–2002* (pp. 1–56). Cambridge: Cambridge University Press.

Weir, C. J. (2005). *Language testing and validation: An evidence-based approach*. Basingstoke, UK: Palgrave Macmillan.

Weisskirch, R. S. (2005). The relationship of language brokering to ethnic identity for Latino early adolescents. *Hispanic Journal of Behavioral Sciences, 27*(3), 286–299.

Weisskirch, R. S., & Alva, S. A. (2002). Language brokering and the acculturation of Latino children. *Hispanic Journal of Behavioral Sciences, 24*, 369–378.

Wheatley, M., & Pabsch, A. (2010). *Sign language legislation in the European Union*. Brussels: European Union of the Deaf.

Wheatley, M., & Pabsch, A. (2012). *Sign language legislation in the European Union* (2nd ed.). Brussels: European Union of the Deaf.

White, J. A. (2014). Cognitive spaces: Expanding participation framework by looking at signed language interpreters' discourse and conceptual blending. *International Journal for Translation & Interpreting Research, 6*(1), 144–157.

Wilbur, R. (1987). *American Sign Language: Linguistic and applied dimensions* (2nd ed.). Boston: Little, Brown.

Wilbur, R. (2006). What does the study of signed languages tell us about 'language'? *Sign Language Linguistics, 9*(1/2), 5–32.

Wilcox, S. (2004a). Gesture and language: Cross-linguistic and historical data from signed languages. *Gesture, 4*(1), 43–73.

Wilcox, S. (2004b). Cognitive iconicity: Conceptual spaces, meaning and gesture in signed languages. *Cognitive Linguistics, 15*(2), 119–147.

Wilcox, S. (1988). Introduction: Academic acceptance of American Sign Language. *Sign Language Studies, 59*, 101–108.

Wilcox, S., & Shaffer, B. (2005). Towards a cognitive model of interpreting. In T. Janzen (Ed.), *Topics in signed language interpreting* (pp. 27–50). Amsterdam: John Benjamins.

Williamson, A. (2012). The cost of invisibility: Codas and the sign language interpreting profession. Available: www.streetleverage.com/2012/11/the-cost-of-invisibility-codas-and-the-sign-language-interpreting-profession/

Williamson, A. (2015). *Nourishing our roots: Deaf-parented interpreters' onramp experiences.* Unpublished Masters dissertation, Western Oregon University.

Willie, S. S. (2003). *Acting Black: College identity and the performance of race.* New York: Routledge.

Wilson, C. W. (2010, July). *Working through, with or despite technology? A study of interpreter-mediated encounters when interpreting is provided by video conferencing link.* Paper presented at Critical Link 6: Interpreters in the Community, Birmingham, UK.

Winston, E. (2004). Interpretability and accessibility of mainstream classrooms. In E. A. Winston (Ed.), *Educational interpreting: How it can succeed* (pp. 132–168). Washington, DC: Gallaudet University Press.

Woll, B. (2003). Modality, universality and the similarities across sign anguages: An historical perspective. In A. Baker, B. van den Bogaerde, & O. Crasborn (Eds), *Cross-linguistic perspectives in sign language research: Selected Papers from TISLR 2000* (pp. 17–27). Hamburg: Signum.

Woll, B. (2013). Sign language and spoken language development in young children: Measuring vocabulary by means of the CDI. In L. Meurant, A. Sinte, M. Van Herreweghe, & M. Vermeerbergen (Eds), *Sign language research, uses and practices: Crossing views on theoretical and applied sign language linguistics* (pp. 15–34). Nijmegan, The Netherlands: De Gruyter Mouton and Ishara Press.

Woodcock, K., Rohan, M., & Campbell, L. (2007). Equitable representation of deaf people in mainstream academia: Why not? *Higher Education, 53*, 359–379.

Woodward, J. (1972). Implications for sociolinguistics research among the Deaf. *Sign Language Studies, 1*, 1–7.

Woolfe, T., Herman, R., Roy, P., & Woll, B. (2010). Early lexical development in native signers: A BSL adaptation of the MacArthur-Bates CDI. *Child Language and Psychiatry, 51*(3), 322–331.

Woll, B., Sutton-Spence, r., & Elton, F. (2001). Multilingualism: The global approach to sign languages. In C. Lucas (Ed.), *The Sociolinguistics of Sign Languages* (pp. 8–32). Cambridge: Cambridge University.

World Federation of the Deaf. (2014). *WFD statement on sign language work.* Helsinki, Finland: World Federation of the Deaf.

Wurm, S. (2014). Deconstructing translation and interpreting prototypes: A case of written-to-signed-language translation. *Translation Studies.* doi:10.1080/14781700. 2013.819293

Xiao, X., Chen, X., & Palmer, J. L. (2015). Chinese Deaf viewers' comprehension of sign language interpreting on television: An experimental study. *Interpreting, 17*(1), 91–117.

Xiao, X., & Li, F. (2013). Sign language interpreting on Chinese TV: A survey on user perspectives. *Perspectives: Studies in Translatology, 21*(1), 100–116.

Xiao, X., & Yu, R. (2009). Survey on sign language interpreting in China. *Interpreting, 11*(2), 137–163.

Young, A., & Ackerman, J. (2001). Reflections on validity and epistemology in a study of working relations between Deaf and hearing professionals. *Qualitative Health Research, 11,* 179–189.

Young, A., Ackerman, J., & Kyle, J. (2000). On creating a workable signing environment: Deaf and hearing perspectives. *Journal of Deaf Studies and Deaf Education, 5*(2), 186–195.

Young, A., & Temple, B. (2014). *Approaches to social research: The case of Deaf Studies.* New York: Oxford University Press.

Young, A., & Hunt, R. (2011). *Research with D/deaf people* (Unpublished research report). School for Social Care Research, National Institute for Health Research, Methods Review 9.

Young, L., Morris, C., & Langdon, C. (2012). "He Said What?!": Constructed dialogue in various interface modes. *Sign Language Studies, 12*(3), 398–413.

Zeshan, U. (Ed.). (2006). *Negatives and interrogatives across signed languages.* Nijmegen, The Netherlands: Ishara Press.

Zeshan, U., & Perniss, P. (Eds). (2008). *Possessive and existential constructions in sign languages: Sign language typology series* (Vol. 2). Nijmegen, The Netherlands: Ishara Press.

Zhao, X. (2015). Constructing linguistic identity and interpreting: A case study of sign language interpreting on Chinese television for political conferences. Unpublished doctoral dissertation, Heriot–Watt University.

Zimmer, J. (1989). Toward a description of register variation in American Sign Language. In C. Lucas (Ed.), *The sociolinguistics of the Deaf community* (pp. 253–272). San Diego, CA: Academic Press.

Zimmer, J. (1992). Appropriateness and naturalness in ASL/English interpreting. In J. Plant-Moeller (Ed.), *Expanding horizons: Proceedings of the 12th National Convention of the Registry of Interpreters for the Deaf* (pp. 81–92). Silver Spring, MD: RID Publications.

Index

Printed and bound by CPI Group (UK) Ltd, Croydon, CR0 4YY